Commissioned with Power

An Overview of the Gifts of the Spirit

by GORDON LINDSAY

**This book is a compilation and revision of several smaller books
written by Gordon Lindsay.**

Published by
Christ For The Nations Inc.
Dallas, Texas
Commissioned With Power - An Overview of the Gifts of the Spirit
Copyright © 2001 Christ For The Nations Inc.
P.O. Box 769000
Dallas, Texas 75376-9000
Phone: 1-800-933-2364
Web-site: http://www.cfni.org
ISBN 0-89985-198-3
Printed in the United States of America
Revised and compiled by Rebecca Walker
Cover design by Gustavo Morán
Cover illustration by Gustave Doré
Graphic layout by Angela Lucas

Table of Contents

PART III — *The Gift of Miracles and the Gift of Prophecy*

Introduction

The gifts of the Spirit are among the most important topics in the New Testament. In I Corinthians 12:27, Paul described the Church as the body of Christ. He explained that the parts of this body are believers who exercise various gifts, just as the parts of the human body have different functions and purposes. In light of this, it follows that without the gifts of the Spirit, the Church would become something very different from what God intended. Instead of being a supernatural organism, the Church would be only another human organization.

It is a historical fact that shortly after the apostolic period, the gifts of the Spirit began to gradually disappear from the Church. Why? One common explanation is that when the New Testament canon was completed, they were no longer needed. But as the well-known writer, Donald Gee, points out in his excellent book, Concerning Spiritual Gifts, there is no evidence in the New Testament to support this view. He writes:

> Such an argument rests upon a complete misconception of the true nature and purpose of the gifts of the Spirit. It assumes that in the Early Church, utterances through these gifts had all the authority of the Scriptures, but the New Testament utterly disproves such an idea. The Early Church is consistently found always appealing to the Scriptures of the Old Testament (never to their own "prophets" be it noted), for support for all doctrine and final settlement in every dispute (Acts 2:16; 15:15; 26:22). The "prophecy of Scripture" provided (II Peter 1:20) a totally different level of authority to the spiritual gifts among them, and it does so still.

Although the manifestation of the gifts ceased to a great

extent after the apostolic age, there is no evidence that this occurred because the Lord withdrew them. They ceased because the Church left its first love. This problem already existed by A.D. 96 when the Apostle John received the Revelation. Note his warning to the Ephesian Church (which prophetic students usually agree symbolizes the apostolic period in Church history):

> "Nevertheless I have *this* against you, that you have left your first love. Remember therefore from where you have fallen; repent and do the first works, or else I will come to you quickly and remove your lampstand from its place — unless you repent" (Rev. 2:4, 5).

During the great persecutions of the second and third centuries, the gifts of the Spirit continued to be observable. But shortly after Constantine's Edict, which brought the Church into imperial favor and made Christianity the national religion, the ministry of the gifts rapidly declined.

However, it is important to note that the operation of the gifts of the Spirit never completely ceased. The story of St. Francis contains thrilling accounts of miraculous healings. When he sent his preachers out, he gave them the same command Jesus gave His disciples in Matthew:

> "And as you go, preach, saying, 'The kingdom of heaven is at hand.' Heal the sick, cleanse the lepers, raise the dead, cast out demons" (Matt. 10:7, 8).

The histories of the persecuted Waldensian and Albigensian sects show that the gifts of the Spirit were still functioning during the Middle Ages. In the 18th century, John Wesley recorded in his journals some of the remarkable Pentecostal phenomena which took place in the meetings of early Methodists. The Moravians and other contemporary groups also experienced many unusual supernatural manifestations. So, while the operation of the gifts greatly diminished over the centuries, they never entirely disappeared. And when believers finally began to earnestly pray for their restoration to the Church, the present latter-day outpouring of the Spirit resulted.

Part I

A Survey of the Gifts, the Word of Wisdom and the Word of Knowledge

Chapter One

Are the Gifts of the Spirit for the Modern Church?

> Love never fails. But whether *there are* prophecies, they will fail; whether *there are* tongues, they will cease; whether *there is* knowledge, it will vanish away. For we know in part and we prophesy in part. But when that which is perfect has come, then that which is in part will be done away (I Cor. 13:8-10).

This passage of Scripture is commonly used as a proof-text by those who believe the gifts of the Spirit have left the Church. Here we are told that prophecies, tongues and knowledge will cease, or pass away. However, just one glance at the verses shows that the period referred to is not this age, but the future perfect age. We all know that "that which is perfect" has not yet come!

In the Great Commission, Jesus promised that miraculous signs would follow and confirm the preaching of the Word (Mk. 16:15-18). These signs were to prove the genuineness of the gospel message to unbelievers. There is no indication in the passage that the terms of the Great Commission were to be changed in any way. In fact, Jesus implied that each generation to come until the end of the age, is to observe "all things that I have commanded you."

> "Go therefore and make disciples of all the nations, baptizing them in the name of the Father and of the Son and of the Holy Spirit, teaching them to observe all things that I have commanded you; and lo, I am with you always, *even* to the end of the age" (Matt. 28:19, 20).

The above are the very last words written by the Apostle Matthew. Who would deny that the Great Commission is still in effect?

The need for supernatural signs to capture the attention of the masses is illustrated in Elijah's challenge of the prophets of Baal on Mt. Carmel. Elijah asked the people, "'How long will you falter between two opinions? If the LORD *is* God, follow Him; but if Baal, follow him.' But the people answered him not a word" (I Ki. 18:21). However, when the fire miraculously fell from heaven in answer to Elijah's prayer, the people fell on their faces and cried, "'The LORD, He *is* God! The LORD, He *is* God!'" (I Ki. 18:39).

Is the World Evangelized Yet?

Some assume that the world is now evangelized, and that the signs are therefore no longer needed. This assumption is obviously far removed from the truth. The fact is, that the population of unbelieving nations is multiplying at such a fantastic rate that unless the spread of the Gospel is accelerated somehow, the Great Commission can never be accomplished. So far, the only successful means of mass evangelism ever demonstrated is the ministry of healing and miracles. That is not to criticize any sincere effort to reach the unsaved — such as medical missions or the building of schools and hospitals. However, these efforts are entirely too slow if we are to reach the lost in our generation. With the fearful increase of weapons of mass destruction, those who predict that the Church will have time to evangelize beyond this generation are indeed optimistic.

Shall we not face the truth? The real reason the gifts of the Spirit are missing from the Church is because we have been satisfied without them. Believers need to realize that without the gifts of the Spirit in our midst, we can never fulfill our destiny. As Paul admonished Timothy to stir up the gift that was within him, we also need to awaken to the fact that Christ has given certain gifts to His body that we need to put into action.

Return of the Gifts Anticipated

It is interesting to note that discerning Bible scholars of the 19th century realized that the disappearance of the gifts of the Spirit from the main body of the Church was due to lethargy and lukewarmness. They looked forward to, and even predicted, a last-day outpouring of the Spirit that would include a reappearance of the gifts.

In 1866, Michael Baxter — many of whose predictions have been fulfilled — wrote about the reappearance of the supernatural in the Church in his famous book *Baxter's Forty Wonders:*

> Increased faith to work miracles ... and unparalleled boldness in preaching the Gospel will characterize the coming Pentecostal outpouring of the Spirit — the various gifts of the Spirit were bestowed upon pastors, prophets, evangelists, teachers, for the perfecting of the saints and the gathering and completing of a perfect Church. But this end is not yet attained, therefore these gifts cannot altogether have ceased, or been entirely withdrawn, although they have been suspended and temporarily withdrawn as mark of displeasure for the apostatizing of the Church from her first love.

At the turn of this century, Michael Baxter's prediction came true. The great Pentecostal outpouring, with a new manifestation of the gifts, began in the United States and spread throughout the world. Some of those who were most used in this outpouring foresaw an even greater move of the supernatural that is yet to come.

In the book *New Zealand's Greatest Revival* by Roberts, a believer remarked to Smith Wigglesworth, "One is tempted to envy you when you have had such great success." He received the following reply:

> "Young man, it is the other way around. I feel

like envying you. I have had three visions —
three only. The first two have already come to
pass, but the third is yet to be fulfilled. I will
most likely pass on to my reward, but you are a
young man and will most likely be in what I
saw." He burst out, "O, it was amazing." He
was asked what was amazing, "O," he said, "I
cannot tell God's secrets, but you remember
what I say — this revival we have had is nothing
to what God is yet going to do." The one to
whom Brother Wigglesworth addressed these
words commented: "It was quite evident that the
evangelist had a special vision granted him of the
coming outpouring of the Spirit in an unprecedented effusion in the days just before our Lord
comes to snatch away the Church."

Dr. Charles S. Price, noted evangelist, said in a sermon he
preached shortly before his death:

Yesterday we sang, "Showers of Blessing," but
now we are waiting for the deluge! It is coming
and nothing can stop it. Like every previous outpouring, this glorious experience which is about
to burst upon the world will not be the product
of any established system. Established systems
may experience it and enjoy it and flow along in
the clear stream of its beautiful, onward flowing.
Even then they may not do it as systems, but
only as the multiplied thousands within their
borders, who are hungry for God and are spiritually conscious of the fact that there is more to
follow.

You have thought, have you not, that you have
been in some glorious healing services? Perhaps
you have and for them we praise the Lord. But
wait a little while. I declare unto you that God is

going to do better in your tomorrows than He has ever done in the past.

Fear of the Devil's Power

One thing that prevents some from seeking the gifts of the Spirit is an almost morbid fear of the devil. They see demon power and delusion everywhere. Of course, there are many deceiving spirits, but the Bible gives us means to discern which are from God and which are not (I Jn. 4:1-3). One of the gifts, the discerning of spirits, is designed to detect the presence of evil powers. Those who fear that if they seek the gifts of the Spirit they might receive something from the devil, should remember Christ's words:

> "If a son asks for bread from any father among you, will he give him a stone? Or if *he asks* for a fish, will he give him a serpent instead of a fish? Or if he asks for an egg, will he offer him a scorpion? If you then, being evil, know how to give good gifts to your children, how much more will *your* heavenly Father give the Holy Spirit to those who ask Him!" (Lk. 11:11-13).

If earthly fathers give good gifts to their children, certainly the Heavenly Father will not do worse by *His* children!

It is also significant to note that this statement was followed by the healing of a mute man. After the man was healed, opposers claimed that the miracle was performed by the power of Beelzebub. But Jesus pointed out that if Satan cast out Satan, then his kingdom would be divided and would not stand (Lk. 11:18-20).

On the basis of Christ's words, we should not fear to press forward and claim the ministry of the gifts. Fear kept the children of Israel from possessing the land that had been promised to them. The 10 spies cautioned the people to play it safe because the inhabitants of the land were giants, and they thought the risks were too great. Because of their fear, that generation never entered into the land of promise. They were doomed to wander and die in the wilderness. God grant that we do not repeat their foolish error.

We need the spiritual gifts to empower us for the battle. Only when equipped with them will the Church accomplish its purpose.

Purpose of the Gifts of the Spirit

What was God's reason for bestowing these special gifts upon the Church? His paramount purpose was for the Church to become the functioning body of Christ on earth through the operation of these gifts.

1. To manifest the body of Christ on earth

> For as the body is one and has many members, but all the members of that one body, being many, are one body, so also *is* Christ. For by one Spirit we were all baptized into one body — whether Jews or Greeks, whether slaves or free — and have all been made to drink into one Spirit. For in fact the body is not one member but many. ... Now you are the body of Christ, and members individually (I Cor. 12:12-14, 27).

Here we are told that the Church is the body of Christ, and each believer is an individual member. The point is this: As long as Christ was on earth, He could be in only one location at a time. He could minister to only a few at a time. But after the Spirit was poured out, it was possible for Him to manifest Himself through an unlimited number of believers. These members of His body can go into all parts of the world ministering to people, as He did when He was on earth. The Church is indeed the body of Christ, doing His works and ministering His love and compassion to the needy. In this way, the ministry of Christ was multiplied many-fold, and in a real way, we are His eyes, ears, feet and hands, continuing His work on earth.

This truth also shows us that when the Church loses the manifestation of the gifts, it becomes weak, ineffective and something totally different from what God intended.

2. *To assist in evangelizing the world*

The Lord gave the Great Commission as a command for believers to evangelize the world.

> And He said to them, "Go into all the world and preach the gospel to every creature. He who believes and is baptized will be saved; but he who does not believe will be condemned. And these signs will follow those who believe: In My name they will cast out demons; they will speak with new tongues; they will take up serpents; and if they drink anything deadly, it will by no means hurt them; they will lay hands on the sick, and they will recover" (Mk. 16:15-18).

World evangelization was not to be done through the use of gimmicks or gadgets, but through miraculous signs manifested through the gifts of the Spirit.

Evangelizing the nations has not been easy. It has often been a slow and tedious process. Some missionaries have labored all their lives to win a few souls. William Carey, the first missionary of modern times, worked six years to win a single convert. Contrast this with the results of the great mass revivals conducted by those with sign/gift ministries.

A few years ago, one of our associates began a campaign in an Islamic country. Approximately 10,000 Muslims gathered to hear him speak. They were not really hostile, but neither were they convinced that Jesus is the Son of God, or that He is alive. They had been taught that He was a prophet such as Mohammed.

The evangelist asked the people if they would believe in Jesus if He healed people before their eyes — giving sight to the blind, hearing to the deaf and making the lame to walk. They readily signified that they would. When these miracles actually began to occur, the vast audience of Muslims began to shout, "Jesus is alive, He is alive! Jesus is the Son of God! He heals our people!"

3. To edify the Church

> But he who prophesies speaks edification and exhortation and comfort to men. ... Even so you, since you are zealous for spiritual *gifts, let it be* for the edification of the church *that* you seek to excel. ... How is it then, brethren? Whenever you come together, each of you has a psalm, has a teaching, has a tongue, has a revelation, has an interpretation. Let all things be done for edification (I Cor. 14:3, 12, 26).

The 14th chapter of I Corinthians gives instructions regarding the order of an apostolic service. For example, we are advised that before giving a message in an unknown tongue, we should make sure there is an interpreter present. Several times in this chapter, Paul emphasizes that edification is one of the greatest purposes of the gifts. Though any gift manifested in the assembly can result in blessing the believers, the gifts of prophecy and speaking in tongues with interpretation are especially adapted for the edification of believers.

4. Deliverance for God's people

Almost all the gifts of the Spirit may serve at times to effect a supernatural deliverance for the people of God, but some of the gifts are ordained for deliverance. The Old Testament is full of occurrences in which the people of God received supernatural deliverance. Jesus' ministry was marked by miracles of supply, such as turning water into wine, the feeding of the 5,000, and miracles of deliverance such as calming the sea.

The gifts designed specifically for delivering God's people in times of crisis are the word of wisdom, the word of knowledge, gifts of healings, working of miracles and the gift of faith.

5. For the perfecting of the Church

And He Himself gave some *to be* apostles, some prophets, some evangelists, and some pastors and teachers, for the equipping of the saints for the work of ministry, for the edifying of the body of Christ, till we all come to the unity of the faith and of the knowledge of the Son of God, to a perfect man, to the measure of the stature of the fullness of Christ; that we should no longer be children, tossed to and fro and carried about with every wind of doctrine, by the trickery of men, in the cunning craftiness of deceitful plotting (Eph. 4:11-14).

Closely associated with edification is God's eternal purpose to perfect the Church. The gifts of the Spirit are manifest through chosen individuals — apostles, prophets, evangelists, pastors and teachers — so that the Church may be made ready for His Second Coming.

Even though people become devout Christians, there is always a possibility that they may be misled by a self-deceived leader who happens to win their confidence. The Church needs teaching by God-anointed men who can discern between true and false.

Are the Gifts of the Spirit Actually Imparted to Believers?

Before we go further in the study of this fascinating subject, we need to give careful consideration to the question of whether the individual members of the body of Christ actually receive these gifts, or if they are given to the Church as a body, and manifested by the Spirit through its various members by a sort of rotation. It is very important for us to know the answer to this question.

There are three possibilities of how the gifts of the Spirit might be distributed, each of which would directly effect how they operate:

First, God could give the gifts to a person as an outright

legacy. The gifts would be his to use exactly as he pleased, with no accountability. There would be no need for instructions on how to take care of the inheritance. Obviously, the gifts of the Spirit are not given on that basis.

Secondly, all initiative in the operation of the gifts might belong to the Holy Spirit, with the members of the body of Christ being passive instruments. A notable illustration of this kind of gift manifestation is the incident when God spoke through Balaam's donkey. In this case, it is apparent that God manifested Himself through the animal, though it obviously did not receive any gift.

That brings us to the third possibility, and the one that I believe is scriptural: The believer is an actual recipient of a gift and is an active partner (not just a figurehead, nor a passive instrument as in the case of the donkey) in its manifestation. It is very important that this is clear. Serious error creeps in when individuals get the impression that the gifts are entirely sovereign manifestations of the Spirit, apart from human responsibility and cooperation. If people suppose that the responsibility for the operation of the gifts is only God's, there is danger that they will confuse their own faulty actions with those of the Spirit. If and when such people get out of order, they will resist instruction, claiming that the Spirit of God makes them do what they do.

Paul refuted this fallacy when he said, "The spirits of the prophets are subject to the prophets" (I Cor. 14:32). The operation of a gift is clearly in the hands of the prophet, who is responsible for the manner in which the gift is manifested, its timing and its proper exercise (I Cor. 14:23-32).

Wrong as it would be to deny the believer's responsibility in the manifestation of the gifts, it would be even more serious to fail to emphasize the importance of the Holy Spirit in their operation. No one receives spiritual gifts like an inheritance. A partnership exists between God and man, and the cooperation of both is indispensable.

Believers receive gifts, but only in the sense of stewardship, as illustrated in the parable of the talents (Matt. 25:14, 15). The talents did not belong to the servants. All of the talents and the increase were to be presented for accounting at the return of the Lord. One of the servants acted as if the talent was his to do with as he pleased and instead of using it, he hid it in the earth. That wicked servant paid a terrible penalty for his disobedience.

It is extremely important that we have a balanced understanding of the basis on which gifts are given. They are not something to be "turned on or off" at the person's will. Nor are they to be used for personal gain. The gifts are given by the Spirit to qualify a person for a special service in the body, as Paul declares:

> Now you are the body of Christ, and members individually. And God has appointed these in the church: first apostles, second prophets, third teachers, after that miracles, then gifts of healings, helps, administrations, varieties of tongues (I Cor. 12:27, 28).

One person is set in a church in a prominent position as pastor or teacher. Another may be given the position of helps, a ministry which may include many things. Romans 12:8 even speaks of giving as one of the "helps." God may bless some individuals more than others financially so they are enabled to help the Church in a special way. God uses each member of the body differently.

The Bible plainly teaches that a gift is given in such a way that we can say one person has it and another does not. God wants every Spirit-filled believer to have at least one manifestation of the Spirit. We are responsible to see that it is exercised, and we will stand before the judgment seat of Christ to give an account of our stewardship.

Scriptural Evidence

Now let us consider the scriptural evidence that the gifts of the Spirit are actually imparted to believers.

1. Both Gifts and Manifestations

The spiritual gifts that Paul speaks of in I Corinthians 12:4-11 are both gifts of the Spirit and manifestations. "But the manifestation of the Spirit is given to each one for the profit *of all*" (ver. 7). Here we are informed that everyone should have at least one of the manifestations. But they are also called gifts, as verse 4 plainly says: "There are diversities of gifts, but the same Spirit."

Paul is plainly giving an introduction to the nine gifts that he lists in verses 8-10. (These gifts of the Spirit should not be confused with the ministry gifts listed in I Corinthians 12:28.) If Paul speaks of these manifestations as gifts, then we should also.

2. Desiring the Best Gifts

But earnestly desire the best gifts. And yet I show you a more excellent way (I Cor. 12:31).

In this verse, is Paul referring to the gifts of the Spirit, or to the ministry-gifts of verse 28 which include apostles and prophets? Surely, Paul does not mean that all Christians are to desire the offices of the apostle and prophet! The first few verses of chapter 13 show that Paul is referring to the gifts of the Spirit, for he mentions several of them — speaking in tongues, prophecy, the word of knowledge, faith and miracles.

In the King James Version, the word desire as used in I Corinthians 12:31 is translated "covet." Covet means to strongly desire possession of something. The tenth commandment warns against coveting or seeking possession of something that belongs to another, but Paul encourages the coveting of God's best gifts!

3. Gifts of Healings

Is more proof needed than this that the manifestations of the Spirit are gifts of the Spirit? Note that Paul actually speaks of one manifestation of the Spirit as "gifts of healings" (I Cor. 12:9). It is by virtue of having this gift that one qualifies for the office of "gifts of healings" which is listed along with apostles, prophets, teachers, etc. in I Corinthians 12:30. The gifts of healings are made available to the Church, but they are given only to certain members. Thus, the conclusion is inevitable, that believers have gifts of the Spirit.

4. *Distributed to Individuals*

> But the manifestation of the Spirit is given to each one for the profit *of all*: for to one is given the word of wisdom through the Spirit, to another the word of knowledge through the same Spirit, to another faith by the same Spirit, to another gifts of healings by the same Spirit, to another the working of miracles, to another prophecy, to another discerning of spirits, to another *different* kinds of tongues, to another the interpretation of tongues (I Cor. 12:7-10).

We have noted that Paul says, "There are diversities of gifts" (ver. 4). In verses 7 and 8, we are told that the manifestation of these gifts is "given to each one for the profit *of all*. For to one is given the word of wisdom ... to another the word of knowledge ..."

After listing these nine manifestations of the gifts, he then adds, "But one and the same Spirit works all these things, distributing to each one individually as He wills" (ver. 11). Notice that Paul devotes the rest of the chapter to explaining that through the operation of these gifts each of the members of the body of Christ have a special function of their own. By virtue of this function, the individual, through his/her office, becomes a gift to the Church. God sets them in the body to fulfill a certain purpose (ver. 28-30).

It seems logical that God would give gifts to individuals who by nature and temperament are best fitted for them, rather than rotating them indiscriminately through all members of the body. Observation confirms that this is what happens. But, only God knows what is in the heart of man. Some that we would never suppose would be qualified for a certain ministry, receive it. God reserves the right to manifest His gifts through anyone, at anytime, and on any occasion. Neither Samuel nor Jesse expected David to be the one who would receive the kingly anointing, but God gave it to him anyway.

5. Impartation

> For I long to see you, that I may impart to you some spiritual gift, so that you may be established (Rom. 1:11).

When the Apostle Paul, wrote to the saints at Rome, he was filled with concern for the spiritual growth of Christians in that city. He declared that they were on his heart, and he hoped God would permit him to visit them. For what reason? That he might impart a spiritual gift to them. Did Paul mean that the spiritual gift to be imparted was to the Church as a whole, and not to the individual? The epistle to the Romans considers not only the gifts of the Church, but also those of its individual members. He points out that believers have "gifts differing according to the grace that is given to us" (Rom. 12:6). Let us read the entire passage:

> For as we have many members in one body, but all the members do not have the same function, so we, *being* many, are one body in Christ, and individually members of one another. Having then gifts differing according to the grace that is given to us, *let us use them*: if prophecy, *let us prophesy* in proportion to our faith; or ministry, *let us use it* in *our* ministering; he who teaches, in teaching (Rom. 12:4-7).

6. Translation of Greek Terms

> Do not neglect the gift that is in you, which was

given to you by prophecy with the laying on of the hands of the eldership (I Tim. 4:14).

Therefore I remind you to stir up the gift of God which is in you through the laying on of my hands (II Tim. 1:6).

Was the gift that Paul told Timothy to stir up the gift of the Holy Spirit? Or did Timothy receive a gift of the Spirit for some special ministry that was ahead, and which was announced by prophecy?

It is true that the Holy Spirit is called a gift. The New Testament uses the term "gift of the Holy Spirit" several times. (See Acts 2:38; 8:20; 10:45; Heb. 6:4.) But in each case *dorea*, the Greek word for gift, is used.

On the other hand, whenever gifts of the Spirit are mentioned, the word *charisma* is used. *Charisma* is never used in connection with the Holy Spirit as a gift, and *dorea* is never used in any instance in connection with the gifts of the Spirit.

The word *charisma*, which the Bible uses with the gifts of the Spirit, was used in connection with Timothy's gift. The reference therefore is to a *gift* of the Spirit, not to receiving the Holy Spirit. Besides, one would hardly expect Paul to tell him to stir up the Holy Spirit. Instead, he was telling Timothy to stir up the *gift* of the Spirit (the ministry) he had received by prophecy.

There is one passage in which the term "gifts of the Holy Spirit" appears where it is not translated from the word *charisma*. It is Hebrews 2:4 which says, "... God also bearing witness both with signs and wonders, with various miracles, and gifts of the Holy Spirit, according to His own will?" (Heb. 2:4). In this case, the term comes from the Greek word *merismos*, meaning distributions. When the translators used the word gift, they were not out of line since the word "distributions" conveys the idea of gifts. Thus the gifts are distributed to the members of the body of Christ.

7. *Misuse of the Gifts*

If the operation of the gifts were wholly the initiative of the Spirit, it would be impossible for them to be misused. But Scripture gives overwhelming evidence that it is possible for gifts to be abused.

In the wilderness, when Moses struck the rock twice, he erred because he did not sanctify the Lord before the children of Israel (Num. 20:11, 12). However, the water flowed out of the rock anyway. Moses' faith caused the miracle to take place, even though he had misused his gift.

In another instance, if Christ had not restrained the disciples, they would have brought fire down from heaven upon the people in a village of Samaria (Lk. 9:51-55).

Paul makes it very clear that speaking in other tongues can be misused by being exercised at the wrong time (I Cor. 14:23). Prophets are instructed to manifest their gift in an assembly in proper order, and to restrain it under certain circumstances (I Cor. 14:29-32).

Because it is possible to misuse the gifts of God, it is evident that there is a joint responsibility between God and man in their manifestation.

Chapter Two

How the Gifts are Received

I Corinthians 12, teaches that spiritual gifts are distributed by the will of the Spirit. This truth is made abundantly clear by many examples throughout the Scriptures. No one can take the callings of God upon himself by an act of his own will. "And no man takes this honor to himself, but he who is called by God, just as Aaron *was*" (Heb. 5:4). It is the Spirit of God who chooses who receives these gifts.

> But one and the same Spirit works all these things, distributing to each one individually as He wills. ... But now God has set the members, each one of them, in the body just as He pleased (I Cor. 12:11, 18).

David du Plessis, whose ministry had an unprecedented acceptance in many areas of the Church, including the historic denominations, had some interesting and enlightening remarks to make on this subject. I take the liberty to quote from his book, *The Spirit Bade Me Go.*

> The ministry in the Church is of tremendous importance. I shall never forget years ago when I read the fourth chapter of the book of Ephesians. I came to the 8th verse which said: "He led captivity captive, and gave *gifts* unto men." Immediately I thought of the "gifts of the Spirit." But when I came to the 11th verse I read: "And He gave some, apostles; and some, prophets; and some, evangelists; and some, pastors and teachers; for the perfecting of the saints." This is where many stop and then seek perfect saints. But I believe it means that Christ

gave these ministries that by them the saints may be "trained or perfected, or matured" — "for the work of the ministry," (by all saints in the church), "for the edifying of the body of Christ." When I check with I Cor. 12:28, I find that — "God hath *set* some in the church, first apostles, secondarily prophets, thirdly teachers," etc. These were not gifts of the Spirit; they were ministries *given* by Christ and *set* by God.

When I realized all this, I asked myself, "Did Christ give me a *ministry gift*? Has God *set* me in the Church for any particular *ministry*?" From that time on, I have been less concerned about my career and more about the *ministry*. Am I doing the will of God? Am I obedient to the guidance of the Holy Spirit? Am I perfecting the saints that they may be able to build the Church? *No longer* did I look for "gifts of the Spirit." I know that *if* I am faithful in the *ministry*, the Holy Spirit will *manifest* His gifts through me that I might bring them to the saints for their edification.

Now let us stop in the 12th chapter of I Corinthians for a while. In a retreat with a score or more theologians and ecumenical leaders in 1956, I dealt with this matter. I gave my personal testimony of how the Lord had blessed me, and I had seen a manifestation of *all the gifts* of the Spirit at one time or another in my ministry. Then Dr. Henry P. van Dusen asked me, "How can we get those gifts?" I replied, "Gentlemen, it is not a question of seeking for *gifts*, but rather a matter of *receiving* the *giver* of these gifts." Once you have the Spirit, and the Spirit has full control of *you*, the gifts will follow, or be manifested by the Spirit through you.

I know the general idea is that the Holy Spirit *gives* certain gifts to certain men and thus enables them to do specific things. There is a sense in which this is true, but it is not true that He gives any man a gift that he may *use*. No man can *use* the Holy Spirit, but rather the Holy Spirit *uses* the man as His channel to manifest *His gifts* to the church. The key to the entire operation is found in the 7th verse: "*But* the *manifestation* of the Spirit is *given* to every man to profit withal." It is the *manifestation* that is most important.

Reading from the King James Version, I would put it this way: "For to one (in a specific assembly of the church) is given *by the Spirit*, (here I add — *the manifestation* of) the word of wisdom. To another (the *manifestation* of) the word of knowledge, *by the same spirit*. ..." *All* may have occasional manifestations of *all the gifts*, but some have more frequent manifestations of the same gift, and thus we have the *ministries* which are listed in verse 28. Verse 29 only emphasizes the fact that all have not the same ministry, nor do all have ministries, *but* the fact still remains that — "*the manifestation of the spirit* is given to *every man*."

David du Plessis had the deep conviction that if he moved into the ministry the Lord had intended for him, God would equip him with the gifts necessary to fulfill it. God remarkably fulfilled those anticipations, opening doors for du Plessis that were not open to other men in his generation. The word of wisdom manifested through him in such richness that it enabled him to give satisfying answers to the many questions he was asked by the world's outstanding theologians. As a result, he was able, directly or indirectly, to lead literally hundreds of denominational minsters into the experience of the baptism of the Holy Spirit. Only supernatural ministry could make such a remarkable thing possible.

Too often, ministers try to copy the ministry of another. The attempt to wear Saul's armor never makes a satisfying ministry. Every young person feeling the call of God, should seek to learn what ministry he/she has been set in the Church to accomplish by waiting on God with an open heart in prayer and fasting. *The great question then is not how we can use God, but how can God use us?*

The gifts of the Spirit are therefore given to equip people for the ministry God has chosen for them, whatever that may be. Such gifts are effective only if they are motivated by the Spirit of God, and used for His glory. They are in no sense to be used for personal convenience, or for promotional purposes.

God Chooses the Humble

It is a common observation that the gifts of the Spirit are not usually given to those who are endowed with unusual natural abilities. The fact that one has exceptional human talents provides a strong temptation for that person to rely upon those gifts. This is not always true, of course. The Apostle Paul certainly was endowed with outstanding natural abilities before he became a Christian (Phil. 3:4-7). Nevertheless, Paul himself declared that not many of those with natural abilities receive the call of God (I Cor. 1:26-29).

It is strange but true that people who possess unusual natural talents have an almost fatal tendency to develop pride in those abilities. We are told that the archangel Lucifer fell because of his wisdom and beauty. "Your heart was lifted up because of your beauty; you corrupted your wisdom for the sake of your splendor" (Ezek. 28:17).

Because of this, God chooses people who are small in their own eyes to perform His special work. Notice the kind of men God called to deliver His people in the days of the judges. Moses was the meekest man on the face of the earth (Num. 12:3). Caleb was a mighty man of war (Josh. 14:10, 11), but his nephew, Othniel, was chosen as Israel's first judge (Judg. 3:9). God chose two women, Deborah and Jael, to deliver

Israel from the power of Sisera, the cruel commander of Canaan's forces (Judg. 4:9, 21). Gideon, the son of a poor man, was the least in his father's house (Judg. 6:15), and Jephthah, an illegitimate child, was driven out of his father's house by his half brothers (Judg. 11:1-3). Even Saul, the first king of Israel, was a humble man until he became prideful because of his position (I Sam. 9:21; 15:17).

David was the youngest of Jesse's sons. Neither Jesse nor Samuel supposed that the Lord would choose David to be king. Jesse didn't even bother to call him in from herding the sheep at the time the choice was to be made (I Sam. 16:11).

The twelve apostles were chosen from lowly or humble positions. None of them were trained or schooled in Judaism.

God does not impart His blessings and ministry-gifts indiscriminately. He takes into consideration the person's temperament and general makeup. One person may have natural talents that lend themselves to evangelism, but also have hidden tendencies that might lead to self-exaltation or conceit. As one writer puts it:

> It seems that in some cases the Spirit's distribution of gifts is determined in a measure by the makeup and inherited characteristics of the individual person. Usually, He imparts such gifts as the person can most readily lend himself to. The natural orator is anointed to become a preacher and the one with an analytical mind becomes a teacher. The one for whom it is more natural to have great faith receives the gifts of healings, and such as have a combination of strong willpower, great faith and a fiery nature, become endued with power to work miracles or cast out demons. Others who are very susceptible to spiritual influences are given the gift of discerning spirits.

Conditions for Receiving the Gifts

1. Receiving the Holy Spirit

It is self-evident that if the gifts are of the Spirit, we must have the Holy Spirit in order for them to manifest properly. While it is true that every saved person has the Holy Spirit operating in his/her life, the full baptism of the Holy Spirit is necessary for a normal working of the gifts.

However, it is also apparent that the apostles exercised gifts of healings, and perhaps some working of miracles, before the Day of Pentecost. Indeed, they were commanded to "Heal the sick, cleanse the lepers, raise the dead, cast out demons" (Matt. 10:8). Yet, we know that the baptism in the Holy Spirit is an important factor in the full manifestation of the gifts.

2. Desire (I Cor. 12:31)

Since the Holy Spirit is the Giver of the gifts, some think that there is little we can do about it — that we must wait patiently for God to move in His own good time and in His own way. This is a very inadequate view of the matter, and has encouraged the Church in times past to become lethargic and lukewarm. Using the same reasoning, certain theologians have argued that because the new birth is a supernatural work, the sinner must await the Lord's time for him/her to be saved. Still others have taught that since healing is a work of God, we must leave the matter entirely in His hands, and wait until He is ready to heal.

Putting all the responsibility on God may sound fine, but the Bible plainly teaches that man has a very definite responsibility also. God always fulfills His part if we are faithful in doing ours.

Therefore, although the distributing of the gifts is the Spirit's prerogative, Paul urges us to "earnestly desire the best gifts." We must have a deep desire for them, and our hearts need to be prepared in order to properly exercise the gifts we do receive. Just as children receive the gifts they ask of their fathers, so are God's gifts given to those who ask for them (Matt. 7:11). As an illustration of this, Paul instructs those who speak in tongues in the assembly to pray that they may interpret (I Cor. 14:13).

Another example of earnestly desiring a certain gift or ministry is found in the story of Elisha. He followed Elijah, refusing to accept anything less than a double portion of the spirit that Elijah possessed. Elijah, knowing that God's best is not given lightly, pointed out that Elisha had asked a difficult thing. However, Elisha passed every test, and after Elijah's translation, the sons of the prophets observed, "'The spirit of Elijah rests on Elisha'" (II Ki. 2:15).

What are the "best gifts" that the believer should covet? We would not attempt to decide which are most valuable, for just as with a human body, even the loss of a little finger can cause severe suffering. Paul tells us that we are not to say to the weaker members, "'I have no need of you'" (I Cor. 12:21). The best gifts for each member of the body are the ones the Holy Spirit chooses to manifest through them.

And while we are on the subject, it can be stated without fear of contradiction that one of the best gifts is wisdom, since it is needed in the successful manifestation of all other gifts. James declares that any of us may ask for and receive wisdom.

> If any of you lacks wisdom, let him ask of God,
> who gives to all liberally and without reproach,
> and it will be given to him (Jas. 1:5).

Some may argue that James is not speaking of the gift of the word of wisdom, but verse 17 indicates that he *is* speaking of gifts.

> Every good gift and every perfect gift is from
> above, and comes down from the Father of lights,
> with whom there is no variation or shadow of
> turning (Jas. 1:17).

3. Dedication to God

Those who manifest the gifts of the Spirit are responsible to live a holy lifestyle. Since they possess special tools for wreaking severe damage upon the kingdom of Satan, they become special targets for the enemy's attacks. Satan tries to intensify the temptations of anointed ministers, and sometimes only the most steadfast and continual resistance brings victory. This is seen in Christ's spiritual conflict in the Garden of Gethsemane (Heb. 5:7; Lk. 22:44). The gifts of the Spirit bring the recipient into realms of warfare in the heavenlies, therefore a letdown in prayer life is very dangerous.

We have only to turn to the examples of men like Balaam, Saul, Samson and Judas to understand these warnings. Each of these men was given an unusual ministry. Yet, they were not adequately prepared for the responsibilities they undertook, and as a result, their earthly careers closed in tragedy.

One of the most important preparations for receiving the gifts of the Spirit is to be completely surrendered and consecrated to God. We must be as consecrated to God as the three Hebrew children who were cast into the fiery furnace for their faith.

> "If that *is the case*, our God whom we serve is able to deliver us from the burning fiery furnace, and He will deliver us from your hand, O king. But if not, let it be known to you, O king, that we do not serve your gods, nor will we worship the gold image which you have set up" (Dan. 3:17, 18).

4. The laying on of hands

Paul said, "Do not lay hands on anyone hastily" (I Tim. 5:22). This must include reference to the laying on of hands for the gifts of the Spirit. Simon the sorcerer wanted power so that anyone he laid hands on would receive the Holy Spirit (Acts 8:19). Peter's rebuke settled the question about the matter of indiscriminately laying hands on people.

Caution should also be used when laying hands on people to receive the gifts of the Spirit. While the Holy Spirit is promised to all whom "the Lord our God shall call," the gift-ministries are given only as the Holy Spirit chooses. The Spirit of

God may lead anointed ministers to lay hands upon certain people to receive a gift-ministry. This was evidently true when Paul laid hands on Timothy:

> Do not neglect the gift that is in you, which was given to you by prophecy with the laying on of the hands of the eldership (I Tim. 4:14).

Clearly, the direct guidance of the Spirit of God is all-important in the matter of laying on hands. It appears that Paul and the presbyters did not lay hands on Timothy to give him a predetermined ministry. Instead, it was the Spirit that spoke by means of a prophecy and told them what his ministry would be. Overzealous people can, by their well-meant but unscriptural actions, do things that are out of order, and which lead to expectations that can never be fulfilled. Paul laid hands on Timothy, but he knew all about him, his mother and even his grandmother. It is not insignificant that Paul refers to the young man's background in connection with laying hands on Timothy (II Tim. 1:5, 6). Likewise, Moses laid hands on Joshua in order for him to receive the spirit of wisdom (Deut. 34:9). But, he did this only after he had known Joshua for a long time and he had thoroughly proved himself.

Chapter Three

The Nine Gifts

The nine gifts of the Spirit fall into three general classifications.

First, there are the revelatory gifts:
1. Word of wisdom
2. Word of knowledge
3. Discerning of spirits

Second, there are the power gifts:
1. Faith
2. Gifts of healings
3. Working of miracles

Third, there are the inspirational gifts:
1. Prophecy
2. Different kinds of tongues
3. Interpretation of tongues

It must not be thought that the gifts of the Spirit are all sharply defined one from another. Actually, the gifts in these three groups tend to merge from one into another, as the spectrum of a rainbow. Thus, the word of knowledge and the discerning of spirits are similar gifts. The supernatural knowledge obtained through discerning of spirits is really a specialized kind of knowledge.

Again, gifts of healings are for the deliverance of the human body from sickness and disease. Yet, a healing which requires creative work would seem to be more correctly classified under the working of miracles. Certainly, the resurrection of the dead is beyond the scope of the gifts of healings, yet healing is involved. It is evident that the boundaries between the two gifts are not sharply defined.

Those familiar with Pentecostal meetings will observe that an utterance in tongues may move into the realm of prophecy. The two gifts are similar in operation except that with prophecy, one speaks in his/her native tongue and therefore has no need of an interpreter.

Often, two or more gifts operate simultaneously. The word of wisdom and the word of knowledge work closely together. Knowledge is the raw material, but we must have wisdom to know how to use it. In II Kings 6 we see as many as seven of the gifts in operation on one occasion!

But, can the supernatural manifestations recorded in the Old Testament be regarded as gifts of the Spirit? It is hard to see how they could be considered in any other light, since the operations were clearly acts of God's Spirit. However, in Old Testament times, the manifestations of the Spirit were on a far more limited scale, with only a comparatively few enjoying these supernatural gifts. In the New Testament dispensation, "the manifestation of the Spirit is given to each one for the profit *of all*" (I Cor. 12:7).

In the Old Testament, the emphasis was on working miracles and predicting future events. The gifts of tongues and interpretation were not evident at all. In the New Testament, the working of miracles is balanced by the operation of other gifts, and the gift of prophecy is used more for the edification of the members of the body than foretelling future events.

Another important factor in the operation of the gifts in the New Testament period is that the Spirit of God is active in the earth during this age. The Holy Spirit manifests His presence in a more direct way to God's people now than during Old Testament times. This is clearly seen from the words of Jesus:

> "Nevertheless I tell you the truth. It is to your advantage that I go away; for if I do not go away, the Helper will not come to you; but if I depart, I will send Him to you" (Jn. 16:7).

Differences of Administrations and Operations

There are differences of ministries, but the same Lord. And there are diversities of activities, but it is the same God who works all in all. (I Cor. 12:5, 6).

The fact that there is a diversity of gifts and gift-ministries is more or less recognized, but that there are different administrations and operations of gifts is not so clearly understood. For example, both Isaiah and Hosea were prophets, and their writings are inspired, but there is certainly a big difference in their prophecies.

Among the Old Testament prophets, the messages of some were only warnings for the people to repent. Other prophets went much deeper into the mind of the Spirit and brought forth deep revelatory truths. Yet, both were anointed by the same Holy Spirit. This variation in prophetic ministers still exists among the New Testament prophets.

Likewise, the operation of the gifts of healings varies in the ministries of different men. This is also true in the manifestation of the other gifts. Our God is a God of variety, whether it is in the realm of nature, or in the spiritual world.

Expect Persecution

Despite the blessings that come from the operation of the gifts, there will be carnal people who, for various reasons, will oppose their manifestation. This is not a modern attitude. During Christ's earthly ministry, there was a certain religious group, the Sadducees, who denied the miraculous. They did not believe in the resurrection, angels or spirits (Acts 23:8).

Even during Paul's ministry, there were some in the Church who began to draw back from supernatural ministry. They had a form of godliness, but denied its power, and Paul warned Timothy to turn away from such people (II Tim. 3:5).

Only 35 years after Pentecost, some from within the Church's own ranks, such as Hymenaeus and Philetus, were teaching that the resurrection had already past (II Tim. 2:17, 18). Others had not gone that far, but were obviously moving away from the supernatural ministry. Ritualists learned quickly that it was easier for them to maintain a smooth-running religious organization if it was conducted on purely natural lines. In the Church at Thessalonica, there was a trend to hold down the operation of the prophetic gifts, no doubt because of the problems presented by this ministry. Notice Paul's admonition to the Thessalonians:

> Do not quench the Spirit. Do not despise prophecies. Test all things; hold fast what is good (I Thes. 5:19-21).

To those in the Corinthian Church who wanted to eliminate speaking in tongues because some had misused the gift, Paul admonished, "do not forbid to speak with tongues" (I Cor. 14:39).

Stirring Up the Gifts

There is a danger that some who have gifts will be tempted to allow them to become dormant. Apparently, this was true to some extent in the case of Timothy, a young man in whom Paul had a fatherly interest and affection. If Paul had an heir, it was Timothy. Yet, we note that twice in his letters the apostle had to admonish the young man to stir up his gift. Both times Paul reminded Timothy of the occasion when hands were laid upon him, and a prophecy was given foretelling the ministry that would be his.

With the gifts, come serious responsibilities. Some neglect the responsibility, perhaps desiring a quieter ministry. This is a dangerous thing to do. All gifts of the Spirit are given by the Lord to accomplish a certain work. Failure to exercise the gift would probably leave that work undone. This is serious and brings to mind the parable of the slothful servant who buried the talent the Lord had given him. The judgment that fell upon that servant should be a warning sufficient to any believer who is allowing his/her gifts to lie dormant.

Some individuals do not manifest their gifts as they should

because of a lack of faith. There must be a boldness of faith in the operation of the gifts or they will not work properly. An excellent illustration of this is when Peter walked on water. When he got his eyes off of Christ and upon the waves, down he went.

God has given all His people a certain amount of faith, as Romans 12:3 declares: "God has dealt to each one a measure of faith." Nevertheless, even this faith can become passive unless we exercise it. We must put our faith into action.

> Having then gifts differing according to the grace that is given to us, *let us use them*: if prophecy, *let us prophesy* in proportion to our faith (Rom. 12:6).

While it is not wise to attempt things beyond our faith, neither should we lag behind in the measure of faith that God has given to us.

Donald Gee, in his book *Concerning Spiritual Gifts*, makes the following remarks:

> These passages suggest at once the thought that many believers do not need to pray for the bestowal of spiritual gifts half so much as they need to attend to the exercise of those they already possess. In such a case it is no use trying to throw the responsibility on the Lord, as though He had never given, or else had withdrawn the gift. The believer himself is responsible for stirring up his gift as the Holy Spirit moves upon him and seeks to bring the sluggish manifestation of His presence into operation once more. How firmly Paul's inspired advice to Timothy insists on the human side of responsibility for the exercise of the Spirit's gifts. It is almost as though God had made Himself sovereign in the bestowal of the gifts, and then left man sovereign as to their free and profitable

exercise. The whole teaching of I Cor. 14 implies the same principle.

If the believer is convicted that he is not in perfect liberty regarding the exercise of gifts once bestowed, then the obvious remedy is repentance concerning whatever may have hindered; a placing of ourselves as far as possible in the flow of the Spirit, and a definite exercise of the will to stir up the neglected gifts. Failure to do this means personal loss, means loss to the Church, and loss thereby to the glory of God.

Are the Gifts Under Control of the Believer?

We believe that, with possible rare exceptions, the recipient of a gift has complete control of his faculties. It is true that on occasion a person, while receiving the Holy Spirit or some special revelation, can be so lost in the Spirit that he/she is not aware of what is going on nearby. But, during public ministry, even while deep in the Spirit, the speaker almost always knows what he is doing and saying. If he chooses, he can stop speaking in tongues or prophesying. Of course, when the Spirit prompts him to do these things, he should obey the Lord. But, what he is doing *is* under his control.

Regarding this, Donald Gee writes in his book *Concerning Spiritual Gifts*:

> There is a mistaken idea quite prevalent that in the exercise of a spiritual gift, the believer is practically forced by the Holy Spirit, almost in spite of the human will. This is never so when God is the source of inspiration to either utterance or action. He always leaves the freedom of the human will entirely unimpaired. The manifestation of the Spirit can be "quenched;" on the other hand the impulses of the Holy Spirit can be yielded to so readily and intelligently that there can be an instant and beautiful exercise of

any spiritual gift. This should be our aim, and it reveals "God and man in oneness blending," not the driving of slave by its master.

Can the Gifts of the Spirit be Counterfeited?

Many people take for granted that every manifestation resembling the operation of the gifts of the Spirit is genuine. But, the Apostle John warns us to test the spirits, for they are not all from God.

> Beloved, do not believe every spirit, but test the spirits, whether they are of God; because many false prophets have gone out into the world. By this you know the Spirit of God: Every spirit that confesses that Jesus Christ has come in the flesh is of God, and every spirit that does not confess that Jesus Christ has come in the flesh is not of God. And this is the *spirit* of the Antichrist, which you have heard was coming, and is now already in the world (I Jn. 4:1-3).

Jesus warned that as the Great Tribulation draws near, there will be many false prophets showing signs and wonders.

> "For false christs and false prophets will rise and show great signs and wonders to deceive, if possible, even the elect" (Matt. 24:24).

The Book of Revelation informs us that during this time, demonic spirits will work miracles and deceive the whole world (Rev. 16:14).

In view of these warnings, there can be no doubt that the gifts of the Spirit can be imitated. Just as Satan deceived Eve through the snake in the Garden of Eden, his false prophets continue to allure many into paths of deception and error. However, the Bible provides information on discerning between the true and the false. Those who prayerfully study the Word of God will never fall victim to these deceptions.

1. The Magicians and Moses

Perhaps the most striking illustration of Satan's ability to imitate God's work is found in the story of Moses. When God gave Moses and Aaron the authority to execute judgment on Egypt, He also gave them a sign to prove this authority to Pharaoh (Ex. 7:9). When Moses threw his rod on the ground, it became a snake (Ex. 4:3).

Moses and Aaron went to Pharaoh and did as the Lord commanded. Aaron threw down the rod and it turned into a snake (Ex. 7:10). But the Egyptian magicians were able to do the same thing (ver. 11, 12)! How could one tell which miracle was of God and which was of the devil? Notice what happened. *Aaron's rod swallowed up the magicians' rods!* Divine power swallowed up the magicians' snakes.

Spiritualists and sorcerers are able to perform many mystifying acts. Sorcery is the art of producing false miracles such as materialization and dematerialization. Elijah and Elisha created oil, but the *oil did not dematerialize; it remained to bless.* Sorcery may imitate a creative miracle, but its miracles are illusionary. Satan does not possess true creative power.

The magicians kept trying. Aaron stretched out his rod over the waters of Egypt and they became blood. The magicians tried their enchantments. They could not counteract the plague, but they were able to imitate what had been done (Ex. 7:19-22).

Pharaoh hardened his heart, refusing to repent, so another judgment came upon him — the plague of frogs (Ex. 8:5, 6). Once again, the magicians were able to imitate what Moses and Aaron had done. But, they were nearing the end of their resources. The magicians failed in their attempts to imitate the next plague — the plague of lice. Then the magicians recognized that the miracles were judgments of God. However, the perverse, self-willed Pharaoh refused to repent.

> Now the magicians so worked with their enchantments to bring forth lice, but they could not. So there were lice on man and beast. Then the magicians said to Pharaoh, "This *is* the finger of God." But Pharaoh's heart grew hard,

and he did not heed them, just as the LORD had said (Ex. 8:18, 19).

Satan has only a certain degree of power. He can imitate some of the gifts of God, so we must be alert to his deceptions. Nevertheless, there is a definite limit to what Satan is able to do. He is not all-powerful.

2. *Human Failure and Evil Spirits*

People are prone to suppose that someone manifesting a gift is practically infallible. Though we should extend honor to the office, we should not surrender our powers of discrimination to the point where we cannot recognize wrong when it exists. A person ministering with the gifts of the Spirit is just as accountable to God and man as anyone else.

There was an incident of a young man who apparently had a genuine experience with God, but due to certain inconsistencies in his life, he opened the door to evil spirits. Since that experience is an excellent example of the matter we are considering, we quote from it here:

> During the time shortly after my conversion, I made it a habit to set aside certain periods for seeking the Lord. My heart was hungry for a deeper revelation of God's wisdom and power. Sometimes I would give hours, even nights waiting upon the Lord. During this period I was joined by another brother, who often spent considerable time with me in prayer. He was almost a full-blooded Indian and we called him "Indian Bill." Indian Bill seemed quite sincere, and it was not until some time later that I learned that he indulged periodically in heavy potations of strong liquor, at which time he became quite another man. Actually, I believe that he desired to be a real Christian, but when temptation pressed him, he would yield to it, thus opening

the way for the operation of demon powers.

Being a new convert, I was rather naive in my understanding of spiritual things. At the time, I supposed that most Christians were only a little less than perfect, and altogether I possessed a very inadequate knowledge of the cunning and subtlety of Satan.

One night while we were praying, Indian Bill began to hear a voice. The voice claimed to be of God. It then informed him that he had been specially favored of God to receive certain "revelations." Bill was far from an educated person, and the "revelations" certainly indicated that another intelligence than his was doing the speaking. In fact, most of the subjects discussed were well beyond the ken of my companion's knowledge. Such subjects as heaven and hell were minutely discussed, and the conditions of those places described in detail. I had a novice's fascination by all this, and at the time had no doubt but that the communications were of God. Having reached the place where we had unreserved confidence in the "messages," the voice then began to play on our human ego. Foolish dupes that we were, we were elated over the thought of being the recipients of what seemed to us to be revelations as great as those in the Bible.

After a time, the voice began to speak against certain ones in the church who, it warned, would not accept these "revelations." We were told that these people were jealous, and that under no circumstances should we give them heed.

Then came the climaxing "revelation." Indian Bill was told that he was "Elijah" returned to earth! (Poor Elijah! How many people in the course of history have supposed that they were Elijah, and have gone to extreme efforts to prove the alleged identity!) Indian Bill was soon convinced that he was Elijah, and the voice warned me that I must accept him as God's special prophet. Naive as I was, now for the first time I began to entertain suspicions. When the young man began to publicly declare his office as that prophet, I at last saw that something was decidedly wrong. It might appear to the reader that I should have become suspicious sooner, but it must be remembered that I was just a young convert, and was fair game for the enemy. Nor did I, at that time, know about my companion's addiction to alcoholic beverages and his periodic relapses — which made possible the operation of seducing spirits.

Nevertheless, inexperienced as I was, I became convinced that the voice must be a seducing or familiar spirit, and I was shocked to realize that I had been so easily taken in. I then earnestly plead with my companion to seek God for deliverance from the deceiving spirit. In justice to him, I must say that he was willing to listen. We knelt together to pray. But the voice, with great urgency, warned us that we must not doubt, that all was well if we did not doubt. Finally, the spirit said, "I will prove to you that I am of God." At that very moment, a guitar standing in the corner made a sound as if a hand had been drawn over the strings, producing a set of chords! This was repeated several times. ...

However, I was no longer deceived. I realized that actually we were having a demonstration of spiritualism, and that the spirit speaking through Indian Bill was evidently a seducing spirit. I then challenged the voice, declaring it was not God but was in fact a familiar spirit. Immediately, there was a surprising result. The devil unmasked, plainly confessed, "Yes, I am the devil. God has permitted me to deceive you because you have committed the unpardonable sin! You are forever lost!"

For several days, I was almost ready to believe this, and I went through great anguish of soul. I thought perhaps I had committed the unpardonable sin. However, God came to me with the following Scripture: "Let not your heart be troubled: ye believe in God, believe also in me" (Jn. 14:1). The Lord then made me to know that He had permitted me to go through this experience for a purpose. That I must not trust every spirit, but I must try the spirits and learn the difference between the true and the false. It was a valuable lesson to me in the years to come and one that I never forgot.

Indian Bill finally recovered from the control of the evil spirit, and I hope, overcame his fondness for alcoholic beverages. However, there are some who go so far in their rebellion that the Spirit of God finally leaves them. Such is the sad story of one of the apostles of Christ.

It should be understood that just because a person rebels doesn't mean that the gift of God will immediately stop working through him. In fact, we are told that "the gifts and the calling of God *are* irrevocable" (Rom. 11:29). This is something that is hard for people to understand. However, an individual with a sign-gift ministry may actually fall into a state of disobedience to God and still continue his/her ministry. This is clearly portrayed in the life of Saul, who was not only king of Israel, but also had a prophetic ministry.

"Then the Spirit of the LORD will come upon you, and you will prophesy with them and be turned into another man." ... When they came there to the hill, there was a group of prophets to meet him; then the Spirit of God came upon him, and he prophesied among them (I Sam. 10:6, 10).

Unfortunately, Saul was unstable. Self-will, envy and a violent temper marked his erratic temperament. Eventually, the Spirit of the Lord left him and an evil spirit took control. His servants apparently discerned what had happened and took action to ensure his deliverance. The Spirit of the Lord had come upon David, and Saul's servants brought him into the palace to minister to the king by playing the harp. During this ministry, the evil spirit left Saul.

But the Spirit of the LORD departed from Saul, and a distressing spirit from the LORD troubled him. And Saul's servants said to him, "Surely, a distressing spirit from God is troubling you. Let our master now command your servants, *who are* before you, to seek out a man *who is* a skill-ful player on the harp. And it shall be that he will play it with his hand when the distressing spirit from God is upon you, and you shall be well." ... And so it was, whenever the spirit from God was upon Saul, that David would take a harp and play *it* with his hand. Then Saul would become refreshed and well, and the distressing spirit would depart from him (I Sam. 16:14-16, 23).

Nevertheless, after David killed Goliath, jealousy entered Saul's heart, opening the door for the evil spirit to return.

> And it happened on the next day that the distressing spirit from God came upon Saul, and he prophesied inside the house. So David played *music* with his hand, as at other times; but *there was* a spear in Saul's hand (I Sam. 18:10).

Saul became murderous under the influence of this demon, and tried to kill David (ver. 11, 12). From that time on, evil influenced Saul's life (I Sam. 19:9).

Yet, a very strange thing happened when David fled and Saul followed him to Naioth. Apparently, Samuel and David had called the prophets of the Lord together to wait upon God and ask for the wisdom to meet the threat against their lives. As Saul's messengers came into the camp, instead of taking David captive, they began to prophesy! Then Saul himself went down. And on his way to David and Samuel's camp, he too began to prophesy — even though an evil spirit had taken possession of him.

> So he went there to Naioth in Ramah. Then the Spirit of God was upon him also, and he went on and prophesied until he came to Naioth in Ramah. And he also stripped off his clothes and prophesied before Samuel in like manner, and lay down naked all that day and all that night. Therefore they say, "*Is* Saul also among the prophets?"(I Sam. 19:23, 24).

The only explanation of this is that the gifts and callings of God are irrevocable. The Spirit of God came upon Saul and he prophesied, causing a conflict between God's Spirit and the evil spirit that had been controlling him. In the conflict, the evil spirit caused him to tear off his clothes and lay naked publicly. What an example of the flesh warring against the Spirit! Those who have gifts of the Spirit should walk humbly before God, lest evil powers move in and hinder or prevent the operation of their gifts. Saul's sad confession was, "I have played the fool and erred exceedingly" (I Sam. 26:21).

The state of affairs that existed with Saul could not go on forever. Toward the end, Saul's prophetic gift was no longer manifesting, and God no longer answered him. In this hopeless condition, he turned to spiritualism and paid a visit to the witch of En Dor.

> And when Saul inquired of the LORD, the LORD did not answer him, either by dreams or by Urim or by the prophets. Then Saul said to his servants, "Find me a woman who is a medium, that I may go to her and inquire of her." And his servants said to him, "In fact, *there is* a woman who is a medium at En Dor"(I Sam. 28:6, 7).

The next day he lost a battle and died on the point of his own spear.

The story of Saul has been repeated more than once. One minister, in particular, once possessed an outstanding anointing. Certain gifts of the Spirit were clearly seen in his ministry. However, he moved at a fast pace and failed to take time to wait on God. Because of this, he lapsed into an old habit formed before his conversion — seeking relaxation through the use of alcohol. Caught in an intoxicated condition on a public highway, he was arrested and charged with driving while under the influence of alcohol.

He confessed what had happened to several of his fellow ministers, and had he only stayed with his confession, God would have delivered him. However, he was pressured by those who believed a cover-up was necessary to save his ministry, and he publicly declared that the whole thing had been a set up. Thus, like Saul, he gave in to the temptation to try to save face with the people at any cost.

> Then he said, "I have sinned; *yet* honor me now, please, before the elders of my people and before Israel, and return with me, that I may worship the LORD your God" (I Sam. 15:30).

Strange as it may seem, even after this deceit, this leader continued to increase in popularity. The gifts of the Spirit continued to be evident in his meetings, and his followers could not believe that he would be party to such a lie. They considered him a martyr. For a long time, it seemed that God had sanctioned his decision. Nevertheless, the time came when this strange Dr. Jekyll and Mr. Hyde performance came out, and those who encouraged the minister to live a lie began to reap the bitter fruit of deception.

Gifts of the Spirit and Godly Living

Unfortunately, there are some who manifest genuine gifts but fall into sin, and in so doing, bring confusion into the house of God.

1. David

David was the sweet psalmist of Israel, a man in which the prophetic gifts were manifest in a special way, and whose psalms have provided inspiration to millions of people. Yet, this inspired writer committed adultery with Bathsheba, and to cover that up, he was a conspirator in the death of her husband.

God forgave David, because he became deeply repentant for his sin. But, the consequences of his actions were beyond calculation. Because his sin brought reproach upon the Lord's cause (II Sam. 12:14), David paid the penalty for his sin for the rest of his life — with treachery and betrayal occurring within his own household. The prophetic anointing continued to work through David (see Psalm 51), but he paid a fearful price for his sins.

2. Balaam

Balaam was a prophet for hire, but he was not a false prophet. Some of his prophecies are among the most beautiful in the Scriptures. Consider his prophecy of Christ:

> "I see Him, but not now; I behold Him, but not near; a Star shall come out of Jacob; a Scepter

shall rise out of Israel, and batter the brow of
Moab, and destroy all the sons of tumult" (Num.
24:17).

Balaam's besetting sin was his love of money. God forbade
him to go with Balak, the Moabite king, who wanted him to
curse the children of Israel (Num. 22:12). But, Balak promised
him riches and honor, so he asked the Lord again for permission to go. Balaam gained neither riches nor honor. He
retained his position as a seer, but his ministry degenerated
into soothsaying and divination.

The children of Israel also killed with the sword
Balaam the son of Beor, the soothsayer, among
those who were killed by them (Josh. 13:22).

According to Acts 16:16, divination is the work of familiar
spirits. As in the case of King Saul, the Spirit of God evidently
forsook Balaam and an evil spirit took its place.

3. Samson

Samson was one of the judges of Israel. His birth was foretold by an angel, at which time God ordained him to be a
Nazarite. Early in his life, the Spirit of God began to move
upon him at his home in the camp of Dan (Judg. 13:25; 14:6).
Samson's supernatural strength enabled him to confound
Israel's enemies, the Philistines, and put them to flight. His col-
orful exploits are familiar stories to all Bible readers.

But Samson had one fatal weakness; he continually ignored
his Nazarite vow of separation. One night, he visited a prostitute in Gaza. Yet, the gift of God did not immediately leave
him. At midnight, he carried away the gates of the city and left
them at the top of a nearby hill (Judg. 16:1-3). It might seem
to the casual observer that the Lord winked at his immoral
conduct. But God does not always collect His accounts on the
day evil is committed.

Samson, morally weakened by sleeping with prostitutes,
now dallied with the treacherous Delilah. As a result of her

seduction, he permitted his hair to be cut. Because of this, his strength left him. Samson deliberately played with fire, and he became a victim of his own foolishness. His eyes were put out, and he was forced to grind in the prison house of the Philistines.

> And she said, "The Philistines *are* upon you, Samson!" So he awoke from his sleep, and said, "I will go out as before, at other times, and shake myself free!" But he did not know that the LORD had departed from him. Then the Philistines took him and put out his eyes, and brought him down to Gaza. They bound him with bronze fetters, and he became a grinder in the prison (Judg. 16:20, 21).

But Samson's gift had not completely left. He was to perform one more great exploit. When his hair finally grew out again, he was brought before the Philistines for them to make fun of him. The Lord, in answer to his prayer, allowed him to collapse the pillars of the Philistine temple, killing about 3,000 men and women including himself (Judg. 16:27-30).

4. Judas Iscariot

Judas Iscariot is a solemn example of a man who manifested genuine gifts of the Spirit, yet totally failed God. He was one of the 12 apostles Jesus sent out to heal the sick, perform miracles, and even raise the dead (Matt. 10:1-8). Likewise, the 70, who were sent out at a later time, returned to testify that even devils were subject to them (Lk. 10:17-20). There is no record that all the others succeeded while Judas failed. We have no record of any particular miracle that he performed, but it is evident that all the twelve had success in this ministry. In fact, he must have achieved a certain prominence, since he was elected treasurer of the group (Jn. 12:4-6).

Apparently, none of the disciples suspected that Judas would betray Christ. When Jesus revealed that one of them would betray Him, everyone of them, including Judas asked, "'Lord, is it I?'" (Matt. 26:22). Acts 1:17 declares that Judas had obtained and shared the ministry that the other disciples had. Peter says, "'For he was numbered with us and obtained a part in this ministry.'" Yet, he betrayed Christ, and after a fruitless repentance, went out and committed suicide.

Certainly, these biblical examples show that the gifts of the Spirit are not meant to be infallible proofs that a person is living a lifestyle that pleases God. They also show that people may continue in their own momentum for a season, but if they persist in a course of self-will, it will destroy them. Repentance will bring God's forgiveness, although like David, the consequences of wrongdoing may be unavoidable.

By Their Fruits You Will Know Them

Jesus taught that a person's character is not to be judged by the gifts, but by the fruits. He added that at the day of judgment, many will say that they prophesied, possessed gifts of healings or worked miracles, offering this as proof that they were true believers. However, they will be judged as workers of iniquity!

> "Not everyone who says to Me, 'Lord, Lord,' shall enter the kingdom of heaven, but he who does the will of My Father in heaven. Many will say to Me in that day, 'Lord, Lord, have we not prophesied in Your name, cast out demons in Your name, and done many wonders in Your name?' And then I will declare to them, 'I never knew you; depart from Me, you who practice lawlessness!'" (Matt. 7:21-23).

The true test of a genuine follower of Christ is in the fruits of the Spirit.

> "Beware of false prophets, who come to you in sheep's clothing, but inwardly they are ravenous wolves. You will know them by their fruits. Do men gather grapes from thornbushes or figs

from thistles? Even so, every good tree bears
good fruit, but a bad tree bears bad fruit. A good
tree cannot bear bad fruit, nor *can* a bad tree
bear good fruit" (Matt. 7:15-18).

The implication is clear. Even though someone demonstrates unusual gifts, they should not be followed unless they
also manifest the fruits. In Paul's discussion on the gifts of the
Spirit, he urges believers to covet the best gifts. He then adds
that they must seek the fruits, or the others will not profit
them. "But earnestly desire the best gifts. And yet I show you
a more excellent way" (I Cor. 12:31).

Chapter Four

The Importance of the Fruits of the Spirit

Today, the gifts of the Spirit are being re-emphasized and restored to the Church, and rightly so. God did not give them as a matter of option, they are necessary to prepare His people for the Second Coming of Christ (I Cor. 1:7, 8). Yet many, in their zeal for the gifts, have forgotten the most important instruction Paul gave for their use. Paul wrote I Corinthians 13 because many in his day, just as in ours, were entranced by the gifts, and overlooked the fact that the fruits of the Spirit must accompany them.

> Though I speak with the tongues of men and of angels, but have not love, I have become sounding brass or a clanging cymbal. And though I have *the gift of* prophecy, and understand all mysteries and all knowledge, and though I have all faith, so that I could remove mountains, but have not love, I am nothing. And though I bestow all my goods to feed *the poor*, and though I give my body to be burned, but have not love, it profits me nothing (I Cor. 13:1-3).

Paul's epistle to the Corinthians showed that he strongly believed in the ministry of the gifts. He even claimed to speak in tongues more than any of them. Miracles, supernatural deliverance, visions, even a visit to paradise, mark the events of his life. Paul, by his example, set the pattern for apostolic ministry. He alone, of the Bible writers, gave instructions on how the gifts should be manifested. But, he also made plain that they have value only if divine love accompanies them.

The Gift of Prophecy Not Enough Without Love

The ministry of the prophet was the most important office in Old Testament times. In the New Testament, it is reckoned second only to the apostolic office. The foretelling or prediction of events far into the future, is perhaps the greatest proof of the inspiration of the Scriptures, although the prophets themselves understood little of their own prophecies (I Pet. 1:10-12). Paul placed a high value on the gift of prophecy, but also emphasized the point that if a prophet understood all prophecies and mysteries, but did not have love, it would profit nothing.

Next, the apostle drew a picture of a man who gave all his goods to feed the poor, and was even willing to suffer martyrdom. Certainly, one who dies for the Gospel stands high on the list of Christ's disciples! When Stephen was stoned, he was allowed to see Christ standing at the right hand of God, as if to welcome him home. Stephen had so much love for his enemies that he could pray, "'Lord, do not charge them with this sin'" (Acts 7:60). His prayer was evidently answered, for Saul, who held the coats of the assassins, was later converted and became the great champion of the Christian faith.

But even martyrdom, *without love*, is not enough. A communist also endures great hardships, personal danger and sometimes dies for the cause. Why? It is not because of love. While there may be mixed motives, it is generally because of a grievance against humanity. Communists live for the day when they can seize power, as the Bolsheviks did in Russia.

The Importance of Love

After showing the importance of having love accompany the manifestation of the gifts, Paul proceeds to analyze it. In Paul's analysis, we find that just as there are nine gifts of the Spirit, there are also nine ingredients in divine love. Let us look at these one by one. They are the graces desperately needed in the Church today.

1. Patience — Love Suffers Long

"Love suffers long. ... bears all things, believes all things, hopes all things, endures all things" (I Cor. 13:4, 7). Love gives a person the power to be patient when everything goes wrong — the power to keep cool and collected, when others lose their equilibrium. There are some people with exceptional talents and abilities that panic when unexpected situations arise.

Patience is an important quality of love. It takes into account the limitations and weaknesses of humanity. Love also hopes for good in everyone. Notice how a mother's love reveals this quality. If a child rebels, and all others give up hope for him/her, the mother will keep praying and hoping — and often her prayers are answered!

R.A. Torrey left home as a youth to escape his mother's prayers. In his determination to have nothing to do with religion, he claimed to be an atheist. He believed he was the maker of his own destiny. But everything went against him, and finally, in a state of desperation, he decided to commit suicide. It was then that God was able to reach him. Gloriously converted to Christ, young Torrey returned to bless his mother who had so faithfully prayed for him. He became one of the world's greatest evangelists.

Had his mother lost patience and faith in God's promise, the story would probably have had a very different ending. How we need patience in the Church today!

2. Kindness — Love is Kind

Kindness is love in action. A young girl, valedictorian of her class, was representing her school in the graduation exercises. As the time approached for her to take part in the program, she became extremely nervous. The main speaker was sitting beside her and, noticing her nervousness, whispered a few encouraging words. Though she soon forgot his name, his manner had been so kind and helpful that her fears vanished and she was able to perform the part required of her in a creditable manner.

Many years later, while looking over her old school papers, she saw the announcement card with the name of the guest speaker. It read *Franklin Delano Roosevelt*. Great men tend to be kind. It is little people who do mean, uncharitable things. Kind people do not willingly hurt others. They get no pleasure out of making someone else's lot harder to bear.

3. *Generosity — Love Does Not Envy*

Generosity is often sorely lacking today because people compare themselves with others. Can we rejoice when others are being blessed, or do we criticize them? No one ever gains by kicking others down.

Love does not envy. Jesus taught that the value of our lives is not based on the abundance of things we possess. If that is not true, Livingstone made a dreadful mistake. Leaving comfort and friends behind, he went to Africa and literally poured out his life to take the Gospel to the people there. But, at his death, his work had so inspired his followers, that they carried his body 1,000 miles to a ship that took it back to England where it was buried with honors in Westminster Abbey.

The relentless drive for status results in neuroses, frustration and nervous breakdowns, with many seeking help on the psychiatrist's couch. This insane effort to outdo each other has been well-named "the great American rat race."

Parents sometimes try to plan their children's lives for them — making plans that are far beyond the child's capabilities. These artificial success standards have littered the road of life with tragic victims. People are left with heartbreaking disillusionment, and often a sense of inferiority and failure. Even some Christians get caught in this. We should never forget that promotion does not come from the east, west or south, "But God *is* the Judge: He puts down one, and exalts another" (Psa. 75:7).

4. *Humility — Love Does Not Parade Itself, is Not Puffed Up*

God earnestly desires to give the Church more power. He said, "'But you shall receive power when the Holy Spirit has come upon you'"(Acts 1:8). We need power to evangelize the world, but a great obstacle to this is that God can find few people He can trust. Too often when people gain a degree of influence, they become insufferable. This drive for power can destroy the good in people.

The cure for unholy ambition is divine love. God did not

choose the ambitious Korah to lead His people out of Egypt, but Moses, the humblest man on earth (Num. 12:3). He even turned down God's offer to establish a new nation from his family alone (Ex. 32:9, 10). God exalted him and made him the deliverer of his people because of his humility.

5. Courtesy — Love Does Not Behave Rudely

Love reveals itself by its pattern of behavior. Customary etiquette is largely superficial, but true courtesy goes far beyond social protocol. A woman may carry a book of etiquette under her arm and still violate courtesy with her nagging tongue. A man may have an impressive testimony at church, but make life miserable for his wife by being stingy with the finances. True courtesy involves all the relationships of life. It causes an employer to treat his employees as he desires to be treated himself. It will also keep Christians from discussing the faults of others in a malicious spirit.

Love does not behave inappropriately. Sadly, some who manifest the gifts of the Spirit are barren of the fruits. They present one image publicly and in private they are totally different. We should understand that common courtesy and thoughtfulness are important. We can win more souls to Christ if we are gracious in our words and manners than if we are awkward and inconsiderate.

6. Unselfishness — Love Does Not Seek Its Own

Paul wrote the following comment on the ministry of his day: "For all seek their own, not the things which are of Christ Jesus" (Phil. 2:21). What a revolution there would be in the ministry today if men would build for Christ, instead of for themselves!

When C.T. Studd was called to the ministry, he was the cricket champion of England and heir to a fortune. Yet, the love that filled his heart when he was converted caused him to give away his wealth and go to the mission field. Many said he was a fool, but his sacrifice resulted in multitudes of people accepting Christ. This same love dominated Paul who said, "I also count all things loss ... that I may gain Christ" (Phil. 3:8).

That is the kind of love we need in the Church today if we are to see the gifts of the Spirit function in the power they should.

7. *Good Temper — Love Is Not Provoked*

Paul does not say that one who has love will never be provoked. In the King James Version, I Corinthians 13:5 says that love "is not easily provoked." No one demonstrated love in a greater degree than Jesus, but even He was angry at times. On one occasion, He drove the money changers out of the temple with a whip of small cords (Jn. 2:15).

One who has divine love will not be easily provoked. Some Christians have a fearfully quick temper. They are terribly sensitive and cannot bear to have anything cross them. In order to master the situations of life, one must be able to control his/her own spirit.

8. *Love Thinks No Evil*

Love does not think evil thoughts. It is sad that some people live in a constant state of suspicion. Being crafty themselves, they naturally expect others to do what they would do. Usually, people respond the way you expect them to. If you show confidence in people, they will usually strive to live up to that confidence. Of course, this is not always true, and some will betray a confidence. However, in the long run, people who have faith in others will come out the best.

9. *Love Does Not Rejoice in Iniquity, but in the Truth*

Some people are never happier than when they hear a bad report about others. In fact, they may even be elated when someone falls by the wayside, believing that they will somehow profit by that person's failure. True Christian love does not respond in this manner. When David heard of the death of his enemy, King Saul, he mourned instead of rejoicing.

> "The beauty of Israel is slain on your high places! How the mighty have fallen! Tell *it* not in Gath, proclaim *it* not in the streets of Ashkelon — lest the daughters of

the Philistines rejoice, lest the daughters of the uncircumcised triumph" (II Sam. 1:19, 20).

With the return of the gifts to the Church, there must be an
emphasis on holiness and the fruits of the Spirit. Implementing
cheap, shoddy schemes to attract attention, and employing the
sensational as a substitute for the working of the gifts of the
Spirit, is not a good omen. Out-of-control human ambition
can result in disaster and bring great harm to the cause. Let
divine love flow, and let humility be the spirit in which we fulfill our ministry to the people. Then, we shall see the Church
come forth in its power, "fair as the moon, clear as the sun,
awesome as *an army* with banners"(S. Sol. 6:10). Then, we
will see the gifts of the Spirit manifested in purity and beauty,
and the Church will fulfill its responsibility to evangelize the
world and be ready for the return of the Bridegroom.

Chapter Five

The Word of Wisdom

> For to one is given the word of wisdom through the Spirit, to another the word of knowledge through the same Spirit, to another faith by the same Spirit, to another gifts of healings by the same Spirit, to another the working of miracles, to another prophecy, to another discerning of spirits, to another *different* kinds of tongues, to another the interpretation of tongues (I Cor. 12:8-10).

In his outline of the gifts of the Spirit, Paul makes it clear that the nine supernatural gifts are not given indiscriminately to all members of the Church, but to the various members as they are chosen by the Holy Spirit. But, just because some are given special gifts of healings, does not mean that they are the only ones in the Church qualified to pray for the sick. Any believer may lay hands on the sick and pray for healing (Mk. 16:15-18). Likewise, some are given the word of wisdom, but again, this does not mean that others in the Church cannot pray for and receive divine wisdom. In fact, all members of the body of Christ are encouraged to do so. "If any of you lacks wisdom, let him ask of God, who gives to all liberally and without reproach, and it will be given to him" (Jas. 1:5). "Wisdom *is* the principal thing; *therefore* get wisdom. And in all your getting, get understanding" (Prov. 4:7).

Three Kinds of Wisdom

To understand the purpose and working of the word of wisdom, note that the Bible makes a moral distinction in defining wisdom. There is divine wisdom, human or natural wisdom and there is the wisdom of Satan. All three kinds of wisdom have this in common: They are dedicated to using the best possible means to secure a desired result. Divine wisdom, therefore, adopts the best means possible to advance the Kingdom of God. Natural or human wisdom is limited to the interests of this life. The third kind is the wisdom of devils, or wisdom that is employed for distinctly evil purposes.

1. The Wisdom of Satan

Ezekiel tells us much about the wisdom of Lucifer. At his creation, Lucifer was a perfect, sinless being and "full of wisdom."

> "You *were* the seal of perfection, full of wisdom and perfect in beauty. ... Your heart was lifted up because of your beauty; you corrupted your wisdom for the sake of your splendor" (Ezek. 28:12, 17).

Here we see that Satan was originally a sinless creature, but through pride his wisdom was corrupted. He chose to use his wisdom for self-exaltation, rather than for the good of God and the universe. As a result, he fell from heaven. Even after his fall, Satan still retained wisdom — only it was now perverted and totally in opposition to God.

Satan's corrupted wisdom is seen in his carefully calculated steps to seduce Eve in the Garden of Eden. First, he chose the snake, the most cunning beast of the field, in which to incarnate himself. Next, he selected to tempt the woman, who being created after Adam, had less experience than her husband. The method he used to present the temptation to Eve (Gen. 3) was an object lesson in craft and deceit. First, he challenged God's truthfulness and goodness. "Has God indeed said?" (ver. 1). Then, an appeal was made to her natural appetite. "The woman saw that the tree *was* good for food" (ver. 6). Next, the appeal was to her soul. "It *was* pleasant to the eyes" (ver. 6). The last temptation was of the spirit. It was a "tree desirable to make *one* wise" (ver. 6). Through the combined effect of these temptations, the woman was persuaded, and yielded to Satan's suggestion to eat the forbidden fruit.

Though his objectives are always evil, Satan's strategies are admittedly sound. For example, in the case of Job, his purpose was to prove that no man served God for nothing. Had he succeeded in his temptation, it would have been a severe blow to God's claim about the loyalty of His subjects. Satan, however, failed to prove his point because of Job's faithfulness.

Satan's temptation of Christ (Matt. 4) was not only a masterpiece of cunning, but was also a perversion of the Scriptures. He promised to give Christ the kingdoms and the glory of this world. Christ, however, was absolutely consecrated to the Father's will, and therefore spurned the devil's offer. He wanted no part in a kingdom that the Father did not give Him. Satan's temptations are diametrically opposed to the will of God, but they often have a deceptive allure and fascination to them.

2. *The Wisdom of Man*

There are countless illustrations in the Scriptures of the use of man's wisdom in everyday life. For example, Jesus showed in one parable that if a man plans to build a tower, it is wise for him to count the cost, in order to be sure he will be able to finish the project. Otherwise, he may become a laughingstock. Also, if a king faces a superior military force, he should consider whether or not he has a reasonable chance to win. If not, it would be wise for him to send an envoy and ask for peace (Lk. 14:28-32). Jesus was referring to natural wisdom in this parable. Supernatural wisdom, by contrast, might make it possible to defeat an enemy even though one may have a much smaller force. This was the case in the story of Gideon.

However, human wisdom primarily pertains to the present life, and is often used to serve selfish purposes. It is a sobering fact that in human society we find people totally dedicated to furthering their own selfish purposes. They will do anything to attain personal advantage regardless of how much their actions hurt others. The Book of James describes this kind of wisdom:

> But if you have bitter envy and self-seeking in your hearts, do not boast and lie against the truth. This wisdom does not descend from above, but *is* earthly, sensual, demonic. For where envy and self-seeking *exist*, confusion and every evil thing *are* there (Jas. 3:14-16).

People may have human wisdom without knowing God. Such wisdom can make us successful in this life, but fail to prepare us for the life to come. Solomon gives an interesting testimony of his search for human wisdom:

> I communed with my heart, saying, "Look, I have attained greatness, and have gained more wisdom than all who were before me in Jerusalem. My heart has understood great wisdom and knowledge." And I set my heart to know wisdom and to know madness and folly. I perceived that this also is grasping for the wind. For in much wisdom *is* much grief, and he who increases knowledge increases sorrow (Eccl. 1:16-18).

Solomon's pursuit of human wisdom left him vexed and with an empty soul. Worldly wisdom is often opposed to the wisdom of God. Paul declares that God will *"destroy the wisdom of the wise, and bring to nothing the understanding of the prudent"* (I Cor. 1:19).

3. The Wisdom of the Spiritual Man

Now, we come to the third kind of wisdom — the wisdom of the spiritual person. Paul contrasts spiritual and natural wisdom in I Corinthians 2:6:

> However, we speak wisdom among those who are mature, yet not the wisdom of this age, nor of the rulers of this age, who are coming to nothing.

Natural wisdom places supreme value on the things of this world — how to make money in order to enjoy the good things in life. It does not consider how quickly those things can be taken away. Spiritual wisdom, on the other hand, thinks beyond this life, and enables people to make good decisions. Who would build a home on the seashore where the tide can destroy it? Who, with a truly sane mind, would spend the major part of his energy laying up treasures on earth where moth and rust corrupt and thieves steal? A spiritual person plans for eternity, so that he might say with the Apostle Paul, "I have fought the good fight, I have finished the race, I have kept the faith. Finally, there is laid up for me the crown of righteousness, which the Lord, the righteous Judge, will give to me on that Day, and not to me only but also to all who have loved His appearing" (II Tim. 4:7, 8).

The wisdom of God does not necessarily come through a *special gift* of the Spirit, for we have noted that divine wisdom is available to all. So, if everyone is invited to ask for and receive divine wisdom, what is the significance and purpose of the word of wisdom, which is given to a limited number?

It is the means by which it comes that is different. One may learn divine wisdom through studying Scripture, hearing a sermon, reading the writings of wise men, or through observation. However, the wisdom which comes through the word of wisdom is supernaturally given.

Acquiring godly wisdom, apart from the word of wisdom, is seen in the life of Christ. We are told that Jesus grew "in wisdom and stature, and in favor with God and men" (Lk. 2:52). At that time, Jesus had not received the Holy Spirit. The wisdom that He received as He grew into manhood was godly wisdom but not the word of wisdom — at least not in its full operation.

What is the Word of Wisdom?

The word of wisdom is a fragment of divine wisdom that is given by supernatural means. Closely associated with the word of wisdom is the word of knowledge. The latter is a supernatural impartation of facts. But facts in themselves are not sufficient; there must be wisdom to handle the facts.

Harold Horton wrote the following in his book *Gifts of the Spirit*:

> God keeps before Him in the same divine store-
> house all the facts of heaven and earth. But we
> must add that He also keeps before Him in the
> same divine storehouse all the facts of time and
> eternity; all the facts that shall be throughout the
> eternal ages. ... For since God is ever conscious
> of all present things and all future things, He
> must also be ever conscious of that infinite gra-
> dation of things that lie between present and far
> future. ... This constant development of God's
> known present into God's known future is really
> the expression of His sovereign purpose, His
> determinate counsel, His applied knowledge and
> experience, His wisdom. So the moment that
> God shows a man a glimpse of some event that
> has not yet transpired, He has really given him a
> fragmentary revelation of His infinite purpose;
> He has virtually shown him what He is going to
> do between now and then and His reason for
> doing it; He has given him a word of divine
> wisdom.

In the broad sense, divine wisdom and divine knowledge
are the sum total of the knowledge of God — past, present and
future. As we shall see, the word of wisdom and the word of
knowledge work closely together and both may be imparted
through still other gifts. For example, the gift of prophecy
deals with future events and reveals how God applies the
knowledge and wisdom of the past to make it serve His future
purposes.

One of the most widespread errors is the supposition that
the word of wisdom is a God-endowed faculty of human wisdom. This is no more true than to suppose that the medical
profession represents the gifts of healings.

So, how does the word of wisdom fit into the picture? It is the active, supernatural agent through which either spiritual or natural wisdom may be imparted, depending on what is needed at the time. As we study the Scriptures, we see that there are varied kinds of natural and divine wisdom, and any of them can be manifested through the word of wisdom. This is in line with Paul's words concerning the gifts, "There are differences of ministries ... and there are diversities of activities" (I Cor. 12:5, 6).

Examples of Supernatural Wisdom

1. God's Wisdom in Creation

Wisdom was present at creation and participated in preparing the heavens and the earth (Prov. 8:1, 27). The universe as we know it is the grand result of divine wisdom and power. Satan has attempted to ruin God's beautiful creation, but the results of his rebellion are only temporary and will eventually be completely overruled.

2. Wisdom for Craftsmanship, Leadership and Everyday Problems

> "See I have called by name Bezalel the son of Uri, the son of Hur, of the tribe of Judah. And I have filled him with the Spirit of God, in wisdom, in understanding, in knowledge, and in all *manner of* workmanship, to design artistic works, to work in gold, in silver, in bronze" (Ex. 31:2-4).

Here, we see that God gave Bezalel special wisdom and understanding so that he would have the knowledge necessary to build the tabernacle and its furnishings. It was more than ordinary human wisdom; it came from the Holy Spirit. In a similar way, God gave Noah the wisdom needed to build the ark.

Some people possess natural talents for leadership. There is, however, a supernaturally imparted wisdom for leadership, which is given by the Spirit of God. We see this in the case of Joshua:

> Now Joshua the son of Nun was full of the spirit
> of wisdom, for Moses had laid his hands on him;
> so the children of Israel heeded him, and did as
> the LORD had commanded Moses (Deut. 34:9).

Joshua, received divine instruction for crossing the Jordan River as well as conquering Jericho. He also received special wisdom regarding how Achan, the man who stole and hid some of the cursed spoil from Jericho, should be punished. Divine wisdom was imparted to Joshua, enabling him to command the sun to stand still in the heavens.

There are some who argue that Solomon's wisdom was only natural wisdom, but the Bible definitely states that Solomon's unique wisdom was a special gift from God (I Ki. 3:11, 12, 28). Whether or not Solomon's gift of wisdom was exactly the same as the New Testament word of wisdom, it certainly was supernaturally given.

In a dream, the Lord asked Solomon what gift he would like to receive (I Ki. 3:5). Solomon asked for God to give him an understanding heart so he would be able to "discern between good and evil. For who is able to judge this great people of Yours?" (I Ki. 3:9). God was pleased by this request and not only gave Solomon great wisdom, but also riches and honor.

How and why did Solomon receive this special gift? Divine sovereignty is always involved in the giving of spiritual gifts (I Cor. 12:11), but there must be human cooperation. We are commanded to "earnestly desire the best gifts" (I Cor. 12:31). As a young man, "Solomon loved the LORD, walking in the statutes of his father David" (I Ki. 3:3). There was a spiritual background in Solomon's life, that prepared him to receive this special ministry.

Solomon's wisdom gave him a special ability to deal with difficult human problems. In one case, two women both claimed to be the mother of the same child. His method of discerning who was the true mother was unique, and revealed a penetrating understanding of human motivation. Solomon called for a sword. He ordered that the child be cut in half, and half given to each woman. The false mother was willing to permit the child to be killed, but the true mother said, "O my lord, give her the living child, and by no means kill him!" (I Ki. 3:26). Solomon then ordered the child to be given to this woman who he perceived was the true mother.

There is an interesting parallel that can be drawn from this story which relates to the body of Christ. Those who yearn for the Church to not be divided, but become one body, are the true members of the body. Those who are willing to divide the Church for selfish purposes are false leaders.

Solomon's two books on wisdom, Proverbs and Ecclesiastes, describe the two main kinds of wisdom. In Ecclesiastes, the writer concerns himself with the search for natural wisdom — a pursuit which he declares finally resulted in vanity and vexation of the spirit. In contrast, Proverbs speaks particularly of desiring divine wisdom, which is recommended, as stated in Proverbs 3:5, "Trust in the LORD with all your heart, and lean not on your own understanding."

Some people are born with a natural discernment which enables them to succeed in business, etc. Others who lacked wisdom have received both natural and spiritual wisdom by seeking the Lord (Jas. 1:5). When such wisdom is given through divine means, it can be called the word of wisdom.

3. Wisdom of the Ages to Come

Beyond the wisdom of this world is the infinite wisdom of God concerning His everlasting Kingdom and plan for the ages to come. The Apostle Paul speaks of this wisdom in Romans 11:33 indicating that we cannot search out the wisdom of God with our finite minds:

> Oh, the depth of the riches both of the wisdom
> and knowledge of God! How unsearchable *are*
> His judgments and His ways past finding out!

The word of wisdom and the word of knowledge draw from the great storehouse of God's wisdom. "For the Spirit searches all things, yes, the deep things of God" (I Cor. 2:10). Paul goes on to explain that these things are not seen or heard by natural means, but are revealed by the Spirit. Therefore, only those who are spiritual can understand this wisdom.

> These things we also speak, not in words which man's wisdom teaches but which the Holy Spirit teaches, comparing spiritual things with spiritual. But the natural man does not receive the things of the Spirit of God, for they are foolishness to him; nor can he know *them*, because they are spiritually discerned (I Cor. 2:13, 14).

The word of wisdom and the word of knowledge, as well as certain other gifts, are designed to reveal certain portions of the divine knowledge when it is needed. We should not forget however, that much of one's spiritual knowledge comes through the study of the Bible, not through possession of these gifts. The Scriptures are our great fountain of divine wisdom.

The New Testament is a revelation of the wisdom and knowledge of God. Paul's teachings in the New Testament are basically devoted to unveiling the wisdom pertaining to God, the Church and God's ways. It was Paul's constant prayer that the people of God possess "the spirit of wisdom and revelation in the knowledge of Him" (Eph. 1:17).

How the Gift Manifests

In character with God's ways of doing things, this gift manifests in more than one way.

1. Audible Voice

One method by which the Lord imparts the word of wisdom is by audible voice. For example, Moses heard the voice of the Lord speaking to him out of the burning bush. God also imparted wisdom to Samuel in this way. When he was a child, Samuel heard a voice calling to him saying, "Samuel, Samuel."

This was followed by a message concerning the house of Eli.

There are many instances in the Scriptures where the voice of God was heard by His prophets. Once, when Elijah was on the Mount of God he heard the sound of a strong wind, followed by an earthquake and a fire, but the Lord was not in these. After all this, Elijah heard a still small voice (I Ki. 19:11, 12). It was that voice that commissioned him to continue his work against Baal, and to train his great successor, Elisha.

2. *Direct Intuition*

God can and does speak without an audible voice. Undoubtedly, some receive the word of wisdom by direct intuition. A certain course of action may seem logical to the natural senses, but suddenly the person may be stopped in their tracks. Nothing was said, but they know beyond all doubt that God has spoken, and subsequent events prove that the change of plan was the wisest thing that could have happened.

Yet, a word of caution must be given here. We are told in the Scripture to prove all things. To yield simply to any impulse, may cause us to make serious mistakes. The words of prophets are to be judged (I Cor. 14:29). Peter thought he knew the will of God when he warned the Lord against going to Jerusalem to fulfill His mission. Actually, Peter's advice was the suggestion of Satan (Matt. 16:21-23).

3. *Visions and Dreams*

There are many instances in the Bible of God speaking to people through visions or dreams.

> *"And it shall come to pass in the last days, says God, that I will pour out of My Spirit on all flesh; your sons and your daughters shall prophesy, your young men shall see visions, your old men shall dream dreams"* (Acts 2:17).

An instance of the word of wisdom being given through a dream is Paul's vision in Asia Minor. He intended to expand his evangelistic efforts in that area, but the Spirit forbade him.

Then, in a night vision, Paul saw a man from Macedonia saying, "Come over to Macedonia and help us" (Acts 16:9). This is definitely an instance of the word of wisdom in operation.

4. Prophecy

The word of wisdom may also come through prophecy. Paul occasionally received guidance through such means. This occurred just before his last trip to Jerusalem, when he was warned of what awaited him if he went there (Acts 21:10-12).

The New Testament does not especially recommend that we seek guidance this way, though it was a method quite common in the Old Testament. In the present dispensation, every believer is a priest in his own right and may secure his own guidance directly from the Lord. Since the person giving the prophecy is not infallible (though a true prophecy of the Spirit of God is infallible), it is possible for people to be led astray by this means. We are instructed to test the spirits (I Cor. 14:29; I Jn. 4:1). Nevertheless, divine leading can and does come through prophetic messages. In such cases, however, other providential circumstances will usually confirm the special leading.

5. Studying Scripture

Ordinarily, the study of the Scriptures, which is our principal source of adding to our knowledge of God, is not in itself a manifestation of the word of wisdom. Nevertheless, there are times when people seeking divine guidance in prayer and Bible study will suddenly sense that God is illuminating a verse of Scripture in a striking way. This is not to be confused with the rather naive practice of opening the Bible and expecting the first verse you see, to be the answer to your special problem. True, some people have received help from the Lord in that manner, but it should not be advocated as a regular means of securing guidance.

Chapter Six

The Word of Wisdom's Purpose

As previously stated, the word of wisdom is the active, supernatural agent by which either natural or spiritual wisdom may be imparted to God's people. There are many instances in Scripture in which natural wisdom was supernaturally given. For example, the wisdom Bezalel needed to construct the tabernacle in the wilderness could be learned at a trade school today. But, since there were no such schools available in his time, the wisdom necessary was supernaturally imparted (Ex. 31:1-4). Likewise, a ship similar to the ark Noah built can be constructed by using modern engineering. Noah, however, had no such source of knowledge, so the wisdom necessary to build the ark was supernaturally given to him.

God's people are continually in need of wisdom in their ordinary, everyday living. We need wisdom to properly conduct business affairs. It is a notorious fact that many Christians, especially ministers, are poor business managers, and as a result, the cause of Christ suffers.

Jesus took special note of this in His parable of the unjust steward when He said, "'For the sons of this world are more shrewd in their generation than the sons of light'" (Lk. 16:8). In other words, the unsaved are often wiser in handling their business affairs than Christians are.

However, it is God's will that we be good business managers. We are instructed not to be "lagging in diligence" (Rom. 12:11). Christians should ask and expect God to give them wisdom in their ordinary business dealings.

Wisdom to Solve Human Problems

One of the great needs in the Christian Church is wisdom to solve difficult human problems. We should not leave this entirely to the psychiatrists. God is able, through the word of wisdom, to impart such knowledge. This is evident in Paul's chapter on marriage counseling. His instructions are so sound that they are as applicable today as they were then. He mentions the marital duties that each mate owes the other, counsels against long separations and advises against divorce or leaving a mate on the grounds that he/she is an unbeliever. Paul's writings are full of common sense advice for solving complex problems.

Not all believers are naturally adapted to minister in every gift, but all can ask for wisdom. It is the one gift which in itself teaches the possessor how it can be most profitably used. "If any of you lacks wisdom, let him ask of God, who gives to all liberally and without reproach" (Jas. 1:5).

Wisdom to Guide the Church

God has set administrators in the church, and those given this authority need the word of wisdom above all other gifts (I Cor. 12:28). The word of wisdom played an important role in the story of the Early Church. When the problem of ministering to the Grecian widows came before the apostles, they immediately called for men who could oversee this task who were, "of *good* reputation, full of the Holy Spirit and wisdom, whom we may appoint over this business" (Acts 6:3).

When Stephen, one of these deacons, emerged as one of the great preachers and leaders in the Early Church, we are told that his adversaries, "were not able to resist the wisdom and the Spirit by which he spoke" (Acts 6:10).

As problems arose regarding the fundamental doctrines of the Church, the apostles, under the guidance of the Holy Spirit, came up with the right answers. For example, they settled the debate of whether circumcision was necessary for salvation by issuing the following statement:

> "For it seemed good to the Holy Spirit, and to us, to lay upon you no greater burden than these necessary things: that you abstain from things offered to idols, from blood, from things strangled, and from sexual immorality. If you keep yourselves from these, you will do well." (Acts 15:28, 29).

This was a word of wisdom applicable for that particular situation. It was the best solution at that time for a people who were just coming out of raw heathenism. Surely, the word of wisdom is just as urgently needed to help shepherd and guide the people of God today, as it was in the days of the Early Church.

Wisdom When Called Before Magistrates

Jesus anticipated that His disciples would be brought before magistrates and even governors and kings to answer for their faith and testimonies. When facing such a situation, He instructed them to not depend upon their own wisdom, but the word of wisdom.

> "You will be brought before governors and kings for My sake, as a testimony to them and to the Gentiles. But when they deliver you up, do not worry about how or what you should speak. For it will be given to you in that hour what you should speak" (Matt. 10:18, 19).

Some years ago we were called to Miami, Florida, to assist the defense in the trial of Jack Coe, an evangelist being prosecuted on charges of practicing medicine without a license. He called me at two o'clock in the morning to say he had been arrested and, before being released, had to post a $5,000 bail. Brother Coe said, "If they could make the charge stick, they can sentence me up to five years in prison."

We decided to go to Miami. When we arrived, we quickly learned the unpleasant truth. A reporter from the *Miami Herald* had run a series of articles accusing Brother Coe of being a religious racketeer. The violence of the attack created sufficient attention to result in an article in *Time* magazine. Hundreds of testimonies of healing were produced by Rev. Coe, but they were ignored.

Then, Joseph Lewis, an unbeliever and a leading freethinker in America at the time, read with pleasure of the attack made by the *Miami Herald*, and decided to join forces with it.

After making a hurried search, he learned of a woman who had brought her child to a meeting to be prayed for, but who apparently did not receive healing. He promised free medical help for the child if the mother would sign a warrant against the evangelist. The distracted woman fell for the bait.

Actually, the woman knew nothing about the conditions upon which divine healing is based. But, she had heard that miracles were taking place in the tent. When she was told to wait her turn in the line, she became hysterical and soundly abused the workers for not letting her child in the healing line at once. She later testified in court that she had not attended church for eight years, and was not serving God in any sense. However, the workers permitted her and her son to get in the line on the second night because she had made herself such a nuisance. When Brother Coe, saw the woman and the boy, he said, "If you believe Jesus heals the child, take the braces off and leave them off."

This was the kind of act of faith Jesus commonly called for when He ministered to the sick. But, a minister of divine healing cannot guarantee that people not serving God will be healed — neither they, nor their children. Divine healing is "the children's bread" (Matt. 15:26). The parents were disappointed and voiced their dissatisfaction to their neighbors over the fact that a miracle did not take place.

As we have said, this information reached Joseph Lewis, president of the Freethinkers. Testifying in court, the woman said Lewis told her that Jack Coe was a religious racketeer, and if she would sign a warrant against him, he would see that the child received free medical treatment.

The newspapers cooperated with Lewis, inflaming public opinion by reporting Jack Coe as a charlatan who fattened his purse by preying on victims such as the woman and her little boy. The child was put on television to further prejudice public opinion against the evangelist.

A warrant was issued for Jack Coe's arrest by Judge Duvall. The constable who came to take him from the pulpit was a fine Christian gentleman, and told him with tears that this was the hardest thing he had ever had to do.

Such was the state of things when we arrived in Miami. Brother Coe's attorney, Mr. Chertkof, told us that public opinion was so strong against Rev. Coe, that his friends had advised him not to take the case. The full-gospel ministers of the town, however, were supporting Coe. The first thing we did was call for the people of God to pray and fast for a successful outcome of the trial. An adverse verdict could have effected the freedom to preach the Gospel of salvation and healing for years to come.

An article appeared in *Life* as well as other magazines — the case was now commanding national attention.

When the trial opened, the prosecuting attorney was confident of victory, and presented his case in a belligerent manner. Jack Coe, he declared, was in flagrant violation of the law. He had taken advantage of people's misfortunes and fraudulently practiced medicine without a license.

Joseph Lewis failed to show up at the trial, leaving others to carry on his work. Various witnesses were put on the stand by the defense. But, time and again, objections were raised by the prosecution to prevent testimony from being given that would have helped the evangelist. The attorney believed, however, that since I was the president of an evangelistic association that represented ministers of different denominations, the court would be forced to permit my testimony to be given. This proved to be the case, and I was given almost complete freedom in answering the lead questions prepared for the defense attorney.

When I entered the witness stand, I thought of the special promise God had given His disciples:

> "And as you go, preach, saying, 'The kingdom of heaven is at hand.' Heal the sick, cleanse the lepers, raise the dead, cast out demons. ... You will be brought before governors and kings for My sake, as a testimony to them and to the Gentiles. But when they deliver you up, do not worry about how or what you should speak. ... For it is not you who speak, but the Spirit of

your Father who speaks in you" (Matt. 10:7, 8, 18-20).

While on the witness stand, I strongly sensed God's presence. In fact, there was a definite sense of exhilaration. I believed that divine wisdom would be given that would completely change the situation. In response to the questions asked on the stand, I showed that even the Catholic Church, as well as many other denominations, believe in divine healing. The prosecuting attorney, sensing that the atmosphere of the court was changing from hostility to sympathy, still was not ready to lose his advantage. He began his cross-examination in the following manner.

Mr. Marsh: Do you believe a child three years old can exercise faith?

Gordon Lindsay: It can neither exercise faith nor unbelief.

Mr. Marsh: Then the child had nothing to do with its healing?

Gordon Lindsay: That is correct, sir.

The questioning then swung to whose fault it was that the child was not healed. I explained that the Syro-Phoenician woman had come to Christ for the healing of her demon-possessed daughter and that Jesus told her that divine healing was "the children's bread," thus indicating it was not for sinners. In other words, the woman needed to get on healing ground first. When she did, her daughter was healed. I said that the conditions for receiving healing are still the same today.

The prosecutor was now ready to spring his trap.

Mr. Marsh: You speak of the faith of the parents, or that the parents should have faith for the child. If the parents have faith, will their child be healed?

At that moment, the Spirit of God showed me the trap that was being set. Should I say that the mother did not have faith? Why would she spend hours trying to get into the line, if she did not believe the child would be healed? *At that moment, the Lord, in a word of wisdom, showed me what to say.*

Gordon Lindsay: The child would have been healed if the parents had Bible faith.

The prosecutor whirled around and looked hard at me.

Mr. Marsh: Bible faith? Do you mean there is more than one kind of faith?

Gordon Lindsay: Yes, the Bible says there is devil's faith. "Even the demons believe — and tremble!" (Jas. 2:19). Devils do not obey God. Only people who obey God have Bible faith.

The prosecutor saw that his trap had been evaded but he did not know it was God who had helped me evade it. He asked one more question.

Mr. Marsh: Do you believe that God is an all-wise God, a good God?

Gordon Lindsay: I do, one hundred percent.

Mr. Marsh: Then, why would God not heal the child even if its parents did not have faith?

Gordon Lindsay: We have to let God set the rules.

Mr. Marsh: Witness dismissed.

How often our human wisdom fails us at a critical moment, and we realize too late what we ought to have said. But, the Holy Spirit is able to give us, through the word of wisdom, the right answer at just the right moment. The great truth made clear in the courtroom that day, which the prosecutor could not contradict, was that God has certain conditions to healing. He alone has the right to set the rules.

God anointed other witnesses to testify that afternoon. Their testimonies, added to what had already been said, turned the tide. Not only was the opposition forced to back down and the case thrown out of court, but the occasion proved to be a wonderful opportunity to witness that Jesus is the same yesterday, today and forever.

God, through these supernatural gifts, makes it possible for the Church to move forward and accomplish its great purpose in the earth.

Wisdom to Win Souls

Supernatural wisdom is necessary in the field of soulwinning. There is a rather humorous story about a barber who felt a burden to witness to people about their souls. He had a customer lathered and waiting in the chair, and he continued to strap his razor while trying to get up enough courage to witness to him. Finally, he turned to the man, and with the sharpened razor in one hand, asked, "Mister, are you prepared to die?" The story has it that the customer did not wait to reply, but jumped from the chair and fled out the door and down the street!

Winning souls requires wisdom. We need supernatural guidance in our approach to people. "He who wins souls *is* wise" (Prov. 11:30).

Wisdom in Time of War

A successful general knows when to wait, and when to take the initiative. A wise strategist seeks to obtain all the information possible about his enemy. He needs to know the enemy's numbers, the physical condition of his men, the adequacy of his supplies, etc. So it is in spiritual warfare; the believer needs to know the enemy's weak point, and how and when to catch him at a disadvantage.

In Old Testament days, the word of wisdom and the word of knowledge sometimes came to godly men who were engaged in warfare. A good illustration of this is when the Philistines made war against David.

David had learned to wait for the moving of the Spirit in his early years. The Psalms reflect many of his experiences in those days. After he became king, his old enemies, the Philistines, returned to challenge him in battle. They still smarted from the humiliating defeat they had suffered when David killed their champion, Goliath, and thought the time had come to avenge the defeat. They had recently experienced a victory over Saul, and had become very bold. Upon receiving the news that David had become king, the Philistines brought a large army into Israel, and "deployed themselves in the Valley of Rephaim" (II Sam. 5:18).

When Israel's scouts brought back this information, David alerted his army and prepared for the battle. Facing the young king was a serious decision. Would it be wiser to strike quickly before the enemy had opportunity to get organized, or wait until his own small army had been reinforced? David asked God about this, and the word of the Lord came to him:

> So David inquired of the LORD, saying, "Shall I go up against the Philistines? Will You deliver them into my hand?" And the LORD said to David, "Go up, for I will doubtless deliver the Philistines into your hand" (II Sam. 5:19).

In response to this reassurance, David and his men attacked the enemy. Soon the lines of the Philistines broke, and their soldiers fled in every direction. In headlong panic, they left their idols behind, and David and his men gathered them up and burned them.

But the Philistines were stubborn. They decided to strengthen themselves where they were weak, and prepare for every contingency. They were sure that they now understood David's tactics and would be able to defeat him next time.

With the success of the first battle, David might have had reason to think that he could defeat the enemy the second time. But he knew that he needed divine guidance at all times, and went before the Lord again. The word of wisdom came a second time with instructions for David. He was not to make a direct onslaught this time; instead, he was to circle around behind them and strike the enemy on the flanks — a sound military tactic. God told him to wait until just the right moment came.

> Therefore David inquired of the LORD, and He said, "You shall not go up; circle around behind them, and come upon them in front of the mulberry trees. And it shall be, when you hear the sound of marching in the tops of the mulberry trees, then you shall advance quickly. For then the LORD will go out before you to strike the camp of the Philistines" (II Sam. 5:23, 24).

"The sound of marching in the ... mulberry trees" is a type of the moving of the Spirit. At the signal, David and his men attacked and succeeded in completely routing the enemy. The defeat broke the spirit and power of the Philistines forever. There is no record of this warlike people invading Israel again, although several minor skirmishes occurred afterward in the Philistines' own territory. From then on, the Philistines were a subdued people.

Yet, without the supernatural word coming at just the right moment, the battle could have been lost, and Philistia, might have become the dominant nation instead of Israel.

Wisdom to Counsel in Governmental Affairs

One of the most tragic lacks in supposedly Christian nations, is the failure to seek and obtain divine guidance when making vital decisions. We do have historical evidence that during critical periods of the Civil War, Abraham Lincoln sought and obtained supernatural help. Most historians agree that the decisions Lincoln made were in most cases the best possible solutions for that time.

Unfortunately, we cannot say that divine help has been seriously sought very often in recent times regarding the great issues confronting our nation. President Eisenhower did, however, occasionally invoke supernatural assistance in his administration, and he asked congressmen to join him in prayer when he took the oath of office. Yet, the trend has been otherwise. Even the Supreme Court, in a terrible and disastrous decision, declared that prayer in our school rooms is unconstitutional.

Oh, that we had a Daniel to whom our nation could turn today! Daniel was a man who, for the greater part of a century, counseled kings and princes. Kingdoms rose and fell, but his wisdom was eagerly sought throughout his lifetime. It was not human wisdom that Daniel possessed, but supernatural wisdom. When he revealed the details of Nebuchadnezzar's forgotten dream, he said, "'But as for me, this secret has not been revealed to me because I have more wisdom than anyone living'" (Dan. 2:30).

Had our nation received divine guidance, we would not have nourished the communist regime in its hours of mortal peril — a regime which, once the danger was over, turned on us to say, "We'll bury you."

Had our government sought divine wisdom, it would not have allowed the Christian general, Chiang Kai-shek, to be forced into a coalition with the godless, communist element, only to be driven out of China. The missionaries left, many Christians were murdered, and now the 1.26 billion people of China live under communism.

Divine Guidance in the Old Testament

Divine guidance is one of the most important subjects of the Bible. God wishes to lead His people step by step in their journey through life. This is beautifully symbolized by the pillar of cloud and the pillar of fire that guided the children of Israel on their way to the Promised Land.

Let us briefly note some of the other means by which God leads His children. To begin with, the Scriptures are the supreme source of guidance for the believer. God reveals the great principles of His will in them. "Your word *is* a lamp to my feet and a light to my path" (Psa. 119:105). It is useless to look for further direction if we neglect to search the Scriptures for the revelations already given. People who fall into delusion usually do so because they have ignored the instructions already available in the Word of God, preferring instead to listen to fables and religious novelties which have no scriptural basis.

God also intends for good, sanctified common sense to enable Christians to discern between what is sound and what is not. A person who knows the Bible will never participate in foolish actions like climbing upon rooftops, hilltops, haystacks and woodsheds to wait for the world to come to an end simply because some deluded religious leader announced a date for the event.

In many cases, divine providence will indicate God's will. Circumstances will often guide us in what we should do. One man thought he was called to leave his family and preach the Gospel. It did not occur to him that his first duty was to take care of the several children he had helped to bring into the world.

Yet, beyond these common means of receiving guidance is the ministry of the word of wisdom, which sometimes shows us the move we should make. There are many examples of this in the Scriptures. We can consider only a few of these.

1. Noah

One of the first instances of supernatural guidance mentioned in Scripture was when God instructed Noah to build the ark. Noah was a preacher of righteousness. He warned his generation of the coming judgment, as his great-grandfather, Enoch, had done (Jude 14, 15). God told Noah that He was about to destroy the wicked from the earth:

> And God said to Noah, "The end of all flesh has come before Me, for the earth is filled with violence through them; and behold, I will destroy them with the earth" (Gen. 6:13).

Noah and his family found grace in the Lord's eyes (Gen. 6:8), and God gave Noah a word of wisdom by which he and his family and the animal species could escape destruction. He was to build an ark, a great ship that would rise above the Flood. The dimensions of the ark show the mark of divine wisdom. Only in modern times, after much trial and error, did science discover the correct dimensions for such a large ship. But Noah learned them by divine revelation. Noah could never have saved himself by his own wisdom; it came to him supernaturally.

2. Abraham Goes to Another Land

Abraham is distinguished by his submission to the will of God. He was a man of prayer, an intercessor, a pilgrim. He lived in Mesopotamia, a land full of idol worship, yet he was true to the worship of Jehovah. One day, God gave him a word of wisdom, telling him to go into another land that He would show him, and there He would make him a father of many nations.

Now the LORD had said to Abram: "Get out of
your country, from your family and from your
father's house, to a land that I will show you. I
will make you a great nation; I will bless you and
make your name great; and you shall be a blessing" (Gen. 12:1, 2).

3. Joseph and Pharaoh's Dream

Joseph is another Bible character who looked to God for
supernatural guidance. Early in his life, he had dreams which
had prophetic significance. In his youth, he did not show the
wisdom of later years, and told his dreams. They caused him to
be hated by his brothers.

Years later, Pharaoh had a dream and Joseph received the
interpretation — seven plentiful years would be followed by
seven years of famine. He then advised Pharaoh with the following words:

Now therefore, let Pharaoh select a discerning
and wise man, and set him over the land of
Egypt. Let Pharaoh do *this*, and let him appoint
officers over the land, to collect one-fifth *of the
produce* of the land of Egypt in the seven plentiful years. And let them gather all the food of
those good years that are coming, and store up
grain under the authority of Pharaoh, and let
them keep food in the cities. Then that food shall
be as a reserve for the land for the seven years of
famine which shall be in the land of Egypt, that
the land may not perish during the famine (Gen.
41:33-36).

This story is an example of one gift working in unison with
another.

4. Moses and the Rebellion of Korah

In the life of Moses, we see numerous occasions in which
the word of wisdom, the word of knowledge and prophecy

worked together, not to mention miracles and healings. Let us consider the case of Korah's rebellion. This was a serious development. With over two million people out in the desert, good discipline was an absolute necessity for law and order to be preserved. These rebels did not deny religion outright. They were too shrewd for that. Instead, they challenged Moses' authority.

> They gathered together against Moses and Aaron, and said to them, "*You take* too much upon yourselves, for all the congregation is holy, every one of them, and the LORD *is* among them. Why then do you exalt yourselves above the assembly of the LORD?" (Num. 16:3).

This rebellion was the most serious problem Moses had faced at that point. If it succeeded, all would be lost. "So when Moses heard *it*, he fell on his face" (ver. 4). While he was in prayer, God gave him a word of wisdom which showed him what course to take. He was to call Korah and his conspirators to a special meeting.

However, the rebels, gave Moses a curt reply, "We will not come up!" (ver. 12). Since the men would not respond to mercy, Moses resorted to divine discipline. Korah and his confederates were cut off from the assembly. Then came swift judgment.

> Now it came to pass, as he finished speaking all these words, that the ground split apart under them, and the earth opened its mouth and swallowed them up, with their households and all the men with Korah, with all *their* goods. So they and all those with them went down alive into the pit; the earth closed over them, and they perished from among the assembly (Num. 16: 31-33).

The rebellion had grown to such proportions, and the conspirators had become so bold and hardened, that there was no other recourse. The word of wisdom showed that this was the only course of action that would prevent the children of Israel from breaking up into independent companies, with each going its own way.

Divine Guidance in the New Testament

There are countless incidents in the Old Testament in which guidance was given supernaturally to God's people, but what about the New Testament? Divine guidance was also earnestly sought in the Early Church, but with this difference: In the Old Testament, people inquired of the Lord through His prophets, but in the New Testament, the believers could go to God for themselves. While it is true that New Testament prophets did occasionally give guidance to members of the Church, it was the exception rather than the rule.

1. Philip

Philip was suddenly told to leave his ministry in Samaria and to go to Gaza. There he met a eunuch who was reading the book of Isaiah in his chariot. Philip spoke to him, led him into a saving knowledge of the Lord Jesus Christ, and baptized him in water. Immediately after that, Philip was caught away by the Spirit (Acts 8:25-40).

2. Ananias

The Spirit of the Lord told Ananias to go to a certain address and minister to Saul of Tarsus, who was to become Paul, the great apostle to the gentiles (Acts 9:10-19).

3. Commissioning Paul and Barnabas

The Holy Spirit spoke to the Church at Antioch, and directed them to commission Paul and Barnabas for missionary work (Acts 13:2).

Such guidance was given at various times to the disciples of the Early Church. It was the supernatural functioning of the word of wisdom. How the body of Christ needs to be guided by divine wisdom!

Chapter Seven

The Word of Wisdom in Christ's Ministry

The word of wisdom functioned perfectly in Christ's ministry. Many people think that though He was human, Jesus possessed all wisdom. Certainly, prior to His incarnation, He shared with the Father the infinite wisdom of the Godhead. However, Philippians 2:6-8 shows that Christ gave up His omniscience and took the form of man, with all its limitations. Jesus grew up just like other children, and "increased in wisdom and stature, and in favor with God and men" (Lk. 2:52). Such a statement could not be said of one who already had all knowledge and wisdom.

The wisdom that Jesus acquired in His youth was divine wisdom, but it was not the special gift of wisdom, for He had not yet been baptized in the Holy Spirit. It wasn't until He was baptized in the Spirit at the Jordan River, just before He began His active ministry, that gifts of the Spirit began to manifest in His life. Some apocryphal books portray Christ as performing fantastic miracles in His youth, such as giving life to clay birds, but John 2:11 says plainly that His *first* miracle was turning water into wine at Cana of Galilee, and this took place after His baptism.

It was this amazing, supernatural wisdom that made Christ's work perfect in every detail. As we study His life, we can only marvel at the perfection with which He handled every situation.

Wisdom in Answering Satan

The first event of Christ's ministry after He received the Holy Spirit, was to use divine wisdom to triumph over the craftiness of Satan. We do not fully understand how Satan took Jesus up to the pinnacle of the temple, nor do we know how he showed Him all the kingdoms of the world in a moment of time. Nevertheless, these were real temptations and very subtly presented. Satan was willing to give Jesus the kingdoms and glory of this world if He would worship him — an offer which Jesus spurned. It is interesting to note that Jesus did not argue with the devil. Instead, He met Satan each time by quoting Scripture.

When Satan tempted Jesus to jump from the pinnacle of the temple to prove He was the Son of God, He replied, "'It has been said, *"You shall not tempt the LORD your God"'"* (Lk. 4:12). Could any answer have been more effective? Satan had misapplied the Scriptures, using the promise that angels would bear Him up *"'lest [He] dash [His] foot against a stone'"* (ver. 11). But Christ exposed this perversion of the Word of God by quoting another Scripture, and showing that the power of God is never to be used for sensational or spectacular purposes. Jesus had come to this world to humble Himself, not to be cast into the role of a superman. Yet when the need arose, and His disciples were in jeopardy on a wind-tossed sea, he defied gravity by walking on the water as He went out to meet them.

Christians would do better in resisting Satan if they would use the Scriptures against him rather than their own arguments or reasoning.

Jesus' Reply to John the Baptist

Jesus' ministry must have been a little disappointing to John the Baptist. By his fearless preaching of God's Word, John had prepared the way for the coming of the Messiah. He no doubt looked forward to being able to sit under His ministry. Nevertheless, after he baptized Jesus in the Jordan River, there is no record that they ever met again, although reports that Christ's ministry was outshining his occasionally came to him from zealous disciples (Jn. 3:26).

Shortly after this, John was thrown into prison. Perhaps the prophet thought Jesus would secure his release somehow. But, John continued to languish in prison, until he finally realized that nothing was going to be done for him. It was then that a faint doubt crept into his mind, and he sent two of his disciples to Jesus with a special message: "'Are You the Coming One, or do we look for another?'" (Matt. 11:3).

How did Jesus answer His great forerunner? Did He explain to John that his ministry must fade away to make room for that of the Messiah? Did He make any explanation at all? No, He did something infinitely wiser. Instead of giving a long complicated explanation, He merely told the messengers to wait and see whether or not His ministry bore the signs of the Messiah.

> And that very hour He cured many of infirmities, afflictions, and evil spirits; and to many blind He gave sight. Jesus answered and said to them, "Go and tell John the things you have seen and heard: that *the* blind see, *the* lame walk, *the* lepers are cleansed, *the* deaf hear, *the* dead are raised, *the* poor have the gospel preached to them" (Lk. 7:21, 22).

Surely, this answer showed perfect wisdom.

Answering the Samaritan Woman

In the incident of the woman at the well, we first see the word of knowledge operating to reveal the woman's past life. Secondly, the word of wisdom is clearly seen through Christ's use of this knowledge to make her conscious of her sinfulness and need of a Savior. The woman started to argue, like most sinners will when in a discussion about religion. The Samaritans, like most sectarian groups, had a pet doctrine. They believed that people should worship God on *their* mountain, and that God was a Samaritan god. The Samaritans had placed such emphasis on this teaching, that the woman supposed it was the main religious question to settle. Basically, it was the old question of "which church is the true church?" So when she believed that Jesus was a prophet, this was the first question she wanted answered.

> The woman said to Him, "Sir, I perceive that You are a prophet. Our fathers worshiped on this mountain, and you *Jews* say that in Jerusalem is the place where one ought to worship" (Jn. 4:19, 20).

The average Jewish teacher would have immediately plunged into an academic discussion on the subject, claiming that the Jews were the "true church." But notice that Jesus did not do this. The word of wisdom dictated a different answer. Christ did not take sides between the Samaritans and the Jews, which would have merely aroused religious prejudice. Instead, He led the woman into a great truth — worship is more than a place, or a location. God is a Spirit, therefore worship of God must be in spirit.

This turned the woman's attention from natural to spiritual things. She expressed her hope that the Messiah would come someday and make all things plain. This was Jesus' opportunity to reveal His identity to her.

Christ Answers His Enemies

Almost every act that Jesus did was an example of divine wisdom in some way. Jesus said He received His wisdom from the Father, "'I speak to the world those things which I heard from Him'"(Jn. 8:26).

A good example of the word of wisdom manifesting in Jesus' ministry is the case when His enemies asked Him if they should give tribute money to Caesar. It was a trick question. They thought that He would be trapped by anything He said. If He replied that they should pay tribute to Caesar, the people would be offended. If He said they shouldn't, the Roman government would be displeased. His answer was a masterpiece. First, He asked those who posed the question to look at the tribute money and tell Him whose image and inscription was on it. When they replied that it was Caesar's, He answered, "'Render therefore to Caesar the things that are Caesar's, and to God the things that are God's'" (Matt. 22:21). Not only did Jesus answer their question in a way that His enemies could not twist, but He got in a timely word on man's obligation to God!

To the doubters who argued over whose wife belonged to whom in the resurrection, Jesus not only pointed out that marriage is for this present age only, but went straight to eternal realities. "'God is not the God of the dead, but of the living'" (Matt. 22:32).

On another occasion, they asked Him what the greatest commandment is. His answer was supreme love to God, and to love your neighbor as yourself. "'On these two commandments hang all the Law and the Prophets'" (Matt. 22:40). This answer has stood ever since as the final word on the subject.

How wonderful it would be if Church leaders could draw upon the word of wisdom for the right answer instead of leaning on their own poor wisdom.

Chapter Eight

The Word of Knowledge

The word of knowledge is the second in Paul's list of spiritual gifts (I Cor. 12:8), and is one of the most valuable. Not only is it very useful, but its operation has a solemn effect upon those who witness it in action.

Just as any believer can pray for the sick and expect an answer, it is also not unusual for lay members to have the gift of knowledge operate through them on occasion. Nevertheless, Paul's words "to another the word of knowledge," indicate that the gift was to be ministered in a special way through people specifically chosen by the Spirit, rather than by the members of the Church as a whole. In both the Old and New Testaments, we find numerous instances in which the word of knowledge operated through men of God such as Moses, Samuel, Elijah, Elisha, Daniel, Peter, Paul and of course, Christ Himself.

The word of knowledge involves a supernatural impartation of facts which, by natural means, the individual has no way of knowing at the moment. We live in a world in which facts are continually changing. What was true yesterday may not be true today. And what is true today may not be true tomorrow. Births, deaths, marriages, accidents and a thousand other occurrences, are constantly changing the status of things. Circumstances may develop that can be extremely important to know quickly. For example, if the Lord had not revealed Nebuchadnezzar's dream to Daniel when He did, both he and his companions would have been executed. In many instances in the Scriptures, the word of knowledge came at a crucial moment — sometimes making the difference between life and death.

A Fragment of Divine Knowledge

The word of knowledge has been defined as a fragment of divine knowledge. "For we know in part and we prophesy in part" (I Cor. 13:9). It should be understood that those through whom this gift functions will not automatically have all knowledge at their fingertips, any more than one who has the gift of miracles can perform all miracles at will.

Elisha was a man through whom the word of knowledge operated. Yet, there were occasions when he had to wait and learn the facts in the ordinary way. This was the case when the Shunammite woman's son died. Elisha was puzzled by her grief, which for the moment had rendered her speechless. When Gehazi tried to make her go away, the prophet restrained his servant saying, "'Let her alone; for her soul *is* in deep distress, and the LORD has hidden *it* from me, and has not told me'" (II Ki. 4:27).

Paul indicates in I Corinthians 13:2 that neither he nor any other human has complete omniscience, and that even if possession of all knowledge was possible, it would be profitless without divine love. This leads us to conclude that the gifts of the Spirit are of little value without the fruits of the Spirit. Elsewhere, Paul declares, "Knowledge puffs up, but love edifies"(I Cor. 8:1).

The gifts of the Spirit and the fruits of the Spirit should work together. For this or any other gift to function properly, a generous measure of humility and wisdom is needed.

The word of knowledge is never to function simply to satisfy mere human curiosity. It doesn't have anything to do with the vulgar pseudo-professions of mind-reading or fortune-telling. The gift is not intended to invade the privacy of another person's thoughts either. However, there are exceptions when hypocrisy or evil purposes need to be exposed and thwarted. Sometimes God reveals a secret that should not be publicly disclosed. In view of these and other considerations, it is understandable why wisdom is needed along with the word of knowledge.

The word of knowledge is not something we learn through the educational process or glean from books or commentaries. Neither is it knowledge accumulated through the direct study of the Scriptures — although that is the usual method by which we obtain our knowledge of God, and it should be strongly emphasized that God does not intend for any of the gifts to supplant or render unnecessary the systematic study of Scripture. Those who presume that the gifts are intended to spare them the necessity of studying the Scriptures, lay themselves open to the possibility of serious error.

There are many so-called "revelations" in the world today which are totally at variance with the Word of God. They lead some astray, but these people would never have gotten into such error had they possessed a basic knowledge of the Bible. Jesus commanded us to search the Scriptures (Jn. 5:39). Likewise, the Apostle Paul advises that we study the Word in order to become true workers for God.

> Be diligent to present yourself approved to God,
> a worker who does not need to be ashamed,
> rightly dividing the word of truth (II Tim. 2:15).

Even those who possess unusual revelatory gifts need to search the Scriptures. This is seen in the life of Daniel. This prophet received some of the most profound revelations found in the Bible. Yet, to understand previously-revealed prophecies, Daniel had to refer to the Scriptures as any other Bible student. This was the case when he inquired about the length of the Babylonian captivity. By reading the prophecies of Jeremiah, he learned that the captivity would last 70 years (Dan. 9:2).

The gift of the word of knowledge, therefore, does not take the place of regular study of God's Word, but is supplemental and intended to serve special needs for specific occasions.

The Varied Operation of the Gift

> There are diversities of gifts, but the same Spirit. There are differences of ministries, but the same Lord. And there are diversities of activities, but it is the same God who works all in all. But the manifestation of the Spirit is given to each one for the profit *of all* (I Cor. 12:4-7).

From the above words, it can be seen that there are varied manifestations in the operation of the gifts. This is very true in the operation of the word of knowledge, which may operate as a distinct and separate gift, or through other gifts. Here are some ways in which the word of knowledge operates:

1. God may impart the word of knowledge by audible voice as He did to Samuel (I Sam. 3:11-14).

2. It may come through dreams or visions as it did to Joseph (Gen. 41:25-36), or Daniel (Dan. 2:19).

3. It may come through prophecy.

4. It can come through the gift of interpretation. However, this gift is usually used in public for edification rather than imparting special revelation.

5. There are times during prayer or meditation when we are made aware of certain things although we have not had it declared to us by actual words. Many Christians can testify to this.

We once planned a trip through Latin America to promote the Native Church Crusade. The tour required at least two or three weeks, but proved to be very successful. All of the missionaries with whom we discussed the issue were enthusiastic about the proposed venture which would involve building hundreds of native churches.

After completing our survey in Panama, I prepared to go to Trinidad, as planned. That day, however, I received a strong and almost overwhelming impression that I should return to the States at once. All day the feeling grew stronger, and I was unable to shake it off. Finally, I called the airline, cancelled my Caribbean tour and reserved a ticket to Texas.

When I arrived in Houston, I called my wife. She immediately told me that my father, almost 89 years of age, had passed away on the day I flew into Panama. She had been calling all over Central America trying to reach me, but just missed me each time. The family was resigned to having the memorial service on the following day without me. The Spirit of God had definitely led me to return, though He had not given me the reason. It is comforting to know that God is considerate of our purely personal matters, apart from the great overall responsibilities of His Kingdom.

Some years ago, my brother-in-law, Rev. L.D. Hall, also had an experience where the word of knowledge was needed. He made a trip into the Sierras to preach in a little town hidden away in a mountain valley. His wife and small baby were with him. After he was well up in the mountains, he stopped to perform some minor repairs on his car. Having completed the repairs, he drove on. When he stopped at a gas station sometime later, he found that his billfold was gone! He searched through the car but could not locate it. With a sinking heart, he realized that he was in the mountains with his family, penniless, and unable to buy food or gasoline to take them to their destination. He drove back to the place where he had made the repairs, but found nothing. He thoroughly searched the car again, but to no avail, and it would soon be night.

In desperation, he asked God to help him. At this point, God gave him a word of knowledge. The billfold was somewhere in the car! My brother-in-law resolved to take his luggage apart, piece by piece, until he found it. His wife protested, saying that he had already searched the car several times. He did it anyway. After taking everything out of the car, he paused to consider what his next step should be. There were some tools and a few other things packed on the running board. It was the only place he had not thought to search, so he took the objects off the running board, and there, behind one of the articles, was the missing billfold!

God is always willing to help His people when they are in trouble.

The Anointed Teaching Ministry

We have considered the various operations of the word of knowledge that are demonstrated in the Old Testament, but what about the function of this gift in New Testament ministry? We are told that various gifts have been set in the Church, and through them distinct ministries are manifested in order to perfect the Church.

> Now you are the body of Christ, and members individually. And God has appointed these in the church: first apostles, second prophets, third teachers, after that miracles, then gifts of healings, helps, administrations, varieties of tongues (I Cor. 12:27, 28).

The gifts of the Spirit are given to implement the regular ministries that have been set in the Church such as apostles, prophets, teachers, etc. Does the word of knowledge have any relation to the ministry of teaching? Isn't there more to this gift than giving aid to God's people in times of emergency? Let us note I Corinthians 14:24-26:

> But if all prophesy, and an unbeliever or an uninformed person comes in, he is convinced by all, he is convicted by all. And thus the secrets of his heart are revealed; and so, falling down on *his* face, he will worship God and report that God is truly among you. How is it then, brethren? Whenever you come together, each of you has a psalm, has a teaching, has a tongue, has a revelation, has an interpretation. Let all things be done for edification.

Notice that as used here, the term "to prophesy" includes teaching, singing in the Spirit, speaking in other tongues (with its interpretation, verse 13) and the imparting of revelation. Through God-inspired teaching, the secrets of people's hearts are revealed!

Occasionally, a minister who is under a strong anointing of the Spirit of God, may move into the realm of prophecy — though it may not be revelatory prophecy. The preacher may not foretell future events, but the Spirit of God may move upon the preached Word, and have a supernatural effect upon the hearers. Ordinary gospel truth suddenly seems alive with divine inspiration.

Likewise, God-anointed teachers sometimes bring forth truths that enlighten the listeners in a way that a routine exposition could never do.

Donald Gee says in his book, *Concerning Spiritual Gifts*:

> But it seems strangely inconsistent not to expect a supernatural manifestation of the Spirit to occur in such an important ministry as that of teaching, if we allow it in other, and dare we say lesser, spheres. Happy experience compels us to testify that such a manifestation does occur. There come times when the Spirit of revelation is so operating through a teacher, exercising an anointed ministry, that we become conscious of an illumination transcending all natural ability either to gain or to impart. It is in such hours that the sheep hear the voice of their Good Shepherd speaking through human lips; even as the early Christians of Asia had heard Christ speaking and had been taught by Him at Ephesus (Eph. 4:20, 21). We know it because our hearts burn within us as surely as theirs did upon the Emmaus road when the risen Christ "expounded unto them in all the Scriptures the things concerning himself." By the gifts of the Spirit that Voice still expounds the Scriptures on that sweetest of all themes — Himself.

Just how far God-anointed teaching can be said to be a manifestation of the word of knowledge is difficult to say, but a finely drawn definition is unnecessary. It is enough to say that we believe such a ministry of the gift exists.

The Use of the Word of Knowledge

Having outlined some of the purposes and the nature of the word of knowledge, let us take note of some of the instances in Scripture when this gift manifested. It usually came forth at critical times.

1. To Inform of Impending Judgment

Because of the extreme wickedness of the inhabitants of Sodom and Gomorrah, God found it necessary to send a terrible judgment upon them. Yet, before He executed this judgment, He felt obligated to inform His faithful servant, Abraham, of what was about to occur. On this occasion, the warning was given by the Lord Himself in a theophonic appearance — God, in human or angelic form.

> Then the LORD appeared to him ... And the LORD said, "Shall I hide from Abraham what I am doing? ... For I have known him, in order that he may command his children and his household after him, that they keep the way of the LORD, to do righteousness and justice, that the LORD may bring to Abraham what He has spoken to him" (Gen. 18:1, 17, 19).

God not only forewarned Abraham of Sodom and Gomorrah's imminent destruction, but explained that the reason for it was "because the outcry against Sodom and Gomorrah is great, and because their sin is very grave" (ver. 20). The Lord showed Abraham that His judgments are not arbitrary, but are sent only when the cup of iniquity is full. It is also evident that Abraham was forewarned so he could intercede for the city.

God withholds His anger toward the wicked until He is without further recourse. Before carrying out judgment, He seeks for intercessors to plead the cause of those who are under indictment. God's mercy always hopes for repentance. Centuries after the destruction of Sodom and Gomorrah, the city of Nineveh came under divine denunciation, but repented as a result of Jonah's preaching.

Though Abraham's intercession for Sodom is one of the classic prayers of the Old Testament, it did not save the city, since not even 10 righteous people could be found within it. However, his prayer did help Lot and his two daughters. Through angelic warning, they were able to escape to the mountains before judgment fell.

This unusual manifestation of divine knowledge shows the variety of ways it may be imparted. (If the destruction of Sodom had been a future event, the revelation would have been prophecy. But, the angels were already poised to execute judgment, so the facts revealed fall more into the category of the word of knowledge than prophecy.)

2. To Reveal the Secrets of Men

> And thus the secrets of his heart are revealed; and so, falling down on *his* face, he will worship God and report that God is truly among you (I Cor. 14:25).

There are times when the hearts of men need to be exposed. Jesus did not depend upon what others told Him; "He knew what was in man" (Jn. 2:25). When He met Peter, Jesus perceived that he was an impetuous fisherman. But beneath the exterior He saw a diamond in the rough. Of Nathaniel, He said, "'Behold, an Israelite indeed, in whom is no deceit!'" (Jn. 1:47).

The word of knowledge functioned in this way in the ministry of Samuel the prophet as well. Through it, the Lord showed him what the new king would be like (I Sam. 8). When Saul and his servant came to Samuel to ask where to find his father's lost donkeys, the prophet not only told Saul what had happened to the donkeys, but what was in his heart!

> Samuel answered Saul and said, "I *am* the seer. Go up before me to the high place, for you shall

eat with me today; and tomorrow I will let you go and will tell you all that *is* in your heart" (I Sam. 9:19).

Revealing the secrets of people's hearts is a specialized manifestation of the word of knowledge, and no doubt in many cases can also be considered a manifestation of the gift of discerning of spirits.

3. To Encourage a Discouraged Prophet

Many Christians have regarded Elijah as a sort of superman. However, the Apostle James refutes this notion by saying, "Elijah was a man with a nature like ours" (Jas. 5:17).

After Elijah's great victory over the Baal prophets, which was obtained as a result of a supernatural display of fire from heaven and the drought breaking, it might be thought that he would have been invincible. But the very next day, he panicked and fled from Jezebel.

The reaction that often follows a great victory is a well-known phenomenon to those who study human emotions. The weakness and depression that sometimes occurs may temporarily unnerve an individual — causing strong people to do foolish things that seem out of keeping with their real character.

Elijah was convinced that he was the last one in Israel who was faithful to Jehovah. What was the use of struggling any longer when the whole nation had given itself to idolatry? Jezebel now wanted him dead and was having him hunted. He thought he was the only one left and he might as well die too.

> And he said, "I have been very zealous for the LORD God of hosts; because the children of Israel have forsaken Your covenant, torn down Your altars, and killed Your prophets with the sword. I alone am left; and they seek to take my life" (I Ki. 19:14).

But, then came the word of knowledge. Elijah was not

standing alone. There were others in Israel who had not bowed the knee to Baal!

> "Yet I have reserved seven thousand in Israel, all whose knees have not bowed to Baal, and every mouth that has not kissed him" (I Ki. 19:18).

So, God encouraged His prophet. Chastened for his lack of faith, Elijah returned to his task with renewed vigor. He anointed Elisha, the man who was to become his famous successor. The false religion of Baal would be completely destroyed. Elijah would go back to Ahab and Jezebel's palace and denounce their wickedness. And God did not answer Elijah's prayer to die either. There was an *uppertaker* not an *undertaker* waiting to take Elijah to heaven in a blaze of glory and a chariot of fire!

So God's Word sometimes comes to His people to let them know He is still on the throne, that He has other faithful saints on earth, and that they must not allow conditions or circumstances to depress them or cause them to give up.

4. To Recall Forgotten Knowledge

The story of Nebuchadnezzar and his forgotten dream is a familiar one. The failure of the Chaldean wise men to recall the king's dream not only exposed their pretensions and deceitfulness, but almost resulted in the death of all the wise men, astrologers and magicians of the region (Dan. 2:1-13).

Fortunately, there was a young Hebrew prophet by the name of Daniel who had been brought to Babylon as the result of the captivity. He requested and was granted a delay in the execution of the king's decree. During the reprieve, God revealed to him the details of the forgotten dream, and Daniel was not only able to tell it to the king, but also give its interpretation.

Here, we see two gifts operating together. The word of knowledge enabled Daniel to tell the king his dream, but it was the gift of prophecy in operation that enabled him to interpret its meaning.

5. To Convert a Sinner

A certain woman with a bad reputation lived in the city of Samaria. She had had five husbands, and had not taken the trouble to go through the formality of a marriage ceremony with the one with whom she now lived. She was naturally looked down upon by her neighbors. Therefore, probably as a habit, she went to the well to draw water when others ordinarily would not be present. But, on one occasion, she discovered a stranger at the well.

Jesus had deliberately chosen this route through Samaria on His way to Galilee. This was rather unusual, for the Jews had no dealings with the Samaritans. Yet, Jesus apparently had this woman in mind when He made the journey. He perceived that deep in her heart there was a longing for reality, a desire to escape the shabby life she had been living. To this woman, the Lord began to reveal some of the greatest truths of the Gospel. He told her that if she drank the true water of everlasting life, she would never thirst again.

But, how could His message get through to her? There was so much confusion regarding religion in Palestine. There was the mixed worship of the Samaritans. There was the decadent Judaism of the Pharisees with the many traditions they had added to the Scriptures. Christ saw that two things were needed. First, she must be convicted of her sinful life. Second, He must cause her to recognize His divine authority so that He could point her to the true way of salvation. He accomplished this in a few brief words — words which showed He knew all about her past life. This was made possible through the word of knowledge.

> Jesus said to her, "Go, call your husband, and come here." The woman answered and said, "I have no husband." Jesus said to her, "You have well said, 'I have no husband,' for you have had five husbands, and the one whom you now have is not your husband; in that you spoke truly" (Jn. 4:16-18).

The woman was greatly impressed. When she returned to the city, she testified to her neighbors, "'Come, see a Man who told me all things that I ever did. Could this be the Christ?'" (ver. 29). Many of the people believed her testimony, and because of this word of knowledge spoken by Christ, a great work of grace took place in the city. "And many of the Samaritans of that city believed in Him because of the word of the woman who testified, 'He told me all that I ever did'" (ver. 39).

It is obvious that if it is used in the right way and at the right time, the word of knowledge is helpful in getting the attention of sinners and turning them to God. (Note that the word of wisdom was also manifested on this occasion.)

Chapter Nine

The Word of Knowledge in Scripture

When Moses was receiving the holy commandments on the Mount of God, he was suddenly told by the Lord that the people had corrupted themselves during his absence. At that very moment, they were dancing nude in drunken revelry around a golden calf. At that time, Moses made his historic intercession for Israel which saved the nation from annihilation. Nevertheless, the most flagrant offenders were executed — 3,000 people perished (Ex. 32).

Then, there was the case of Achan, who sinned by taking some silver, a wedge of gold and a Babylonian garment during the conquest of Jericho. Joshua knew that something had gone wrong when his army was defeated at Ai, but he was unable to determine the cause, until a word of knowledge from the Lord revealed it to him.

> So the LORD said to Joshua: "Get up! Why do you lie thus on your face? Israel has sinned, and they have also transgressed My covenant which I commanded them. For they have even taken some of the accursed things, and have both stolen and deceived; and they have also put *it* among their own stuff" (Josh. 7:10, 11).

The actual identity of the individual who had done this was revealed after lots were cast, and Achan from the tribe of Judah was taken.

Also, when Gehazi asked Naaman for a talent of silver and two changes of clothes, pretending that two sons of the prophets had unexpectedly arrived and needed help (II Ki. 5:20-27), his deception was discovered by supernatural means.

Word of Knowledge in Samuel's Ministry

As we have already noted, the word of knowledge worked through Samuel. That God sovereignly gave this gift to Samuel is clearly evident. While he was a small boy, and before he had any definite experience with the Lord, God revealed certain things to him about Eli's family. Samuel faithfully delivered the message to Eli. It was a grim warning. Eli had failed to restrain his wayward sons, and as a result, judgment was coming upon his house (I Sam. 3).

The people soon recognized that Samuel possessed this remarkable gift. When Saul failed to find his father's donkeys, his servant suggested that they consult Samuel (I Sam. 9:6).

In the meantime, the Word of the Lord had already come to Samuel, informing him all about Saul and his search for the lost animals.

> Now the LORD had told Samuel in his ear the day before Saul came, saying, "Tomorrow about this time I will send you a man from the land of Benjamin, and you shall anoint him commander over My people Israel, that he may save My people from the hand of the Philistines; for I have looked upon My people, because their cry has come to Me" (I Sam. 9:15, 16).

After Samuel met Saul and his servant, he invited them to eat with him the following day. Samuel promised Saul, "I will ... tell you all that *is* in your heart" (I Sam. 9:19). The next day, Saul learned that the donkeys had been found, and was informed that he had been chosen to be king of Israel!

When it came time to present Saul to the people, the word of knowledge was again required. He had disappeared and could not be found. When they inquired of God, "the LORD answered, 'There he is, hidden among the equipment'" (I Sam. 10:22).

Unfortunately, as the Lord had forewarned, Saul's humility was short-lived. He became self-willed, with fitful and sullen moods. Sometimes, he showed a generous spirit, but at other times he was moody, jealous and stubborn. On one occasion, the Lord commissioned Saul to execute judgment on the Amalekites. But Saul, in His self-will, was disobedient, only partially fulfilling the command.

The word of the Lord came to Samuel informing him of Saul's disobedience, making necessary his rejection. It so grieved Samuel that "he cried out to the LORD all night" (I Sam. 15:11).

Having rejected Saul as king, the Lord commissioned Samuel to anoint one of Jesse's sons to replace him. Samuel would have anointed one of the other sons of Jesse, rather than David whom the Lord had actually chosen, but the word of knowledge and the word of wisdom kept him from making that mistake.

> But the LORD said to Samuel, "Do not look at his appearance or at his physical stature, because I have refused him. For *the LORD does* not *see* as man sees; for man looks at the outward appearance, but the LORD looks at the heart" (I Sam. 16:7).

This is one of the finest examples of the manifestation of this gift. We often make wrong judgments concerning people. However, the word of knowledge, and the similar gift of discerning of spirits can give us true insight into the character of those to whom we must delegate important tasks. The word of wisdom shows us what steps to take as the result of this knowledge.

Years after Samuel died, Saul was desperate to receive information about the outcome of an impending battle with the Philistines. So, he tried to have the witch of En Dor call up Samuel from the grave. Whether it was actually Samuel that the witch called up is controversial. Some people believe that God permitted Samuel to appear on this particular occasion. Others believe it was an evil spirit. Regardless of who it was, the message Saul received was a true one; it foretold his doom.

Paul and the Word of Knowledge

The operation of the word of knowledge is clearly evident in the life and ministry of the Apostle Paul. However, this gift was not reserved only for notables such as Paul and the apostles. The Lord might have given Saul of Tarsus his instructions while he was lying prostrate on the Road to Damascus. Instead, he gave the message through an obscure disciple by the name of Ananias.

Along with other disciples, Ananias had been awaiting the arrival of the "wolf" with fear and apprehension. News of Saul's intention to take into custody men and women who professed faith in Christ, had preceded his arrival. Ananias was surprised to receive instructions from the Lord to visit this man, lay hands upon him, and pray for him to be healed of his blindness and filled with the Holy Spirit.

> So the LORD *said* to him, "Arise and go to the street called Straight, and inquire at the house of Judas for *one* called Saul of Tarsus, for behold, he is praying. And in a vision he has seen a man named Ananias coming in and putting *his* hand on him, so that he might receive his sight" (Acts 9:11, 12).

Notice that Saul's name was given, along with the street on which he was staying and the name of the man in whose house he was staying. Incidentally, this was not the only time a street address was given through direct revelation. In the next chapter, while a centurion by the name of Cornelius was praying, he was directed to send for Peter, who was living in Joppa, to come and preach to his household.

> "Now send men to Joppa, and send for Simon whose surname is Peter. He is lodging with Simon, a tanner, whose house is by the sea. He will tell you what you must do" (Acts 10:5, 6).

Throughout Paul's ministry, the word of knowledge often

came to his aid at critical moments, enabling him to make the right move at the right time.

Through the word of knowledge and the word of wisdom, Paul was forbidden to preach in Asia and was directed instead to go to Macedonia and preach the Gospel in Europe, where people were awaiting his help (Acts 16:9).

Through this gift, Paul was forewarned by others that if he went to Jerusalem, he would be bound and put in prison (Acts 21:4-13).

On another occasion, Paul warned the captain of the ship which was to take him to Rome, that he should remain in the harbor to avoid a violent storm that was gathering upon the Mediterranean (Acts 27:10, 11).

When the captain ignored Paul's advice, disaster followed just as Paul had said. Yet Paul, after praying and fasting, was able to bring words of cheer to his companions — the ship would be lost, but all those on board would be saved (Acts 27:21-26).

Elisha and the Word of Knowledge

Of all the Old Testament prophets, it is in Elisha's life that the ministry of the word of knowledge appears in greatest emphasis. It is obvious that much of his success lay in the power this gift gave him. Immediately after Elijah's mantle fell upon Elisha and he received a double portion of the Spirit, the ministry of the word of knowledge began to work through him.

The effectiveness of any gift depends on a strong anointing of the Holy Spirit. A gift may work to some degree with a weak faith, but its proper functioning is only possible where there is a firm and unwavering faith such as Elisha had immediately following the translation of Elijah. The sons of the prophets apparently had a prior knowledge of that event, but they had only enough faith to believe that Elijah had been transported to some valley or distant mountain (II Ki. 2:16).

Jehoram, the son of wicked Ahab, was faced with a rebellion by Moab. He managed to persuade the godly Jehoshaphat, as well as the King of Edom, to join him in an alliance against the Moabite king. They soon ran into trouble. Their armies found themselves in a desert area where there was no water. Seven days passed and the situation was becoming very critical.

During this dilemma, Jehoshaphat, King of Judah, asked if there was a prophet in the camp. The King of Israel and his servants did not seem to hold a very high opinion of Elisha. One of them said "'Elisha the son of Shaphat *is* here, who poured water on the hands of Elijah'" (II Ki. 3:11). Apparently, Elisha was a man who made no pretensions, and was content to be known as Elijah's servant.

Elisha flatly said that if it were not for the presence of Jehoshaphat, he would not look at or see the King of Israel. But, because Jehoshaphat *was* there, he called for a musician. "Then it happened, when the musician played, that the hand of the LORD came upon him" (II Ki. 3:15). (It is interesting to note that on more than one occasion recorded in Scripture, music played an important part in the ministry of the Spirit.)

As the musician played, the word of knowledge came to Elisha. There would be no wind or rain like there was when Elijah prayed to end the drought. God often chooses the most simple method to achieve an end. There was actually water already in the valley, but it lay hidden beneath the surface of the land. Elisha instructed the kings, "'Make this valley full of ditches'" (ver. 16). And, that night, as the armies dug waterways through the valley, springs of water flowed out upon the ground. There was plenty of water for the soldiers and their animals.

But, that was not all. An interesting thing happened when the morning light fell upon the scene, which played an important part in the outcome of the day's events. When the Moabite army arose early in the morning, they saw the water, but it appeared red under the reflection of the morning sun. They jumped to the hasty and erroneous conclusion that the kings had turned on one another, and that the reddish hue of the water was caused by the blood of those who had been killed.

Unaware of the true state of affairs and intent upon taking the spoil, the Moabites rushed pell-mell into the camp of the Israelites. Suddenly, to their dismay, they found that they had fallen into a trap. They panicked and scattered in a desperate retreat, with the armies of the confederate kings hot on their trail. The Moabite army was completely defeated.

The Word of Knowledge and War in the Heavenlies

The sixth chapter of II Kings is one of the most interesting chapters in the Bible. It shows the manner in which various gifts of the Spirit may operate in harmony and coordination. This chapter also shows that the real warfare of God's people is not on earth but in the heavenlies. As Ephesians 6:12 declares, "... we do not wrestle against flesh and blood, but against principalities, against powers, against the rulers of the darkness of this age, against spiritual *hosts* of wickedness in the heavenly *places.*"

Since our battle is a spiritual one, we should not make the mistake of waging it against flesh and blood. We must fight against the powers of darkness which have carnal people under their control. To fight such a war, we need the gifts of the Spirit as well as the whole armor of God, in order to be protected against the attacks of the enemy. Through the manifestation of these gifts, we can turn from the defensive to the offensive.

In this chapter, all the gifts of the Spirit were in operation, with the exception of speaking in other tongues and interpretation — gifts reserved exclusively for the New Testament Church.

1. *The Word of Knowledge*

Despite the fact that Elisha performed a great service for the King of Syria by healing Naaman, the captain of his military forces, he treacherously made a covert invasion of Israel. But, Elisha saw all that was going on, and sent word to the King of Israel that a trap was being prepared for him. This happened not once, but several times, as Elisha, through the word of knowledge, anticipated the moves of the Syrian army and forewarned the King of Israel (II Ki. 6:8).

2. Discerning of Spirits

The King of Syria was "very troubled" by this and came to the conclusion that there was a spy in their midst. But, one of his aids disclosed that Elisha was the true reason the King of Israel was able to evade the traps he set. "'Elisha, the prophet who *is* in Israel, tells the king of Israel the words that you speak in your bedroom'"(II Ki. 6:12).

The Syrian king therefore decided to capture Elisha, and sent an army to Dothan during the night to completely surround the city. When Elisha's servant got up the next morning and saw the great army of chariots, he cried out in distress, "'Alas, my master! What shall we do?'" (ver. 15). Elisha responded by praying for the young man's eyes to be opened so he could see. And, when the young man looked, "he saw. And behold, the mountain *was* full of horses and chariots of fire all around Elisha" (ver. 17). What Elisha had said was true; there were more on their side than on their enemies' side (ver. 16).

The gift of discernment or "discerning of spirits" is not exclusively used for the detection of evil spirits. There are actually more good spirits than evil spirits. Therefore, at times this gift should enable us to see the angels who are ministering to the heirs of salvation and who encamp around them that fear the Lord.

3. The Working of Miracles

As the leaders of the army drew near to take Elisha prisoner, the prophet called upon the Lord saying, "'Strike this people, I pray, with blindness'" (ver. 18). And, it happened. This was the gift of miracles in operation — a gift designed to perform supernatural acts. Through the operation of this one gift, the power of that great army was nullified.

4. The Gifts of Healings

The Syrian army, stunned by this calamity, was easily led to the King of Israel in Samaria. The king was amazed by the strange procession Elisha led into town. After learning what had happened, he prepared to kill them. But, instead, Elisha restrained him, asked God to restore their sight, and a mass healing took place (ver. 20).

5. *The Word of Wisdom*

We have mentioned that the King of Israel proposed executing the whole army. But the word of wisdom through Elisha vetoed the plan. He said, "'You shall not kill *them*. Would you kill those whom you have taken captive with your sword and your bow? Set food and water before them, that they may eat and drink and go to their master'" (ver. 22). As a result, these particular bands of Syrians, grateful for their lives, did not invade Israel again. (Later however, their king himself treacherously violated the kindness that was shown to him.)

6. *The Gift of Faith*

Backing up the operation of all these gifts was the unusual faith that Elisha had. Handling a great army in such a daring way could not have been accomplished with natural faith. It required the operation of supernatural faith that is born as the result of walking with God and becoming accustomed to how spiritual laws operate.

7. *The Gift of Prophecy*

Elisha was a prophet. Therefore, he spoke and did these things by the spirit of prophecy.

As Elijah and Elisha needed these gifts in their day, so the Church must have them today.

Christ and the Word of Knowledge

> But Jesus did not commit Himself to them, because He knew all *men*, and had no need that anyone should testify of man, for He knew what was in man (Jn. 2:24, 25).

Since Jesus emptied Himself of the divine glory He possessed before His incarnation, He needed to have the gifts of the Spirit, just as His followers need them. As we observe Christ operating in these gifts, we see Him using them only for the glory of the Father, and never for personal convenience. Christ could have turned stones to bread to prove that He was the Son of God, but He disdained this suggestion of the devil. On the other hand, He did not hesitate to miraculously feed the multitude when they fainted for hunger. He refused to perform a miracle to satisfy Herod's curiosity, nor would He produce a sign for the unbelieving Pharisees. Yet, He performed many miracles and showed His glory to all who believed Him.

Jesus never used His supernatural powers to satisfy mere human curiosity. Yet, He never failed to use this resource when it enabled Him to perform a service for the glory of the Father. Through the word of knowledge, and the discerning of spirits, He was able to understand the hidden motives of those who came to him. Because of this, He was always able to speak the words that were exactly appropriate for the situation.

Christ Knew His Own Disciples

Jesus said, "'I know My *sheep*'" (Jn. 10:14). He knew the hearts, temperament and character of each of His disciples. He did not know this by means of the wisdom He had with the Father before He came into the world, but through the knowledge that came to Him by the Holy Spirit. In the natural, Christ "increased in wisdom and stature" (Lk. 2:52) as any other person born into this world. But, when it was time for His ministry to begin, the Holy Spirit came upon Him, and through it, He received the spiritual equipment necessary to fulfill His ministry.

It was by the word of knowledge that Jesus understood Peter's temperament, strength and weaknesses as soon as He met him, and was able to say to him, "'You shall be called Cephas' (which is translated, A Stone)" (Jn. 1:42). To Nathaniel, He said, "'Behold, an Israelite indeed, in whom is no deceit!'" (Jn. 1:47). When the astonished Nathaniel wanted to know how Jesus knew this, He replied, "'Before Philip called you, when you were under the fig tree, I saw you'" (Jn. 1:48). He knew all about Judas too. He knew that under his smooth exterior there was deceit and treachery. Without identifying who the false disciple was, Jesus said, "'Did I not choose you, the twelve, and one of you is a devil?'" (Jn. 6:70).

Christ knew the hearts of all, whether it was Mary Magdalene whom He delivered of seven devils, or the Samaritan woman to whom He revealed that He was the Messiah, or Nicodemus, a master in Israel, to whom He said, "'You must be born again'" (Jn. 3:7).

As we have already noted, this phase of the word of knowledge blends into the gift of discerning of spirits, so it is not always possible to determine where the exercise of one gift begins and the other ends. Since the working of these gifts depends upon the same Spirit, this circumstance is of minor importance. The above ministry probably comes within the range of both gifts, just as in some respects, speaking by the gift of prophecy or by interpretation of tongues is very similar in operation.

It is understandable that Satan would attempt, by one means or another, to destroy the disciples of Christ and thus overthrow the divine program. He knew that to carry on the work of the Church after Jesus returned to heaven, trained disciples would be necessary. Therefore, if they lost their lives at sea, Satan's purpose would benefit.

So, one night when the disciples were crossing the Sea of Galilee, a fierce wind arose, putting their lives in jeopardy. At that critical moment, Jesus, Who was praying on a nearby mountain, became aware of the danger. He arose from His prayer in the fourth watch of the night, and came to them, walking upon the water. Here is another beautiful example of two gifts operating simultaneously — the word of knowledge and the ministry of miracles.

The Word of Knowledge and Other Gifts in Christ's Ministry

When the word of knowledge is freely operating, the actions of those through whom it is manifested may sometimes seem puzzling. For instance, when Jesus received the news that

Lazarus was sick, He stayed two more days in the place where He had been ministering. Christ did not cut His ministry short because unforeseen things arose; He was never caught off guard. Jesus explained to His disciples, "'This sickness is not unto death, but for the glory of God'" (Jn. 11:4). From this statement, it is not surprising that the disciples supposed that Lazarus would recover. When Christ finally started toward Bethany, His followers tried to dissuade Him, seeing no reason for Him to return to the vicinity of Jerusalem where He would be exposed to attempts on His life.

Jesus informed them that the reason for His journey was to awaken Lazarus. The disciples still did not understand, so the Lord had to speak plainly. Lazarus' sudden turn for the worse, his untimely death, the funeral, the grieving survivors — all this Jesus knew by the word of knowledge, and shaped His actions accordingly. It was, of course, all very mysterious to His puzzled disciples. But, they were soon to learn that Lazarus had died, but would be raised from the dead!

It is interesting to note how each gift supported and worked in harmony with the other in this remarkable event. First, the word of knowledge acquainted Jesus with what had happened in Bethany. Second, the word of wisdom dictated His actions — He decided to finish His work beyond Jordan, even though the sickness would be fatal. Third, supernatural faith was operating, making it possible for Christ to take dominion over the situation — to turn sorrow into joy, and death into glorious victory. Fourth, there was the prophetic announcement that Lazarus would rise again. And fifth, there was the working of miracles which restored the body of Lazarus, already in a state of decomposition, to perfect health and life.

The Word of Knowledge During the Passion Week

The word of knowledge was very evident in the ministry of Christ during the closing days of His earthly life. Immediately after Peter confessed His Lordship, Jesus began to speak of the events that would terminate His life.

From that time Jesus began to show to His disciples that He must go to Jerusalem, and suffer many things from the elders and chief priests and scribes, and be killed, and be raised the third day (Matt. 16:21).

As He and His disciples approached Jerusalem, He sent two disciples ahead to get a donkey for Him to ride into Jerusalem.

"Go into the village opposite you, and immediately you will find a donkey tied, and a colt with her. Loose *them* and bring *them* to Me. And if anyone says anything to you, you shall say, 'The Lord has need of them,' and immediately he will send them" (Matt. 21:2, 3).

Here, Jesus outlined a course of action that was possible only because He had a supernatural source of information. He needed an animal to ride into the city so that the prophecy of Zechariah could be fulfilled. He told His disciples what to do, and they found everything just as He said.

Upon reaching Jerusalem, they needed a place to prepare the Passover. Jesus told them that as they entered the city they would meet a man carrying a pitcher of water. They were to follow him.

And He said to them, "Behold, when you have entered the city, a man will meet you carrying a pitcher of water; follow him into the house which he enters. Then you shall say to the master of the house, 'The Teacher says to you, "Where is the guest room where I may eat the Passover with My disciples?"' Then he will show you a large, furnished upper room; there make ready" (Lk. 22:10-12).

This also was the direct operation of the word of knowledge. The disciples found things just as Jesus had said, and the Passover was prepared.

When the disciples took the Last Supper with Jesus, they had no knowledge that Judas was about to betray Him. But, Jesus knew and indicated the one who would betray Him, by giving him the piece of bread He had dipped (Jn. 13:26).

Jesus also knew that Peter's courage would fail, and he would deny Him three times.

> "I tell you, Peter, the rooster shall not crow this day before you will deny three times that you know Me" (Lk. 22:34).

Thus, we see that the word of knowledge working in harmony with prophecy and other gifts played a very important part in the ministry of Christ. It was by this means that Jesus was able to fulfill the prophecies, and complete His work on earth to the last detail.

Is it not true that as this age closes, if the Church is to fulfill its destiny as the body of Christ on earth, it must have this important gift operating too?

Part II

Discerning of Spirits, the Gift of Faith and the Gifts of Healings

Chapter Ten

Discerning of Spirits

The first chapters of the Bible emphasize the importance of being able to discern evil when it is present. It is ironic that although Eve, the mother of the human race, desired to learn the difference between good and evil, she was unable to discern the true identity of her tempter — a failure which resulted in not only her fall, but that of the whole human race. Persuaded by the smooth coaxing of the snake of which Satan had taken possession, she ate the forbidden fruit, thereby ushering sin and death into the world.

As we begin to study the gift of discerning of spirits, let us first look at its range and purpose. Discerning of spirits is closely related to the word of knowledge, but as we shall see, it is restricted to specialized knowledge. It is a supernatural ability to identify the nature and character of spirits, seen and unseen. These include:

1. Angelic spirits
2. Demonic or satanic spirits
3. Human spirits
4. The Spirit of God

What the Gift is Not

The discerning of spirits has often been confused with other things, and there are a number of popular misconceptions about its purpose and how it works. It may help us to understand the gift better if we first determine what the gift is not.

1. *Seeing faults in others*

Many believe that discerning of spirits gives one the ability to discern the faults of others, and more often than not, these people suppose that they possess such a gift! Harold Horton, in his excellent book *Gifts of the Spirit,* makes the following pertinent remarks on this subject:

> Discerning of spirits is not the power to discover faults in others. Not one of us requires the baptism in the Holy Spirit to endow us with the gift of criticism and faultfinding. We are all richly endowed by fallen nature with this particular "gift." The use of such a gift is indeed forbidden in the Scriptures. "Judge not, that ye be not judged." One of the purposes of the Holy Ghost baptism is to destroy this gift of criticism and replace it with the sweet "gift" of gentle forbearance. But these things are of course not supernatural at all. This spiritual gift is not discerning of character nor of faults, but of *spirits.*
>
> How often unguarded beginners tell us after their baptism, they have received "the gift of discernment!" In substantiation whereof they immediately begin to point out failings in fellow-believers! There need be no spiritual gift to uncover human failings, but there needs to be a good deal of Christly love to cover them.

2. *Mind reading*

Discerning of spirits should not be confused with the so-called art of mind reading. Professional mind readers in the entertainment field have sometimes mystified large audiences with what they call extrasensory perception. They allegedly read the minds of people, locate lost items, and in some cases, claim to discover the perpetrators of crimes.

These purely psychic demonstrations, which the performers concede have no religious significance, certainly have no relation to the gift of discerning of spirits. The gifts of God are never given to provide cheap entertainment for those looking for a new sensation. Neither are they included in the repertoire of a magician nor mind reader.

3. *Spiritist phenomena*

Mediums, who commonly claim to possess the gift of discerning of spirits, are patent frauds. They yield themselves to the control of familiar spirits. These unclean spirits have access to information of which the medium often is ignorant, and thus the mediums are able to stage demonstrations which amaze and convince the unwary. King Saul visited the Witch of En Dor incognito. But as soon as the woman went into her trance, she knew the identity of her visitor (I Sam. 28:7-12).

These spirits have power to impersonate the dead, deceiving bereaved people into believing that they are in communication with deceased loved ones. This is nothing but a cruel hoax. All such communications, if not outright frauds (as is often the case), are the work of lying spirits. Because spiritualist mediums are able, through these impersonating spirits, to reveal information that people thought was secret, or happened years ago, many are convinced that spiritualism is authentic.

The gift of discerning of spirits has nothing to do with the practice of witchcraft or black arts either. Instead, the gift boldly exposes the satanic character of these practices.

4. *Psychiatry*

Psychiatry is a profession that has recently gained considerable popularity. People who are emotionally disturbed go to these practitioners of the mind, and are told to relax and answer questions relating to their childhood. The theory of psychiatry is that probing the minds of these disturbed persons for mental blocks releases hidden hostilities.

While we believe that counselors are urgently needed in the Church, we do not believe that psychiatry has the answer for Christian people. It has no relation to the gift of discerning of spirits, and most psychiatrists are not born-again believers. They are usually ignorant of the Scriptures and ordinarily deny the existence of demonic spirits.

Purpose of the Gift

Discerning of spirits has a much broader field than is

generally understood. In fact, as we study the gift, we shall see that it is a doorway into the spiritual world. By it, God's people may discern good spirits as well as evil spirits. Angels are often present, but ordinarily we cannot see them. Sometimes, however, people have seen and conversed with angels. Occasionally, angels take on human form and appear to people, but on other occasions, they have been seen as spirit beings. By what power is this possible? It must be through the gift of discerning of spirits. The Apostle Paul, on the Damascus Road, saw a vision from the Lord. Yet those who were with him saw nothing (Acts 9:7). Paul was able to see what others could not.

Let us now consider some of the purposes of discerning of spirits:

1. *To see within the spirit world*

When God permits, discerning of spirits enables one to see into the spiritual realm. When Elisha was separated from Elijah, he saw the chariot and horses of fire that took the prophet away (II Ki. 2:11). When the Syrian army surrounded his house at Dothan, Elisha was undisturbed. Why? His eyes were open to the spiritual world. He saw the chariots of the Lord and could encourage his servant, saying, "Those who *are* with us *are* more than those who *are* with them" (II Ki. 6:16).

2. *To discern evil spirits*

There are various tests for detecting and distinguishing evil spirits from good spirits, but some of them cannot always be conducted immediately (I Jn. 4:1-3). Sometimes evil spirits deceive Christians by pretending to be the Spirit of God. They occasionally pretended to worship Christ when He was on earth, but Jesus always unmasked these demonic spirits and cast them out of their victims.

Discerning of spirits enables one to instantly detect the presence of an evil or seducing spirit. For example, Paul identified the spirit of divination in the girl at Philippi (Acts 16:16-19).

3. *To discern evil and hypocrisy among God's people*

We have already noted that discerning of spirits is not for mind-reading purposes. There are times, however, when Christians need to know what evil people are planning. There are times when deception is practiced among God's people and if it is left unchecked, it might cause great harm. The cases of Achan, Gehazi, and Ananias and Sapphira are scriptural examples of hypocrisy and lying being detected and dealt with. It is evident that such a gift is needed in the Church today, to keep it cleansed of evil.

In a certain meeting, an experienced evangelist who possessed a ministry in the word of knowledge and discerning of spirits, was praying for the sick. A young woman came to be prayed for, and her husband stood right behind her. The evangelist suddenly became aware that the woman had been committing adultery. He spoke in a tone low enough that the audience could not hear, but loud enough that the husband could. Her spouse immediately stepped forward with an angry expression on his face. Nearby workers wondered what was going to happen, but at that moment, the word came forth that the husband had committed the same sin, and the time and place were given. The husband stepped back embarrassed and speechless. When the couple realized that both were equally guilty, their heads dropped in shame. They began to weep and sought each other's forgiveness.

In the hands of a novice, this kind of a situation could be extremely dangerous. However, in this case, wisdom, knowledge and discernment worked together, and both individuals were brought to repentance as a result.

Doorway to the Spirit World

In order to more fully understand the discerning of spirits and how it works, it is necessary to review the background of this gift as it is unfolded in the Old Testament. As we consider these incidents, it will become evident that the gift has a broad field of operation.

A basic biblical revelation is that there are two distinct worlds — one natural and the other spiritual. Through our physical senses we can perceive the natural world, but they give us no contact with the spiritual world. It is only possible to pierce the veil that divides the two by some supernatural ability, such as the gift which we are considering.

Originally, mankind was created to be a citizen of both worlds. God provided Adam and Eve with a home in the Garden of Eden, where they were given lordship over the natural creation. In the evening, during the cool of the day, God came down and communed with them. But the Fall changed this. Severing the connection between people and God, sin caused them to hide from Him. No longer could the natural eye look upon its Creator, nor was it possible for the spirit of man to abide with deity. A veil or wall had come between the two worlds.

Although man's contact with the spiritual world has not yet been fully restored, redemption and God's ultimate condescension have restored the broken communion and the discerning of spirits gives man the ability to occasionally glimpse into these realms.

As we have already noted, it has been customary to limit this gift to the discerning of evil spirits. Actually, there are more good spirits than evil spirits in the universe (Rev. 12:4). These good spirits, usually called angels, have a special responsibility to the redeemed. Hebrews 1:14 refers to them declaring, "Are they not all ministering spirits sent forth to minister for those who will inherit salvation?" We are told that these celestial beings constantly attend the righteous. "The angel of the LORD encamps all around those who fear Him, and delivers them" (Psa. 34:7). Jesus said that even God's little ones have guardian angels:

> "Take heed that you do not despise one of these little ones, for I say to you that in heaven their angels always see the face of My Father who is in heaven" (Matt. 18:10).

When Adam and Eve were evicted from the Garden of Eden, an angel was sent to guard the way to the Tree of Life so they would not eat its fruit and live forever in their fallen state (Gen. 3:24). Now through Christ, mankind once again has access to the Tree of Life. The angels no longer keep us away, but guard and protect us until the day comes when we actually eat of its fruit (Rev. 2:7).

In order for communication between angels and humans to be possible, angels must either take on physical form, which they can do, or the person with whom they wish to communicate must receive a special gift of spiritual perception. Such powers are evidently associated with discerning of spirits.

In Bible times, when angelic visitations took place, it was always in connection with unfolding some important event in the divine plan. Such an occurrence naturally had a tremendous impact upon the individual, as illustrated in the lives of Elijah and Elisha. The latter possessed a burning desire to receive Elijah's ministry. Just before he was taken away in a chariot of fire, Elijah inquired what he might do for Elisha. His successor-to-be answered, "'Please let a double portion of your spirit be upon me'" (II Ki. 2:9). Elijah's reply was strange, but as we shall see, it had a very important significance.

> So he said, "You have asked a hard thing. *Nevertheless*, if you see me *when I am* taken from you, it shall be so for you; but if not, it shall not be so" (II Ki. 2:10).

Just what did Elijah mean by these words? He was telling Elisha that if his eyes could pierce the veil and see him at the moment of translation, then his request would be granted.

As we know, Elisha did see Elijah at his departing. He did see the chariot drawn by horses of fire. He did see and receive the mantle that fell to him from the prophet. From that moment on, Elisha was another man — he, too, lived in two worlds. No longer was he a mere servant, pouring "water on the hands of Elijah." The mantle of Elijah was now upon him, and he exercised this new power and authority in a befitting manner (II Ki. 2:15).

This power revolutionized Elisha's life. On one occasion,

the King of Syria invaded Israel. Through this gift, Elisha was able to keep the King of Israel informed of the enemy's plans. Because his plans kept being thwarted by Elisha's disclosures, the Syrian king sent a large detachment of chariots to Dothan to apprehend the prophet.

By morning light, the Syrian army had surrounded Elisha's house. When the prophet's servant looked out the next morning, he was utterly dismayed by the chariots and horses of the Syrian army. Despite the young man's understandable dismay, Elisha seemed undisturbed. There was a reason for this; the prophet could see what was happening in both worlds! True, there was an army of Syrians surrounding them, but he could also see the angelic army which outnumbered the Syrians. Thus his reply to his servant, "'Do not fear, for those who *are* with us *are* more than those who *are* with them'"(II Ki. 6:16). Elisha realized that his servant could not see what he saw, so he prayed and the young man's eyes were opened.

Elijah and the Angel

Elisha's ministry causes us to ask about the ministry of Elijah, from whom he received the double portion. When did Elijah obtain the ability to see into the spiritual realm? Was it when he raised the widow's son? Was it when he called fire down out of heaven? Or did it come when he prayed until the heavens opened and there was an abundance of rain? No, as mighty as the ministry of Elijah was at that time, he had not yet entered into the two-world ministry that was to make him absolutely fearless.

When the message reached him that the notorious Queen Jezebel was after his head, Elijah fled in terror to Beersheba, the last outpost of Israel. He then went a full day's journey into the wilderness, laid down under a juniper tree, and prayed that he might die.

This hour of death, however, became the hour of a new life for Elijah — the beginning of a new ministry for him. The angel of God touched him, and he awoke to see a visitor from another world, who offered him "angel's food." Elijah ate and went back to sleep, after which the angel awoke him a second time and told him to eat again. This was the turning point of Elijah's life. In the strength of that food, he journeyed to the Mount of God where he heard the still, small voice and received divine instructions for the vital ministry God still had for him to perform.

Never again would Elijah run from his enemies. Instead, he returned to the very place from which he had fled — to the very shadow of Ahab's palace. There he pronounced judgment on the wicked king and his execrable wife, Jezebel. Elijah's life was now a march of triumph, ever forward and onward until the moment of his translation. Elijah was now a citizen of two worlds!

Chapter Eleven

Discerning Angelic Spirits

"Do not forget to entertain strangers, for by so *doing* some have unwittingly entertained angels" (Heb. 13:2).

It is an interesting fact that when angels appeared in Old Testament times, often their identity as angels was not immediately recognized. Their solemn manner and conversation, however, usually caused them to be recognized as men of God. This indicates that angels resemble human beings in appearance.

When the angels appeared to Abraham (and later to Lot) they were recognized only as men of God. Abraham instinctively knew they were holy individuals, but their angelic identity was not immediately perceived. One of the three visitors, however, was the Lord Himself, and He not only revealed His identity to Abraham, but the purpose of His mission. "'Shall I hide from Abraham what I am doing?'" (Gen. 18:17).

This visit from the Lord and the angels was the outstanding event in Abraham's life. Jesus said, "'Your father Abraham rejoiced to see My day, and he saw *it* and was glad'" (Jn. 8:56). It was at that time that Abraham became the great intercessor. His prayer for Lot and the city of Sodom is a classic prayer of intercession (Gen. 18:23-33). Abraham's absolute surrender to the will of God from that time on was beautifully illustrated in his willingness to give up his son, Isaac.

This visit from the unseen world undoubtedly had much to do with the great faith which marked his life. It is interesting to note that after Abraham's death, and after he had entered the abode of the righteous, that place became known as Abraham's bosom (Lk. 16:22).

Moses — Man of Two Worlds

Moses was a man of 80 when God called him at the burning bush. Human ambition had burned out during his 40 years in exile, but God had not forgotten him. At the appointed time, God called him to deliver the children of Israel from bondage in Egypt.

The outstanding experience of Moses' life took place on the Mount of God. He hid there from human companionship, and interceded for the children of Israel who had, by a particularly flagrant act of idolatry, jeopardized their existence as a nation. God not only accepted Moses' intercession, but granted him a rare privilege. He was permitted to see God's form and glory from a hidden place in a rock (Ex. 33:11-23).

When Moses went down from the mountain, his face shone with divine glory. He was now a man of two worlds. When he died, God, Himself, buried him. The next time Moses appeared in Scripture, he was one of the figures on the Mount of Transfiguration.

Joshua and the Messenger

Joshua, a young man when Israel left Egypt, was the first captain of the Israelite army. He was also one of the two spies who brought back a good report concerning the land (Num. 14:6-9). Later, in anticipation of the fact that Joshua was to be his successor, Moses laid hands upon him so he would receive the spirit of wisdom (Deut. 34:9).

After the death of Moses, God commissioned Joshua to lead the children of Israel across the Jordan. Behind them was the river, before them was the city of Jericho. It was too late to turn back now! How would he accomplish this great task? Joshua had reached the most critical hour of his life.

It was at this moment that Joshua got a glimpse of a messenger from another world. As he stood alone, he saw a man with a drawn sword in his hand. Who was this? How did this stranger get into the camp? Joshua boldly asked, "'*Are* You for us or for our adversaries?'" (Josh. 5:13). The angel replied, "'No, but *as* Commander of the army of the LORD I have now come'" (ver. 14).

This was the encouragement Joshua needed. He saw that the armies of heaven were present and ready to help him. In recognition of that fact, the angel told Joshua to take off his shoes. This was a symbolic act; it showed that the battle was not Joshua's but the Lord's, and that Joshua did not have to depend upon his own strength. Joshua had joined the ranks of those who had become citizens of two worlds.

Gideon and the Angel

Although Gideon eventually proved himself to be a man of rare courage, his actions and conduct at the beginning were far from those of a hero. He was threshing wheat behind a winepress where he was hidden from view of the Midianites when he met the angel of the Lord.

Gideon seemed to have a deep inferiority complex. His family was poor and he considered himself least in his father's house (Judg. 6:15). When he recognized the angel as a heavenly messenger, he was so frightened he thought he was going to die (ver. 22, 23). When the Lord instructed him to tear down the altar of Baal, he did it at night when no one would see him (ver. 27).

Gideon is remembered particularly for his reluctance to venture against the Midianites. The Lord granted him special signs, and finally had to send him to the enemy's camp to hear for himself certain things that would give him confidence (Judg. 7:10-15).

It is clear that without the angel's visitation and the supernatural confirmation, Gideon would not have had the courage to attack the Midianites. It was not until Gideon knew that he had reinforcements from another world — "the sword of the Lord, and of Gideon" — that he was changed from a fearful man into a hero.

God help the modern Church realize that there are invisible forces that will fight its battles, if believers will only put their trust in God! We need spiritual discernment to perceive the forces of the other world; then we shall not be tempted to rely on carnal devices.

Manoah, His Wife and the Angel

Angelic ministry played an important role in the days of the judges. During one of the periods when Israel suffered from Philistine oppression, an angel appeared to Manoah's wife and informed her about the coming birth of Samson, who would deliver Israel from the enemy. The woman knew the visitor was a man of God and thought he might even be an angel, but she was not absolutely certain (Judg. 13:6).

Her husband also had a strong desire to meet this man of God, and prayed for the angel to pay them another visit. Manoah's prayer was answered and the angel reappeared, confirming his first message. Then, after Manoah had prepared a sacrifice to the Lord, the angel did a wondrous thing; he "ascended in the flame of the altar!" (Judg. 13:20). Manoah, who apparently had less courage than his wife, was afraid that this strange occurrence was an omen of their death. His wife sensibly pointed out that the angel would not have told them all the things he had if he had intended to take their lives.

Daniel and the Unseen World

Of all characters of the Old Testament, Daniel seems to have had the greatest understanding of the unseen world. When word came to him of the royal decree to kill all the wise men of Babylon, he had the assurance that God would send deliverance. For nearly three quarters of a century, he was a confidant of kings and princes, always ready with the wisdom necessary for the situation at hand.

On one occasion, Gabriel the archangel appeared to him (Dan. 9:21). At another time, while he and others were praying and fasting, an angel appeared to him in heavenly glory, "like the appearance of lightning" (Dan. 10:6). It is interesting to note that while others knew something was happening and were terrified, only Daniel had the power to see the angel — only he had discerning of spirits.

> And I, Daniel, alone saw the vision, for the men who were with me did not see the vision; but a

great terror fell upon them, so that they fled to hide themselves (Dan. 10:7).

The angel then gave him special information regarding the great conflict going on in the unseen world between the powers of righteousness and the powers of evil.

Angelic Ministry in the New Testament

We can note only a few of the angelic visitations recorded in the New Testament. But, they show that messengers from the unseen world appear to certain individuals on special occasions.

Gabriel, the angel of the Lord appeared to Zacharias to inform him of the coming birth of John the Baptist (Lk. 1:11-22). He doubted Gabriel's message, and this caused him to remain mute until after the birth of his son.

Gabriel also appeared to Mary, the mother of Jesus, informing her of the great privilege that was to be hers — that she was to become the mother of the Son of God (Lk. 1:26-38).

A band of angels appeared to the shepherds who were guarding their sheep in the fields outside of Bethlehem, proclaiming to them that the Christ-child had been born (Lk. 2:9-14).

An angel of the Lord appeared to the apostles while they were in prison and released them, saying, "'Go, stand in the temple and speak to the people all the words of this life'" (Acts 5:20).

Angelic ministry was involved when the Gospel was first preached to the gentiles. While Cornelius was in his house praying, an angel appeared to him and instructed him to send for Peter who would tell him what he needed to do (Acts 10:6).

An angel came into the prison where Peter was being kept in custody. It instructed him to get up and dress, and then took him through the gate of the prison which opened on its own. He was free to continue his ministry (Acts 12:5-10).

The angel of God stood before Paul when he was aboard a ship that was caught in a storm and said, "'Do not be afraid, Paul; you must be brought before Caesar; and indeed God has granted you all those who sail with you'" (Acts 27:24).

These examples indicate that the gift of discerning spirits is associated with the ministry of angels. This gift enabled many in both Old and New Testament times to perceive beings of the unseen world and thereby receive strength, encouragement and guidance to accomplish the tasks entrusted to them.

The Mount of Transfiguration

Peter left his own testimony of how the transfiguration effected his life and ministry. "For we did not follow cunningly devised fables when we made known to you the power and coming of our Lord Jesus Christ, but were eyewitnesses of His majesty. ... And we heard this voice which came from heaven when we were with Him on the holy mountain" (II Pet. 1:16, 18). Peter was referring to the experience on the Mount of Transfiguration. Not only did Christ appear in a glorified state, but Elijah and Moses appeared with Him. To Peter, seeing these Old Testament prophets actually alive and conversing with Christ concerning His approaching death, was a very convincing demonstration of supernatural power. He, James and John had been permitted to pierce the veil and see into another world.

Chapter Twelve

Discerning Evil Spirits

There are, as most of us well know, many evil forces on the loose in the spiritual world. The Apostle John warns us that we must always be on the alert for their activity.

> Beloved, do not believe every spirit, but test the spirits, whether they are of God; because many false prophets have gone out into the world. By this you know the Spirit of God: Every spirit that confesses that Jesus Christ has come in the flesh is of God, and every spirit that does not confess that Jesus Christ has come in the flesh is not of God. And this is the *spirit* of the Antichrist, which you have heard was coming, and is now already in the world (I Jn. 4:1-3).

Here John informs us of a method by which any believer can identify an evil spirit. Circumstances, however, do not always make it possible to use this method of identification. The gift of discerning spirits provides effective means at all times for detecting evil spirits, and is therefore of great service to the cause of Christ. If, for example, such a gift had been available to Eve, the course of history might have differed greatly. Had she known the identity of the one who was tempting her, she probably would have fled from him in mortal terror. Her ignorance, added to the fact that doubt had entered her heart concerning God's justice in withholding the fruit of the Tree of Knowledge from them, led to Eve's fateful error. There are many people today who do not realize who is tempting them either.

Methods by Which Satan Misleads

It is very important for God's people to know the various means and methods which Satan uses to deceive and mislead. The story of Job is a good example. Satan was able to send a cyclone and take the lives of Job's sons and daughters (Job 1:18, 19). Through the Sabeans, he killed the patriarch's servants and stole his cattle (ver. 14, 15). Lightning struck more of Job's servants and only one escaped (ver. 16). The Chaldeans invaded and robbed him of his camels (ver. 17). Finally, Job was struck by the devil with painful boils from head to foot (Job 2:7).

The remarkable thing about all this was that, although Satan was responsible for these things, everybody, including Job, blamed God for it. The servant who escaped said, "'The fire of God fell from heaven'" (Job 1:16). Job's three friends declared that undoubtedly, God had sent these disasters as punishment on Job, and that he should repent. His wife felt that God was responsible and advised her husband to, "'Curse God and die!'" (Job 2:9). Although Job refused to curse God, he did believe her charge that God was responsible. He replied, "'Shall we indeed accept good from God, and shall we not accept adversity?'" (Job 2:10).

What a help it would have been to Job if he had known the true identity of the one responsible for these disasters! It is said that the Book of Job was the first book of the Bible to be written. If so, then the first written revelation God made to mankind was that the devil is the cause of so many of our troubles and illnesses. This remarkable circumstance surely emphasizes the importance of being able to discern when evil powers are operating.

Satan attempts, and often succeeds, in leading God's people into delusions and causing them to do things completely outside God's will. "For false christs and false prophets will rise and show great signs and wonders to deceive, if possible, even the elect'" (Matt. 24:24).

We are told in I Chronicles 21:1, "Satan stood up against Israel, and moved David to number Israel." Even the unspiritual Joab saw that David's desire was inspired by pride, and protested strongly against it. But David was determined, and overlooked the fact that the Law of Moses commanded that a special offering be made when a census was taken, to prevent a curse from coming upon the people (Ex. 30:12). David was so absorbed in self-will that he overlooked all these things until judgment fell on the people. When he realized that he had sinned, he sought the Lord and his eyes were opened so that he saw the avenging angel with the drawn sword. David's repentance and intercession for the people was heard, and the hand of the destroying angel was stopped (I Chr. 21:15-27).

That Satan can confuse believers and impress thoughts completely contrary to God's will is fully illustrated in Peter's words to Christ in Matthew 16:22. When this event occurred, Peter had just made the confession that Jesus was the Christ, and the Lord had replied to Peter that this great truth had not come through human wisdom, but was a direct revelation from the heavenly Father.

> Jesus answered and said to him, "Blessed are you, Simon Bar-Jonah, for flesh and blood has not revealed *this* to you, but My Father who is in heaven" (Matt. 16:17).

Yet, immediately after this, when Jesus began to explain what would happen to Him in Jerusalem, Peter rebuked the Lord saying, "'Far be it from You, Lord; this shall not happen to You!'" (Matt. 16:22). Notice the significance of Christ's reply. It was not directed to Peter as much as it was to Satan!

> But He turned and said to Peter, "Get behind Me, Satan! You are an offense to Me, for you are not mindful of the things of God, but the things of men" (Matt. 16:23).

Jesus attributed Peter's words to the direct suggestion of Satan, even though shortly before, Christ acknowledged that Peter's confession had come directly by revelation from the heavenly Father! It is therefore evident that if we are not alert, believers may occasionally mistake a suggestion of Satan for that of the Spirit of God.

Abimelech

> God sent a spirit of ill will between Abimelech and the men of Shechem; and the men of Shechem dealt treacherously with Abimelech (Judg. 9:23).

An evil spirit came upon the usurper, Abimelech. Those who followed him apparently had no idea of the identity of the spirit that dominated their leader, and they blindly followed him to their own destruction. The story of this usurper shows the operation of a certain law; evil spirits have liberty to take over people who seek power by treachery and betrayal.

There is no doubt that a Satanic spirit completely dominated and controlled Adolf Hitler. The people of Germany (and even many in the Church) were not, at least for a long time, able to discern the spirit that controlled his vile and murderous character. It's unfortunate that at times God's people have so little ability to discern between the good and the satanic.

We are told that King Saul of Israel received the Spirit of God. He prophesied under the Spirit, and was "turned into another man" (I Sam. 10:6). But Saul had a perverse self-will, and grieved the Lord until an evil spirit took control of him (I Sam. 16:14).

It is remarkable that the followers of Saul, unlike those of Abimelech, discerned that it was no longer the Spirit of God, but an evil spirit that had taken possession of their king. "And Saul's servants said to him, 'Surely, a distressing spirit from God is troubling you'" (I Sam. 16:15). In this respect, they had better discernment than some Christians today who blindly follow leaders who obviously have departed from the truth.

The servants noted that David had unusual faith and power with God, and they recommended that he come and minister to King Saul. This resulted in the exorcism of the evil spirit (ver. 23). However, Saul's emotional conflicts opened the door for the evil spirit to return. He became excited and insanely jealous over the applause that David received after he killed the giant, Goliath (I Sam. 18:9-11).

The evil spirit strengthened its grip on Saul, and eventually the Lord departed from him once and for all. Evil became Saul's master. It was then that he consulted the Witch of En Dor, a woman possessed with a familiar spirit (I Sam. 28:7-15). It is even more sad that the king's servants discerned that his erratic conduct was opening the door to evil spirits, but he continued in his willful course.

Jehoshaphat was one of Judah's most God-fearing kings, but he had one serious fault — an unfortunate tendency to enter into alliances with the wicked. In this particular situation, Ahab proposed a military campaign against Ramoth-Gilead, and managed to persuade Jehoshaphat to participate in it with him.

Ahab and Jezebel were religious enough, but their religion was rank idolatry, which mixed in the most abominable practices of the heathen. The king and queen maintained a community of hireling prophets to invoke the blessing of the gods on any enterprise in which they chose to engage. Just as some notorious dictators of our time regularly consult oracles and astrologers to secure the favor of mystic powers, Ahab called his hireling prophets to put their blessing upon this enterprise. All of the paid prophets promised the king unqualified success. "So they said, 'Go up, for the Lord will deliver *it* into the hand of the king'" (I Ki. 22:6).

However, Jehoshaphat was not completely satisfied by the smug answers of Ahab's hireling prophets, and insisted on sending for a prophet of the Lord — one who had antagonized Ahab by prophesying evil against him.

Now comes one of the most remarkable revelations in Scripture, one which permits us to learn something about the activities that take place between the opposing powers of good and evil. The only other Old Testament passage that compares to it is Daniel 10.

While the false prophets continued to prophesy prosperity and success for Ahab's adventure, Micaiah exploded a bomb-shell in the camp by predicting both disaster in the coming battle, and the death of the king. Micaiah then related the vision God had given him of lying spirits securing permission from the Lord to deceive the prophets of Ahab (I Ki. 22:20-23).

This was clearly a case of discerning spirits. Through supernatural revelation, Micaiah perceived that the spirit in the mouth of Ahab's prophets was not the Spirit of God, but a lying spirit. Micaiah got no thanks for his honest warning. He was thrown unceremoniously into prison with only bread and water to eat and drink. Ahab ignored the warning and went into battle like an ox to the slaughter. Despite his attempt to make the enemy think Jehoshaphat was the king of Israel, and thereby divert their attack away from himself, Ahab's disguise was penetrated. He was killed in the battle, and dogs licked up his blood as the prophet had said.

Paul Discerns a Spirit of Divination

The classic New Testament example of the discernment and identification of an evil spirit is in Acts 16:

> Now it happened, as we went to prayer, that a certain slave girl possessed with a spirit of divination met us, who brought her masters much profit by fortune-telling. This girl followed Paul and us, and cried out, saying, "These men are the servants of the Most High God, who proclaim to us the way of salvation." And this she did for many days. But Paul, greatly annoyed, turned and said to the spirit, "I command you in the name of Jesus Christ to come out of her." And he came out that very hour (Acts 16:16-18).

Notice the details of the incident. The evil spirit in the girl was masquerading as the Spirit of God. There are some things about this situation that are similar to the case of Simon the Sorcerer, who pretended that his black arts were the same thing Philip preached (Acts 8:10-13). The familiar spirit in the girl did not speak against Paul's preaching, but pretended to be sympathetic. Some people might have been fooled by this demonstration, but not Paul. Realizing that if he did nothing, the people would confuse the Gospel with soothsaying, he cast out the evil spirit in the Name of Jesus.

Of course the girl's masters were very displeased with this turn of events, and Paul and Silas were thrown into prison. A miraculous earthquake opened the prison doors and changed the situation. Paul and Silas succeeded in converting the jailer and his family, and were soon released from prison to continue their evangelistic work. As a result of Paul's ministry, Europe became a stronghold of the Christian faith.

Today there is a general lack of understanding, even among Full Gospel people, of the evil powers that are in action. Because of this, hypnotism is commonly being used to assist in childbirth, and by psychiatrists who plumb the minds of their patients in an attempt to relieve them from stresses and complexes. This practice is very dangerous. There can be no doubt that hypnotism, like spiritualism, is associated with the work of evil spirits.

Dr. John G. Lake told of an interesting incident, relating to this subject, that occurred in one of his meetings in Africa:

> In Johannesburg Tabernacle, at a Sunday service God instantly healed a lame girl. She came from Germiston. She had been suffering for three-and-a-half years from what doctors said was either an extreme case of rheumatism, or the first stages of hip disease. She was not able to get up the steps without assistance when she came to the platform to be prayed for. We asked her: "How long have you been sick?" She said, "For three-and-a-half years." "Have the doctors treated you?" "Yes; for two-and-a-half years, and then they gave me up." "Who has been treating you for the last year?" "A hypnotist."

Just then, a well-known hypnotist arose in the audience, and moved forward and took a front seat. I said, "Never mind the hypnotist. Jesus is going to heal you right now. In two minutes you will be well." We laid hands on her and prayed, and instantly the Lord delivered her, and she walked up and down the platform several times to demonstrate to herself and to the audience that she was well.

I stepped back and looked at her, my heart going out in praise to God for His mercy, when suddenly the Spirit of the Lord descended upon me in power, not in any gentle influence, but with a mighty intense power — a spirit of revelation against the spirit of the hypnotist. I stepped from the platform directly in front of him and said, "Are you the man who has been hypnotizing this woman?" He replied, "Yes, I am." He rose to his feet and looked toward me in a challenging attitude. I said to him, "In the Name of Jesus Christ, you will never hypnotize anybody again." And before I realized what I was doing, I reached over the front of the platform, grasped his collar with my left hand, while with my right I slapped him on the back, saying, "In the Name of Jesus Christ, the Son of God, you come out of him." He laughed at me and asked, "Do you mean to tell me that I cannot hypnotize anybody?" I replied, "Yes, sir, that is the end of that thing. The devil that caused you to hypnotize people is out."

He worked all night in an endeavor to hypnotize some subjects, and in the morning at six came to my house saying, "This is a mighty serious business, mister; this is my bread and butter." He wanted me to give him back the power to hypnotize. I explained to him that it was not I but Jesus who cast out the devil. I added, "Brother, it looks to me as if the Lord wanted you to earn an honest living."

He cancelled his engagement at the theater where he was billed to give exhibitions, and the last heard of, he was working in a mine and earning an honest living. That demonstrated that there is a mighty manifestation of the Spirit of God who has dominion over every other power. It is still true that in His Name we shall cast out devils.

Discerning When Sickness is Caused by Satan

Discerning of spirits has a definite relation to the ministry of healing. Many people do not know that Satan is directly, or indirectly, the cause of all sickness. Yet, few things are made more clear in Scripture. For example, in the case of Job, we are told that the devil was responsible for putting the boils on him.

> So Satan went out from the presence of the LORD, and struck Job with painful boils from the sole of his foot to the crown of his head (Job 2:7).

When Paul preached his first sermon to the gentiles, he declared that sickness was caused by the oppression of Satan, and that Christ was revealed to destroy his works.

> "How God anointed Jesus of Nazareth with the Holy Spirit and with power, who went about doing good and healing all who were oppressed by the devil, for God was with Him" (Acts 10:38).

Christ, Himself, attributed to the works of Satan the affliction of the woman who had been bowed over for 18 years.

> "So ought not this woman, being a daughter of
> Abraham, whom Satan has bound — think of it
> — for eighteen years, be loosed from this bond
> on the Sabbath?" (Lk. 13:16).

The words of Jesus indicate that evil spirits are the cause of many afflictions. In this case, the woman was bowed over by a "spirit of infirmity" (Lk. 13:11). When Christ cast out the spirit, she was able to resume a normal position.

Of course, sickness is not always caused by evil spirits. But when this is the case, the person cannot be delivered until the spirit is cast out. There are many kinds of evil spirits. There is the spirit of infirmity, mentioned in Luke 13:11. There are deaf spirits (Mark 9:25), blind spirits (Matt. 12:22), mute spirits (Matt. 9:32, 33), murderous spirits, like the one that caused Saul to become violent (I Sam. 18:9-11), epileptic spirits (Lk. 9:39), insane spirits (Lk. 8:27-35), unclean spirits (Mk. 1:23), and undoubtedly a number of other kinds.

The gift of discernment is of great service in dealing with sickness. For example, the way to deliver an individual will be different if the person is possessed with a spirit of infirmity, than if he/she has an ordinary disease. The plural term "gifts of healings" (I Cor. 12:9) indicates that here are different gifts of healings, each adapted for various kinds of afflictions.

Occasionally, a person may be possessed by more than one evil spirit. Mary Magdalene was delivered from seven devils (Mk. 16:9). In the case of apostasy, a person may become a habitation of as many as eight or more evil spirits (Lk. 11:24-26). The lunatic in the tombs, was possessed by a whole legion of demons (Mk. 5:9). The gift of discernment enables one to detect whether the patient is possessed by more than one evil spirit. All demons need to be discerned and cast out if the person is to get well.

The word of knowledge and discerning of spirits also work together in the ministry of praying for the sick. It goes without saying that people should be sure that they are completely under the anointing before attempting to tell other people what their afflictions are. A mistake could shatter people's confidence, confuse them, or perhaps cause them to believe they have a disease that they do not have. Civil authorities could even consider this to be medical malpractice, and serious legal difficulties could result.

Chapter Thirteen

Discerning the Human Spirit

> But Jesus did not commit Himself to them,
> because He knew all *men,* and had no need that
> anyone should testify of man, for He knew what
> was in man (Jn. 2:24, 25).

The need for the ability to discern the human spirit is illustrated in the story of Jacob. With his mother, Rebekah's advice and assistance, Jacob impersonated his brother Esau and deceived his father, Isaac. Isaac, whose sight had nearly failed, could not distinguish between his two sons. He said, "'The voice *is* Jacob's voice, but the hands *are* the hands of Esau'" (Gen. 27:22). Thus Isaac was deceived into giving the blessing to Jacob instead of Esau.

While the wall around Jerusalem was being rebuilt, Nehemiah was confronted by a lot of opposition. Sanballat and Tobiah tried every scheme and trick they could think of to bring the work to a halt. The prophet not only faced hindrance from without, but he also had a problem of discouragement within.

When subterfuge failed, a mercenary hired by Tobiah and Sanballat came to Nehemiah warning him to hide in the temple because, "' ... they are coming to kill you; indeed, at night they will come to kill you'" (Neh. 6:10). At first, Nehemiah did not recognize that the man was a spy, though he did not think much of his advice. Then a flash of discernment came to him and he recognized that the messenger was from the enemy's camp.

> Then I perceived that God had not sent him at
> all, but that he pronounced *this* prophecy
> against me because Tobiah and Sanballat had
> hired him (Neh. 6:12).

In certain cases, it is important to know what is in the individual's mind in order to help him. There are some instances in which the person is committing a serious sin, and at the same time, publicly seeking healing. When such hypocritical individuals fail to receive deliverance, the impression is often left that the person who prayed failed to have faith. Again, there are individuals who come into church pretending to be believers, but are really wolves in sheep's clothing. How often the Church has suffered because the truth about people was not known! For example, a minister of a large church in Milwaukee appeared to be very zealous in building up his congregation, but was actually a criminal at heart. He set fire to his own church in order to collect the insurance money, so he could build another one in a more fashionable section of the city. What a man to have in charge of the spiritual welfare of a congregation!

In another situation, a minister in Seattle who enjoyed a wide reputation as a spiritual man and as a leader in his denomination, was ultimately found guilty of seducing several of the young women in his congregation. What a need there is for spiritual discernment to detect the rise of evil in the Church before it gains such headway!

Yet, the Spirit of God is reluctant to publicly expose a person if they can possibly be saved. Where there is hope of repentance, God may allow an individual's transgressions to be covered, to prevent their ministry and influence from being ruined. Those who have the gift of discernment should bear in mind that the Lord is merciful. Sometimes, God may reveal a developing situation so it can be stopped before it goes too far. Where true repentance is obtained, the person with discernment should know how to keep God's secrets. If, however, the individual continues to play with fire, God will likely bring the evil to light, even as He did with David's sin (II Sam. 12:12). Once God exposes a situation, nothing can cover it up.

Sometimes it is unclear just where the operation of the word of knowledge ends and the discerning of spirits begins. The gifts are closely related. Generally speaking, however, when the revelation involves exposure for moral considerations, the gift in operation can be said to be discerning of spirits.

Jesus obviously possessed both the word of knowledge and discerning of spirits. When the Pharisees murmured against Him, He understood what was in their hearts. "Jesus perceived in His spirit that they reasoned thus within themselves" (Mk. 2:8). Usually a person with the word of knowledge will have some measure of the kindred gift of discerning of spirits.

Let us now consider some of the examples in the Bible when discernment of the human spirit was needed. There were prophets who spoke from their own hearts and deceived people. There were those who, for the love of money, practiced deception and fraud. They pretended to be religious, but were actually ravening wolves at heart. To prevent such people from leading others astray, the gift of discerning of spirits was, and still is, needed.

Prophets Who Speak From Their Own Spirit

There are false prophets who are possessed by, and speak under the influence of, familiar spirits. On the other hand, there are those who speak presumptuously from their own spirits. One of the purposes for the gift of discerning of spirits is to be able to distinguish the spirit by which a prophet speaks. There is also a way by which anyone can determine if a prophet speaks by the Holy Spirit, although time is required in making the test. This is found in Deut. 18:21, 22:

> "And if you say in your heart, 'How shall we know the word which the LORD has not spoken?' — when a prophet speaks in the name of the LORD, if the thing does not happen or come to pass, that *is* the thing which the LORD has not spoken; the prophet has spoken it presumptuously; you shall not be afraid of him."

Jeremiah Discerns False Prophecies

Hananiah was a false prophet who spoke presumptuously

from his own heart (Jer. 28:1-4). He gave a prophecy claiming that within two years God would break the yoke of Nebuchadnezzar, the King of Babylon, and that the captives of Judah and the vessels taken from the temple would be returned to Jerusalem.

Jeremiah discerned that the prophecy was false. Somehow, Hananiah had deluded himself into believing that what he said was true. He was very likely under satanic suggestion, but we are not told that a familiar spirit spoke directly through him. Hananiah's words came out of a deceived heart. Jeremiah discerned at once that his prophecies were false, and Hananiah's doom was foretold.

> Then the prophet Jeremiah said to Hananiah the prophet, "Hear now, Hananiah, the LORD has not sent you, but you make this people trust in a lie. Therefore thus says the LORD: 'Behold, I will cast you from the face of the earth. This year you shall die, because you have taught rebellion against the LORD.'" So Hananiah the prophet died the same year in the seventh month (Jer. 28:15-17).

Some years ago, there was a brilliant but erratic minister making a series of bold predictions including that within a year the island of Japan would sink beneath the sea and that California would suffer its worst earthquake in history. The brilliance and forcefulness of the speaker held the audience spellbound. So many startling prophecies were made, it is doubtful that more than a few in the audience were able to remember any of the details. Apparently, none of the predictions ever came to pass. The man had merely spoken out of his vivid imagination, and his erratic conduct soon caused him to lose the confidence of many people.

We may expect false prophets to arise and to deceive many, and should be alert against them. If we are not, they will lead others astray with their persuasiveness.

Elisha Discerns Deception

A clue to the secret of Elisha's great power was his utter disregard for earthly and material things. He was completely dedicated to the cause of Jehovah, and was always ready to assist others when they were in trouble, to help them pay their debts or recover their losses. However, he seemed to have little or no concern for his own comfort. Elijah's dramatic translation made the world to come very real for Elisha. Apparently, he lost all ambition for possessions in a world in which he was only a passing pilgrim.

Elisha's outlook was puzzling to his servant Gehazi, who coveted earthly things in the same proportion that his master had contempt for them. Gehazi's patience reached the breaking point when Naaman was healed of leprosy and the prophet turned down the substantial reward he was offered in gratitude. Gehazi thought Elisha was a fool. So with a trumped-up story about two sons of the prophets just arriving from a journey, Gehazi secretly pursued Naaman and pretended he had been sent to ask him for a talent of silver and two changes of clothes. Naaman was glad to comply with his request, and soon the gift obtained by deception was hidden away in a safe place — at least, so Gehazi thought. But Elisha knew all that had taken place. When the servant returned, he was startled to hear the prophet's words, "'Did not my heart go *with you* when the man turned back from his chariot to meet you? *Is it* time to receive money and to receive clothing, olive groves and vineyards, sheep and oxen, male and female servants?'" (II Ki. 5:26).

Gehazi should have known better. He knew that Elisha lived close to God, and that deception could not be hidden from him. But the lust for money and material things blinded him. Gehazi left Elisha's presence taking Naaman's leprosy with him.

There is much corruption in the Church today. Ministers who have had some success, too often forget their spiritual calling and get their eyes on money. In doing so, they lose the spiritual power that brought them into prominence in the first place. The word of knowledge and discerning of spirits need to be restored to the Church to guard against greed.

Keeping Evil From the Church

After the outpouring of the Holy Spirit on the Day of Pentecost, the Church enjoyed continuous and rapid growth — 3,000 converts on one day, 5,000 on another. But as in all great revivals, there were people who joined themselves to the movement whose motives were mixed. Some like Judas Iscariot, considered Christianity a religious enterprise that might prove lucrative to those who got in on the ground floor.

So when Ananias and Sapphira saw others selling their property and giving the proceeds to the movement, they felt that in order to stay in good standing, they must appear to do the same. But, they secretly reserved a substantial portion of the sale price — just in case things didn't turn out as anticipated. As Peter later made clear, their great sin was not that they reserved a part of the money from the sale, but that they deliberately conspired to give the impression that they had given *all* of it. If such deception had gone undetected, the integrity of the newborn Church would have been in jeopardy. If it had become infiltrated with evil and hypocrisy, Satan might have succeeded in subverting the movement at its very inception. But, a supernatural ministry saved the Church.

When Ananias laid the money at the apostle's feet, piously pretending that it was the whole amount, Peter suddenly received a check from the Holy Spirit. He perceived in the Spirit that Ananias and Sapphira had planned together to perjure themselves by lying to the Holy Spirit. Peter, under the Holy Spirit's anointing, pronounced this judgment:

> But Peter said, "Ananias, why has Satan filled your heart to lie to the Holy Spirit and keep back *part* of the price of the land for yourself? While it remained, was it not your own? And after it was sold, was it not in your own control? Why have you conceived this thing in your heart?

You have not lied to men but to God." Then
Ananias, hearing these words, fell down and
breathed his last. So great fear came upon all
those who heard these things. And the young
men arose and wrapped him up, carried *him* out,
and buried *him* (Acts 5:3-6).

Soon afterward, Sapphira came in and the tragic drama
was completed. Judgment fell on both the husband and wife
for daring to lie to God!

This may seem to be severe punishment, but obviously it
had a beneficial effect on the Church. Notice what happened:

1. Fear fell on the Church (ver. 11).
2. The ministry of the supernatural was increased (ver.
   12).
3. The unconverted were restrained from joining the
   Church (ver. 13).
4. Multitudes of converts were added to the Church (ver.
   14).

There is no doubt that the modern Church is urgently in
need of this ministry. There is much evil in the Church and
both the discerning of spirits and divine discipline are sadly
needed to cleanse it.

Simon the Sorcerer

Simon was a man who had achieved a great reputation
among the people of Samaria. He practiced sorcery, but deceived the people into believing that he was orthodox, and that
the mysterious rites he performed were actually miracles of
God (Acts 8:9, 10).

Simon was subtle, so when Philip came preaching Christ
and performing miracles, he did not oppose it. Instead, he let
the people believe that Philip's miracles were of the same kind
as his. However, there was no repentance or change of heart
on his part. When Simon requested the rite of baptism, Philip,
who apparently had gifts of healings and miracles, did not

have the discernment which would have enabled him to understand the motives behind his request. He proceeded to baptize the sorcerer.

Simon, who had been duly impressed by Philip's miracles, observed Peter and John laying hands on the Samaritans to receive the Holy Spirit. He became obsessed with a desire to obtain the same power. Being essentially blind to spiritual things, he supposed that the power Peter and John had was of the same kind as that through which he practiced his arts. He therefore offered the apostles money if they would give him the power they had.

This strange request immediately drew Peter's attention, and he discerned that Simon was of another spirit altogether. The apostle strongly rebuked him.

> But Peter said to him, "Your money perish with you, because you thought that the gift of God could be purchased with money! You have neither part nor portion in this matter, for your heart is not right in the sight of God. Repent therefore of this your wickedness, and pray God if perhaps the thought of your heart may be forgiven you. For I see that you are poisoned by bitterness and bound by iniquity" (Acts 8:20-23).

Peter's severe rebuke made Simon tremble. He begged that judgment would not come upon him. We are not told whether his desire was merely to escape punishment, or if he truly repented.

Chapter Fourteen

The Gift of Faith

The gift of faith contrasts with the working of miracles in that the former appears to be passive, while the working of miracles is distinctly active and immediate in its operation. However, although the gift of faith *appears* to be passive, it sets forces in motion that are irresistible.

When Jesus came to the fig tree that bore no fruit but had only leaves, He said, "'Let no one eat fruit from you ever again'" (Mk. 11:14). Nothing *appeared* to happen, but actually something *did* happen. On the following morning as they passed that way again, the disciples saw that the fig tree had withered away. This gave Christ the opportunity to make the following striking statement on the power of faith:

> So Jesus answered and said to them, "Have faith in God. For assuredly, I say to you, whoever says to this mountain, 'Be removed and be cast into the sea,' and does not doubt in his heart, but believes that those things he says will be done, he will have whatever he says. Therefore I say to you, whatever things you ask when you pray, believe that you receive *them*, and you will have *them*" (Mk. 11:22-24).

While the gift of miracles produces instantaneous action, the gift of faith secures the same results in a less spectacular way. When Elijah asked the widow of Zarephath to take the last of her meal and oil and bake him a cake, promising that the meal would not waste nor the oil fail, he was exercising the gift of miracles. Also, when he prayed and fire fell from heaven and consumed the sacrifice, the gift of miracles was operating. But when Elijah sat by the Brook Cherith in quiet confidence that God would supply his need, he was exercising the gift of faith. Another example of the gift of faith in operation was when the three Hebrew children were thrown alive into the fiery furnace because they would not worship the golden image. Faith delivered them from its flames.

Supernatural faith is available to all believers (Jn. 14:12), as is the gift of speaking in other tongues. This is not true of all the gifts. For instance, the working of miracles in the hands of a novice could result in disaster. If Jesus had not restrained them, James and John would have called down fire from heaven on a Samaritan city because they had received an affront. If the Samaritans had been killed, they would not have experienced the great revival that later occurred when Philip went there. The gift of faith, however, is not so easily misused.

When the gift of miracles is operating, miracles take place at once. When the gift of faith is working, God, through the believer's faith, takes the initiative and brings about the miracle, but it generally does not come to pass immediately. Since God never makes a mistake, it would seem that the will of God is assured in this case. On the other hand, man takes the initiative in the working of miracles, and this may not always be true.

The gift of faith has a wide scope of usefulness, and it is unfortunate that the Church has not reached out and secured the benefits of it in a far greater way. Because of the more spectacular nature of the working of miracles, many have desired and sought after that gift — often in vain. Yet the same results may be achieved through the gift of faith!

There is much to be said about the working of faith, of its human and its supernatural character, of its diversity of operation, and of the way it is manifested in varying intensity in the lives and ministries of different people. The Scriptures speak of little faith, growing faith, mustard seed faith, fruit-of-the-Spirit faith and the gift-of-the-Spirit faith.

Strictly speaking, all faith is a gift of God. "God has dealt to each one a measure of faith" (Rom. 12:3). Unfortunately, many people fall under evil influences and lose their faith. Some who are not rooted in the Word of God, listen to false teachers and shipwreck their faith (I Tim. 1:19; II Tim. 2:18).

Faith, in its primary definition, is that innate capacity within every human being to believe in a Supreme Being. Children recognize that they live in a universe that they did not create, and are therefore confronted with the great question, "How did this world come into existence?" Human reason can never explain it. Reason can only say that creation is here, and since it exists, there must be a Creator.

> For since the creation of the world His invisible *attributes* are clearly seen, being understood by the things that are made, *even* His eternal power and Godhead, so that they are without excuse (Rom. 1:20).

Two Kinds of Faith

There are two principal kinds of faith — natural and supernatural. Natural faith can accomplish many things. It can bring the sinner into a place of forgiveness and salvation. On the strength of this natural faith, people may reach out and receive many blessings. Jesus occasionally reproached His followers because they did not use the natural faith they already had. When the disciples were overtaken by a storm at sea, and became fearful, He said, "'Why are you fearful, O you of little faith?'" (Matt. 8:26).

Faith begins with the recognition that God is. "For he who comes to God must believe that He is, and *that* He is a rewarder of those who diligently seek Him" (Heb. 11:6). This natural faith, if properly nurtured, will grow and become stronger and stronger, until eventually it moves into the supernatural realm. Every victory or answer to prayer inspires more faith. Faith, however, must receive its direction and strength through the Word of God. "So then faith *comes* by hearing, and hearing by the word of God" (Rom. 10:17). Simply stated, faith is our confidence that God will do what He has said He will do.

The Scriptures also speak of faith as a fruit of the Spirit. This kind of faith is not specifically miracle faith. Faith as a fruit of the Spirit refers to the faith of the Christian who has learned to trust absolutely in the goodness and providence of God. It is a faith that is not dismayed by the unexpected, nor disheartened by difficulties. It takes all things in stride. It believes that all things work together for good to them that love the Lord. Faith, as the fruit of the Spirit, has unbounded confidence in the integrity of God and in His providence. It exclaims with the Apostle Paul:

> Oh, the depth of the riches both of the wisdom and knowledge of God! How unsearchable *are* His judgments and His ways past finding out! (Rom. 11:33)

Faith — the Gift of the Spirit

Then there is faith that is a gift of the Spirit. In a certain sense, all faith is a gift of God, just as our physical life is a gift of God. But, there is faith which is a direct impartation from God, a supernatural faith that reaches into the creative realm. This kind of faith becomes the very set of the soul, and counts the things which are not as though they are.

The Church needs faith that will lift its people out of depression and out of the toils of the enemy. We need faith that will stand like a rock when the devil strikes his evil blows and that breaks the grip of sickness and disease, bringing the believer into a realm of divine health. We need faith that will break the fetters of discouragement and defeat, lifting us into a walk of victory and triumph, as well as faith that will supply all that is required when it is needed. We need faith that can open prison doors, calm the stormy sea, bind the powers of darkness, and lift the believers into a life of continuous victory. The writer of Hebrews sums it up eloquently:

> And what more shall I say? For the time would fail me to tell of Gideon and Barak and Samson and Jephthah, also *of* David and Samuel and the prophets: who through faith subdued kingdoms, worked righteousness, obtained promises, stopped the mouths of lions, quenched the violence of fire, escaped the edge of the sword, out of weakness were made strong, became valiant

in battle, turned to flight the armies of the aliens. Women received their dead raised to life again. Others were tortured, not accepting deliverance, that they might obtain a better resurrection (Heb. 11:32-35).

The Laying on of Hands

By faith Isaac blessed Jacob and Esau concerning things to come. By faith Jacob, when he was dying, blessed each of the sons of Joseph, and worshiped, *leaning* on the top of his staff (Heb. 11:20, 21).

In the days of the Patriarchs, the blessing was imparted from father to son through a special dispensation of faith. The case of Isaac's blessing Jacob makes it clear that the gift of faith is independent of the gift of discernment. For while the blessing was supernaturally imparted, the nearly blind Isaac was unable to discern that he was not blessing Esau, but Jacob, his younger son!

Sometimes the patriarchal blessing was administered on the deathbed. This was the case when Jacob called his grandsons Ephraim and Manasseh to him, laid his hands upon them, and gave them his blessing. He intentionally placed his right hand upon the youngest, and his left upon the oldest. Joseph was displeased with this and tried to reverse his father's hands, but Jacob replied, "'I know, my son, I know. He also shall become a people, and he also shall be great; but truly his younger brother shall be greater than he, and his descendants shall become a multitude of nations'" (Gen. 48:19). Shortly after this, and just before he died, Jacob gave his special blessing to all of his sons.

There were several things which seem to have been involved in giving the patriarchal blessing.

1. It was an act of special significance, usually performed through laying on hands.

2. When giving the blessing, the patriarch was so directed by the Spirit of God that his hands went to the right person, though he might even mistake the identity of the one whom he was blessing!

3. The blessing was usually accompanied by a prophecy that related to events many generations in the future.

4. The blessing was often given just before the patriarch's death.

5. This patriarchal sacrament apparently foreshadowed special blessings that would be given to Christians through laying on hands in the New Testament dispensation. In the Old Testament, the blessing was by race and national election. In the Church Age it is for "as many as the Lord our God will call" (Acts 2:39).

Laying on hands in Old Testament days was not only for ministering the tribal blessing. Moses laid hands on Joshua and he received "the spirit of wisdom."

> Now Joshua the son of Nun was full of the spirit of wisdom, for Moses had laid his hands on him; so the children of Israel heeded him, and did as the LORD had commanded Moses (Deut. 34:9).

God is not restricted to any particular method in giving the Holy Spirit. It may fall according to the sovereign grace of God as it did on the Day of Pentecost and at Cornelius' house (Acts 2:1-4; 10:44). Yet on other occasions, such as the revival in Samaria, the gift was given through faith, by the laying on of hands. Despite Philip's noted success, both in the number of conversions and also in the mighty miracles that were taking place, it was not until Peter and John came down that the people received the Holy Spirit.

> Now when the apostles who were at Jerusalem heard that Samaria had received the word of God, they sent Peter and John to them, who, when they had come down, prayed for them that they might receive the Holy Spirit. For as yet He

had fallen upon none of them. They had only
been baptized in the name of the Lord Jesus.
Then they laid hands on them, and they received
the Holy Spirit (Acts 8:14-17).

The Apostle Paul also received the Holy Spirit through laying on of hands (Acts 9:17). In Acts 19:6, we find that Paul
laid hands on the disciples at Ephesus in order for them to
receive the Holy Spirit.

In Galatians 3:5 Paul infers that the Holy Spirit is ministered to Christians through faith. It is evident that the gift of
faith is involved in this. We cannot minister the Spirit to
whomever we choose in our own power. Peter made that clear
to Simon the magician. However, someone who has the special
faith for this ministry may minister the Holy Spirit to many
people in a single service, when people are ready and prepared
to receive Him.

The most unusual Holy Spirit service I ever witnessed was
held by Gayle Jackson at Dothan, Alabama. The meeting had
been a powerful one from the beginning.

Often, an entertainment troupe in a city adversely affects
religious services, but in this case, a carnival that had come to
town had to fold up due to lack of business. Night after night,
as Brother Jackson preached, large numbers were getting saved,
with many miracles taking place. But the evangelist waited to
have the Holy Spirit service. He knew that people's faith was
increasing and was expecting a deluge of blessing to fall when
the service was finally held.

We happened to be present the night of his Holy Spirit
rally. Step by step, the evangelist led the people to a climax of
expectancy, preparing them for the moment when hands would
be laid upon them. And what an outpouring it was! The local
pastor declared that 500 received the Holy Spirit that night.
This was only an estimate; so many people were receiving the
Spirit in every part of the great tent, that it was impossible to
do more than approximate the number. It was a marvelous
demonstration of mighty, supernatural faith in operation!

We know that divine healing may be received in various ways. The ill person can pray, as Hezekiah did and receive deliverance (II Ki. 20:1-11). Church members may pray for one another and be healed (Jas. 5:16). People may be healed through handkerchiefs or cloths that have touched the body of a person of faith (Acts 19:11, 12). And of course, gifts of healings are especially ordained of God for healing the sick.

It is evident that not every member of the Church possesses the special gifts of healings. "Do all have gifts of healings?" (I Cor. 12:30). Yet all believers may lay hands on the sick for healing (Mk. 16:15-18). Sick people can also be healed at a distance through the spoken word of faith. "He sent His word and healed them" (Psa. 107:20).

While some who minister to the sick may have gifts of healings, many people are healed when no special gifts of healings are present. There is no question that the gift of faith often operates in the healing of the sick. People who do not possess special gifts of healings may at times see great miracles of healing take place.

Concerning a particularly difficult affliction which the disciples could not heal, Jesus said, "'If you can believe, all things *are* possible to him who believes'" (Mk. 9:23).

It is certain that the gifts of the Spirit may be ministered from one person to another. Moses laid hands on Joshua and he received the spirit of wisdom (Deut. 34:9). Paul and the elders laid hands on Timothy and he received a gift of the Spirit. In this case, the laying on of hands was accompanied by a special prophecy which may have foretold something about Timothy's future ministry (I Tim. 1:18).

> Therefore I remind you to stir up the gift of God which is in you through the laying on of my hands (II Tim. 1:6).

But here a word of caution is needed. The Holy Spirit is for all believers — not so the gifts. The impartation of the gifts is the Holy Spirit's prerogative. He distributes "to each one individually as He wills" (I Cor. 12:11). It appears, however, that anointed Christians may cooperate and carry out the will of the Spirit through laying on hands, so that the gift that God has chosen may begin to manifest. This is apparently what happened in the case of Timothy.

Chapter Fifteen

The Gift of Faith and Divine Protection

One of the most practical aspects of the gift of faith is that it provides supernatural protection for believers. The world is a dangerous and complex place. Nature is often unpredictable and hostile. Irresponsible people may adversely effect our whole life. But are these things inevitable? Must fate or chance control the destinies of God's children?

I believe that God holds the lives of His people in His own hands, and if they will only believe, His providence will watch over them and theirs. The 91st Psalm makes several promises:

1. Deliverance from traps (ver. 3)
2. Deliverance from fear (ver. 5)
3. Deliverance from accidental death (ver. 6-7)
4. Deliverance from evil (ver. 10)
5. Deliverance from sickness (ver. 10)
6. Deliverance from accidents (ver 11, 12)
7. Deliverance from Satan and beasts (ver. 13)

The 91st Psalm takes us out of the natural and into the supernatural; out of the uncertainties of life and into a realm where all things are possible. This is not reserved only for specifically chosen saints; the door is open to all who will enter it. Unfortunately, most people wait until calamity strikes before they seek God for protection. How much better it would be to pray as Jesus taught us, "'And do not lead us into temptation, but deliver us from the evil one'" (Matt. 6:13).

The Book of Hebrews reminds us of the Old Testament saints who learned to live in that realm. Among these were the three Hebrew children, who were thrown alive into King

Nebuchadnezzar's fiery furnace because of their faith. Let us notice how the gift of faith worked in this remarkable incident.

The Three Hebrew Children

Daniel's three friends, Shadrach, Meshach and Abed-Nego, had been promoted to positions of influence in Babylon. It has been said that we need more Christians in government. Unfortunately, the temptations of politics often rob people of their spirituality. This should not be. The three Hebrew children are examples of those who have stood true to God while in public office. Although they held positions of great responsibility in affairs of state, they never wavered in their devotion to God.

One day, King Nebuchadnezzar set up an image of gold in the Plain of Dura. This image stood as a symbol of the authority and majesty of the proud Babylonian kingdom. A herald declared that at the sound of music, the people from every tongue and nation must bow down and worship the image. "'And whoever does not fall down and worship shall be cast immediately into the midst of a burning fiery furnace'" (Dan. 3:6). The three Hebrew children, however, refused to obey this decree.

Of course, there are always enemies of Jehovah who are eager for an opportunity to make trouble for believers. When they discovered that Shadrach, Meshach, and Abed-Nego were not obeying the decree, they immediately communicated this to the king. Nebuchadnezzar was a man with a terrible temper, and would allow no disobedience. His word was law and no one dared to defy it — not if he regarded his life. Nevertheless, the king was inclined to make a concession for these friends of Daniel. He was willing to overlook this infraction if they would promise to comply with the decree in the future. He made it plain, however, that if they did not, the penalty would be death.

The situation was about as bad as any that believers in Jehovah have ever had to face. They had to choose between being put to death or worshiping the golden image. But God knows how to provide grace and strength in the time of need. It is said that D.L. Moody was asked on one occasion whether he had grace to be a martyr. His reply was, "No." Since he was not facing that situation, he did not need a martyr's faith. However, he said he was sure that if God ever required it of him, He would supply strength and grace when it was needed. This is an excellent illustration of how all the gifts of the Spirit operate. God does not give His gifts to be played with. But for those who put their trust in Him, they are active and ready when the need arises.

The three Hebrew children's answer was heroic:

> Shadrach, Meshach, and Abed-Nego answered and said to the king, "O Nebuchadnezzar, we have no need to answer you in this matter. If that *is the case*, our God whom we serve is able to deliver us from the burning fiery furnace, and He will deliver *us* from your hand, O king" (Dan. 3:16, 17).

The working of miracles is active while the gift of faith is passive. Notice the difference between the operation of the two gifts. When the messengers of the king rudely demanded that Elijah come down from the hill and give an accounting to King Ahaziah, Elijah replied, "'If I *am* a man of God, then let fire come down from heaven and consume you and your fifty men'" (II Ki. 1:10). The miracle took place.

The three Hebrew children apparently did not possess the gift of miracles, but they said, "'If that *is the case*, our God whom we serve is able to deliver us from the burning fiery furnace, and He will deliver *us* from your hand, O king. But if not, let it be known to you, O king, that we do not serve your gods...'" (Dan. 3:17, 18).

Their blunt refusal to comply made the king furious. In his anger, he commanded that the furnace be heated seven times hotter than usual. Then the Hebrew children were tied hand and foot and thrown into it, clothes and all. All the fire did was burn their bands loose, so they were able to walk unharmed in the middle of the furnace! But that was not all; a Fourth

Man appeared and walked in the furnace as well! The king was a witness!

> "Look!" he answered, "I see four men loose, walking in the midst of the fire; and they are not hurt, and the form of the fourth is like the Son of God" (Dan. 3:25).

The astonished king immediately called for the three Hebrew children to come out of the furnace. The subdued and chastened monarch was now ready to listen to whatever they had to say. He now declared that if anyone said anything against the God of the Hebrew children, he would be cut in pieces and his house made into a dunghill.

Students of prophecy see a prophetic significance to this incident. They believe it foreshadows the reign of the Beast, who will also set up an image that men must worship. The measurements of Nebuchadnezzar's image, 60 cubits high and six cubits broad, allude to the number of the Beast — 666. No doubt the gift of faith will operate strongly during the end times, and believers will again obtain deliverance from fire, water and the elements.

Daniel Delivered From the Lions' Den

Daniel's deliverance from the lion's den is one of the finest examples of the gift of faith in action. When the princes of Persia saw that Daniel stood very high in the favor of King Darius, they looked for a reason to find fault with him. They decided that the only way to accomplish their evil plans would be to bring accusations against Daniel regarding his religion. Therefore, pretending to honor the king, they proposed that he declare it illegal for anyone to make a petition to God, or anyone except himself for a period of 30 days. The gullible monarch, not seeing that it was a cunning scheme to injure Daniel, fell into the trap and signed the decree.

> Now when Daniel knew that the writing was signed, he went home. And in his upper room,

> with his windows open toward Jerusalem, he
> knelt down on his knees three times that day,
> and prayed and gave thanks before his God, as
> was his custom since early days. Then these men
> assembled and found Daniel praying and mak-
> ing supplication before his God (Dan. 6:10, 11).

That unholy decree has had its modern counterpart in the United States Supreme Court decision to outlaw prayer in the public schools. America's attitude toward this anti-God ruling should be the same as Daniel's. Although the prophet was a law-abiding citizen, he not only continued to pray, but opened his window so that what he did was public knowledge.

Daniel's enemies lost no time in informing the king of Daniel's refusal to comply with the anti-prayer law. The king, now alert to the scheme and highly displeased with himself for being deceived by these ruthless and ambitious men, tried to save Daniel. However, he was unable to find a way around the inflexible Persian law. He seemed to have faith in Daniel's God, however, for he said, "'Your God, whom you serve con-tinually, He will deliver you'" (Dan. 6:16).

So Daniel was thrown into the den of lions, and the king returned to his palace with a heavy heart. He fasted and was sleepless throughout the night. When morning came, the king arose quickly and went to the lion's den. To his great relief and joy he found Daniel still alive!

> And when he came to the den, he cried out with
> a lamenting voice to Daniel. The king spoke,
> saying to Daniel, "Daniel, servant of the living
> God, has your God, whom you serve continually,
> been able to deliver you from the lions?" Then
> Daniel said to the king, "O king, live forever!
> My God sent His angel and shut the lions'
> mouths, so that they have not hurt me, because
> I was found innocent before Him ..." (Dan.
> 6:20-22).

This situation is an excellent demonstration of the gift of faith in operation:

1. Daniel had made prayer a business in his life. Three times a day he prayed and gave thanks to God. In other words, he had already done his praying. He did not wait until he got in the lions' den to pray.

2. Daniel's personal life caused the king to have confidence in his God. Yet his religion only incited the animosity of treacherous people. It costs something to live wholly for God, but it is with people of such consecration that the gift of faith operates.

3. The gift of faith produces a quiet confidence within the believer. Daniel, having done his praying beforehand, needed only to trust now. The king, on the other hand, spent the night in sleepless anxiety and worry.

4. God often uses angelic messengers to answer the prayer of faith. In this circumstance, He sent His angel to shut the mouths of the lions.

5. Daniel did not move a finger against his enemies. Nevertheless, their evil plans boomeranged against them. They and their families suffered the fate they had intended for Daniel.

6. Out of Daniel's trial, God received glory. The king, convinced of the reality of Daniel's God, wrote a testimony of his faith and sent it to all the peoples of the earth (Dan. 6:25-27).

Even a child can have the supernatural faith necessary for deliverance. Missionary, A.G. Humphry, told of a little girl who was protected from a witch doctor who tied her to a large banyan tree so that she would be killed by lions. Lula had attended the mission school and given her heart to Jesus. The witch doctor was infuriated that his power and influence in the village was lessening, so he used his authority to convince the little girl's mother that the child was possessed by evil spirits.

After tying the girl to the tree in the forest, the witch doctor thought that would be the last of her. But she had learned to trust Jesus that no harm would befall her! In the morning the witch doctor, the girl's mother, and others went out to see what happened during the night. Imagine their astonishment to find her safe and unharmed by the beasts of the forest!

About 20 feet from her was a well-trodden path over which it was evident that the animals had been passing all night long. Divine providence never permitted them to get nearer than the path!

When asked about the lions she said, "Yes, they marched around the tree all night long, roaring and making a terrible noise, but they could not harm me because teacher told me Jesus would always protect us if we trusted Him; so I asked Him to take care of me."

The Apostles Delivered From Prison

We should not suppose that the gift of faith, even in the Christian dispensation, will *always* bring deliverance. Paul was not permitted to have deliverance from his "thorn in the flesh." Examples are recorded in the Scriptures which show that God may allow some of His best disciples to die for their faith. They are given the great honor of becoming members of a select company — the martyrs of the Church.

However, in many cases, they did receive deliverance from situations that meant life or death. In some instances, no doubt, the heroic death of Christians has had the effect of inspiring others to rise up and take their place. In most cases, however, it is God's will for His people to fulfill their natural life span. And it is just as much the devil's will that they do not.

The Church was not very many days old before the hostile Jews gave the apostles a warning that they were not to speak in the Name of Jesus (Acts 4:18). The apostles rejected this ultimatum saying, "'We cannot but speak the things which we have seen and heard'" (ver. 20). When the Church heard what had happened, they had a great prayer meeting.

It is possible that at times the gift of faith is manifested through the Church as a whole. This might have been the case in this situation. When the members of the Church finished praying "the place where they were assembled together was shaken" (Acts 4:31). God answered their prayer that He would perform mighty miracles for them in the Name of Jesus. "And through the hands of the apostles many signs and wonders were done among the people" (Acts 5:12).

Then the High Priest and his followers rose up in great indignation and had the apostles thrown into prison over the stir that was taking place among the people. Notice that the apostles did not attempt to perform a miracle to escape from prison, but apparently had supreme confidence that God would deliver them.

> But at night an angel of the Lord opened the prison doors and brought them out, and said, "Go, stand in the temple and speak to the people all the words of this life" (Acts 5:19, 20).

This supernatural deliverance from prison confounded the opposition. Some of their enemies wanted to have the apostles executed, but they were aware that the people believed in them because of the miracles they did. Therefore, they didn't dare lay a hand upon them, "For they feared the people, lest they should be stoned" (Acts 5:26). They had to content themselves with repeating their order for the apostles not to speak in the Name of Jesus. They might as well have saved their breath. Peter and the apostles replied saying, "'We ought to obey God rather than men'" (Acts 5:29). Peter followed this statement by preaching a sermon to *them*!

The Jews wanted to kill them, but didn't dare. Gamaliel, the great teacher, charged his colleagues to be careful. Was not the fact that the prison doors supernaturally opened something to think about? Gamaliel told them that if this move was of God they could not stop it, and that they needed to be careful lest they be found fighting against God.

> "But if it is of God, you cannot overthrow it — lest you even be found to fight against God" (Acts 5:39).

In this story, faith operated in a united Church. The persecution they were experiencing drew them together. It is in such an atmosphere of harmony that supernatural faith works so mightily.

Peter Delivered From Prison

Several years passed before another great persecution arose. Then Stephen was stoned to death. None other than Saul of Tarsus was standing by, consenting to his death (Acts 7:58-60). Stephen's prayer for God to forgive his murderers did not secure his own deliverance, but it was heard. Many believe that his mantle was transferred to the shoulders of Saul, the Church's chief persecutor, who was converted through a startling, supernatural visitation on the Damascus Road.

Saul's conversion again utterly confounded the opposition, and a considerable amount of time elapsed before another major persecution arose. Then it was Herod Agrippa I, the grandson of Herod the Great (the monarch who had murdered the babies of Bethlehem), who persecuted the Church. He seized James the brother of John and killed him (Acts 12:1, 2). His death alerted the Church to its imminent peril, and the saints, hearing that Peter had also been arrested, began to pray without ceasing for him:

> Peter was therefore kept in prison, but constant prayer was offered to God for him by the church (Acts 12:5).

A miracle took place, but it was not the working of miracles, for Peter was asleep when it took place. The Church, itself, did not seem to have miracle faith for his deliverance. Yet, somehow, supernatural faith was in operation.

The angel of the Lord came to rescue Peter from the hands of Herod. Note that a series of supernatural occurrences were involved:

1. The guard's unnatural sleep
2. The chains falling from Peter's hands
3. The gate opening on its own

The angel did only what Peter could not do. Peter was instructed to get up, clothe himself, put on his sandals, and then follow the angel out of the prison. Once outside, the heavenly visitor departed and Peter was left alone.

It is noteworthy that the individual members of the Church did not seem to have faith for Peter's deliverance. They could hardly be persuaded that Peter was at the gate, but his continued knocking forced them to open the door. However, their praying played an important part in the outcome of the situation. Jesus once said to Peter, "'But I have prayed for you, that your faith should not fail'" (Lk. 22:32). The prayers of the Church evidently strengthened Peter's faith so much that he had confidence in the outcome, and could fall asleep with soldiers on either side of him, knowing that he was scheduled for execution on the following day! This is a beautiful example of the gift of faith in operation.

There is a sequel to this event. Though we are not told that the Christians prayed for Herod's death, they no doubt asked God to deal with the wicked king who was bent on destroying the leaders of the Church. When Herod saw that his prisoner had escaped, he satisfied his blood lust by putting the prison guards to death. Shortly afterward, while accepting a blasphemous deification from the people of Caesarea, the angel of the Lord struck him and he "was eaten by worms and died" (Acts 12:23).

The significance of these events cannot be overlooked. Believers are instructed to pray for their enemies and for those who persecute them. But when the sins of the wicked have reached the full, and they insist on destroying the work of God, they must be turned over to God's hands to be held accountable.

Paul and Silas Delivered

Paul had vigorously persecuted the Church, and though he was eventually converted on the Damascus Road, he did not escape persecution himself. He had held the coats of those who stoned Stephen, and the time would come, more than once, when he too would face an angry mob bent on taking his life (Acts 14:19; II Cor. 11:23-28).

Paul and Silas' ministry in Philippi, which marked the introduction of the Gospel to the continent of Europe, resulted in their arrest. They were whipped and put in the stocks in the innermost part of the local prison. But they were not discouraged! The atmosphere was one of victory rather than of defeat, as they prayed and sang songs at the midnight hour. It is in such an atmosphere that the gift of faith operates.

This story furnishes us with valuable information concerning the operation of this gift. First of all, Paul and Silas were not arrested as the result of foolishness. Some over-zealous ministers today conduct themselves in such an unbecoming way as to draw upon themselves well-deserved criticism. Then they piously claim they are being persecuted for righteousness' sake!

Some years ago, we visited two preachers who were in the Los Angeles County jail. They considered themselves suffering persecution for the Kingdom of God, and proudly compared themselves to Paul and Silas. But the fact of the matter was, they had been convicted in a court of law for libelous attacks upon another minister in the city. They were suffering for foolishly circulating scandalous accusations against others, not for righteousness' sake.

On the other hand, we should not hold back the message of deliverance — regardless of the consequences. Paul saw that a demon-possessed girl was being exploited, and could not refrain from delivering her from the bondage of Satan. Her heartless masters were furious because their source of ill-gotten gain dried up. Under the pretext that the apostles were breaking Roman law, they had them brought before the magistrates who sentenced them to be beaten with a cat-o'-nine-tails — a whip made of nine knotted lines or cords fastened to a handle. Afterwards, bruised and bleeding, they were put into the stocks.

Instead of complaining, as soon as they recovered from the shock of their painful beating, Paul and Silas began to look to God for deliverance. Some people can pray when they go through trials, but it is too much for them to praise God. Instead of having a spirit of victory, they get themselves worked up into such a state of self-pity that they are little good to themselves or to anyone else. But Paul and Silas sang praises to God, to the utter astonishment of the prisoners and the jailer, no doubt.

Then the miracle happened! There was a great earthquake, everyone's chains were loosed and the prison doors opened. The jailer was responsible for the safekeeping of the prisoners — his life for theirs, if any escaped. Thinking they would all escape, he prepared to kill himself.

However, Paul had no intention of leaving. He cried out, "'Do yourself no harm, for we are all here'" (Acts 16:28). The other prisoners, under the spell of these supernatural happenings, also remained. There had been earthquakes before, but none with the effect of this earthquake!

Paul now had the opportunity to preach the Gospel to the jailer and his family. The jailer heard enough to convince him that Paul and Silas had the truth of God. Falling down before them, he said, "'Sirs, what must I do to be saved?'" So they said, "'Believe on the Lord Jesus Christ, and you will be saved, you and your household'" (Acts 16:30, 31). That same hour, the jailer and his whole family were converted and baptized.

The next day, Paul did not spare the magistrates. They had brutally beaten Paul and Silas and thrown them into prison. With their arrogance gone, they begged mercy of those they had grossly mistreated.

The apostles did not stay in Philippi very long, but they left behind the foundations of a strong church. Their faith, while going through great trials, was a mighty inspiration to the young converts. In his letter to the Philippians, Paul expressed confidence that God, who began a good work in Philippi, would complete it (Phil. 1:6). Evidently, the people there loved him, for it was the only church in Macedonia that remembered to help him after he left the region (Phil. 4:15-17).

Chapter Sixteen

The Gift of Faith and Divine Provision

The life of Abraham provides us with some of our greatest lessons on faith. From the moment he appears in the scriptural narrative, Abraham is revealed as a man with a deep and abiding faith in God. It was this faith that caused him to decide to obey God, leave his native country and journey to a land he had never seen before. Yet, this faith was not supernatural. It was the same kind of faith that any believer has.

But, faith is not static. Abraham's faith grew from year to year. Although blessed with silver and gold, and permitted by God to have great possessions, his heart was not set on these things. Instead, he set his heart on "the city which has foundations, whose builder and maker *is* God" (Heb. 11:10).

Abraham's faith was not perfect. As soon as the land experienced a famine, he departed and went to Egypt. Fearful that someone might kill him to get his beautiful wife Sarah, he pretended that she was his sister. This foolish decision soon got him into trouble.

God told Abraham that He would give him a male heir by Sarah. But after a 10 year delay, and with his wife having passed child-bearing age, he consented to take Sarah's handmaid, Hagar, as a wife in an ill-advised attempt to help God out. This union gave Abraham more trouble than all his other mistakes put together. Yet Abraham was a man who stood as a giant of faith above all his contemporaries. So much so that he is called the father of the faithful and a friend of God.

The Ram in the Thicket

Though Abraham's faith lapsed on occasion, it never failed completely. The time came, however, when Abraham needed more than his own natural faith. He needed supernatural faith, to believe that God would fulfill the promise that his son, Isaac, would become a great nation. Abraham needed faith that, if necessary, God would raise Isaac from the dead.

Abraham was greatly sorrowed when the Lord commanded him to take his only son and offer him as a burnt offering on Mt. Moriah. Some have argued that it was immoral for God to ask Abraham to take the life of his only son. This reasoning reflects a superficial knowledge of the circumstances involved. The gruesome fact is that the heathen living in Abraham's day carried out this terrible practice. The Lord was actually teaching Abraham that human sacrifice was never necessary or required by God! God had supplied a sacrifice from the foundation of the world. So, just before Abraham killed his son, the angel of the Lord restrained him and showed him that a ram (a type of the sacrificial Lamb of God) had been caught in a thicket nearby (Gen 22:11-13).

All of us hope that God will meet our need when we are in an emergency, as He did for Abraham. We have the right to expect this, if we are willing to sacrifice everything like Abraham was. But, people who are not willing to put God's promises to a real test should not expect to receive the same blessings that Abraham enjoyed. He was committed to sacrificing everything for God if necessary.

The provision of the ram for the sacrifice was not a manifestation of the gift of miracles, for Abraham was not active in causing it to happen. He simply believed God would keep His promise, and that in some way which he did not fully understand, God would work it out, even if He had to raise Isaac from the dead. Because of that faith, he was ready to risk all for God.

> By faith Abraham, when he was tested, offered up Isaac, and he who had received the promises offered up his only begotten *son*, of whom it was said, "*In Isaac your seed shall be called*," concluding that God *was* able to raise *him* up, even from the dead, from which he also received him in a figurative sense (Heb. 11:17-19).

Other Scriptural Examples

There are many instances in the Scriptures of needs being supernaturally met for God's people through the working of miracles. Examples of these include: Food in the form of manna and quail being provided for the children of Israel in the wilderness, the waters at Marah becoming sweet, and water coming out of the rock at Rephidim.

The gift of faith is more easily adapted to the average ministry than the working of miracles. It operates in the lives of those who have an abiding trust in the promises of God. The working of miracles boldly declares what the miracle is to be; the gift of faith knows that deliverance will come, but does not define just how or when it will occur.

When Jesus told Peter to go down to the sea and get a coin from the mouth of the first fish he caught, a miracle took place. It was a miracle that the right fish came to Peter's hook at just the right moment.

On the other hand, when Jesus told His disciples that their needs would be taken care of and not to take money with them, no apparent miracle took place, but faith saw that their needs were met.

When Elijah was fed by the ravens who brought him flesh twice a day, no actual miracle took place. It was a manifestation of faith that caused these feathered servants to sustain him day by day.

When the widow's oil and meal were multiplied, the working of miracles was demonstrated. But, when Elijah lay down under the juniper tree to die, the miracle-gift was apparently out of his reach. Yet, supernatural faith was so strong in the prophet that it unconsciously rose above the prophet's natural faith. When he awoke, the angel was there to supply his need.

When the children of Israel were at war with the Moabites, they came into a desert where there was no water. This time, no miracle was performed to create water out of a rock, as was done at Rephidim. But the faith working in Elisha assured him that the Lord would provide a way to save the army. Through the word of knowledge, God showed Elisha just where water was in the valley. When the army dug ditches, there was plenty of water (II Ki. 3:16, 17).

During the siege of Samaria, the gift of faith moved upon Elisha, causing him to say:

> "Hear the word of the LORD. Thus says the LORD: 'Tomorrow about this time a seah of fine flour *shall be sold* for a shekel, and two seahs of barley for a shekel, at the gate of Samaria'" (II Ki. 7:1).

The skeptical officer on whose arm the king leaned, said, "'Look, *if* the LORD would make windows in heaven, could this thing be?'" (II Ki. 7:2). Elisha told him that he would see the prophecy come true, but because of his unbelief, he would not taste any of it (ver. 2).

Sometimes God shows His miracles in a spectacular fashion, but more often than not, He prefers to hide the miraculous element. When the gift of faith is operating, He often permits it to appear that only natural forces are at work. Yet, the spiritual person can see and discern the hand of God moving in these events.

The gift of faith has different operations, manifestations and conditions which govern it. The Bible gives an important condition to receiving God's supernatural assistance for physical and financial needs:

> "Will a man rob God? Yet you have robbed Me! But you say, 'In what way have we robbed You?' In tithes and offerings. You are cursed with a curse, for you have robbed Me, *even* this whole nation. Bring all the tithes into the storehouse, that there may be food in My house, and try Me now in this," says the LORD of hosts, "if I will not open for you the windows of heaven and pour out for you *such* blessing that *there will* not *be room* enough *to receive it*" (Mal. 3:8-10).

Do we want faith that opens the windows of heaven? Do we desire for God to prosper us financially? Faith is an act. We must be faithful in the tithe and in our giving to God. If we fail in this, then according to the Scriptures we are thieves and robbers. Indeed, it indicates that we have small faith, and it is unlikely that the Spirit of God will give His gifts to us.

In the New Testament, Christ promises to give a *hundredfold* to a special group of people. This is such an amazing promise!

> So Jesus answered and said, "Assuredly, I say to you, there is no one who has left house or brothers or sisters or father or mother or wife or children or lands, for My sake and the gospel's, who shall not receive a hundredfold now in this time — houses and brothers and sisters and mothers and children and lands, with persecutions — and in the age to come, eternal life" (Mk. 10:29, 30).

Notice the conditions. This promise is given to those who have been willing to leave all and trust God. There is a testing period, and there are few who are willing to go through such a test. Nevertheless, those who meet the conditions learn that God's promises are indeed true. God gives such people the faith for great finances, by which they are able to help advance the Kingdom of God in unusual ways.

Faith Provides for 1,000 Orphans

We have a wonderful example of the gift of faith operating in the life of the late Lillian Trasher, the "Nile Mother," as she cared for 1,000 orphans in Assiut, Egypt. This remarkable event occurred during World War II.

During that time, it became increasingly difficult to get financial assistance from America, and clothing and food became very scarce and expensive in Egypt. Lillian was touched when her little boys came to morning prayer with dirty and badly torn jackets. She went to the storeroom; it was a sad sight. There was nothing there but a few pieces of clothing in worse condition than those which the children were wearing. She looked up to heaven and said, "Oh Lord, you see my dear children. They must have clothes."

At the time, the orphanage did not have a dollar. To buy clothes for hundreds of children would not only be a miracle — but a miracle of the first magnitude!

Shortly after this, one of Lillian's prominent friends in Cairo wrote a letter inviting her to the capital because the American ambassador wished to see her immediately. Lillian left on the next train. She found the ambassador, who had always been very gracious to her, beaming with delight. He told Lillian he had heard many wonderful things about her orphanage and was interested in helping her. He said a large shipment of clothes had been sent by the American Red Cross to Greece, but Greece had fallen to the enemy, and it was impossible to deliver the clothing. He had received orders to distribute it to refugees and charitable institutions in Egypt. He then handed Lillian Trasher $125 and explained that it was a personal gift to pay for shipping these materials from Cairo to Assiut.

The clothing he gave Lillian lasted the orphanage two or three years! There were 2,600 dresses, 1,900 hand-made woolen sweaters of all sizes — 6,017 pieces of clothing altogether! Later, from the same ship, Lillian received blankets, food and more clothes. What a payday!

Everyone had wondered what "poor Lillian" would do when the war was at its height, but they saw that God could direct an entire shipload of clothing and food to Egypt to take care of a faithful woman who was caring for others!

Chapter Seventeen

The Gift of Faith and Divine Health

The gift of faith enables the believer to enter the realm of divine health. We live in a day when divine healing has been greatly emphasized, yet a constantly recurring cycle of sickness and healing is certainly not God's best for the believer. Some people are found in every prayer line and want to be prayed for in every service. Such people are chronically sick in body and mind, and often never rise above this. They tell you over and over that they must have a miracle, but all the while they are wholly committed to their confession of weakness. In some cases, they strongly resent any suggestion that they adopt a different point of view.

The Church has been given the promise of divine healing; yet it is surprising how few passages there are relating to the Christian's healing. Actually, there is little emphasis on healing for the believer. The reason for this is simple. God's plan for His children is divine *health*, rather than divine *healing*. Contrast the few references to sickness among believers in the Early Church, and the amount of sickness in the Church today. The Apostle John said, "Beloved, I pray that you may prosper in all things and be in health, just as your soul prospers" (III Jn. 2). When the Bible mentions sickness in reference to the Church, it is usually in a manner that suggests the individual is, to a large extent, responsible for being in that condition. Paul said that many of the Corinthians were sickly and some had died because they did not discern the Lord's body (I Cor. 11:29, 30). In other words, it was their own fault!

In James, the promise of healing is given, but again the possibility is raised that sickness might be caused by the sins of the believer — sins of commission, or more likely sins of omission, such as lack of prevailing prayer.

And the prayer of faith will save the sick, and the Lord will raise him up. And if he has committed sins, he will be forgiven. Confess *your* trespasses to one another, and pray for one another, that you may be healed. The effective, fervent prayer of a righteous man avails much. Elijah was a man with a nature like ours, and he prayed earnestly that it would not rain; and it did not rain on the land for three years and six months. And he prayed again, and the heaven gave rain, and the earth produced its fruit (Jas. 5:15-18).

Of course, sickness may have its origin from causes which cannot be classified as outright sin — failure to obey the laws of health, indulgence in worry, failure to take proper rest, etc. Then there are people who seem to have inherited a sickly body. All of these people need to move from their position of weakness into the sphere of faith and health.

There are some Christian homes with sickness constantly affecting one or more members of the family, and with frequent trips to the hospital, or operation after operation. Far be it from us to reproach those who are caught in the toils of such circumstances. Yet we would not do our duty before God if we did not point out that there is a realm of dominion and victory. Believers can live without being constantly under the specter of sickness, with its heavy burden of medical and hospital expenses. One of the greatest purposes of the gift of faith is to lift us above the *curse* of sickness — for that is just what the Bible calls it (Deut. 28:15, 27-29).

The human race was created with dominion "over all the earth" (Gen. 1:26) but lost that dominion through the Fall. That loss included the loss of health, but thank God that which was lost through the Fall has now been regained through Christ! This was foreshadowed by Israel's redemption from Egypt:

So he cried out to the LORD, and the LORD showed him a tree. When he cast *it* into the waters, the waters were made sweet. There He made a statute and an ordinance for them, and there He tested them, and said, "If you diligently heed the voice of the LORD your God and do what is right in His sight, give ear to His commandments and keep all His statutes, I will put none of the diseases on you which I have brought on the Egyptians. For I *am* the LORD who heals you" (Ex. 15:25, 26).

Lest any should misunderstand this promise, it was repeated in Ex. 23 and Deut. 7.

"So you shall serve the LORD your God, and He will bless your bread and your water. And I will take sickness away from the midst of you. No one shall suffer miscarriage or be barren in your land; I will fulfill the number of your days" (Ex. 23:25, 26).

"And the LORD will take away from you all sickness, and will afflict you with none of the terrible diseases of Egypt which you have known, but will lay *them* on all those who hate you" (Deut. 7:15).

In the early days of the nation of Israel, we are told that "*there was* none feeble among His tribes" (Psa. 105:37). Listen to the testimony of Caleb, one of the spies that brought back a good report concerning the Promised Land.

"And now, behold, the LORD has kept me alive, as He said, these forty-five years, ever since the LORD spoke this word to Moses while Israel wandered in the wilderness; and now, here I am this day, eighty-five years old. As yet I *am as* strong this day as on the day that Moses sent me; just as my strength *was* then, so now *is* my strength for war, both for going out and for coming in" (Josh. 14:10, 11).

Psalm 91 is a marvelous promise of immunity from sickness and plague. The 103rd Psalm not only promises salvation and healing, but even speaks of the renewing of youth! "Who satisfies your mouth with good *things, so that* your youth is renewed like the eagle's" (ver.5).

Foolish attempts have been made to discredit these great promises of divine health by asserting that Paul's "thorn in the flesh" was sickness — that he was nearly blind, and as one commentator puts it, "Was afflicted with chronic ophthalmia including bodily weakness, and a repulsive appearance."

Therefore, it is reasoned, if the mighty Paul could not get victory over sickness, how could we hope to do so? Such statements are in flat contradiction to the scriptural record. True, Paul went blind on the Damascus Road, but we are told that God healed him (Acts 9:18). Anyone who denies this plain statement is guilty of gross libel against the Word of God.

The actual facts indicate that Paul enjoyed divine health, although throughout his ministry he lived under the strain of violent persecution and often had to endure extremely severe physical hardships. In Lystra, he was stoned and left for dead, yet he got up from the stoning in good health, and continued his ministry without loss of time (Acts 14:19, 20). When a deadly viper bit him, he shook it off and felt no harm (Acts 28:3-6). This is not the story of a sick man, but of one who lived in the realm of divine health with supernatural strength given to him when it was needed. Paul's testimony was that he labored more abundantly than all the other apostles. If Paul's thorn in the flesh was sickness, we could well wish an epidemic of the same disease to visit the entire Church!

The ministry needs to enter into this realm of faith today. It is within the reach of all, for this dominion over sickness is a manifestation of the gift of faith. Following is the testimony of a noted man of God, A.B. Simpson, who tells his experience:

Testimony of A.B. Simpson

For more than twenty years I was a sufferer from many physical infirmities and disabilities. Beginning a life of hard intellectual labor at the age of fourteen, I broke down hopelessly with nervous prostration while preparing for college, and for many months was not permitted by my physician even to look at a book. During this time I came very near death, and on the verge of eternity gave myself at last to God. After my college studies were completed I became the ambitious pastor of a large city church at the age of twenty-one. Plunging headlong into my work, I again broke down with heart trouble and had to go away for months of rest, returning at length, as it seemed to me at the time, to die. Rallying, however, and slowly recovering in part, I labored on for years with the aid of constant remedies and preventatives. I carried a bottle of ammonia in my pocket for years, and would have taken a nervous spasm if I had ventured without it.

God knows how many hundreds of times in my earlier ministry when preaching in my pulpit or ministering by a grave it seemed that I must fall in the midst of the service or drop into that open grave.

Several years later two other collapses of long duration came in my health. Again and again during these terrible seasons it seemed that the last drops of life were ebbing out.

I struggled through my work most of the time and often was considered a hard and successful worker, but my good people always thought me

so delicate, and I grew weary of being sympa-
thized with every time they met me. Many a neglected visit was apologized for by these good
people because I was not strong. When at last I
took the Lord for my Healer, I just asked the
Lord to make me so well that my people would
never sympathize with me again, but that I
should be to them a continual wonder through
the strength and support of God.

I think He has fulfilled this prayer, for they have
often wondered these recent years at the work I
have been permitted to do in His name.

It usually took me till Wednesday to get over the
effects of the Sabbath sermon, and about Thursday I was ready to begin to get ready for the next
Sabbath. Thanks be to God, the first three years
after I was healed I preached more than a thousand sermons, and held sometimes more than
twenty meetings in one week, and do not
remember once feeling exhausted.

A few months before I took Christ as my Healer,
a prominent physician in New York insisted on
speaking to me on the subject of my health, and
told me that I had not constitutional strength
enough left to last more than a few months. He
required my taking immediate measures for the
preservation of my life and usefulness.

During the summer that followed I heard a great
number of people testify that they had been
healed by simply trusting the Word of Christ,
just as they would for their salvation. It drove
me to my Bible. I determined that I must settle
this matter one way or the other. I am glad I did
not go to man. At His feet, alone, with my Bible

open, and with no one to help or guide me, I became convinced that this was part of Christ's glorious gospel for a sinful and suffering world, and the purchase of His blessed Cross, for all who would believe and receive His Word. That was enough. I could not believe this and then refuse to take it for myself, for I felt that I dare not hold any truth in God's Word as a mere theory or teach to others what I had not personally proved. And so one Friday afternoon at the hour of three o'clock, I went out into the silent pine woods, and there I raised my right hand to Heaven and in view of the Judgment Day, I made to God, as if I had seen Him there before me face to face these three great and eternal pledges:

1. As I shall meet Thee in that day, I solemnly accept this truth as part of Thy Word, and of the Gospel of Christ, and, God helping me, I shall never question it until I meet Thee there.

2. As I shall meet Thee in that day I take the Lord Jesus as my physical life, for all the needs of my body until my life's work is done; and helping me, I shall never doubt that Thou dost so become my life and strength from this moment, and wilt keep me under all circumstances until Thy blessed coming, and until all Thy will for me is perfectly fulfilled.

3. As I shall meet Thee in that day I solemnly agree to use this blessing for the glory of God, and the good of others, and to speak of it or minister in connection with it in any way in which God may call me or others may need me in the future.

I arose. It had only been a few moments, but I knew that something was done. Every fibre of my soul was tingling with a sense of God's presence. I do not know whether my body felt better or not — I did not care to feel it — it was so glorious to believe it simply, and to know that henceforth He had it in hand.

Then came the test of faith. The first struck me before I had left the spot. A subtle voice whispered: "Now you have decided to take God as your Healer, it would help if you should just go down to Dr. Cullis' cottage and get him to pray with you." I listened to it for a moment without really thinking. The next, a blow seemed to strike my brain, which made me reel as a man stunned. I staggered and cried: "Lord, what have I done?" I felt I was in some great peril. In a moment the thought came very quickly, "That would have been all right before this, but you have just settled this matter forever, and you told God you will never doubt that it is done."

In that moment I understood what faith meant, and what a solemn and awful thing it was, inexorably and exactly to keep faith with God. I have often thanked God for that blow. I saw that when a thing is settled with God, it was never to be unsettled. When it was done, it was never to be undone or done over again in any sense that could involve a doubt of the finality of the committal already made. I think in the early days of the work of faith to which God afterwards called me, I was as much helped by a holy fear of doubting God as by any of the joys and raptures of His presence or promises. This little word often shone like a living fire in my Bible: "If any man draw back, my soul shall have no pleasure in him." What the enemy desired was to get some element of doubt about the certainty and completeness of the transaction just closed, and God mercifully held me back from it.

I have since known hundreds to fail just at this point. God made me commit myself to Him and His healing covenant before He would fully bless me. I know a dear brother in the ministry, now much used in the gospel and in the ministry of healing, who received a wonderful manifestation of God's power in his body and then went home to his church but said nothing about it, and waited to see how it would hold out. In a few weeks he was worse than ever. When I met him the next time he wore the most dejected face you could imagine. I told him his error, and it all flashed upon him immediately. He went home and gave God the glory for what He had done, and in a little while his church was the center of a blessed work of grace and healing that reached far and wide, and he himself was rejoicing in the fullness of Jesus.

Nearby was a mountain 3,000 feet high; I was asked to join a little party that was to ascend it. I shrank back at once. Did I not remember the dread of heights that had always overshadowed me, and the terror with which I had resolved in Switzerland and Florence never to attempt it again? Did I not know how an ordinary stair exhausted me and distressed my poor heart?

Then came the solemn searching thought, "If you fear or refuse to go, it is because you do not believe that God has healed you. If you have taken Him for your strength, need you fear to do anything to which He calls you?"

I felt it was God's thought. I felt my fear would be, in this case, pure unbelief, and I told God that in His strength I would go.

Just here I would say that I do not wish to imply that we should ever do things just to show how strong we are, or without any real necessity for them. I do not believe God wants His children needlessly to climb mountains or walk miles just because they are asked to. But in this case, and there are such cases in every experience, I needed to step out and claim my victory some time, and this was God's time and way. He will call and show each one for himself. And whenever we are shrinking through fear He will be very likely to call us to the very thing that is necessary for us to do to overcome the fear.

And so I ascended that mountain. At first it seemed as if it would almost take my last breath. I felt all the old weakness and physical dread; I found I had in myself no more strength than ever. But over against my weakness and suffering I became conscious that there was another Presence. There was a divine strength reached out to me if I would have it, take it, claim it, hold it, and persevere in it. On one side there seemed to press upon me a weight of Death, on the other an Infinite Life. And I became overwhelmed with the one, or uplifted with the other, just as I shrank or pressed forward, just as I feared or trusted; I seemed to walk between them and the one that I touched possessed me. The wolf and the Shepherd walked on either side, but the Blessed Shepherd did not let me turn away. I pressed closer, closer, closer, closer to His bosom, and every step seemed stronger until, when I reached that mountain top, I seemed to be at the gate of heaven, and the world of weakness and fear was lying at my feet. Thank God, from that time I have had a new heart in this breast, literally as well as spiritually, and Christ has been its glorious life.

A few weeks later I returned to my work in this city, and with deep gratitude to God I can truly say, hundreds being my witness, that for many years I have been permitted to labor for the dear Lord in summer's heat or winter's cold without interruption, without a single season of protracted rest, and with increasing comfort, strength and delight. Life has had for me a zest, and labor an exhilaration that I never knew in the freshest days of my childhood.

The Lord has permitted the test to be a very severe one. A few months after my healing He called me into the special pastoral, evangelistic and literary work which has since engaged my time and energy, and which I may truthfully say has involved fourfold more labor than any previous period of my life. And yet I desire to record my testimony to the honor and glory of Christ, that it has been a continual delight and seldom any burden or fatigue, and much, very much easier in every way than the far lighter tasks of former years. I have been conscious, however, all the time that I was not using my own natural strength. I would not dare to attempt for a single week what I am now doing on my own constitutional resources.

I am intensely conscious with every breath that I am drawing my vitality from a direct supernatural source, and that it keeps pace with the calls and necessities of my work. Hence, on a day of double labor I will often be conscious, at the close, of double vigor, and feel just like beginning over again — and indeed, almost reluctant to have even sleep place its gentle arrest on the delightful privilege of service. Nor is this a paroxysm of excitement to be followed by a reaction, for the next day comes with equal freshness. I have noticed that my work is easier and seems to draw less upon my vital energy than before. I do not seem to be using up my own life in the work now, but working on a surplusage of vitality supplied from another source. I believe and am sure that is nothing else than "the life of Christ manifested in my mortal flesh."

I would like to add, for my brethren in the ministry, that I have found the same divine help for my mind and brain as for my body. Having much writing and speaking to do, I have given my pen and my tongue to Christ to possess and use, and He has so helped me that my literary work has never been a labor. He has enabled me to think much more rapidly and to accomplish much more work, and with greater facility than ever before. It is very simple and humble work, but such as it is, it is all *through* Him, and I trust *for* Him only. And I believe, with all its simplicity, it has been more used to help His children and glorify His name than all the elaborate preparation and toil of the weary years that went before. To Him be all the praise.

Dr. Simpson's testimony illustrates how the gift of faith operates to produce not only divine healing, but divine health.

Chapter Eighteen

The Gift of Faith and Supernatural Transportation

Jesus Walks on the Water

> But the boat was now in the middle of the sea, tossed by the waves, for the wind was contrary. Now in the fourth watch of the night Jesus went to them, walking on the sea. And when the disciples saw Him walking on the sea, they were troubled, saying, "It is a ghost!" And they cried out for fear. But immediately Jesus spoke to them, saying, "Be of good cheer! It is I; do not be afraid" (Matt. 14:24-27).

The devil suggested that Jesus establish His claims of divinity by a spectacular leap from the pinnacle of the Temple. Jesus refused to comply. *"You shall not tempt the LORD your God,"* (Matt. 4:7) was His rebuke to the adversary. He refused to make a theatrical display of His powers in an effort to win the admiration of men. Yet He was willing to defy gravity and walk upon the surface of the water to aid His disciples when they were in danger.

On the preceding day, Jesus performed the miracle of feeding 5,000 because He had compassion on the multitude of hungry people who were far from their homes. This spectacular miracle inspired the crowd to attempt to make Him king, and He had to slip away into the mountains to prevent this (Jn. 6:15). While He was absent, the disciples left in a ship for Capernaum, and were caught in a storm at sea.

When Jesus came to them walking on the water, Peter's faith was inspired. He requested that he, too, be able to walk on the water. And walk he did, until he took his eyes off the

Lord and looked at the waves. As he began to sink, Jesus took Peter's hand and together they walked back to the ship.

But, this demonstration of Christ's power over physical limitations, was not yet over. Immediately after He stepped in the boat, a miracle of supernatural transportation occurred! But before we consider that event, let us refer to a remarkable incident that took place in the days of Elisha, in which the powers of gravity were overruled.

The Ax That Floated

The story of Christ walking on the water calls to mind the incident of the ax that floated. Although this occurrence involves the working of miracles, because of its nature, it fits properly here.

It is interesting to note that God often performs miracles for the benefit of the most humble. The sons of the prophets had decided that their quarters were too small, so they planned to establish residence in another locality. They asked Elisha, whom they looked upon as a father, to accompany them. Trees grow abundantly along the Jordan, and they planned to cut timber from the area to make a shelter.

In the venture, one of the sons of the prophets' ax head fell off and plunged into the swirling current of the Jordan. He cried out to Elisha:

> "Alas, master! For it was borrowed," So the man of God said, "Where did it fall?" And he showed him the place. So he cut off a stick, and threw *it* in there; and he made the iron float (II Ki. 6:5, 6).

This supernatural happening was performed through the gift of miracles, rather than the gift of faith. Yet faith was certainly involved, and its operation involved a higher law than that of gravity. Faith can suspend gravity's effect on a heavy material such as iron. It can also make supernatural transportation possible. And when Jesus returns, faith will effect the translation of God's people. But let us now return to the incident of the ship that was in the midst of the sea.

The Miracle of Transportation by Ship

> Then they willingly received Him into the boat, and immediately the boat was at the land where they were going (Jn. 6:21).

The Sea of Galilee is seven or eight miles across, and John 6:19 informs us that the disciples had rowed a distance of about three or four miles when Jesus walked out to meet them. So, they were in the very middle of the sea when Jesus entered the ship. (See also Matt. 14:24.) Yet, we are told that "immediately the boat was at the land where they were going," making it clear that a miracle of transportation took place! Here we see faith not only overruling the laws of gravity, but overcoming the laws of inertia, making instantaneous transportation possible! These events at sea no doubt involved both the gift of faith and the working of miracles.

Supernatural Transportation of Elijah

Statements made by some of Elijah's contemporaries tend to strongly support the view that Elijah, prior to his translation, experienced supernatural transportation. There are two very strong pieces of evidence that cause us to believe this conclusion is correct.

The first is in I Kings 18 when Elijah asked Obadiah to inform Ahab that he wanted to see him. Notice Obadiah's strange reply:

> "And now you say, 'Go, tell your master, "Elijah *is here*'"! And it shall come to pass, *as soon as* I am gone from you, that the Spirit of the LORD will carry you to a place I do not know; so when I go and tell Ahab, and he cannot find you, he will kill me. But I your servant have feared the LORD from my youth" (I Ki. 18:11, 12).

Now, why would Obadiah make such a curious remark unless Elijah previously had experienced supernatural transportation, and the event was well-known? It seems likely that at an earlier meeting with Ahab, Elijah had suddenly and mysteriously disappeared. This must have happened, or why else would Obadiah have thought of suggesting that such a thing would happen again? Ahab had been so mystified that he sent messengers into every kingdom in an attempt to locate Elijah. In addition to this, after Elijah was translated to heaven, the sons of the prophets thought he had been transported to another location, as their words clearly show.

> Then they said to him, "Look now, there are fifty strong men with your servants. Please let them go and search for your master, lest perhaps the Spirit of the LORD has taken him up and cast him upon some mountain or into some valley." And he said, "You shall not send anyone" (II Ki. 2:16).

Why did they think this? The conclusion seems inevitable that they had knowledge of such a thing happening to Elijah already. The sons of the prophets naturally supposed that this had occurred again, but they were mistaken. This time, Elijah had been caught up to heaven in a chariot of fire! (II Ki. 2:11). We cannot dwell here on the divine purpose of Elijah's translation, but the last two verses of the Old Testament speak rather plainly of a future ministry for the prophet (Mal. 4:5, 6).

Philip Transported

Incidents of supernatural transportation were not unique to the Old Testament. Philip also experienced such an event. He had begun his ministry as a deacon. Soon, however, he was preaching full time. Feeling called to evangelistic ministry, he went down to conduct a campaign in Samaria. In the historic revival that followed, large numbers of Samaritans accepted Christ and many miracles occurred. News of the special moving of the Spirit reached Jerusalem, and Peter and John went to Samaria, laid hands upon the converts, and many received the baptism in the Holy Spirit.

In the middle of this remarkable revival, Philip was met by an angel and told to go to the desert of Gaza. Not knowing exactly what the Lord had in mind, he obeyed. There in the desert, he met the Ethiopian eunuch who was in charge of the treasure of Queen Candace. The Spirit of the Lord then showed Philip the purpose of his journey. He was to testify to the eunuch and explain to him how the prophecies of Isaiah were fulfilled in Christ. As the chariot proceeded mile after mile, getting farther and farther away from Philip's territory, the eunuch listened to his explanation of the Scriptures. At last they stopped at a watering place and the eunuch, now quite convinced, asked Philip to baptize him.

Would Philip have to walk the many weary miles back through the hot and burning desert? No. Apparently the Lord wanted him immediately back to the cities where, as the Christian Church's first evangelist, he was having such success. So the Spirit of the Lord caught him up and transported him to Azotus — some 40 or 50 miles away!

> Now when they came up out of the water, the Spirit of the Lord caught Philip away, so that the eunuch saw him no more; and he went on his way rejoicing. But Philip was found at Azotus. And passing through, he preached in all the cities till he came to Caesarea (Acts 8:39, 40).

Miracles are given to confirm the Word. The catching away of Philip must have been a profound confirmation to Philip's preaching. Tradition tells us that the eunuch carried the message back to Ethiopia and was responsible for establishing Christianity there — the effects of which have extended to the present day.

Supernatural Transportation in the Last Days

Will such events be repeated again in the last days? No doubt they will. However, such happenings were rare in the Bible, and no doubt will never be common. Jesus could have been transported from place to place by the Spirit had He so chosen. Yet we have record that it happened only once in His ministry, and that was when His disciples, exhausted from battling the wind and waves through the long hours of the night, needed to reach shore so they could rest and sleep.

God does not intend for His people to specialize on the spectacular or sensational. When supernatural transportation is needed by those who preach the Gospel, it no doubt will take place. At other times, God's people will travel from place to place in the normal manner.

Elijah's experience of transportation by the Spirit prepared him for his translation. He looked forward to it calmly, though no doubt with great anticipation. God always prepares His people for new experiences of faith.

Notice the calm faith that Elijah had. He knew that God was going to take him. This is seen in his reply to Elisha, who had requested a double portion of his anointing. "If you see me *when I am* taken from you, it shall be so for you; but if not, it shall not be *so*" (II Ki. 2:10).

Another example is the story of Enoch. "By faith Enoch was taken away so that he did not see death" (Heb. 11:5). It was faith that caused him to be translated.

Chapter Nineteen

The Gift of Faith and Deliverance

And the Lord will deliver me from every evil
work and preserve *me* for His heavenly kingdom. To Him *be* glory forever and ever. Amen!
(II Tim. 4:18).

The above were among Paul's last words, and were certainly a testimony that described God's loving care of the apostle. Although Paul suffered great changes of fortune, in the
end, the Lord delivered him from every circumstance, whether
caused by Satan, wicked men or nature. The shipwreck that
occurred off the island of Malta is a good illustration of the
protection God gave the apostle. Here we see the gift of faith
in operation when all hope seemed lost.

Paul had been warned several times by the Holy Spirit not
to go to Jerusalem; that if he did, he would be apprehended
and sent to prison (Acts 21:4, 11). Apparently, God was willing to spare the aged warrior the hardships that would befall
him if he fell into the hands of the Jews at Jerusalem. However,
Paul believed that if he went to prison, God would use this to
His glory. And if death came, Paul would regard it as a fitting
climax to a life devoted wholly to his Lord. In Jerusalem, he
was arrested, just as he had been told. The imprisonment was
very confining to a man as active as Paul, and he sought
through every means to effect his release. Ironically, his appeal
to Caesar, who happened to be none other than the notorious
Nero, prevented him from being set at liberty (Acts 26:32).

During the journey to Rome, through the Holy Spirit, Paul
foresaw the coming storm and warned the centurion to remain
in the harbor where they had docked. His appeal, while having influence on the centurion, did not prevail. The place where
they were anchored was not an especially good harbor in which
to spend the winter, so the ship sailed. Not long afterward,

they were caught in a fierce storm just as Paul had foreseen.

What caused the storm? Did the powers of darkness play a part in it? Satan, prince of the power of the air, has a certain amount of control over the atmosphere, but we know his power is limited. Storms also depend on physical factors. We are told that "sailing was now dangerous because the Fast was already over" (Acts 27:9). This means that it was about the middle of September, or at the autumnal equinox, a period marked by fierce storms at sea in many parts of the northern hemisphere.

The storm raged, but God was not through with Paul, and the apostle had not given up hope. For 14 days, he fasted and waited before God. On the 14th day, the angel of the Lord appeared to him, and said that all on board would be saved! He then went to the crew and gave them the good news:

> "For there stood by me this night an angel of the God to whom I belong and whom I serve, saying, 'Do not be afraid, Paul; you must be brought before Caesar; and indeed God has granted you all those who sail with you.' Therefore take heart, men, for I believe God that it will be just as it was told me" (Acts 27:23-25).

Although the ship and its cargo were lost, the entire crew, as well as all the passengers, escaped to land. However, the incident brings out an interesting fact about the nature of the gift of faith. Assuming that Satan was an active factor in the violence of the storm, we see that he was able to go only so far. At one time during the tempest, things got so bad that we read "all hope that we would be saved was finally given up" (Acts 27:20).

As we study this incident, we are compelled to believe that in certain cases there are powerful forces of darkness actively fighting against God's people. In fact, it seems that in the closing years of Paul's life, Satan had built up an effective strategy to hinder his ministry. Every move he made seemed to be countered. When writing to the Thessalonians, he said, "Therefore we wanted to come to you — even I, Paul, time and again — but Satan hindered us" (I Thes. 2:18). After two years in prison, he was sent to Rome, where he would spend two more years in confinement. Was his time being wasted? No, for during these years, many of his epistles were written that have become such a valuable legacy to the Church.

Another example is recorded in Daniel 10, where one of the princes of darkness withstood the angel sent to Daniel for 21 days. In such cases, it seems that prayer and fasting are necessary in order to break the grip of evil powers. It is possible for some battles to be lost and certain miracles to fail, simply because those involved give up the fight too soon. The purpose of the gift of faith is to give us such confidence that we will not be moved, but will believe that things shall be as God has said.

The Snowstorm That Ceased

The following incident occurred in the early days of my ministry, and I tell it as I remember it. The occurrence impressed me vividly at the time, and I believe that the details are essentially accurate.

I had been invited by a certain Christian family to hold some services in the Sierras of California, in the little village of Sierraville. I had looked forward to the meeting, and when the time came to make the trip, I was eager to be on my way. It was late in November — the day before Thanksgiving — and bad weather was setting in. A steady rain was falling. An elderly man warned me not to attempt the trip. "I have lived in this country many years," he said, "and I know that a heavy rain here this time of the year means snow up in the mountains."

This information made me pause. However, I had no other meetings arranged, and in my youthful enthusiasm, I disregarded his warning and started on the trip. When I was about halfway up the pass, the rain turned into snow and slush, which gradually got deeper the farther I went. By the time I reached a mountain village, the going was pretty rough, and my car had no chains. I stopped at the general store and bought some rope. Since the wheels of my car had spokes, I wound the rope around all four tires.

By now, the snowfall had almost become a blizzard, and it was long after dark. I asked the storekeeper what the weather forecast was, and he told me that storms like this often lasted for days. When he saw that I was going to attempt to cross the divide that night, he looked at me as if I was out of my mind.

"Young fellow," he said, "no one can get over that pass tonight. The snow is already a foot deep up there, and you can be stranded there for days. At the best, you will suffer from the cold and exposure, and there will be no one to rescue you. If you go on it's your own funeral."

Looking back, I realize that my actions were rather rash, and I am not recommending that anyone else do what I did. Here, in the midst of a blinding snowstorm that might continue for days, I was planning to do the impossible. But something kept urging me to get over the mountain so I could preach the following night. So I started on.

Notwithstanding my youthful zeal, I believe God put a supernatural faith in my heart that night. I seemed to see myself preaching the next day in Sierraville.

As I pushed on, I discovered that the ropes were a great help and, for a while, I was able to make very good time. But it was a false encouragement. The snow got deeper and deeper, and at last it piled up so high in front of the car's bumper, that I could go no further. I looked up the road, but the flakes were falling so thickly that it was impossible to see more than a short distance ahead. For a moment, I thought of what the storekeeper had told me about the storm probably lasting for days, but I pushed the thought out of my mind.

I had carried several heavy blankets along with me so I would be prepared for an emergency. (Automobiles in those days could break down anywhere, even in good weather.) I got into the back of the car and began to pray. I said to myself, "Here is an opportunity to test the promises of God." I began to pray like Elijah did on Mt. Carmel when he was praying for rain. The remarkable thing about it was that I really believed the storm would stop!

How long I prayed, I cannot say. But I could feel the presence of God there with me. Suddenly, I felt that something had happened! I looked out. Did I see a star? I looked again. Why, the whole sky was as clear as a bell! Not a flake of snow was falling! After that, I had a praise meeting right in the car. Afterwards, being quite warm from my exertions, I pulled the heavy blankets over me and went to sleep.

I awoke to the heavy clatter of a powerful gasoline motor. Bright sunshine was streaming through the mountain passage, as I heard the sound drawing nearer and nearer. Soon, I saw that it was a snowplow coming, and the man driving it was a member of the family who had invited me to hold the meeting!

With a little help from him, I got my car into the open roadway, and an hour later I was at the home of my friends, ready to eat Thanksgiving dinner! God gave us a very profitable meeting in that village, with a number of souls saved and some receiving the baptism of the Holy Spirit.

Since then, I have often thought of this incident. It was not the only time something of this nature happened to me, although some of the circumstances were unique. I know that God put faith in my heart that night for the storm to cease, and I was not surprised when it happened. But I certainly would not attempt to pray at just any time for a storm to stop — not unless God put it in my heart to do so. We are not to tempt God, or rush into danger so that God can perform a miracle for us. Yet I know that God gave me supernatural faith that night to believe that the storm would stop.

Deliverance From the Snake

"In My name ... they will take up serpents; and if they drink anything deadly, it will by no means hurt them ..." (Mk. 16:17, 18).

Paul's adventures were not over after he escaped from the ship. Although the passengers were safely on land, the storm had not ended. The falling rain made everyone very uncomfortable. However, with the help of the natives, a fire was kindled and Paul joined with others in gathering fuel for it. The heat of the fire drove a poisonous snake out of the flames, and Paul happened to be the one who was just laying his bundle of sticks on the fire. The viper attached itself to Paul's hand. He shook the snake free and it fell into the fire. The natives then thought he was a criminal and expected him to die suddenly, but changed their minds when they saw he suffered no harm.

> However, they were expecting that he would swell up or suddenly fall down dead. But after they had looked for a long time and saw no harm come to him, they changed their minds and said that he was a god (Acts 28:6).

This was a clear instance of the gift of faith in operation. Paul had been bitten by a poisonous snake. Both Paul and the natives knew its bite was deadly, however, he had faith in the promise of God, and the result was that no harm came to him.

Do Not Tempt the Lord

As we have noted, Mark 16:18 says, "'They will take up serpents; and if they drink anything deadly, it will by no means hurt them.'" Some have interpreted this to mean that Christians should go out and pick up snakes to prove their faith. Occasionally, we hear of people who do just that. As a result, one man had his arm swell to double its normal size. There have been cases where people have died as a result of participating in an orgy of snake handling. This is clearly tempting God. If people would carefully read their Bibles, or even use common sense, they would not make this error. Paul picked up the snake by mistake as he was helping to build a fire, and he did not wave it around to show how much faith he had. Instead, he shook it off into the flames, and God protected him from the viper's deadly fangs (Acts 28:5).

In Mark 16, the fourth sign to follow believers, was, "'If they drink anything deadly, it will by no means hurt them'" (ver. 18). The word "if" indicates that people are not to go out and drink poison or pick up snakes just to prove they are believers. If they do it accidentally, or are forced to drink something poisonous, they may then claim the promise of immunity.

This is an excellent example of the gift of faith in operation. If a snake bites a believer, they can lay hold of the promise and believe that there will be no pain, and that no evil effects will result.

The Noxious Stew Healed

There is the pertinent incident in the Old Testament (II Ki. 4:38-41), in which the sons of the prophets were cooking a pot of stew. A famine was in the land, and food was scarce. The company was hungry and waiting anxiously for dinner, but when the stew was served, they discovered that some of its ingredients — some wild gourds — were poisonous. Elijah said, "'Then bring some flour'" (ver. 41). They threw the flour into the pot and the noxious gourds were neutralized.

Chapter Twenty

The Gift of Faith and Divine Discipline

The Church Age is imperfect and there will always be minor differences of opinion between men who are conscientious and sincere. It is impossible to secure conformity of belief in every detail of doctrine. The Early Church permitted liberty of conscience on matters as important as circumcision (Acts 15). They did, however, require belief in the doctrine of Christ (Heb. 6:1, 2). They were not to bid Godspeed (success) to anyone who denied or violated the doctrine of Christ (II Jn. 9-11).

As is true today, there were those in apostolic days who prevented the doctrine of Christ from being taught. Among them were Hymenaeus, Alexander and Philetus. They denied the basic truth of the resurrection, saying it had already taken place, and overthrew the faith of some people (I Tim. 1:19, 20; II Tim. 2:16-18). This teaching was evidently the beginning of gnosticism, the heretical doctrine which teaches that matter is evil, and therefore, there is no resurrection.

These men got around the truth either by allegorizing it or giving it some kind of mystical application. Many modern false religions such as Christian Science, Spiritualism and Modernism, deny the truth of the physical resurrection. There were those in Paul's day who were involved in this error, and among these was Alexander the coppersmith whom Paul said had greatly resisted their words (II Tim. 4:14, 15).

The teaching of these men resulted in serious confusion in the Church. Paul described these heretics as putting away "a good conscious," and causing those who listened to them to make "shipwreck" of their faith.

What should the Church do about this? We are told that the "servant of the Lord must not quarrel but be gentle to all, able to teach, patient, in humility correcting those who are in opposition" (II Tim. 2:24, 25). But if this fails, and people such as these continue to cause others to lose their faith, what should be done? Should they be left free to continue to injure the body of Christ? No. God has given the Church a method to handle such cases. Sometimes, evil may be removed from the Church through the working of miracles, as in the case of Ananias and Sapphira, or when Moses dealt with the rebellion of Korah, Dathan and Abiram. Divine discipline, however, may also be administered through the gift of faith.

Jesus said, "'Whatever you bind on earth will be bound in heaven, and whatever you loose on earth will be loosed in heaven'" (Matt. 18:18), but this binding and loosing may only be done through faith. In his letter to Timothy, Paul said he had delivered Hymenaeus and Alexander, the men who had introduced heresy into the Church, "to Satan that they may learn not to blaspheme" (I Tim. 1:20).

In the case we are considering, Paul delivered the offenders over to Satan; that is, they were put under divine discipline. He did not desire for these men to lose their souls; they were to receive this chastening "that they may learn not to blaspheme." This was the method used with those who were guilty of bringing evil doctrines into the Church, and who would not listen to advice or take correction.

Divine Discipline for Immorality in the Church

The Scriptures also teach that flagrant immorality should be dealt with through divine discipline. In I Corinthians 5, we are told of an open case of unlawful cohabitation. There was no need for investigation or special discernment such as Peter exercised in the case of Ananias and Sapphira. This was a flagrant violation of common decency, for a man was sleeping with his father's wife! If such a matter was allowed to go unpunished, it would encourage the breakdown of all restraint and discipline in the assembly. The Corinthian saints no doubt deplored what was happening, but it was easier to let the matter go than to do anything about it.

The Apostle Paul, who was in another city, learned of the situation, and warned the Corinthians that if the spread of evil was not checked, it would corrupt and render the whole church ineffective. As long as sin is hidden, the individual alone is responsible for it, but as soon as it is revealed to the Church, the whole assembly becomes responsible. It is a serious matter for young Christians to come into a church where such a condition exists. If they see old saints condoning such practices, they may think that it is all right for them to do likewise.

The Corinthian Church was evidently afraid to handle this matter. If the man was brought to trial, he might cause serious trouble in the church. Some people, no matter what their offense, have a way of causing disunity in the Church by getting others to sympathize with them.

Paul showed how the case was to be handled. The man was to be supernaturally disciplined.

> And you are puffed up, and have not rather mourned, that he who has done this deed might be taken away from among you. For I indeed, as absent in body but present in spirit, have already judged (as though I were present) him who has so done this deed. In the name of our Lord Jesus Christ, when you are gathered together, along with my spirit, with the power of our Lord Jesus Christ, deliver such a one to Satan for the destruction of the flesh, that his spirit may be saved in the day of the Lord Jesus (I Cor. 5:2-5).

This was how the Church was to administer discipline that could not be effectively done otherwise. The power of binding was the divine method of discipline when other means were not effective. Notice that such action was not to be applied in a light way or with a vindictive spirit. The believers were to mourn before God that such action was necessary — mourn that such evil was brought into the Church in the first place, requiring this stern discipline. Second, the action was taken with the man's own good in mind. It was better for him to suffer at that time, than to be eternally lost. Third, the method was to deliver the man over to Satan for the destruction of the flesh. This meant that some severe physical affliction would come upon the man in order to bring him to his senses and teach him that he could not trifle with God's ordinances.

It is evident that this is the only method that will adequately deal with certain deliberate offenders of Church integrity and purity. Church trials are often a laughingstock to the world, but God has a way of dealing with sinners in the Church that will command the respect of the culprit, the world and the Church. It is time that we use the divine method.

Notice the perfection of the divine method. Church trials sometimes render an unjust verdict, but God is the perfect Judge. If a man is right in God's sight, no human can condemn him. Balaam the prophet tried to curse Israel, but it was turned into a blessing instead (Num. 24:9b, 10).

Divine discipline can only be accomplished through faith. Because it involves spiritual forces, the gift of faith is required. Occasionally, as in the situation of the Church at Corinth, the combined faith of all the members of the church is called for.

The Results of Divine Discipline

I vividly recall one instance when divine discipline was necessary. At the time, I was the new pastor of a church which, in the months before my arrival, had gone through some very serious trials.

The previous pastor had unwisely incurred the hostility of the wife of one of the board members. She had become obsessed in her mind that this church would shortly fail. Apparently, to make her own prediction come true, she used every opportunity to discourage those who were supporting the church. We tried to be patient with her and even conceded that she had some just cause for complaint. But eventually, we were forced to admit that our efforts to win her sympathy had proven a complete failure. We perceived that her actions were steadily undermining the faith of other members of the church. Her husband, a good man, was on the verge of backsliding and the whole church was being jeopardized by her conduct.

Realizing that further efforts to appease her were useless, and that the future of the church was hanging in the balance,

I decided one day, after a fruitless talk with her, to discuss the matter with my wife. I told her that I felt led to turn this woman over to divine discipline in order to prevent her and the church from being brought to ruin as a result of her bitter, vindictive spirit. Kneeling down, we agreed in prayer that this offender in the church be bound in the spirit, and turned over to Satan so she might know how serious it was to trifle with the work of God.

In a matter of a few days, we received a call from her husband asking us to come to their home at once. When we arrived we were met with a baffling scene. This headstrong woman, who had so relentlessly sought to destroy the work of God, now lay on her bed, her eyes filled with stark terror. She begged us to do something to help her. She believed a devil had taken possession of her, and said she was about to lose her mind. We observed her frightened expression and saw that she was telling the truth. We told her that we would pray, but gently reminded her that there was something she needed to do.

We left after a few minutes, but the next day or so we were called again. This time, as soon as we entered her room, she began to pour out an awful confession of her rebellion. She accused herself of being the cause of every problem the church had ever had. She went on to say that God had given her up, and that the devil had taken her over. The poor woman believed that she had committed the unpardonable sin, and that her case was hopeless.

We visited her a number of times, and now that she had repented, encouraged her to accept full forgiveness through the blood of Jesus. For quite a time she refused to believe that there was hope for her, but eventually her hope began to return. It was about a month before she was able to get out of bed, but during that time she called, one by one, all the members of the church to her bedside to ask their forgiveness.

She was finally able to return to the church, and from that time on she was humble and submissive, never again saying a word that could adversely affect the welfare of the church. There can be no doubt that divine discipline is God's method of solving problems caused by unruly members when other means fail.

The gift of faith is sadly needed in the Church today to provide the discipline that will keep it healthy. Such discipline must include mercy, and be invoked only in order to restore the guilty person. In serious cases, human methods often result in the individual's becoming incorrigible. Divine discipline does not leave the person free to continue recklessness, as happens only too often with human methods. It should be noted that discipline which is unfair, unjust or contrary to the will of God, will not work.

Balak asked Balaam to curse Israel for a reward. The hireling prophet would have complied with this request if it had been within his power. But no one can curse what God has blessed. All Balaam succeeded in doing was maneuvering himself into a position where the curse boomeranged against himself. He eventually died the death of a soothsayer (Num. 31:8).

Divine discipline should be used only when other means have been exhausted, and then only to bring glory to God and without vindictiveness. It should be done in love by those who are untainted by personal ambition. Only then will heaven ratify that which is done on earth. In all except the most flagrant cases, the restoration of the erring one is the objective of divine discipline.

Chapter Twenty-one

Committal — the Secret of Dynamic Faith

How can God's people receive this gift of faith? How can they have it operating in their lives?

> So Jesus said to them, "... for assuredly, I say to you, if you have faith as a mustard seed, you will say to this mountain, 'Move from here to there,' and it will move; and nothing will be impossible for you. However, this kind does not go out except by prayer and fasting" (Matt. 17:20, 21).

Jesus spoke these words to His disciples after they had experienced failure in casting an epileptic demon out of a boy. Prayer and fasting is undoubtedly an important element in the full exercising of the gift of faith.

Some years ago, there was an article published by Rev. C.H. Pridgeon entitled "The Prayer of Committal." This article, one of the best ever written on the subject, shows how committal to God brings into operation the dynamic power of the gift of faith. It is such a significant article that we take the liberty of quoting a portion of it here:

> Commit your way to the LORD, trust also in Him, and He shall bring *it* to pass [Hebrew, "He works"] (Psa. 37:5).

> To *commit* anything fully to God, it is necessary to have a definite transaction with God.

> We heard of a farmer who had great difficulty in becoming established in his Christian life. He was

always giving himself to God and in a short time the enemy would tell him that nothing was done, that he was not a Christian and that his consecration did not amount to anything; and he would fall into uncertainty and doubting. This up-and-down experience troubled him and he rarely had any peace of mind. The devil seemed to torment him continually. Drawn by a new impulse he made up his mind that, right where he was in the field, he would yield himself to the Lord *once and for all*, and to make it absolutely definite, he would drive a stake in the ground on the very spot. Not long after, as he was at work in another field, Satan attacked him as aforetime and told him that he had not given himself to God. He replied, "Come this way, Devil." Over the fence he went and back to the field where he had driven the stake. "Look, here is the spot where I did it, and this is the stake I drove, and this is the place where God accepted me." This definiteness and decision lifted him far above all doubts and suggestions of the adversary. Many are in doubt because of their lack of definiteness in dealing with God.

Many pray about their needs and keep on praying as though they did not believe, and in consequence, pray themselves out of faith. In Mark 11:24, we see that we are to be definite in making our requests known to God, and it is just as necessary to be definite in believing what God says about the answer. After praying and believing, if the answer doesn't come immediately, do not continue to pray for it in such a way that it is evident you are not believing Him for it. If you do, you will find when you have finished praying that your faith has weakened or is entirely gone. If God keeps you waiting for the *conscious* answer, tell Him that you are waiting and are still believing and praising Him for the answer. Thus, you become one of the Lord's "rememberers," spoken of in Isaiah 62:6, 7 (margin notes in NKJV), by reminding Him of His promise and by still maintaining your stand of faith saying, "Lord, I believe You and praise You."

Other methods of prayer may result in praying yourself out of faith altogether. Going back over the same ground again and again will ruin your faith. There is nothing that so fully clinches faith as to be so sure of the answer that you can thank and praise God for it. We may know we have believed the Lord, because after we pray, we are no longer restlessly planning and working in an attempt to answer our own prayer, but are filled with restful praise because we believe God's Word that He "works."

A sure sign that we have believed is found in Hebrews 4:3: "We who have believed do enter that rest." Prayers that pray us out of faith are the result of centering our thoughts on the difficulties in the way rather than on God's promises. We should not be occupied with our feelings, symptoms, faith or lack of faith, but only with what God has said. The simple way is to begin calling the things we have prayed for *ours* and to thank God for them before we feel or see the answer. God is faithful. He cannot deny Himself.

Joshua dared to claim a promised victory on the authority of God's word alone, while there were no signs of that victory being accomplished. According to their faith, God acted, and when they shouted (praised), He made the walls of Jericho fall. Abraham, "did not consider his own body ... he did not waver at the promise of God" (Rom. 4:19, 20; see also 4:17).

If what we believe for always came immediately, faith would have no chance to grow and be perfected.

What Committal Is

What is true about prayer is also true about committal or consecration. People consecrate and reconsecrate over and over again, not realizing that each repetition discounts the one previously made. If you were to give a book to a friend and then repeated this gift day after day, soon nobody would know to whom the book belonged. We find that in the law of offerings in the Bible, once an offering was laid upon the altar, it belonged to the Lord from that moment on, and no one dared to retake it. Once something has been surrendered to God, the next thing to do is to believe that God accepts it, and to consider it *His*. Don't keep on committing and recommitting your case to God. One of Satan's most subtle traps is to get us to do this.

To *commit* suggests not only bringing the matter to God, but also leaving it there. To bring something to God is hard enough, but to leave it there is harder. Yet, it is necessary to leave it with Him and trust Him if He is to work.

Suppose your watch is broken, so you take it to the watchmaker and ask him if he can repair it. After he looks at it through his magnifying glass, he replies, "Yes." Then you take the watch and say, "Thank you," and go your way. Will your watch be repaired? No. If you want it repaired, you must leave it with the watchmaker. So often, when we ask the Lord to take care of a certain difficult thing for us, He says, "Yes," and yet we fail to leave it with Him and nothing is ever done.

We have to learn to really hand over our requests to God, pray until we believe, and then leave them with Him. So often, when we face difficult or urgent matters, we like to feel that we still have them in the power of our hands. It is difficult for us to give up the control. Why not give God a chance to work?

Let us look at another analogy, a parable in nature that teaches exactly the same lesson. A small boy, who had been born and brought up in a large city, asked his parents for permission to plant some Indian corn in their little garden, and was given a few seed corn. He planted the corn with wonder and responsibility. He committed it to the ground, burying it out of sight and watered it. Although he hardly expected it to come up the first day or two, he could not resist the temptation to dig up each grain to see how it was getting on. Needless to say, no corn grew from that planting. He had to begin all over, and after a long time gathered the little harvest of corn.

We commit some requests to God exactly the same way he did those grains of corn. We commit them to Him and water them with our prayers and tears, but we are too impatient. It is hard to wait. We dig them up and take them in our hands to see how they are getting on. This blocks the working of God.

Never dig up in unbelief what you have sown in faith. There is too much self-effort and too little real committing to God. Some prayers have to be hidden in God's hand until they die, and God wants us to leave them there by faith. God knows that "if it dies, it produces much grain" (Jn. 12:24).

When anything is really committed to God, we must not act as we did before. Usually, He does not want us to do anything but trust Him. If there is anything else, He will make it plain. We must be careful to do only what He directs. We must not do anything that is inconsistent with the faith of committal.

The Word of God tells us, "'When you pray, believe'" (Mk. 11:24). Many simply pray and think there is virtue in saying prayers; but God, in this text, calls our attention to the necessity of believing when we pray. This believing is not simply believing in God, but means to believe for the very thing we have asked of Him.

We must take the definite place of believing God. This is not merely believing that God will answer our prayer some time, for that is putting off God's working until some future time, which would only be *hope* instead of *faith*. We must believe that we *have* the answer, even though we neither see nor feel that we have it (see I Jn. 5:14, 15). God says, "Now faith is" (Heb. 11:1), not faith shall be. That would only be hoping for, not present tense believing and having. Faith begins *now*.

Faith must be more than a mental willingness to believe; it must be a faith founded on God's promise. You must believe it is God's will to answer this particular prayer. If you so believe Him, you can begin to thank Him. If you can honestly thank God from your heart that He has heard you, you can be sure that your faith is sufficiently perfect for Him to work. Then you can say, "Lord, I believe You and praise You."

His Word says, "... by prayer and supplication, with thanksgiving, let your requests be made known to God" (Phil. 4:6). Pray this way until you can believe and thank Him for the answer, and He will begin to work.

Divine Healing Through Committal

Many cases of healing have been accomplished by the same kind of committal and faith. One young woman was suffering from dropsy, and was swollen to twice her natural size. After using all rational means and the help of kind physicians, she seemed to get worse rather than better. She saw that there was nothing else for her to do but commit herself and her case to God and trust Him to work. By a definite act of faith, she committed herself and her disease to God, claiming His promise in Psalm 37:5. Some improvement was noticed at once, but the disease still lingered. Day after day, she would look up to God and say, "Lord, I will believe You and praise You." It was not long until she was entirely restored. She not only recovered her former health and strength, but also gained a blessed nearness and fellowship with God.

Another case which illustrates this truth is that of a woman who was under much pressure because so many things were working against her. It seemed that she was attacked on every side. She became discouraged and then melancholy and was on the verge of committing suicide.

She had been a believer, but her faith seemed shipwrecked. She was approached by a Christian worker and asked if she was a believer. She said, "I used to be, but I am not now." After a few sympathetic words from the worker, she told the worker about some of her troubles. The worker tried to comfort her; but there seemed to be such a deep sense of utter inability and helplessness, and such a spirit of discouragement and darkness that all ordinary methods failed.

The worker, knowing the secret of the prayer of committal offered in faith and continued by praise, asked her if she would commit herself and all her troubles to the Lord by a definite act of faith. She knelt in prayer, but said she could not pray. The worker helped her voice a prayer to God in a few words. She repeated, "Lord, I commit all my troubles and myself to You, and I believe Your promise that if we commit and trust You, You will work. Lord, I believe You and praise You."

The worker told her that God said in His Word to commit to Him and trust Him and He would work, and that the only kind of prayer she would have to offer after she had made such a committal would be, "Lord, I believe You and I praise You."

It was several months before the worker saw her again. The lady's whole countenance and life had been transformed. Her life was filled with praise and God had done more than she had asked or thought. He had not only answered prayer, but had transformed her life into one that was radiant with God and which would be helpful to many struggling with depression.

We have a God who is able to save and help the broken-hearted and discouraged.

Commit Your Children to God

Many Christians have been praying for the salvation of their loved ones, but do not understand the prayer of committal.

A mother had a son who was leading a sinful life. Her neighbor quoted to her the Scriptures, "'For the promise is to you and to your children'" (Acts 2:39), and "'Believe on the Lord Jesus Christ, and you will be saved, you and your household'" (Acts 16:31). The neighbor told her to commit her son to the Lord, believe the promises, tell the Lord that she believed Him, and then praise Him. The mother said, "This came as a revelation to me. I never saw it that way before." She committed her son to God, and he was wonderfully saved shortly afterwards.

Do not keep repeating that you *take* the answer to your prayer, but continue to say, "I *took* and *have* it because God *declares* that we shall *have* what we *take*, and whatsoever we say believing shall come to pass." (See Mk. 11:23.)

Begin to pay the debt of praise and adoration that you owe to your God. Do not hinder God's work, but let your prayer of committal merge into faith and your faith into praise, thus enabling God to defeat the devil on your behalf and pour out such a blessing that there will not be room to receive it.

Chapter Twenty-two

Gifts of Healings

"... to another the gifts of healings by the same Spirit" (I Cor. 12:9).

This short statement by Paul implies several things about the gifts of healings. First, it is a multiple gift. Second, these several gifts are not intended to be divided among a number of persons, instead the entire group of healing gifts are designed to function through one individual.

However, as might be anticipated, in practice, few achieve the ideal goal of having all the healing gifts functioning perfectly and equally in their ministries. This explains why some ministers possessing a healing ministry have greater success with certain afflictions than with others — different gifts are involved.

These gifts, as is the case of the other gifts, are entirely supernatural in character. They should not be confused with the healing arts of the medical profession. Luke was a physician, but after he entered the ministry with the Apostle Paul, there is no record of his practicing medicine. The miracles of healing he recorded were entirely the result of divine power.

The Purpose of the Gifts of Healings

One of the most valuable books dealing with this subject is Harold Horton's, *The Gifts of the Spirit.* We take the liberty to quote from him on the character of the gifts of healings:

> And once again, as in all the other gifts, we must emphasize the entirely supernatural character of the gift. For these gifts of healings are commonly confused with a high degree of medical or surgical or manipulative or scientific ability. These are all of the natural man. They do not occur in

the Scriptures at all, except as they are superseded in Christ. Healings through these gifts are
wrought by the power of Christ through the
Spirit, by ignorant believers with no knowledge
of physiology, diseases, symptoms, drugs or surgery. True, Luke the beloved physician was
among the Lord's disciples. So was John the
beloved fisherman. As the one became a spiritual fisher and supernatural healer, so the other
became a supernatural healer and spiritual fisher. It is entirely dishonest to suggest, as some
writers do, that Paul took Luke with him on his
journeys as a safeguard, in case his miraculous
gifts failed! Those who know God's miraculous
ways in the Scriptures look upon such a statement as an impossible travesty of the truth.

Methods of Administering Divine Healing

Many books have been written on divine healing, and in
the limited scope of this book, we cannot exhaustively cover
the entire subject. We shall therefore confine ourselves to the
study of the actual working of the gifts of healings.

1. *Healing through personal prayer*

"Is anyone among you suffering? Let him pray" (Jas. 5:13).
James 5 is the chapter which invites the sick to call for the elders to pray for them. But note that they are encouraged, unless
too seriously ill, to look to God on their own for healing first.
Jesus gave many promises to His followers to encourage them
to receive deliverance as a result of their own faith.

> So Jesus answered and said to them, "Have faith
> in God. For assuredly, I say to you, whoever says
> to this mountain, 'Be removed and be cast into
> the sea,' and does not doubt in his heart, but
> believes that those things he says will be done,
> he will have whatever he says. Therefore I say to
> you, whatever things you ask when you pray,

> believe that you receive *them*, and you will have
> *them*" (Mk. 11:22-24).

Of course, as the promise indicates, just prayer alone is not sufficient. We must exercise faith when we pray. We must believe we receive. This means we must not look to our senses; we must not give attention to the symptoms; we must look to the promise, and stand firmly upon it. Then we will receive whatever we ask for. One of the finest examples of a man praying for his own healing is the case of Hezekiah. He was terminally ill, but God gave him faith for a great deliverance (II Ki. 20).

Seven times the promise is given by the Lord that if we ask anything in His Name it will be given (Jn. 14:14). This promise certainly includes healing of the body, which is "the children's bread."

2. Healing through the laying on of hands

This method of ministering to the sick may be used by all believers. "'And these signs will follow those who believe ... they will lay hands on the sick, and they will recover'" (Mk. 16:17, 18). Christ evidently considered it important that all of His people be able to minister to the sick when needed. A parent should be able to pray for a sick child and see him/her receive deliverance. Such healing may not come in exactly the same way as it does through someone who possesses gifts of healings, but the result is the same. Healing is healing!

3. Healing through the command of faith

With the exception of James 5, we find prayer spoken of rarely, if at all, in connection with the ministry of healing. The prophecy of Isaiah, quoted by Matthew, indicates that our sicknesses have already been borne by Christ, and therefore it is a matter of appropriation, rather than praying the healing down from heaven.

> When evening had come, they brought to Him
> many who were demon-possessed. And He cast

out the spirits with a word, and healed all who
were sick, that it might be fulfilled which was
spoken by Isaiah the prophet, saying: *"He Himself took our infirmities and bore our sickness"*
(Matt. 8:16, 17).

Since Christ has already borne our sins and sicknesses, it is
therefore our privilege to appropriate what is already ours. In
most cases, we see the apostles commanding the sick to be
healed, rather than praying for them.

4. *Healing through the spoken word*

While laying on hands was the general method used by
Christ and the apostles for healing the sick, people were also
often healed through the simple spoken word of faith. This
happened a number of times in the ministry of Christ. On one
occasion, He was asked to heal a centurion's servant who was
very ill. Jesus said He would go to the servant and heal him.
The centurion, however, said to Jesus, "'But only speak a word,
and my servant will be healed'" (Matt. 8:8). The servant was
healed that very hour!

On another occasion, a nobleman asked Christ to come and
heal his son. Jesus said, "'Go your way; your son lives'"(Jn.
4:50). The Psalmist declared, "He sent His word and healed
them" (Psa. 107:20).

5. *Healing through an anointed cloth*

In using the term "anointed cloth" we do not mean that the
cloth is anointed with oil, but that it has come in contact with
a person anointed by the Spirit of God, who has faith for healing.

In addition to the familiar story of the woman with the
issue of blood who touched the hem of Christ's garment and
was healed, we are told that many others received deliverance
through mere contact with Christ. "And as many as touched
Him were made well" (Mk. 6:56).

This type of ministry was not restricted to Jesus alone. We

are informed that Paul sent out aprons and handkerchiefs that had touched his body, and when these came in contact with the sick, they were healed.

> Now God worked unusual miracles by the hands of Paul, so that even handkerchiefs or aprons were brought from his body to the sick, and the diseases left them and the evil spirits went out of them (Acts 19:11, 12).

6. Healing through performing an act of faith

There are a number of instances in Scripture of people receiving healing as the result of obediently performing an act of faith. A classic example is the case of Naaman, who came to Elisha to be healed of leprosy. Elisha told him to go to the Jordan River and dip himself in the water seven times. It is apparent in the passage (II Ki. 5:14) that he would not have been healed if he had not taken the seventh and final dip!

It is not uncommon for people to be healed today through obedience to the command given by the one praying for the sick. It is not the act itself that heals, but putting one's faith into action.

Faith is an act. On many occasions, the Lord commanded a sick person to do something which at the moment seemed impossible. For instance, He commanded the palsied man to stretch out his withered hand, and the lame man to rise up and walk. Their obedience to the command brought their healing.

The case of the 10 lepers who asked for healing is perhaps one of the most remarkable examples of healing in Scripture. Jesus commanded them to go show themselves to the priests. "And so it was that as they went, they were cleansed" (Lk. 17:14). It was when they *acted* on the command to go, that they were healed.

Healed When She Arose From Her Bed

One of the first healings I remember was of a woman in our community who was a member of the local Methodist church. She received a remarkable deliverance the moment she obeyed the command to rise from her bed.

This woman had been seriously ill, and the physicians decided her only hope was an immediate operation. The cost of the proposed surgery was well beyond the family's financial resources. In desperation, the husband went to the local bank and arranged for a loan. In the meantime, my mother, who had great faith for divine healing, felt a burden for the family. She went to the sick woman and encouraged her to believe God for healing. My mother asked the woman if she wished prayer for her recovery. The woman's church had taught against divine healing and she had never taken any interest in the teaching. But, as is often the case when desperate illness or death faces a person, she was inclined to alter her views.

The lady consented to allow prayer to be offered for her healing. So my mother took the next train to Portland hoping to get Dr. Lake to go pray for the woman. However, he was not available, and mother requested that one of the other ministers go. The brother who went did not have much knowledge of social graces, but his faith in God was strong. Though he had acquired a brusque, unceremonious manner of dealing with the devil, it produced results — even though his mannerisms sometimes offended people of high tastes.

When mother and this preacher arrived at the sick woman's home, and the minister had opportunity to observe her critical condition, he told her that her sickness was the work of the devil. After giving the sick woman some instructions, he proceeded to rebuke the affliction with a loud, booming voice that carried through the whole house. Then, rather roughly, he told the woman that she was healed and for her to get out of bed. The lady at first hesitated to do this, but eventually she obeyed because she was afraid not to. As she arose from her bed, she discovered, to her great joy, that she had been made whole. At that time, the pastor of the local church was very much opposed to divine healing. This miracle was the first step in convincing him of its reality. Eventually, he became convinced of its scriptural foundation and received a notable healing himself.

As a general rule, putting your faith into action has a very decisive effect in bringing the gifts of healings into immediate manifestation.

7. *Healing by the anointing of the elders*

> Is anyone among you sick? Let him call for the elders of the church, and let them pray over him, anointing him with oil in the name of the Lord. And the prayer of faith will save the sick, and the Lord will raise him up. And if he has committed sins, he will be forgiven (Jas. 5:14, 15).

This is the method commonly used by the elders of the Church. Anointing with oil is significant. In large healing campaigns where faith is high, the sick person feels and realizes the presence of God's Spirit. In a sick person's home where faith may be low, and the individual is very aware of pain and suffering, anointing with oil serves a practical purpose. The oil denotes and signifies the presence of the Spirit. The act of anointing marks the precise moment for the individual to exercise faith and claim healing.

We have listed at least seven ways in which divine healing may be ministered to the sick. Most, if not all, of these methods may operate in connection with the gifts of healings. Yet, we must keep in mind that many believers who minister successfully to the sick may not possess actual gifts of healings (I Cor. 12:30).

In this respect, we should not overlook the fact that the gifts of healings are appointed in the Church (I Cor. 12:28). It is quite possible, and experience seems to bear this out, that the Holy Spirit may permit a gift to operate through *any member* of the body in order to meet the need of the moment. God reserves the right to manifest Himself through any individual at any time or on any occasion, as illustrated in the case of Balaam, when God actually spoke through a *donkey* (Num. 22:28-30).

Chapter Twenty-three

The Various Healing Gifts

Different gifts of healings are needed for the different kinds of sicknesses. The question naturally arises as to the grouping of the diseases. The Scriptures do not answer this directly, but experience in ministering to the sick gives us some very good clues as to the probable classifications. For example, there is a similarity between the afflictions caused by certain evil spirits.

1. Casting out blind, deaf and mute spirits

We believe that specific gifts of healings are involved in deliverance from this category of diseases. Scripture consistently speaks of casting out evil spirits as being different from healing the sick. (An example is Matthew 8:16.)

Certain types of demons take possession of the auditory and optical nerves, paralyzing them. Thus, the person afflicted by them may become deaf or blind. Because they cannot hear and therefore have no way of learning how to produce intelligible sounds, many deaf people, unless specially trained, cannot talk. If the spirit is cast out of a deaf person, and someone will patiently teach them to use their voice, they will gradually learn to talk. On the other hand, if a mute spirit actually controls the vocal chords, the person may be able to hear, and yet unable to talk.

There are various other nerve centers in the human body over which spirits may secure control, partially crippling or paralyzing certain muscles. The evil spirits that cause these afflictions are not the most powerful, and usually can be cast out without much difficulty. In these cases, the return of hearing or sight may occur almost instantly.

However, as Jesus pointed out, these exorcised spirits desire a human body and may return. Therefore, the person should be forewarned and prepared to resist any attempt on their part to re-enter. For upon returning, their grip over the individual is greatly strengthened (Lk. 11:24-26).

Healing the Blind Man in Lima, Peru

I recall the healing of a totally blind man in a Lima, Peru campaign. He had lost his sight 25 years previously, and was unable to see a ray of light. The man was standing near the head of the line. Ordinarily, I do not consider it advisable to minister to a totally blind person the first time he attends a meeting. He is engulfed in such a darkness that it is not surprising that he has little hope, let alone faith. He usually needs to be led out of the despair of his spirit first. But, as I observed the eager expression on the face of this man, I perceived that he had faith to be healed. An expression of expectancy lit up his entire countenance.

I determined to pray for him. Apparently, a blind spirit had oppressed the optic nerves, causing him to lose all sight. (See Matt. 12:22). I then laid hands on him rebuking the blindness, and after a moment asked him if he could see. He opened his eyes wide and looked about with great eagerness and anticipation. It was apparent that he saw nothing, yet he was so sure that he could see, that he would not admit he was still blind. He just stood there smiling and looking. I told him to remain standing for a few minutes, while I prayed for some of the others. But I had hardly started, before I heard a tremendous shout coming from the audience. I turned around to see that the man was pointing out the lights, counting them, "Una, dos, tres, cuatro, cinco ...!" The whole congregation had risen to its feet, shouting and worshiping God.

Then I noticed the man pause. A look of bewilderment spread over his face, and he began to shake his head. I said to the interpreter, "Something is wrong; ask him what the trouble is." There was a moment of exchange in Spanish, and then they told me he was saying, "I can see, but all the lights are great long tubes," and he extended his hands indicating the length. Then we understood, for at the time he became blind, fluorescent lights had not been invented! As soon as the matter was explained to him, all was well.

In this particular case, it was evident that the eyeballs were undamaged, but oppressing spirits had deadened the optic nerves. Freed from this, the man was able to see immediately.

2. *Casting out the more powerful devils*

> Then the disciples came to Jesus privately and said, "Why could we not cast it out?" So Jesus said to them, "Because of your unbelief; for assuredly, I say to you, if you have faith as a mustard seed, you will say to this mountain, 'Move from here to there,' and it will move; and nothing will be impossible for you. However, this kind does not go out except by prayer and fasting" (Matt. 17:19-21).

However, someone who has considerable success in casting out evil spirits may run into serious difficulties in dealing with the more powerful demons, such as epileptic and insane spirits. This was true in the case of the epileptic child in Matthew 17:14-21.

The disciples who had experienced great success in this ministry (Lk. 10:17), found that they were unable to cast out an epileptic demon. In defiance of those who tried to cast it out, the demon would throw the child on the ground, causing him to foam at the mouth until it appeared that he was dead.

The disciples came to Jesus in embarrassment, asking what had gone wrong. Jesus, by healing the child, showed that there was no reason for their failure as far as God's will was concerned. Nevertheless, prayer and fasting was needed for deliverance from this type of demon possession.

Casting out demons is a work of the Holy Spirit (Matt. 12:28), but in this case prayer and fasting were evidently necessary to call into operation the particular healing gift needed to cast out this powerful demon.

Jesus also showed that while a single demon may be ejected with comparative ease, deliverance in the case of multiple demon possession is much more difficult (Lk. 11:26). In the event of a legion of demons taking possession of someone, the situation becomes increasingly hopeless, unless the one who ministers to the victim is armed with the same power that Christ possessed (Mk. 5:1-19). The demons that Christ ejected from the lunatic took possession of a herd of pigs, which became so terrified that they rushed headlong into the sea and drowned (ver. 13).

Just as the evil spirits went out of the demoniac into the pigs, under certain conditions they may enter into an unwary person. However, an evil spirit cannot take possession of just anyone. The door must be opened in some way. Fear may permit an evil spirit to enter. Giving in to fits of anger or jealousy may open the door. An irreverent or frivolous person who is present at the time evil spirits are being cast out may become the victim of an attack.

I remember one case in Miami, Florida, in particular. The service had proceeded quietly. The people had listened in a state of reverent awe as they witnessed powerful demons cast out in the Name of Jesus. After the service, a man and woman came to me and rather rudely criticized the meeting because they felt there had not been enough demonstrations. They were accustomed to meetings in which loud demonstrations took place in every service and supposed any other kind of service was a failure. They were almost belligerent in their attitude.

While I was wondering how I should answer them, the woman was suddenly struck by an evil spirit and began to tremble violently. At first, her husband supposed the power of God had come upon her. But, soon he saw that something had gone seriously wrong. What a change of attitude took place! Was there any help for her? I took the woman away from where people were engaging in conversation, and behind a curtain I rebuked the evil spirit. In a moment she was free. Nothing more needed to be said. The couple, much humbled and grateful for the deliverance, had learned their lesson. They realized that more than shouting is required to cast out an evil spirit; it requires authority.

Deliverance of the Insane Woman

A remarkable case of deliverance from insane demons took place in the John G. Lake Healing Rooms in Spokane. The woman's name was Lena Lakey. In her testimony, she said she had become violently insane while working as a cook at a lumber camp. Several men were required to overpower her. They tied her in bed, but she was able to wrench herself free and tore the bed to pieces. She struck one man with the side of the bed and rendered him unconscious. Another was in the hospital three weeks recovering from injuries. She escaped into the woods during a drenching rain, and eventually fell exhausted in a thicket of trees, where she lay unconscious until a search party found her six hours later. She was brought to Spokane by six men in a car and was tied with ropes.

Before taking her to court to be committed to the insane asylum, they decided to bring her to the Healing Rooms. Dr. Lake laid his hands on her in prayer, and the insane demons were cast out and she was instantly healed. An abscess on her side, from which she had suffered for 15 years, totally disappeared within 24 hours, and a rheumatic bone deposit between two joints of the fingers and toes, so extensive that it forced the joints apart, was gone in 48 hours. She was made completely whole.

Special gifts of healings are obviously involved in casting out the more powerful demons, as in the case just described. Jesus indicated in His teaching that a higher operation of the spiritual gifts is needed to cast out these powerful demons. Those who attempt to exorcize such evil powers, without possessing the authority to back up their words, might find themselves in grave danger, as did the sons of Sceva (Acts 19:13-16).

3. *General healing of the sick*

Not all sickness is caused by demonic spirits, although we may correctly say that all disease directly or indirectly comes from Satan (Acts 10:38). Take for example Job's boils. They were not caused by demonic spirits, although we are told they indirectly originated from Satan (Job 2:7).

Modern medical science affirms that boils are caused by germs. A carbuncle, such as Hezekiah had, is caused by a very serious infection that spreads faster than the body can rally its defenses. In many cases, a carbuncle results in death. Obviously, for a healing to take place in such a case, the infection must first be destroyed since the body can no longer cope with it.

Until recently, cancer was thought to have no connection with micro-organisms of any kind. However, it is now believed, and there is much evidence to substantiate the belief, that a minute virus (so small it may be a living molecule) in some way penetrates the cells and causes them to act insanely. They begin to multiply wildly without plan or design. For healing to occur, the evil virus inside these cells must be killed. (Surgery is only effective when the diseased cancer cells can be completely cut away from the healthy flesh.)

Diseases caused by infectious parasites (germs, bacteria or virus) account for a very large amount of sickness. The gift designed to cure such diseases must be among the foremost of the healing gifts.

4. Creative miracles

It is obvious to even the casual observer that there is a difference between the healing of an eye in which the organic structure is retained, and one in which the eyeball has been destroyed or seriously damaged. In the former, when pressure on the optic nerve is released, the eye may be able to see immediately. On the other hand, the person with the destroyed eyeball or one that is malformed at birth, would still not be able to see. In this case, a creative miracle is needed besides healing.

John 9 tells us of a man who was not afflicted with diseased eyes, but who was born blind. This was a different situation from those who had lost sight later in life, and a creative miracle was required to heal him.

Man was originally made from the dust of the earth. Therefore, Jesus took dust from the ground, mingled it with His spit, and "anointed the eyes of the blind man with the clay" (Jn. 9:6). After the man washed in the pool of Siloam, he could see. This was a miracle of such a high degree that the

Pharisees refused to believe it until the evidence compelled them to (ver. 18). The man who was healed knew that a creative work had been done, and told the Pharisees, "'Since the world began it has been unheard of that anyone opened the eyes of one who was born blind'" (ver. 32). Creative healing miracles verge on the gift of working miracles, and will be given further consideration in chapter 26.

The Healing of Congressman Upshaw

The remarkable healing of former Congressman William D. Upshaw was of such a nature, and the circumstances were so well known, that skeptics had a hard time explaining it. It was more than a healing; there was a work of creation done in his body which enabled him to walk again — after being crippled for nearly 60 years! The former congressman served four terms for the state of Georgia. Once he ran on an independent ticket for the presidency of the United States. He was an unusually gifted speaker, and his name was known by millions of people.

When William Upshaw was 18, he fell on the crosspiece of a wagon frame and fractured his spine. For seven years, he was a total invalid. Because of his own determination and exertion, he finally learned to walk with the aid of crutches. When I first met him he had used the crutches for nearly 60 years, but he was able to make his way about in this painful and tedious fashion. He had been attending our salvation/healing campaign in Los Angeles, where thousands were being saved and healed.

One day during the meeting, he asked to see me. He told me about the injury which had kept him on crutches for so many years. The accident had evidently severed vital nerves, and a creative work would have to be done before he could walk. I encouraged him to continue to attend the healing services. I told him God would heal him, but his faith needed to grow until it could take hold of the promise for the needed miracle. I do not recall whether he was prayed for at that time or not, but I know he continued to attend the meetings regularly.

Two years later, I was present at the Branham meetings in the same city. Brother Branham told me that in a vision he had seen the healing of a statesman. The following night as he left the platform, and while still under the anointing, he said, "The congressman is healed." William Upshaw's heart leaped, and believing that what had been said was true, he rose to his feet and started walking! In his own words, he testified, "I laid aside my crutches and started toward my happy, shouting wife … and the bottom of heaven fell out! Heaven came down our souls to greet us, and glory crowned the mercy seat."

For several years after that, the Honorable William D. Upshaw criss-crossed the country, giving his testimony in many cities, including Washington, D.C., where he had spent many years as a congressman. His testimony was published in a number of America's leading newspapers. Just as the healing of the blind man who washed in the pool of Siloam astonished many, so the healing of this statesman became one of the most outstanding testimonies of God's power in the 20th century.

We may add further that faith must reach a certain intensity for the more powerful gifts of healings to come into operation. God never denies persistent faith.

5. Ministering with healing power

In many cases of sickness, all that is needed is for divine power to destroy the disease agent, and then the body's natural restorative powers may bring a rapid return to health. In other cases, the disease may have destroyed certain vital organs to the extent that supernatural healing is also needed.

This was evidently the case with the woman who had suffered from an issue of blood for 12 years (Lk. 8:43). She touched the border of Jesus' garment, and "immediately her flow of blood stopped" (ver. 44). Certainly, more happened in this situation than the mere destroying of the disease. Healing virtue flowed into her body and made her whole. Jesus Himself confirmed this when He said, "'I perceived power going out from Me'" (ver. 46). This remarkable phenomenon occurred at other times in Christ's ministry. The "healing virtue" flowed into His clothes, and whoever touched the hem of His garment was made whole (Mk. 6:56).

This particular kind of healing also appeared in the ministry of the Apostle Paul (Acts 19:11, 12).

The healing virtue mentioned in Scripture is apparently a tangible thing. When hands anointed of God are laid on cloths or handkerchiefs, there is an actual flow of healing power into the cloths. When these come in contact with the bodies of sick people, the healing virtue flows into them and heals them. This kind of power resided in the bones of Elisha, for when a dead man came in contact with those bones, he was restored to life (II Ki. 13:21).

Dr. John G. Lake, who had unprecedented success in the healing ministry, makes this remarkable comment concerning the intensity of a healing:

> Healing is by degree, based on two conditions. First, the degree of healing virtue administered; second, the degree of faith that gives action and power to the virtue administered.

This statement is worth careful study.

The Healing of a Paralyzed Woman

The results of a powerful anointing on the one who is ministering to the sick, and when there is a flow of healing virtue, are obvious in the miracle that took place when Dr. John G. Lake received the baptism in the Holy Spirit. We shall let Dr. Lake tell it in his own words:

> One afternoon, a brother minister called and invited me to accompany him to visit a lady who was sick. Arriving at the home, we found the lady in a wheelchair. All her joints were set with inflammatory rheumatism. She had been in the condition for ten years.
>
> While my friend was conversing with her, preparing her to be prayed with that she might be healed, I sat in a deep chair on the opposite side of a

large room. My soul was crying out to God in yearning too deep for words, when suddenly it seemed to me that I had passed under a shower of warm tropical rain, which was not falling upon me but through me. My spirit and soul and body, under this influence, was soothed into such a deep, still calm as I had never known. My brain, which had always been so active, became perfectly still. An awe of the presence of God settled over me. I knew it was God.

Some moments passed; I do not know how many. The Spirit said, "I have heard your prayers, I have seen your tears. You are now baptized in the Holy Spirit." Then curents of power began to rush through my being from the crown of my head to the soles of my feet. The shocks of power increased in rapidity and voltage. As these currents of power would pass through me, they seemed to come upon my head, rush through my body and through my feet into the floor. The power was so great that my body began to vibrate intensely, so that I believed if I had not been sitting in such a deep low chair, I might have fallen upon the floor.

At that moment, I observed my friend was motioning me to come and join him in prayer for the woman who was sick. In his absorption, he had not noticed that anything had taken place in me. I arose to go to him, but I found my body trembling so violently that I had difficulty in walking across the room, and especially in controlling the trembling of my hands and arms. I knew that it would not be wise to thus lay my hands upon the sick woman as I was likely to jar her. It occurred to me that all that was necessary was to touch the tips of my finger on the top of the patient's head and then the vibrations would not jar her. This I did. At once, the currents of holy power passed through my being, and I knew that it likewise passed through the one who was sick. She did not speak, but apparently was amazed at the effect in her body.

My friend, who had been talking to her in his great earnestness, had been kneeling as he talked to her. He arose saying, "Let us pray that the Lord will now heal you." As he did so, he took her by the hand. At the instant their hands touched, a flash of dynamic power went through my person and through the sick woman, and as my friend held her hand, the shock of the power went through her hand into him. The rush of power into his person was so great that it caused him to fall on the floor. He looked up at me with joy and surprise, and springing to his feet said, "Praise the Lord, John, Jesus has baptized you in the Holy Ghost!"

Then he took the crippled hand that had been set for so many years. The clenched hands opened and the joints began to work — first the fingers, then the hand and the wrist, then the elbow and shoulder. The woman was completely and gloriously delivered.

When Lake received the baptism in the Holy Spirit, he received, as his subsequent ministry proved, powerful gifts of healings.

6. *Raising the dead*

Raising the dead is associated with the ministry of healing, but with the added consideration that the person's spirit must be recalled to the body. If the body has been dead for any length of time, there will be physical degeneration in the vital organs, including irreversible brain damage. In the case of Lazarus who had been dead four days, physical decay was well advanced (Jn. 11:39). His raising was indeed a miracle! It was, in fact, proof of Christ's resurrection power (Jn. 11:23-25).

Many cases of people being raised from the dead have come to our attention, although in practically all such cases, the person was dead less than an hour. Certainly, very special gifts are involved in these miracles.

7. *Healing from drug addiction*

There is one area of the gifts of healings probably not mentioned in Scripture — that is deliverance from drug addiction. Nicotine, which is inhaled into the system through cigarette smoking has been proven by research at John Hopkins University to be a deadly killer. Many people find it extremely difficult to break the smoking habit, and many never will without the power of God.

The more powerful drugs obtain such a powerful grip on the victim, that in over 90 percent of cases, no deliverance is possible without divine help. However, many remarkable deliverances from these habits have occurred as the result of the prayer of faith. It is probable that special gifts of healings are involved in the deliverance.

Healing of Lillian Yeomans

Many people have heard of Dr. Lillian Yeomans, and have read her excellent writings on divine healing, including *Healing From Heaven*.

Lillian Yeomans came from a family of physicians. Her father was a physician, and she became one as well upon graduation from Ann Arbor in 1882. Lillian was a Christian, but she was like Peter, following afar off. Needless to say, she did not intend to become a drug victim. But, due to the strenuous work of practicing medicine and surgery, she occasionally resorted to morphine to steady her nerves and enable her to sleep. One day she made the terrible discovery that the drug had become her master. What anguish of soul she experienced when she realized she could not break its grip. Here is a portion of her story, as taken from Volume IV, page 350 of *Leaves of Healing*, and also from her own book *Healing From Heaven*:

> When by tremendous exercise of willpower I abstained from the drug for twenty-four hours, my condition became truly pitiable. Trembling with weakness, my whole body bathed in cold sweat, heart palpitating and fluttering, respiration irregular, my stomach unable to retain even as much as a drop of water, intestines racked with pain and tortured with persistent diarrhea, I was unable to stand erect, to articulate clearly, or even to sign my name. I could not think connectedly; my mind was filled with horrid imaginings and awful forebodings, and worst of all, my whole being was possessed with the specific, irresistible, indescribable craving for the drug. No one that has not felt it can imagine what it is. Every cell in your body seems to be shrieking for it. It established a periodicity for itself in my case, and I found that at five o'clock each afternoon I had to have it.
>
> "Like a skeleton with a devil inside," one of my nurses said, and I think that her description, if not flattering, was accurate enough. My friends had lost all hope of ever seeing me delivered, and far from urging me to give up drugs, advised me to take them as the only means of preserving the little reason that remained to me. They expected my wretched life to come to an early close, and really could not desire to see so miserable an existence prolonged.
>
> Well, my reason for coming to Zion was not that I had lost confidence in the efficiency of means, but because it seemed to me God told me very

> clearly that He would not deliver me from this by means. God seemed to say plainly, "I am the Lord that healeth thee," so I came down to Zion, and brought a large quantity of morphine and chloral with me which Dr. Speicher promptly took away.
>
> Now I am perfectly free from that craving for morphine. I have gained fully twenty-five pounds I think, and I have a ravenous appetite. I have been sleeping well, and I feel I am completely delivered from morphine and chloral, for which I give God the praise.

Divine deliverance from alcoholism and the more powerful drugs involves the operation of special gifts of healings. It would be interesting to know just what all is involved in the working of such a gift. However, science is not able to study this phenomenon in the way they analyze the working of electricity or some natural force. Nevertheless, the effects of these gifts can be readily seen and proved.

8. *Other gifts of healing*

Obviously, these various methods of healing reflect the operation of different gifts, each particularly suited for a given need. We have not attempted to cover the whole range of the healing gifts. Deliverance from allergies no doubt involves a particular gift. There are probably other special gifts involved in healing the more desperate kinds of diseases, including unusual congenital malformations caused by defective genes, degenerative diseases, cerebral palsy, water-head babies, brain damage, etc. Special and unusual gifts of healings, perhaps closely associated with working of miracles, are needed to secure effective deliverance for such cases. God is able to heal anyone of anything, yet, it is plain that the Church has not fully entered into a ministry that brings consistent deliverance for those so seriously afflicted.

Chapter Twenty-four

Ministering in the Healing Gifts

How do the gifts of healings operate? Sceptics claim that those who possess genuine gifts of healings should be able to heal anybody, anytime, anywhere. They also claim that healing ministers should be willing to accept all challenges and satisfy the whims of any person demanding a demonstration of a miracle for his/her private benefit. Such irreverence toward divine gifts is hardly worthy of passing consideration.

Since Christ Himself ministered to people through these gifts, we have a considerable amount of pertinent material to study. This information gives a fairly definite understanding of how the gifts of healings manifest, and the conditions under which they operate.

Healing Anybody, Anytime?

One of the questions posed by those who challenge the ministry of healing is: Are the gifts of healings intended to heal anybody, anytime? They avow that Christ healed anybody and everybody — that there were no conditions. But the Bible flatly contradicts such a view. For example, in Christ's own city of Nazareth, "He could do no mighty work there, except that He laid His hands on a few sick people and healed *them*" (Mk. 6:5).

Notice, it does not say that Christ *would* not do mighty works there, but that He *could* not do mighty works there. This implies that God laid down laws for healing to which Christ made Himself subject. Moreover, as if to emphasize the point, Jesus referred to the prophet Elisha who ministered healing to Naaman, saying, "'And many lepers were in Israel in the time of Elisha the prophet, and none of them was cleansed except Naaman the Syrian'" (Lk. 4:27).

It is clear that the gifts of healings are not designed for indiscriminate healing. There are important conditions to be met first. As someone has wisely said, "All sicknesses can be healed, but not all sick people can be healed."

Arousing Satan's Hostility

Men may deny the miraculous, but demons quickly recognize the threat that this ministry poses to them. When Jesus entered the synagogue at Capernaum, an unclean spirit that possessed a man recognized Christ as the Son of God and cried out in fear:

> Now in the synagogue there was a man who had a spirit of an unclean demon. And he cried out with a loud voice, saying, "Let *us* alone! What have we to do with You, Jesus of Nazareth? Did You come to destroy us? I know who You are — the Holy One of God!" (Lk. 4:33, 34).

Christ, however, commanded the demon to be quiet and cast it out.

Operating in the Supernatural Realm

Under the Mosaic Law, lepers were segregated from the congregation (Lev. 13:46). Lepers were considered unclean, and to prevent contracting the disease no one was allowed to touch them. Yet, when a leper came to Christ asking Him to make him whole, Jesus reached out His hand and, "touched him, saying, 'I am willing; be cleansed'" (Matt. 8:3).

From this, we conclude that the person operating in the gifts of healings should have dominion over the diseases and evil powers that afflict those he/she ministers to.

Healing at a Distance

Some people don't have enough faith for healing unless they receive personal ministry. These people usually will be healed only if hands are actually laid upon them. There are others, however, who will believe when the Word is spoken for their deliverance. This is beautifully illustrated in the case of the centurion and his servant:

The centurion answered and said, "Lord, I am not worthy that You should come under my roof. But only speak a word, and my servant will be healed. For I also am a man under authority, having soldiers under me. And I say to this *one*, 'Go,' and he goes; and to another, 'Come,' and he comes; and to my servant, 'Do this,' and he does *it*" (Matt. 8:8, 9).

Jesus, marvelling at the centurion's faith, spoke the word, and "his servant was healed that same hour" (ver. 13).

Because healing may be accomplished by the spoken Word, mass healing is possible when faith is present. Hundreds of people have been healed at the same moment in large campaigns in which faith reached a high level.

Many, who were sick and lying in the streets, were healed when Peter's shadow fell on them as he passed by (Acts 5:15). The gifts of healings will operate whenever faith makes a real contact, regardless of time or distance.

I shall never forget one morning years ago, when I was doing evangelistic work 3,000 miles from home. I received a letter from my father. Mother usually did the writing, and when I saw that the letter was written in my father's handwriting, I knew something was wrong. And there was. Mother was desperately ill. Examinations had determined that the disease was cancer of the stomach. The physician recommended an immediate operation which would be expensive, and with no promise of more than a brief postponement of the inevitable. Mother determined to trust God for healing, and father, in deep distress, wrote to tell me the grave circumstances.

Far from home and having no money to return, I drove out to an old schoolhouse. Kneeling by a bench, I laid my Bible down and opened it to one of the great promises: "'Whatever things you ask when you pray, believe that you receive *them*, and you will have *them*'" (Mk. 11:24). I do not recall that I prayed long, but as I did, my soul seemed to reach out to God in an unusual way. I felt the power of the Holy Spirit come upon me, and praying, I said, "O God, although mother is

251

3,000 miles away, You have all power. You know that I have prayed for many others and they have been healed; now mother's life is at stake. At this moment, I believe that Your power destroys the cancer and she shall live." When I arose, I received a strong assurance that deliverance had come.

About three days later, I went to the post office and found an air mail letter waiting for me. It was addressed in mother's handwriting, and standing in the post office lobby, I hastily tore it open. Down the page I could see the words, "Hallelujah! Praise the Lord! God has done a miracle. The cancer is gone!"

She was gloriously healed. A few months later, she made a trip to California to testify to friends and relatives. I met her there. God had done the miraculous and healed my mother, although she was nearly 3,000 miles from where I prayed.

Rights of Evicted Demons

Some ask if it would be possible to bind a demon and cast it into the Bottomless Pit where it could do no further harm. Apparently, however, demons have certain legal rights that must be respected. Although all demons will eventually be cast into the Pit, the time for that has not yet come. The legion of demons cast out of the demoniac called Jesus' attention to this fact:

> And suddenly they cried out, saying, "What have we to do with You, Jesus, You Son of God? Have You come here to torment us before the time?" (Matt. 8:29).

Additional information concerning these demons is given in the book of Luke. We are informed that the evil spirits begged Jesus not to cast them into the Pit.

> And they begged Him that He would not command them to go out into the abyss (Lk. 8:31).

Certainly, a demon is under obligation to obey God's ministers, so we pose the question: If a demon does not readily obey the one who has been given power over it, does it not jeopardize any legal rights it may have in this respect? We believe that, under certain circumstances, it is possible to bind the power of a demon so that it can never again enter into that particular person.

Cooperation and Faith of the Sick Person

Faith is an act. When about to minister to a sick person, Jesus would often tell them to put their faith into action. Thus, He said to the man sick with palsy, "'Arise, take up your bed, and go to your house'" (Matt. 9:6). To the woman who touched the hem of His garment, Jesus said, "'Be of good cheer, daughter; your faith has made you well'" (Matt. 9:22). To the blind man who asked for healing, He said, "'According to your faith let it be to you'" (Matt. 9:29). To the man with the withered hand, Christ said, "'Stretch out your hand'" (Matt. 12:13). This was a physical impossibility; yet when he made the effort, his hand was healed.

When the 10 lepers asked Jesus for healing, He commanded them to go show themselves to the priest. "And so it was that as they went, they were cleansed" (Lk. 17:14).

These examples make it clear that the gifts of healings are not designed to operate independently of the sick person's faith. They are required to cooperate — to show faith by action; to do the things they were unable to do. Those who minister gifts of healings should seek to secure some physical act of faith from the person who comes for healing.

Healing Ground

While it is true that God may impart healing grace and saving grace at the same time, the ideal method is for the person to become aware of his spiritual need first. Divine healing is the "children's bread," and people need to get on healing ground to be able to retain their healing.

The Canaanite woman (Matt. 15:22-28) who came to Christ to obtain deliverance for her demon-possessed daughter, was not on healing ground. Christ, in His infinite wisdom, did not respond to her plea at first. This drew out the woman's faith. Notice the progressive revelation:

At first, she addressed Him as "Son of David." But, as the "Son of David," Christ could not help a woman who was a gentile.

Next, she called Him "Lord" and worshiped Him. But, she was still a sinner, and His reply was that healing was the "children's bread," and as such, it should not be cast to dogs.

The woman rose to the occasion. In her great humility, she was willing to be included with the dogs, and gave her amazing reply, "'Yes, Lord, yet even the little dogs eat the crumbs which fall from their masters' table'" (ver. 27). She received both her request and a commendation from the Lord for her great faith.

It is important that those who minister in the gifts of healings direct people to Christ as their Lord and Savior before they minister "the children's bread" to them.

Prayer and Fasting

The question is often asked, "Shouldn't results always take place if one actually has gifts of healings?" However, the apostles, who had consistent results in ministering to the sick, experienced at least one notable failure. In this case, they tried to cast an epileptic demon out of a child, and were unable to do so. The father said to Jesus, "'So I brought him to your disciples, but they could not cure him'" (Matt. 17:16).

Some have said that this failure proves that in certain cases it is not the will of God for the person to be healed. This myth is disproved by the fact that Jesus delivered the child (ver. 18).

When the disciples asked why they could not cast out the demon, Jesus replied:

> "Because of your unbelief; for assuredly, I say to you, if you have faith as a mustard seed, you will say to this mountain, 'Move from here to there,'" and it will move; and nothing will be impossible for you. However, this kind does not go out except by prayer and fasting" (Matt. 17:20, 21).

Jesus' words reveal that prayer and fasting are sometimes required even of those who have gifts of healings, in order to achieve deliverance over the more powerful demons.

John Alexander Dowie lived at a time when the ministry of divine healing had almost disappeared from the Church. He gave himself to prayer and fasting and waiting on God for the return of apostolic ministry. Eventually, God answered his prayer. He received an anointing that enabled him to have mastery over powerful demonic spirits. The healing of the famous songwriter, Rev. F.A. Graves, composer of "There's Honey in the Rock," was one of the more noted miracles of this nature that occurred under Dowie's ministry.

Rev. Graves was a victim of epilepsy. He was an orphan, and added to this misfortune, he never knew what hour during the day the epileptic demon might throw him to the floor, wallowing, foaming and gnashing his teeth. For 20 years, he endured this horrible suffering.

Rev. Graves happened to attend one of Dr. Dowie's meetings when he was in Minneapolis, Minnesota. His friends went to Dr. Dowie and talked to him at length about the affliction of this evangelist-singer. The following day, word was sent that Rev. Graves had met with a serious accident and was dying. Dr. Dowie immediately got in a carriage and drove as rapidly as possible to where Rev. Graves was staying.

Rev. Graves had been taking a bath in a friend's home, and had shut the bathroom door and locked it. He had just filled the deep bathtub with water when he had a seizure and fell over with his head in the water. His fall was heard outside, and the people of the house rushed to the door and tried to communicate with him, but could not. They tried to break the door down, but were not strong enough. Someone ran outside for help, and a large, heavy man who was passing by was summoned in. When he managed to break down the door, they found Rev. Graves not only suffering from a seizure, but also nearly drowned from the fall into the water. The people worked with him and brought him back to consciousness, but he suffered a hemorrhage and lost a great quantity of blood.

At that moment, Dr. Dowie arrived and laid hands upon

him. The flow of blood immediately stopped. Dr. Dowie also prayed for the attacks of epilepsy to cease.

The next day, Rev. Graves realized that he was delivered, and rushed to where Dr. Dowie was to tell him that he had been healed. A few times afterward, the enemy tried to retake possession of him, but his deliverance became perfect, and for many years, he testified in various cities of being healed of one of the most terrible forms of epilepsy.

After Rev. Graves' healing, God specially endued him with a gift of song writing; a number of his hymns find a place in hymnals and are still sung today.

Challenges Against the Ministry of Healing

Sometimes, when confronted with an especially harmful attack against divine healing, we might find it necessary to defend the ministry. Such defense must be made only in a way that is compatible with the dignity of the Spirit of God.

The story of Herod is a case in point. This ungodly king, who had yielded to the murderous spite of Herodias, and had John the Baptist beheaded, had heard of Jesus' miracles. He was curious and wanted to see Him. The opportunity presented itself when Jesus was taken from Pilate's judgement hall and sent to him for judgement. Herod desired for Jesus to perfom a miracle for him, and had He obliged him, it is quite likely that Jesus would not only have been freed, but Herod would have given Him special honors. History might have been quite different.

> Now when Herod saw Jesus, he was exceedingly glad; for he had desired for a long *time* to see Him, because he had heard many things about Him, and he hoped to see some miracle done by Him (Lk. 23:8).

Herod questioned Jesus at great length, and was obviously deeply disappointed that the Lord refused to answer him a single word. Thus, rebuffed in the presence of his men of war, Herod sent Christ back to Pilate, and from there, He went to the cross (ver. 11).

One miracle performed before Herod would have changed everything. But Jesus refused to use the gifts of God to humor or convince a wicked man. Miracles are not to be used for unworthy purposes. Gifts of healings are an expression of God's compassion for the sick, the penitent, the humble and the needy.

Always Instantaneous?

While many healings are instantaneous, it would be misleading to say all of them are, or even that all the people Jesus healed were instantly made whole.

> Then He came to Bethsaida; and they brought a blind man to Him, and begged Him to touch him. So He took the blind man by the hand and led him out of the town. And when He had spit on his eyes and put His hands on him, He asked him if he saw anything. And he looked up and said, "I see men like trees, walking." Then He put *His* hands on his eyes again and made him look up. And he was restored and saw everyone clearly (Mk. 8:22-25).

People must be encouraged to believe, even though an instantaneous miracle does not take place.

Not Praying Indiscriminately

Some challenge those who minister divine healing, saying that those who minister to the sick should visit the hospitals and sanitariums and heal everyone who is ill. Such a proposition is completely unscriptural, of course. When Jesus went to the pool of Bethesda, there were many sick people there, anxiously awaiting healing. But Jesus healed only one of them and then left. The reason He did this is obvious; He had no opportunity at Bethesda to lay the proper foundation for faith. The people wanted healing, but their attention was not on the One Who had come into their midst. Instead, it was focused on the water in the pool.

Indirect Defense Against the Forces of Opposition

Miracles of healing are an effective answer to opposition. The exercise of such a ministry has tremendous impact upon people, and often results in drawing to Christ people who have previously shown little or no interest in the Gospel. Revivals resulting from a powerful demonstration of healing occurred repeatedly in the Early Church. Because the lame man at the Beautiful Gate was healed, 5,000 believed (Acts 4:4). The miracle was also effective in preventing the Pharisees from forcefully opposing the spread of Christianity.

> But when they had commanded them to go aside out of the council, they conferred among themselves, saying, "What shall we do to these men? For, indeed, that a notable miracle has been done through them *is* evident to all who dwell in Jerusalem, and we cannot deny *it*. ... So when they had further threatened them, they let them go, finding no way of punishing them, because of the people, since they all glorified God for what had been done" (Acts 4:15, 21).

Again, in Acts 5, we are told of multitudes believing as a result of the signs and wonders performed at the hands of the apostles.

> And through the hands of the apostles many signs and wonders were done among the people. And they were all with one accord in Solomon's Porch. ... And believers were increasingly added to the Lord, multitudes of both men and women" (Acts 5:12, 14).

Although the Jewish rulers desired to stop the movement at all costs, they did not because these miracles had such an impact upon the populace, that they were afraid they would be stoned if they harmed the apostles (Acts 5:26).

Part III

The Gift of Miracles and the Gift of Prophecy

Chapter Twenty-five

The Working of Miracles

To another the working of miracles ... (I Cor. 12:10).

What is the gift of working miracles? Even a casual study of Scripture reveals that this gift has a wide scope of operation. At one end of the spectrum it merges with the gifts of healing. Certain healings that involve creative action are true miracles. At the other end of the spectrum are miraculous interventions in the very course of nature — such as breaking droughts, overruling gravity, rolling back the sea and making the sun stand still.

The gift of working miracles involves various kinds of supernatural phenomena, such as raising the dead, miracles of supply, miraculously delivering God's people and invoking special judgments against wicked people or nations.

Not to Amuse or Entertain

It is important to understand that miracles are never given for the purpose of amazing, astounding, amusing, or entertaining. They have a much more serious purpose that is compatible with God's dignity and majesty. The vulgar and cheap displays of supernatural phenomena smack of sorcery and leave no doubt that they are not of God, but are the work of depraved demon spirits.

Challengers of the apostolic ministry who want miracles performed at their whim and fancy, merely repeat the irreverent demands of the Pharisees who wanted Jesus to show them a sign from heaven. The Lord answered their request with a sharp rebuke (Matt. 16:4).

After Jesus had fasted 40 days, the devil tempted Him to make bread out of stones to prove He was the Son of God. Christ refused to make bread in order to demonstrate His power to the devil (Matt. 4:3, 4). Yet later, when the multitudes were hungry, He made bread enough to satisfy their need, and then some.

The devil also suggested that Jesus jump from the pinnacle of the temple to prove He was the Son of God, but Jesus refused to establish His claims by theatrical displays of power that would make Him appear as a superman (Matt. 4:6, 7). Yet as mentioned in a previous chapter, when His disciples were in danger at sea, He did not hesitate to overrule the forces of gravity and walk on the surface of the water to go to their aid (Matt 14:24, 25).

When Jesus was arraigned before Herod, the king was "exceedingly glad" because "he hoped to see some miracle done by Him" (Lk. 23:8). This was Jesus' last opportunity to escape the cross, but that was not His intention. Jesus knew that Herod's motives were inspired only by curiosity and superstition, not from any honest desire to know God or to do His will, so He refused to even talk with him (ver. 9).

God's Use of Natural Means

While a miracle is entirely supernatural in its source, it is in harmony with divine wisdom to use natural means in connection with the miracle. At the time of the Flood, God could have created water out of nothing to submerge the earth. Instead, He allowed two things to happen: "That day all the fountains of the great deep were broken up, and the windows of heaven were opened" (Gen. 7:11). This apparently means that natural rain came down from the clouds, as well as the oceans being affected by powerful gravitational tides.

In Moses' day, God could have used some mysterious method to force the Red Sea back and make a pathway for His people. Instead, He sent a strong east wind that made the sea become dry land (Ex. 14:21). The wind, a natural force, was used to roll the sea back, but the power that caused it to move was entirely miraculous.

When Jesus fed the 4,000, He multiplied five barley loaves and two small fish to feed the multitude (Jn. 6:9). Likewise, during Elijah's day, the widow's oil and handful of flour lasted for the remaining months of famine (I Ki. 17:10-16).

We may therefore consider it God's way to use whatever natural forces or supplies are at hand when performing a miracle. This does not in any way detract from the fact that the miracle is supernatural, for no barley loaves or fish will multiply *themselves*, so that a multitude may be fed!

Miracles Out of the Natural Realm

In his book *The Gifts of the Spirit*, Harold Horton says the following about the working of miracles:

> A miracle, therefore, is a supernatural intervention in the ordinary course of nature; a temporary suspension of the accustomed order; an interruption of the system of nature, as we know it. The gift of the working of miracles operates by the energy or dynamic force of the Spirit in reversals or suspensions of natural laws. A miracle is a sovereign act of the Spirit of God, irrespective of the laws or systems. A miracle has no explanation other than the sovereign power of the Lord. God is not bound by His own laws. God acts as He will[s] either within or outside of what we understand to be laws, whether natural or supernatural. To speak of God as though He were circumscribed by the laws of His own making is to reduce Him to the creature plane and impair the very essence of His eternal attributes. When in a sudden and sovereign act, God steps outside the circle by which His creatures or creation are boundaried, we call it a miracle. And so does God in the Scriptures.

When the Bible speaks of the gift of working miracles, it refers to miracles that are *performed through humans*. The Bible also records many miracles that occurred as the result of the sovereign action of God. That is, no human agent was used in the operation of the miracle. These supernatural interventions include such events as the destruction of Sodom and Gomorrah, the burning bush, the pillar of fire, the confusion of tongues at Babel, the appearance of the star to the wise men, etc. Since these miracles were performed entirely as divine, sovereign actions, they cannot be classified as the result of the gift of miracles in operation.

Signs, Wonders and Various Miracles

> God also bearing witness both with signs and wonders, with various miracles, and gifts of the Holy Spirit, according to His own will? (Heb. 2:4).

The various kinds of miracles tend to fall into distinct classifications. We can classify most of the miracles into the following groups:

1. Miracles of supply
2. Raising the dead
3. Miracles of judgment
4. Miracles of deliverance
5. Miracles that overrule nature

There are some miracles that are not so easily classified. For example, in certain cases the divine manifestation may be partly a miracle and partly a healing. There are also unusual or unique miracles that have happened only once, or that occur very rarely.

One of the best modern illustrations of a unique miracle is the case of Ronnie Coyne. He lost sight in his right eye as a result of an accident with a piece of barbed wire. The eye had to be removed and a plastic eye was inserted to take its place. Sometime afterward, he was prayed for by a female evangelist, Mrs. Gillock. The miracle that resulted was so outstanding that it was challenged by skeptics, but public demonstrations of his ability to see are overwhelming, unanswerable and beyond contradiction. The story taken from the February, 1954 issue of *The Voice of Healing* is as follows:

The Miracle of the Plastic Eye

In May 1950, the Coyne family moved to Sapulpa, Oklahoma. One day in August of that year, while the mother was taking a nap, she was aroused by a cry coming from her son, Ronald, who was a short distance down the street. His brother came in saying Ronald had stuck a wire into his eye.

At first the mother thought little about it, but the boy continued to cry, and late in the afternoon she noticed a white spot on the eyeball. The parents took Ronald to a doctor and later to one of the best eye specialists in Tulsa — Dr. Otis Lee at the Springer Clinic. He realized the seriousness of the accident and rushed the boy to St. John's Hospital.

Surgery was performed in an attempt to save the eye, but during the operation it was discovered that an abscess had formed and there was no way to drain it. The parents were informed that Ronald might lose the other eye, or even his life, if the infected eyeball was not removed.

For hours the mother desperately held on to God, hoping that the eye might not be lost. She would not give her consent for the removal of the eyeball, but finally her husband gave his permission for the operation to proceed. A plastic eyeball was fitted to take the place of the eye that had been removed. Four days later, Ronald went home. Since the eyeball is the eye's camera, there can be no sight once it is removed — at least, according to medical science.

About 10 months later, Ronald asked his mother the question, "If Jesus comes tonight, will I be ready?" Shortly after this he went to a Vacation Bible School and came home one day with a big smile saying, "Mother, I got saved!"

About two weeks after Ronald's salvation, the family began attending a revival in Sapulpa. Ronald had an infection in his tonsils, so his mother, not wanting to have the tonsils removed by surgery, told him to go up and be prayed for. The female evangelist, Sister Gillock, prayed for him and then noticed that something was wrong with his eye. She asked the boy if he believed the Lord could heal his eye, not knowing the eyeball had been removed and the one she saw was plastic. When Ronald said he believed he could be healed, she prayed for him to see. God heard the prayer of faith — Ronald began to see objects with his right eye! First he saw the steps, then the microphone, and then was able to count fingers.

Everyone who knew the facts was astonished. The parents and others tested him for four days. The absolute conclusion was that the boy was seeing!

Soon the news spread. The local newspapers wrote an article on the healing. Reporters came from *The Tulsa World* and *The Tulsa Tribune*, and these papers carried the story. The Lord visited the mother and told her to "go and tell the people." She took Ronald to many meetings with vast audiences, demonstrating what God had done.

At the Dallas Voice of Healing Convention in December 1952, Ronald stood before the congregation and showed the people how he was able to see through the plastic eye. I personally tested the boy a number of times, and there was no doubt in my mind that he was able to see equally well with the plastic eye in, or the plastic eye out. It was a miracle!

Ten years later, Ronald spoke at our 1962 Voice of Healing Convention at Harrisburg, Pennsylvania. He had become a fiery young evangelist, and not only delivered a splendid and anointed message, but demonstrated that the miracle still enabled him to see perfectly out of the plastic eye.

The Preservation of Clothing

"And I have led you forty years in the wilderness. Your clothes have not worn out on you, and your sandals have not worn out on your feet" (Deut. 29:5).

The miracle of the preservation of the Israelites' clothing is one of the most interesting and unique miracles, but is rarely mentioned or discussed. If the children of Israel were to remain in the wilderness for 40 years, it was necessary that they have some way to clothe themselves. There were no clothing stores or shoe shops in the desert of Sinai. Just a few months of walking on the abrasive desert sands would have worn the soles of their shoes completely through. How could this great multitude have continued the many years in the wilderness if there had not been some kind of miracle to preserve their clothing? God had foreseen this need, and through a continuous miracle, He preserved their garments and shoes during the 40 years in the wilderness.

The Miracle of the Wet and Dry Fleeces

> So Gideon said to God, "If You will save Israel by my hand as You have said — look, I shall put a fleece of wool on the threshing floor; if there is dew on the fleece only, and *it is* dry on all the ground, then I shall know that You will save Israel by my hand, as You have said." And it was so. When he rose early the next morning and squeezed the fleece together, he wrung the dew out of the fleece, a bowlful of water. Then Gideon said to God, "Do not be angry with me, but let me speak just once more: Let me test, I pray, just once more with the fleece; let it now be dry only on the fleece, but on all the ground let there be dew." And God did so that night. It was dry on the fleece only, but there was dew on all the ground (Judg. 6:36-40).

This was a very special miracle — a sign to Gideon that God would be with him in his battle against the Midianites. Many people seek to imitate Gideon by also putting out "fleeces." Sometimes they ask for a sign as to whether they should or should not do a thing which they already know is not God's will. That was the case with Balaam. This hireling prophet had already been informed by the Lord that he should not go with Balak. Yet he asked again, like a spoiled child, for permission to go.

Even Gideon showed that he knew he was carrying the matter too far, when he asked for the *second sign*, for he said, "'Do not be angry with me, but let me speak just once more ...'" (Judg. 6:39). As for Balaam, who was attracted by the king's silver and gold, God answered his insistent request with an unusual miracle — one, however, which showed His stern displeasure, rather than His approval.

Miracle of the Donkey That Talked

> Then God's anger was aroused because he went, and the Angel of the LORD took His stand in the way as an adversary against him. And he was riding on his donkey, and his two servants *were* with him. Now the donkey saw the Angel of the LORD standing in the way with His drawn sword in His hand, and the donkey turned aside out of the way and went into the field. So Balaam struck the donkey to turn her back onto the road. ... Then the LORD opened the mouth of the donkey, and she said to Balaam, "What have I done to you, that you have struck me these three times?" And Balaam said to the donkey, "Because you have abused me. I wish there were a sword in my hand, for now I would kill you!" So the donkey said to Balaam, "*Am* I not your donkey on which you have ridden, ever since I *became* yours, to this day? Was I ever disposed to do this to you?" And he said, "No." Then the LORD opened Balaam's eyes, and he saw the Angel of the LORD standing in the way with His drawn sword in His hand; and he bowed his head and fell flat on his face (Num. 22:22, 23; 28-31).

In this case, we see that God provided a miracle in response to Balaam's actions — a miracle for which he had not asked. The donkey's speaking was not a prophetic gift, for there is no record that the donkey ever spoke afterward. Neither do we have any record that a miracle of this type ever occurred again. This miracle demonstrates that if God can speak through an animal, He has the power to speak through anyone He chooses.

The Confusion of Tongues

We mention this next event, not because it was performed through the working of miracles, for there is no record that there was any human involved, but because it throws light upon God's miraculous manifestations.

On the Day of Pentecost, the 120 disciples in the Upper Room spoke in other tongues — in the languages of 17 different nations — praising and blessing God. This miracle made it possible for people who spoke these various languages to understand the new work that God was doing.

At the Tower of Babel, the miracle was similar; people began to speak in other languages. Yet in this case, the purpose was different; it was not to make the people understand each other, but to confuse them. It was an act of judgment upon the people who were in rebellion against God.

> "Come, let Us go down and there confuse their language, that they may not understand one another's speech." So the LORD scattered them abroad from there over the face of all the earth, and they ceased building the city. Therefore its name is called Babel, because there the LORD confused the language of all the earth; and from there the LORD scattered them abroad over the face of all the earth (Gen. 11:7-9).

It is interesting to note that the miracle of speaking in other tongues which may occur either as a blessing, or in this case as a judgment, may be performed as a sovereign act of God, or take place through a human agent, as we see in the laying on of hands:

And when Paul had laid hands on them, the Holy

Spirit came upon them, and they spoke with tongues and prophesied (Acts 19:6).

Though there are some unique miracles that appear in the scriptural record, most miracles fall into definite classifications.

Chapter Twenty-six

Raising the Dead

The act of raising the dead is related to, yet distinct from, the operation of the gifts of healings. In restoring life to one who has died, more than a healing miracle is required. The spirit of the departed must return to the body. Just as God determines who comes into the world, it is also His prerogative to decide whether a spirit should return once it has departed. Admittedly, occasions of the dead returning to life are rare.

God has given many promises of divine healing to His people. It is almost as universal in its application as the promise of salvation (Psalm 103:2, 3). On the other hand, though Jesus promised that His disciples would raise the dead, there is nothing to indicate that they were to do this in the same way they healed the sick.

News had come to Jesus that John the Baptist had been put in prison. Two of John's disciples arrived asking Jesus the question, "'Are You the Coming One, or do we look for another?'" (Matt. 11:3). Instead of immediately answering their question, He told them to stay and observe His ministry, and to judge for themselves whether it possessed the signs of the Messiah or not:

> Jesus answered and said to them, "Go and tell John the things which you hear and see: *The* blind see and *the* lame walk; *the* lepers are cleansed and *the* deaf hear; *the* dead are raised up and *the* poor have the gospel preached to them" (Matt. 11:4, 5).

Although Jesus told John's disciples that one of the signs of His ministry was raising the dead, when the news came that John the Baptist had been executed, He made no effort to restore him to life (Matt. 14:12). There were rumors that John would rise from the dead — rumors which had reached the ears of King Herod (Matt. 14:2). He was in the prime of life at the time of his death, but it was evidently not God's will for the prophet to be raised from the dead.

None of us born into this world are here by any merit or power of our own. No other creature is as helpless and utterly dependent on the help of others as a human newborn. When death comes as it universally does to all, man is again just as helpless. He cannot call himself back to life and once death strikes, there are few who ever return. If and when this does happen, there must be some compelling reason for it. When the heart stops beating, medical science can occasionally stimulate and restore it to action through some powerful drug. But once the spirit leaves the body, no medical ingenuity or device can bring it back. The situation is forever out of the hands of man.

Nevertheless, God can cause the human spirit to return if He so wills it. Obviously, it is not His will except in certain cases. Jesus raised Lazarus from the grave. But when the rich man requested that another Lazarus return from the dead to warn his wicked brothers to turn from their sins, the request was denied (Lk. 16:30, 31).

But God has promised that in certain cases, even in this time, the dead will be restored to life. In such circumstances, however, the person who has died usually has been dead for only a brief time. Where corruption of the body has already set in, a high type of miracle is necessary. Jesus raised Lazarus who had been dead four days. Decay was already so far advanced (Jn. 11:39) that the miracle was in reality a type of resurrection (Jn. 11:23-26). When God intends such a miracle to take place, there is usually a strong witness on the part of the one who prays that God will restore the person to life. Also, those who are raised from the dead are in most cases, though not all, comparatively young people.

We shall now study various accounts of people who died and were restored to life.

The Raising of the Widow's Son by Elijah (I Ki. 17:9-24)

The first instance the Bible describes in detail, is the case of Elijah raising the widow's son. The fact that the Prophet Elijah had been sent to the widow of Zarapheth's home indicates that she was a woman with unusual faith. Elijah's unceremonious request for her to give him the last bit of food she possessed, and her willingness to comply, certainly shows this. This last morsel of food was all that stood between them and starvation when the prophet appeared on the scene. Yet she was asked to risk what little she had, on the strength of Elijah's promise that there would be more flour in the barrel! The widow was not disappointed. She and her son lived for many days on the flour that was in the barrel.

But even though Elijah was in the house, death somehow succeeded in striking down the woman's only son. Men who are mightily used of God do not always escape embarrassing situations which may raise the question, "If the preacher has so much faith, how did this happen in his home?"

It was indeed embarrassing to Elijah. The widow, under the strain of her grief, hinted that the disaster was somehow connected to Elijah's presence. Apparently, she had committed some sin in her earlier years which weighed upon her conscience, and Elijah's austere and holy life no doubt called it to her mind:

> So she said to Elijah, "What have I to do with you, O man of God? Have you come to me to bring my sin to remembrance, and to kill my son?" (I Ki. 17:18).

Elijah found himself in a rather uncomfortable position. He was a guest in a home where he was being made indirectly responsible for the death of the son. What was he to do? Never before, as far as Elijah knew, had a dead person returned to life. Never before had the grim reaper been forced to yield its prey. But Elijah saw only one way that the situation could be fully redeemed, and he determined to seek that solution — as

273

remote as it seemed. The child must be restored to life! Let us see how the prophet went about the task.

1. He took the boy away from his mother; though she had faith, it was not the faith necessary to raise the dead. Moreover, overwhelming grief hinders the faith one has. Hysterical attempts to get prayers answered are rarely effective. We do not invoke divine power through frantic desperation. Conscious of this, Elijah wanted to get alone with God.

2. Elijah began to reason with God. Why did He allow this to happen? He made a mistake not uncommon in our day; he concluded that God had killed her son. He apparently did not realize that the devil has the power of death, a fact that has been made clear in the Church Age.

> Inasmuch then as the children have partaken of flesh and blood, He Himself likewise shared in the same, that through death He might destroy him who had the power of death, that is, the devil (Heb. 2:14).

3. Elijah was a man of action. After complaining to God, he stretched himself on the child and prayed, "'O LORD my God, I pray, let this child's soul come back to him'"(I Ki. 17:21). Elijah knew that a peculiar anointing rested upon him, and that this power, if it could be released, was able to bring the boy back to life. God did not disappoint the prophet's great faith. The boy's spirit returned and he lived again. This miracle proved to the widow that Elijah was indeed a man of God.

> Then the woman said to Elijah, "Now by this I know that you *are* a man of God, *and* that the word of the LORD in your mouth *is* the truth" (Ki. 17:24).

Raising the Dead Boy in Finland

I personally witnessed the following remarkable incident, in which a dead boy was raised to life. Concerning the accident, I wrote at the time: "I saw the boy run over by a car, moving at a fairly high rate of speed. I witnessed his being brought into our car; he was without breath or heartbeat. I witnessed William Branham pray for the child and saw the return to life as the evangelist spoke the words 'In Jesus' Name, may the spirit of this lad return to the body.'"

Other witnesses such as Jack Moore were present. The pastor of the local church, Vilho Soininen of Kuopio, Finland, who was with us at the time of the accident and saw the miracle take place, wrote the following:

> Three carloads of us made an unforgettable trip to nearby Puijo Observation Tower situated on a beautiful scenic elevation. As we were returning from Puijo, a terrible accident occurred. A car ahead was unable to avoid striking two small boys who ran out into the street in front of it, throwing one down on the sidewalk, and the other five yards away in a field. One unconscious boy was carried into a car just ahead of us, and the other, Kari Holma, was lifted into our car and placed in the arms of Brother Branham and Miss Isaacson, who were sitting in the back seat. Brothers Moore and Lindsay were in the front seat with me.
>
> As we hurried to the hospital, I asked, through Miss Isaacson the interpreter, how the boy was. Brother Branham, with his finger on the boy's pulse, answered that the boy seemed to be dead, since the pulse did not beat at all. Then he placed his hand over the boy's heart and realized that it was not functioning. He further checked the boy's respiration and could detect no breath. Then he knelt down on the floor of the car and began to pray. Brothers Lindsay and Moore prayed, too, that the Lord would have mercy. As we neared the hospital, about five or six minutes later, I glanced back, and to my surprise, the boy

opened his eyes. As we carried the boy into the hospital, he began to cry, and I realized that a miracle had taken place.

Raising the Shunammite Woman's Son (II Ki. 4)

The points of similarity between when Elijah raised the widow of Zarapheth's son and when Elisha raised the Shunammite woman's son are remarkable. This is not surprising, however, since Elisha had taken up Elijah's mantle, received a double portion of his spirit, and was now carrying on his ministry in undiminished vigor.

The Shunammite woman is spoken of by the Scriptures as a "great woman." She did not merit this description because she was famous or had worldly ambitions. Indeed, when Elisha asked if he could speak to the king for her, she replied, "'I dwell among my own people'" (II Ki. 4:13). There was no desire on her part to be great as the world calls great, or be numbered among those in high places. But there had been a deep desire in her heart to do something for the cause of Jehovah. So she provided a room for Elisha, asking nothing in return for her services.

But Elisha did learn of something that the woman had long desired — she wanted a child, although by this time, her hope had faded. The birth of a child would be a miracle, for she and her husband were up in years. Nevertheless, the prophet told her she would bear a son the following year.

The child was born as Elisha had promised. He grew and the mother's heart was happy. Yet, all the time she had an unexplained foreboding that some evil loomed ahead for the child (ver. 16, 28). Then one day, while the boy was watching the reapers, he was struck with a sudden attack of pain. He was immediately carried to his mother, and rested in her arms until noon. Then he died.

His mother was a woman of action. She had her animal saddled and rode to the man of God to tell him what had happened. This is where her great faith shows. Her husband, a good, but unimaginative man and conventional in his thinking, tried to dissuade her from making the trip by saying,

"'Why are you going to him today? *It is* neither the New Moon nor the Sabbath'" (II Ki. 4:23). The woman was not to be deterred, however, and when she found Elisha, she poured out her story. But now that the child was dead, what could Elisha do other than express his sympathy?

1. First, he sent Gehazi ahead with his staff. This suggests that a material object might absorb and retain a tangible part of the divine anointing. The staff, which had been in contact with Elisha, might carry with it sufficient healing virtue to restore the boy to life (see Acts 19:11, 12). However, even though Elisha's staff may have contained a measure of healing power, it was not sufficient to restore the child to life.

2. Elisha, upon arriving at the house, went at once to the room where the boy had been laid, and closed the door. Just as Elijah had done, Elisha shut himself away from the mother's grief. Then he prayed to the Lord. Since no promise had been given for the general raising of the dead in that age, it would seem that in this, as well as in other cases, the mind of God needed to be learned before attempting a miracle of this nature.

3. Elisha also laid upon the dead child, just as Elijah had done:

> And he went up and lay on the child, and put his mouth on his mouth, his eyes on his eyes, and his hands on his hands; and he stretched himself out on the child, and the flesh of the child became warm (II Ki. 4:34).

Here is another demonstration of the impartation of divine power through direct physical contact. Elisha prayed to the Lord for the child's spirit to return to him. The gift of faith and the gift of miracles were probably working in unison as "the flesh of the child became warm." Life had returned to the boy!

This miracle naturally had a tremendous effect upon the woman. She came in "and bowed to the ground; then she picked up her son and went out" (ver. 37).

Child Restored to Life in Mexico

My wife and I made a trip to Mexico in the spring of 1949 to personally test what reaction the deliverance ministry would have in a foreign country. We were amazed. The effect of this ministry was far beyond our expectations — churches were packed, and the people had such faith that startling miracles took place.

While we were in Monterrey, a family brought a seriously ill child to the meeting. But the crowd pressed in so tightly that it did not seem possible to get the child to the front to be prayed for. Because the child's condition had become so serious, they decided to return home. When they had nearly reached their house, the child gave a final gasp and quit breathing. Their baby was dead.

In desperate hope that God would do something, they returned to the auditorium, believing that if Jesus could perform miracles, He could restore their child to life. When the congregation learned that the baby was dead, they made a way for the parents to get to the front. At the moment, I was praying for a long line of people. My interpreter, seeing that the people were excited, interrupted to tell me that a serious case had just been brought in, and asked if I would pray for it. I did not understand that the child was dead. But when I prayed for the child, who had been very still, it suddenly began to show movement. I did not learn until a few minutes later why such excitement followed in the congregation — the Lord had brought back to life a child that was dead!

Raising the Widow of Nain's Son (Lk. 7:11-16)

Since Jesus is the resurrection and the life (Jn. 11:25), it is fitting that during His ministry, He should demonstrate His power over death, giving authenticity to His claims.

It is significant that death never had any power in Jesus' presence. Christ attended no funerals. On the contrary, Scripture records only one occasion where Jesus became part of a funeral procession. He walked up to the open coffin, touched it, spoke to the dead body, and death was broken by His presence. Death could not stand before Him except when He willingly, of His own accord, laid down His life for ours (Jn. 10:18). Even the two thieves crucified on either side of Him could not die while He was alive (Jn. 19:32, 33).

Let us notice what occurred when Jesus raised the widow of Nain's son — the first time He raised the dead.

1. The dead person was a youth, for Jesus addressed him as a "young man." Unless there is some special reason, it is the will of God for His people to live out their natural life span. This life is a school to prepare us for the world to come.

2. The young man's mother was a widow. He was an only son, and likely her only means of support. She had raised him to manhood. Now he was taken from her, and she was left alone and destitute. In sympathy for the widow, a large number of people of the city were following her to the grave to pay their last respects.

While the Scriptures do not actually state this, we may justifiably assume that the widow was a godly woman. There would be cause, therefore, for Christ, Who had been brought face to face with death that day in the city of Nain, to manifest His power over the enemy of mankind (I Cor. 15:26). It was an opportunity for the Prince of Life to show that death could not stand before Him.

3. Jesus touched the bier and the dead man sat up and began to speak! What a dramatic moment! What tears of joy and rejoicing! It is not difficult to imagine what the main topic of conversation was in the village of Nain for many days to come. They would listen again and again to the words of the young man, as he related his experiences, after he had drawn his last breath. They would ask where he had been and what he had seen after his spirit left his body.

However, the purpose of the miracle was not to create a sensation. As far as we know, Jesus had never met the widow before. He first saw her as she followed the funeral procession with her head bowed in grief. He had been moved with compassion over the plight of the sorrowing widow who was left alone and without help. By raising the dead boy, God would receive glory.

Then fear came upon all, and they glorified God, saying, "A great prophet has risen up among us"; and, "God has visited His people" (Lk. 7:16).

The Miracle of Thomas Welch

Compassion was certainly the reason for raising Thomas Welch from death, after he suffered a fatal accident while working on a trestle in a mountain village. There was nothing he had done for which he should have received mercy. Reared as an unbeliever, he had heard the gospel message before the accident but according to his own testimony, "just couldn't believe it."

At the age of 18, he went to work at a lumber mill in Bridal Veil, Oregon. One day, he was working on a high trestle 55 feet above the ground. He lost his footing and fell over backward, striking the jutting cross-members on the way down. His body was battered, bones were broken, and his skull was fractured. For a period of 20 minutes, he lay in a pool of dirty engine water. Swept along by the dark currents of the Nether World, he felt himself irresistibly gravitating into the hell which he had never believed was real. He cried to God for mercy, but it seemed the day of mercy was past, and he could see no way to escape. The moments passed. Then, to his unspeakable relief, he saw Christ coming his way. But even then, it didn't appear that the Lord would notice him. At the last moment, just before He had completely disappeared from view, Jesus turned and His compassionate gaze fell upon Thomas. At that moment, Thomas came back to life!

What had happened? Mrs. Finn Brocke, a Christian lady whose husband was an engineer at the lumber camp, had taken a deep interest in the orphan boy. She was like a mother to him, and when the news of the accident reached her, she hurried to him. All she could think of was to pray that the Lord would not let him go out of this world in his unsaved condition. The great compassion that flooded her heart gave her faith for a mighty miracle, and Thomas came back to life.

They took Thomas to the hospital, but as he says, "I didn't

die. I had already been dead." During the next four days, he did more thinking than he had ever done in his life, and he talked with God. When the Lord finally asked him if he would preach the Gospel, he answered, "Yes."

At the end of the four days, the miracle was complete. It was fully documented and amazed the physicians, as well as hundreds of others who knew about the accident. Every broken bone had been healed, and the young man went to church to testify about what God had done for him.

Thomas kept his word to preach the Gospel. I know this incident to be absolutely true, for he and I started out together in the ministry, and preached our first sermons under the same tent.

Raising Jairus' Daughter (Lk. 8:41-56)

Jarius was a ruler of a synagogue who asked Jesus to go to his home where his 12-year-old daughter lay dying. There are some significant things about this miracle. By asking Jesus to heal his daughter, he marked himself as a disciple of the Lord and brought upon himself the hostility of other religious leaders. When he came to Jesus, he knelt at His feet and worshiped Him (Matt. 9:18), thus becoming one of the very first to acknowledge Christ as worthy of worship.

On the way to his home, the woman with the issue of blood touched the hem of Jesus' garment and the procession came to a halt. The father then experienced the agony of delay. While his daughter was at the point of death, this woman touched Jesus' garment and was healed. The woman testified about her healing, and Christ used her faith as an object lesson for His listeners. The precious moments were slipping away — time was running out at Jairus' home.

There was an atmosphere of faith at the time this miracle occurred. The ruler of the synagogue had just worshiped Jesus. One woman had shown such faith in Him that she had touched the hem of His garment and received healing. The people were in a state of expectancy. We notice also that the citizens of this city had been very receptive to the message of the Lord. We are told that "the multitude welcomed Him, for they were all waiting for Him" (Lk. 8:40). But they were not looking for a miracle as great as raising a dead person to life. When the messenger announced that the girl had died, he said there was no purpose in troubling the Master any further. But Jesus said, "'Do not be afraid; only believe, and she will be made well'" (Lk. 8:50).

Upon arrival, they found the neighbors and relatives weeping in hopelessness and despair. Jesus said, "'Do not weep; she is not dead, but sleeping'" (Lk. 8:52). We say people are sleeping only when we know we can awaken them. Christ *could* awaken the dead; therefore He was able to say that the dead girl was only asleep! This, however, was beyond the comprehension of His audience.

Christ dismissed everyone from the room except Peter, James, John and the parents. Even a little unbelief can hinder a miracle like raising the dead. The parents had a hope born of desperation — a hope that is sometimes seen in the bereaved — a refusal to let go of a loved one. While others openly ridiculed the idea that any hope remained, the faith of the parents somehow rose to the occasion.

The Lord took the girl by the hand and said, "'Little girl, arise'" (ver. 54). Notice that each time Jesus required death to relinquish its prey, He limited His command to the person He was raising. Now, in answer to His command, the spirit of the young girl returned! She opened her eyes, was helped to her feet, and to the astonishment of all present, walked out of the room.

Jesus told them to feed her immediately. Even after a great miracle takes place, the recuperative powers of the body need to be put into action. Food would bring strength to her body, which had been weakened by the consuming sickness through which she had passed.

Raising Lazarus (Jn. 11)

The raising of Lazarus from the dead stands out above all other cases recorded in the Bible, except for the resurrection of Christ Himself. We are specifically informed that he had been dead four days. Martha, his sister, protested having the grave opened because in that warm climate, offensive decomposition had already set in. In the raising of Lazarus, the elements of the resurrection appear to have been involved. Certain statements found in the chapter indicate that the event may be considered a preview of the resurrection:

> Jesus said to her, "Your brother will rise again." Martha said to Him, "I know that he will rise again in the resurrection at the last day." Jesus said to her, "I am the resurrection and the life. He who believes in Me, though he may die, he shall live. And whoever lives and believes in Me shall never die. Do you believe this?" (Jn. 11:23-26).

There were many significant circumstances involved in raising Lazarus which throw light on this type of miracle.

1. Lazarus' family was devoted to the Lord. While many believed Jesus was a prophet, these friends believed He was the Messiah — the fulfillment of Old Testament prophecy (ver. 27). Mary had unusual spiritual intuition. When she sat at the feet of Jesus and listened to His words, she forgot everything else. She apparently was one of the few who truly understood the significance of His approaching death at Jerusalem, as evidenced when she anointed Jesus with the costly spikenard (Jn. 12:3). Lazarus' own devotion to Him is shown in the words the messengers spoke to Jesus, "'Lord, behold, he whom You love is sick'" (Jn. 11:3).

This was the setting for the greatest of all Jesus' miracles.

2. Jesus said that this event was "'for the glory of God, that the Son of God may be glorified through it'" (ver. 4). The raising of Lazarus reveals the compassion of Christ for all the heartbroken and grief-stricken. On the way to the tomb, He wept because of the sorrow of the people.

3. Before performing the miracle, the Lord drew forth a confession of faith. Martha was moving in the right direction when she said, "'But even now I know that whatever You ask of God, God will give You'" (ver. 22). From this she advanced to a statement of faith in the resurrection which would take place at the last day (ver. 24). She finally made the confession, "'Yes, Lord, I believe that You are the Christ, the Son of God, Who is to come into the world'" (ver. 27).

4. Then came the prayer of Christ at the grave that preceded the raising of Lazarus. When He healed the sick, we have no record that Jesus prayed individually for them. Instead, He *commanded* the sick person to be healed, and the work was done.

But in this case, Jesus paused to thank God for what was about to be done. Why did He do this? The people needed to know that what He was about to do was a work of God, not of man (ver. 42). Jesus said in John 5:19, 20 that all the miracles He performed were the work of His Father.

5. Then came the word of command. In a loud voice, Jesus cried, "'Lazarus, come forth!'" (Jn. 11:43). It has been said many times, that had the Lord not limited His command to Lazarus, all the dead would have come forth! Some day that cry *will* be made universal, and all that are in the graves will hear His voice (Jn. 5:28, 29).

In response to His command, the decaying corpse felt the impact of life-giving power! A billion cells felt the resurrection of life! The decomposing elements were chemically changed and reversed from the chaotic conditions of death to their normal arrangement. The spirit of Lazarus returned to his body and heard the command to come forth. The dead arose, hampered only by the grave clothes which were quickly removed by eager friends.

Can you imagine the dramatic moment, the excitement, the joyful cries that rang out from those who a moment before had been weeping around the grave? Tears of sorrow became tears of joy.

Bringing a Sister Back to Life
This great biblical miracle brings to mind the incident when John G. Lake's sister passed away. He tells the story in his own words:

I sometimes have thought that there was no other circumstance in my own life that ever called out so much faith in God and determination of soul to see God's will done, as in the healing of a sister. One of my sisters and I had been chums from our childhood; she was a little older than I. The vision of Christ as the Healer had just opened to my soul.

She was dying of an issue of blood. My mother called me one night and said, "John, if you want to see your sister alive, you must come at once." When I arrived, my mother said, "You are too late, she is gone." I stepped to her bedside, and laid my hand on her forehead; it was cold and white. I slipped my hand down over her heart; it had ceased to beat. I picked up a small mirror and held it over her mouth, but there was no discoloration. The breath was gone. I stood there stunned. Her husband knelt at the foot of the bed weeping. Her baby was asleep in the crib at the opposite side of the room. My old father and mother knelt, sobbing at the side of the bed. They had seen eight of their children die; she was apparently the ninth. My soul was in a storm.

Just a few weeks before, my wife had been healed when almost dead. Prior to that, my brother had been healed, after having been an invalid for 22 years. A short time before that, my older sister, with five cancers in the breast, who had been operated on five times and given up to die, was healed. As I looked at this sister, I said, "O God, this is not Your will. I cannot accept it! It is the work of the devil and darkness. It is the devil who has the power of death."

I discovered this strange fact, that there are times when one's spirit lays hold on the spirit of another. Somehow, I just felt my spirit lay hold of the spirit of that sister. And I prayed, "Dear Lord, she cannot go." I walked up and down the room for some time. My spirit was crying out for somebody with faith in God that I could call upon to help me.

As I walked up and down my sister's room, I could think of but one man who had faith on this line. That was John Alexander Dowie, six hundred miles away. I went to the phone, called Western Union and told them I wanted to get a telegram through to Doctor Dowie with an answer back as quickly as possible. I sent this wire: "My sister has apparently died, but my spirit will not let her go. I believe if you will pray, God will heal her."

I received this answer back: "Hold on to God. I am praying. She will live."

I have said a thousand times, what would it have meant if instead of that telegram of faith, I had received one from a weakling preacher who might have said: "I am afraid you are on the wrong track," or, "Brother, you are excited," or, "The days of miracles are past."

It was the strength of his faith that came over the wire and while I stood at the telephone and listened, the very lightnings of God began to flash in my spirit. I prayed, "This is of hell, it cannot be, it will not be. In the name of Jesus Christ, I abolish this death and sickness, and she shall live."

As I finished praying, I turned my eyes toward the bed, and I saw her eyelids blink. But I was so wrought up, I said, "Maybe I am deceiving myself." So I stood a little while at the telephone, the lightnings of God still flashing through my soul. Presently, I observed her husband get up and tiptoe to her head, and I knew that he had seen it. I said, "What is it, Peter?" He replied, "I thought I saw her eyelids move." And just then they moved again. Five days later, she came to father's home and the Lake family sat down to Christmas dinner, the first time in their lives when they all were well.

Raising Dorcas (Acts 9:36-43)

In the Apostolic Church, there was a woman named Dorcas who was noted for her unselfishness and devotion to good deeds and works. Dorcas became sick and died. The grieving Church felt that they could not afford to lose such a worthy worker. Why should she be cut off in the middle of her years, when they needed her so badly? Jesus had raised certain people from the dead, and had promised that His disciples would do the same (Matt. 10:8). Perhaps the Lord would give Dorcas back to them. Peter was not far away, and messengers were immediately dispatched requesting he come at once.

When Peter arrived, the people were weeping and "showing the tunics and garments which Dorcas had made while she was with them" (Acts 9:39). He was apparently impressed by their recital of the virtues of this woman of God, and his faith was challenged to believe God for a miracle. However, the weeping and grieving were not going to change things. As Christ did at the home of Jairus, Peter sent out the mourners. Then he knelt down and prayed.

Convinced that God would perform a miracle, he turned to the body and gave the command, "'Tabitha, arise'"(ver. 40). Dorcas opened her eyes and Peter helped her get up. He then called the saints and presented her alive (ver. 41). This miracle caused a stir throughout the countryside, and many were converted to Christ. "And it became known throughout all Joppa; and many believed on the Lord" (ver. 42).

Eutychus Raised From the Dead (Acts 20:7-12)

We now come to the final incident recorded in the Scriptures of a person being restored to life. Paul was occasionally a lengthy speaker. At Troas, he "continued his message until midnight" (Acts 20:7). Eutychus, a young man, went to sleep. Unfortunately, he chose the wrong place to fall asleep. As he drowsed in a window, he lost his balance and fell to the ground three stories below. Those who picked him up pronounced him dead.

Paul, however, went down and fell on the boy, embracing him and asking for God to restore him to life. The apostle realized that this would probably be the last time he would be in this city, and he certainly did not want the people to associate his last visit with the death of a young man who went to sleep because of his long preaching. What seemed to be a disaster turned into a miracle. Paul told the people that life was still in Eutychus. Then he returned, to preach until dawn! By that time, the young man had fully recovered.

This incident is especially interesting, since it shows how God grants extraordinary miracles when the need arises. Paul may have felt somewhat responsible for the young man's death, and therefore, believed that God would answer his prayer and restore him to life — he was not disappointed.

Chapter Twenty-seven

The Plague Miracles

The story of Moses gives us much valuable information concerning the working of the gift of miracles, especially in the matter of the following 10 plagues that fell upon Egypt as punishment for its wickedness and its cruel treatment of God's people, Israel:

1. The plague of water turned to blood (Ex. 7:20-25).
2. The plague of frogs (Ex. 8:1-5).
3. The plague of lice (Ex. 8:16-19).
4. The plague of flies (Ex. 8:20-24).
5. The plague of the death of livestock (Ex. 9:1-7).
6. The plague of boils (Ex. 9:8-12)
7. The plague of hail (Ex. 9:13-35).
8. The plague of locusts (Ex. 10:1-20).
9. The plague of darkness (Ex. 10:21-23).
10. The plague of the death of the first-born (Ex. 11; 12).

Now let us consider what these 10 plagues teach us about the gift of working miracles.

This Was Not the Gift of Faith

Moses probably received the gift of faith later, during his stay on the Mount, but it was not the gift in operation during the 10 plagues that came upon Egypt.

Notice how timid and reluctant Moses was regarding the commission God had given him. He made excuses, telling the Lord that he was slow of speech and therefore could not effectively present Israel's case to Pharaoh (Ex. 4:10). He did not feel that his people, who were groaning under the heavy hand of slavery, would listen to him. Lacking self-confidence, he asked the Lord for someone who was able to speak better than he could to act as his spokesman (Ex. 4:13). After the first confrontation with Pharaoh, Moses returned discouraged. It appeared to him that he had accomplished nothing, except to further stir up Pharaoh's enmity.

> So Moses returned to the LORD and said, "LORD, why have You brought trouble on this people? Why *is* it You have sent me? For since I came to Pharaoh to speak in Your name, he has done evil to this people; neither have You delivered Your people at all"(Ex. 5:22, 23).

Moses did not manifest the quiet assurance that is inherent in the gift of faith.

New Dispensations are Ushered in with Supernatural Events

It seems to be in accordance with the divine purpose that when a new dispensation is ushered in, it is accomplished and marked with special supernatural events. These events may occur as sovereign manifestations of God, or they may transpire through the working of miracles. The miracle of the burning bush was a sovereign manifestation of God, but the visitation of the plagues was accomplished through the gift of working miracles.

There were supernatural manifestations in the days of Enoch and Noah. Likewise, miraculous events occurred while Christ was on earth and at the beginning of the Church Age. Today, as the Second Coming draws near, there has been a revival of the miracle ministry. This no doubt will increase as time goes on. This gift will also be powerfully manifested in the ministry of the two witnesses during the Great Tribulation.

Man Takes the Initiative in the Working of Miracles

God took the initiative in sending the judgment of the Flood. This was also true of the destruction of Sodom and Gomorrah, which was accomplished through two angels sent for that purpose. But in the working of miracles it is man who takes the initiative, even though he performs the miracles at God's command.

Notice the first Egyptian plague when the waters were turned to blood. The Lord said, "'Say to Aaron, "Take your rod and stretch out your hand over the waters of Egypt ... that they may become blood ...."'" (Ex. 7:19). Nothing happened until Aaron "lifted up the rod and struck the waters that *were* in the river" (ver. 20). Then, and only then, did the waters turn to blood.

When the Israelites needed to cross the Red Sea in order to escape the Egyptian army, Moses encouraged the children of Israel to believe for their deliverance. Yet instead of lifting up his rod and dividing the sea, as he should have done, Moses resorted to prayer. The Lord showed him that there is a time to pray and a time to act! Notice the Lord's words:

> And the LORD said to Moses, "Why do you cry to Me? Tell the children of Israel to go forward. But lift up your rod, and stretch out your hand over the sea and divide it. And the children of Israel shall go on dry *ground* through the midst of the sea" (Ex. 14:15, 16).

Satan Can Imitate Some Miracles

The events that occurred during the 10 plagues reveal that Satan has power to imitate some miracles, although his power has definite limitations. When Aaron threw the rod down before Pharaoh, it became a snake, but Pharaoh's magicians did the same thing! Through the magic and enchantments of the magicians, Satan was able to duplicate this astonishing feat and thus nullify the miracle's effect upon Pharaoh. However, there was one difference which showed the supremacy of Jehovah: "Aaron's rod swallowed up their rods" (Ex. 7:12).

The magicians were able to imitate the plague of blood also (Ex. 7:22). This work of the magicians effectively kept Pharaoh blind to the fact that God was behind Moses' demands, so he hardened his heart and went on to receive further judgments.

When Aaron lifted up his rod and frogs came up out of the

waters and covered the land of Egypt, the magicians successfully imitated this plague also (Ex. 8:7).

Pharaoh was convinced that Moses and Aaron had certain mystical powers, but the fact that his magicians were able to duplicate their miracles convinced him that it was all the same kind of magic. Moses apparently just had a little stronger kind.

A fact to be observed here is the delusive power of sorcery, which today is called spiritualism. People who dabble in it soon lose the ability to discriminate between the supernatural and the psychic. Miracles of God have little effect upon them because they have lost their moral sensibilities, and they conclude that everything supernatural is of the same nature. Demonic manifestations have power to astonish, but they bring no moral conviction. Those who deal with these deceiving spirits soon lose all conception of God as holy.

When invoking the third plague, Aaron lifted up his rod and struck the dust, turning it into lice. But when the magicians tried to do this with their enchantments, they failed. They had gone as far as they could go (Ex. 8:17, 18). God has set definite limits to Satan's power.

Pharaoh's sorcerers were now convinced that what they were up against was "the finger of God," and they told Pharaoh so. But their own magic had contributed to bringing Pharaoh into a state of delusion and madness. He was beyond persuasion. He had hardened his heart to the point of no remedy.

Miracles are a Sign

At the burning bush, the Lord explained to Moses that he would be given certain miracles to perform as signs to Pharaoh. But as God forewarned, the stubborn monarch hardened his heart and refused to pay attention to them.

The Lord has also given certain miracles to the Church, to confirm the Word and convince the unbelievers.

> And they went out and preached everywhere, the Lord working with *them* and confirming the word through the accompanying signs (Mk. 16: 20).

Miracles do one of two things; they either convince and bring people to repentance, or they harden and make them like Pharaoh — irrevocably unrepentant. The great miracles of Christ in the cities of Capernaum, Bethsaida and Chorazin produced many believers, including James, John, Peter and Andrew. However, many people were deeply absorbed in acquiring material things. These cities which were located on the great trade routes, were flourishing and prosperous, offering unusual opportunities to gain wealth. Even though the people's curiosity was aroused at the time, they soon settled back into a state of worldliness and unconcern. As a consequence, these communities received a very solemn denunciation from Christ.

> "Woe to you, Chorazin! Woe to you, Bethsaida! For if the mighty works which were done in you had been done in Tyre and Sidon, they would have repented long ago in sackcloth and ashes. ... And you, Capernaum, who are exalted to heaven, will be brought down to Hades; for if the mighty works which were done in you had been done in Sodom, it would have remained until this day" (Matt. 11:21, 23).

The Working of Miracles and Obedience to God

It is assumed by many people that anyone exercising the gift of miracles must be walking close to God and can do no wrong. Actually, a person to whom the working of miracles is given has moved into the realm of the heavenlies, and is especially vulnerable to satanic attack. Such people have a serious responsibility to walk in close obedience to God.

After Moses met with the Lord at the burning bush and received his commission, it was his solemn duty to stay in covenant relationship with God. Yet Moses neglected the very foundational sign of the covenant relationship — circumcision. Spiritual carelessness can have the most serious consequences.

Just before Israel was to be delivered, Moses' first-born

had a close brush with death. The child had not been circumcised and was therefore outside of covenant. His mother, however, took a sharp stone, performed the operation, and saved the child's life.

> And it came to pass on the way, at the encampment, that the LORD met him and sought to kill him. Then Zipporah took a sharp stone and cut off the foreskin of her son and cast *it* at *Moses'* feet, and said, "Surely you *are* a husband of blood to me!" So He let him go. Then she said, "*You are* a husband of blood!" — because of the circumcision (Ex. 4:24-26).[1]

---

[1]Modern translations of the Bible translate this passage of Scripture to mean that the Lord tried to kill Moses, not the child, and that Zipporah saved her *husband's* life by circumcising her son.

Chapter Twenty-eight

Miracles in the Life of Samson

Samson, with his miracle ministry, is in a class all by himself. His birth and ministry were announced by an angel, but his life and work are hard to explain. He was a Nazarite, yet he continually violated his vow of separation by indulging his fleshly appetites. As Samson grew into manhood, he desired a wife from the Philistines, Israel's mortal enemies. "And Samson said to his father, 'Get her for me, for she pleases me well'" (Judg. 14:3). That was Samson's besetting sin: When he wanted something, he was determined to get it regardless of the consequences. We may wonder why the Lord chose Samson in the first place. Yet his story helps us to understand how some ministers, mightily used of God, can allow themselves to become victims of their fleshly appetites. The story of Samson is a warning of how great the penalty is for giving in to carnal temptations.

Samson's Strength

The miracle of Samson was his amazing physical strength. When Daniel was thrown into the lion's den, he was protected from the hungry lions. In Samson's case, the Spirit of the Lord came upon him and gave him strength to kill a young lion that came roaring against him.

> And the Spirit of the LORD came mightily upon him, and he tore the lion apart as one would have torn apart a young goat, though *he had* nothing in his hand (Judg. 14:6).

In Daniel's case, the gift of faith was in operation. In Samson's, it was the working of miracles.

Samson, in a way, was a child of nature. By some kind of

cunning, he was able to trap 300 foxes. Tying them tail to tail, he fastened torches to them and let the foxes run through the standing grain of the Philistines, setting their fields on fire (Judg. 15:4, 5).

The Philistines decided to teach Samson a lesson by burning his wife and her father with fire. He retaliated, and single-handedly "attacked them hip and thigh with a great slaughter" (Judg. 15:8). We may note that Samson's motto was not the Golden Rule, but one quite different: "'As they did to me, so I have done to them'" (ver. 11).

The children of Israel, fearing that the Philistines would take vengeance on them for Samson's exploits, decided to deliver him into their hands. He seemed to realize that his great strength was not to be used against his own countrymen, and allowed them to bind him with new cords (ver. 12, 13). The gifts of the Spirit are never to be used against the people of God, except when flagrant acts have been committed requiring divine discipline.

When the Philistines were ready to kill Samson, "the Spirit of the LORD came mightily upon him; and the ropes that *were* on his arms became like flax that is burned with fire, and his bonds broke loose from his hands" (ver. 14). Then Samson took a jawbone of a donkey and killed 1,000 Philistines with it. After this tremendous exertion, he was about to die from thirst. He cried to God and water flowed from a hollow place (ver. 19). The Philistines by this time had had enough, and there was apparently a long period of quiet lasting for nearly 20 years (ver. 20).

But Samson never quite got victory over his besetting sin. The Philistines could not subdue him, but the prostitutes of Philistia accomplished what their army could not. Samson went down to Gaza and slept with a prostitute (Judg. 16:1). The Philistines knew Samson was there and surrounded the place where he was. Nevertheless, his great strength remained with him. At midnight, he arose and took the doors of the gate of the city and the two gate posts, and like a youth playing pranks, carried them to the top of a hill that faces Hebron.

Samson was like some people today who will condone sin

as long as they seem to be getting away with it. Yet, as the saying goes, "The mills of God grind slowly, but they grind exceedingly fine." Before long, Samson would participate in the grinding.

Samson and Delilah

The last stage of Samson's drama was about to unfold. The carnal prophet slept with another temptress by the name of Delilah. It was getting easy for Samson to believe that he could do as he pleased. He seemed to have a charmed life. So it was that as "an ox to the slaughter," he went down to Delilah's house to sleep upon her knees. This totally unscrupulous woman, through the employment of her seductive charms, learned the secret of his great strength, and while he slept, she had his hair cut.

> And she said, "The Philistines *are* upon you, Samson!" So he awoke from his sleep, and said, "I will go out as before, at other times, and shake myself free!" But he did not know that the LORD had departed from him (Judg. 16:20).

Samson shook himself all right, but no one else shook. The Philistines took him, put out his eyes, bound him with fetters of brass, and made him grind grain in the prison.

The story is not quite finished, however. Samson's hair began to grow again, and later, when the Philistines brought Samson out to make fun of him at one of their heathen festivals, he asked the Lord for one more chance to avenge himself of his enemies. He reached out his arms and pulled on the two key pillars in the center of the temple. The building fell upon the lords of the Philistines, as well as on himself. "So the dead that he killed at his death were more than he had killed in his life" (Judg. 16:30).

There are a number of important truths in the story of Samson that can help us to understand certain things about the gift of working miracles.

1. People who are given the gift of working miracles are

usually specially prepared for their ministry by the Lord.

2. Certain operations of the gift are peculiar to particular people. With Samson, it was a manifestation of great physical strength. But Samson's gift was not exclusively confined to the area of strength, as shown when the water miraculously flowed out of the hollow place to quench his thirst.

3. An especially powerful anointing of the Holy Spirit usually accompanies the gift.

4. Samson was a Nazarite, indicating that one whom God prepares for a miracle ministry should live a separated life. An individual is in grave danger if the separation is defiled.

5. People who have the gift of working miracles, may violate their vow of separation and still manifest their gift for a time. This was true in Samson's case.

6. Eventually, disobedience will weaken any person. Sin grieves the Holy Spirit. In time, He may depart from the person walking in disobedience as He did from Samson. Without the Holy Spirit, the gift cannot operate successfully.

7. People may not immediately recognize that the Spirit has left, and like Samson, may "shake themselves" and think that they can do as they have done before. Eventually, however, they will discover that their power is gone.

8. When people truly repent, they may, like Samson, have a temporary return of their old ministry. Often, however, if they have lived a long time in sin, it will only be a shadow of what it once was. Samson had one more great miracle, and then it was all over.

Defiling the Separation

I am reminded of a man once mightily endowed with the Holy Spirit, with results perhaps equaling that of any other minister in America. But with his great success, he became overconfident and felt he no longer needed the counsel of those who had helped to get him to the top. On his own, he felt free to order his life as he pleased. For a time, God's blessing was upon him. The usual sycophants clustered around him and told him what a great man he was. Soon, he reached a place where he was completely unaware that the devil was slowly closing the trap. Pitfalls lay ahead, but he didn't know it. Like Samson, he developed a relationship with a woman who was not his wife. He returned to secular employment — another Samson, once wonderfully used of God, who found himself grinding in the mill of lost opportunity!

Chapter Twenty-nine

Miracles of Supply

Throughout the Bible, we find accounts in which God, by supernatural means, provided for His people. One of God's seven great redemptive names which He revealed to the children of Israel is "Jehovah-Jireh" — the Lord will provide (Gen. 22:14).

During his harrowing experiences in the wilderness, the psalmist, David, learned to say, "The LORD *is* my shepherd; I shall not want" (Psa. 23:1). Christ taught His disciples to put their trust in the God Who fed the sparrows and clothed the lilies of the field. His ability to provide for His children in time of need, even when miraculous means are required, is just the same today.

In considering the supplying of needs through the supernatural gift of working miracles, we are dealing with a very practical matter — one that any child of God may face sometime during his lifetime.

The Manna Miracle
One of the first miracles of supply recorded in the Scriptures was when God sent the manna to feed the children of Israel.

> Then the LORD said to Moses, "Behold, I will rain bread from heaven for you. And the people shall go out and gather a certain quota every day, that I may test them, whether they will walk in My law or not" (Ex. 16:4).

There are a number of valuable lessons to be learned from this miracle, which was witnessed by the children of Israel each day for 40 years. God wants us to depend upon Him daily.

Thus Jesus taught His disciples to pray: "'Give us this day our daily bread'" (Matt. 6:11). While God does not require us to live hand-to-mouth, neither does He want us to depend on laid-up wealth, so that we are trusting in our riches rather than in God. Therefore, He told the children of Israel that (with the exception of the Sabbath) they were to gather the manna *daily*. Some of the people disobeyed these instructions, thinking they should gather enough to last for several days, just in case something went wrong! Those who did this found that the manna they had stored in their tents "bred worms, and stank" (Ex. 16:20). Others were lazy and failed to gather enough for the Sabbath, the day which God had set aside for them to rest. Then they violated the Sabbath by going out to gather manna on that day (Ex. 16:26-30).

Those who insist on working every day of the week not only incur the displeasure of God, but will find that their own body suffers for their failure to give it proper rest.

It should also be observed that a miracle of supply is given only when it is definitely needed. One who already has a full table should not expect a miracle of supply to be performed. The very day the children of Israel ate the corn of the land of Canaan, the manna which had appeared over 12,000 times, ceased to fall.

Note that the manna was a beautiful type of Christ, the Bread from heaven which "gives life to the world."

> Then Jesus said to them, "Most assuredly, I say to you, Moses did not give you the bread from heaven, but My Father gives you the true bread from heaven. For the bread of God is He who comes down from heaven and gives life to the world" (Jn. 6:32, 33).

Water From the Rock

The children of Israel had journeyed until they were deep in the desert of Sinai. News came that the fierce warriors of Amalak were on their way to contest their passage through the wilderness. To make matters worse, the report circulated through the camp that there was no water to drink. The lack of water soon precipitated a desperate crisis; the people murmured against Moses, saying that they were about to die from thirst. In fact, we are told that some of the people were ready to stone their leader (Ex. 17:4). It was then that the Lord told Moses what he should do:

> "Behold, I will stand before you there on the rock in Horeb; and you shall strike the rock, and water will come out of it, that the people may drink." And Moses did so in the sight of the elders of Israel (Ex. 17:6).

Just as the manna was a type of Christ, so was the rock that gave the water. Striking the rock typified the crucifixion of Christ. On the cross, Jesus' side was pierced with a spear, and blood and water came out (Jn. 19:34). The Lamb of God suffered *once* to put away sin, and may not be crucified again (Heb. 6:6). Therefore, Moses was only to strike the rock once. Here, we see the possiblity for the gift of miracles to be misused.

All was well the first time the miracle of water coming out of the rock occurred. However, the second time the congregation was without water, trouble occurred. The Lord commanded Moses to bring water out of a rock again, but the rock had already been struck once. This time God's command was, "'Speak to the rock before their eyes, and it will yield its water; thus you shall bring water for them out of the rock ...'" (Num. 20:8).

But Moses was angry with the children of Israel, and instead of following God's instructions and speaking to the rock, he struck it as he had done before (ver. 11). Moses had made a great mistake. In consequence, the Lord said to him, "'Because you did not believe Me, to hallow Me in the eyes of the children of Israel, therefore you shall not bring this assembly into the land which I have given them'" (ver. 12).

Therefore, is it not clear that a minister may perform miracles, yet manifest the gift in the wrong way? If God is not given the glory, even though the miracle comes to pass, there may be consequences for misusing the gift of God.

The Meal in the Barrel

During the famine, Elijah hid himself by the Brook Cherith. Twice a day, the ravens brought him flesh to eat. This, in itself, was a miracle of supply, but it was apparently associated with the gift of faith, rather than the working of miracles. This did not go on indefinitely. After a time, the brook dried up. Without water, Elijah would die. So God commanded the prophet to go to a widow of Zarephath, who would sustain him.

Elijah found, upon arrival, that this widow was one of the poorest inhabitants of the country, and the most unlikely prospect he could have found to give him help. In fact, all she and her son had left between themselves and starvation was "a handful of flour in a bin, and a little oil in a jar" (I Ki. 17:12). She told Elijah that she was about to make this into a little cake, "'that we may eat it, and die.'"

Elijah told her to go ahead and make the cake, only she was to give it to him! Then she could make cakes for herself and her son. What kind of proposition was this? It was a profound lesson on giving. If we want God to perform miracles of supply, we must show Him that we completely trust Him and are willing to give Him all we have if He asks — even if it seems to mean great sacrifice.

It must have been a real test for the woman to take the last food in her house and give it to Elijah, instead of keeping it for her son and herself. Nevertheless, she took the risk, and when she looked into the flour barrel again, there was still flour in it, just as Elijah had said (I Ki. 17:14, 16).

Jesus mentioned this miracle in His sermon to the people of Nazareth. He was pointing out the truth that people who have few opportunities often have more faith than those who have enjoyed great privileges.

> "But I tell you truly, many widows were in Israel
> in the days of Elijah, when the heaven was shut
> up three years and six months, and there was a

great famine throughout all the land; but to none of them was Elijah sent except to Zarephath, *in the region* of Sidon, to a woman *who was* a widow" (Lk. 4:25, 26).

The Widow's Oil Increased

A widow of one of the sons of the prophets went to Elisha in deep distress. Her husband had died in debt, and for payment, the creditors had come to take her two sons as slaves. She was desperate and went to Elisha for help.

Elisha asked, "'What shall I do for you? Tell me, what do you have in the house?'" (II Ki. 4:2). *Miracles of supply begin with what is at hand.* This principle is illustrated in many of the biblical miracles:

- When Elisha miraculously fed 100 men, he began with 20 loaves of barley (II Ki. 4:42).
- When Jesus turned the water into wine, He commanded that the pots first be filled with water (Jn. 2:7).
- When Jesus fed the 5,000, He began with five loaves of bread and two fish (Matt. 14:17).
- When Jesus fed the 4,000, He received and broke the seven loaves and a few little fish (Matt. 15:34).

Elisha was ready to help the widow, but first asked her what she had in the house. She replied that all she had was a jar of oil (II Ki. 4:2). He told her, "'Go borrow vessels from everywhere, from all your neighbors — empty vessels; do not gather just a few'" (ver. 3). Here is a very important lesson on the working of miracles. You cannot receive more than you have faith for. Elisha told the woman why she should gather the vessels; she was to pour the oil from the full vessel into the empty ones!

If her faith was small, she would probably only borrow from her nearest neighbors. But if her faith was large, she would take the trouble to visit her more distant friends. We are not told how many vessels she and her sons were able to collect, but apparently, the number was considerable. Faith is an act. Our actions show how much faith we have.

Elisha told the widow to close the door behind herself and her sons before she started pouring out the oil (ver. 4). Miracles are not performed to satisfy curiosity seekers, or convince the skeptic. Some of the greatest miracles occur before the smallest audiences, not because God doesn't want to bless the multitude, but because a miracle performed before a carnal audience sometimes produces the wrong effect.

The woman kept pouring the oil into the pots, and when the last vessel was filled, "the oil ceased" (ver. 6).

There is a story about a woman who was known throughout the community as a devoted Christian with strong faith that God would always supply her need. There was also an unbeliever in the same town who was well-known for his opposition to Christianity. He mocked at the thought that God would answer the prayers of His people.

One day, the woman found herself with a serious problem. She was completely out of food, and there was no immediate prospect of replenishing her cupboard. She fell on her knees and asked God, who had never failed her, to supply her need.

As chance would have it, the unbeliever was passing by her open window and overheard her prayer. He paused to listen as she itemized the various things she needed. The skeptic was struck by the idea that it would be a good joke to trick the woman by securing the very things that she had prayed for himself. When the woman saw them on her porch, she would likely conclude that the Lord had answered her prayer. He would then appear from his hiding place and show her that it was *not* the Lord who had answered her prayer.

So he carried out his plan, and everything happened exactly as he anticipated. When the woman opened her door and discovered the exact things she had requested, she threw her hands in the air and began praising the Lord. The unbeliever stepped from concealment nearby, and proceeded to inform the woman that the Lord had not sent the groceries. It was he who had heard her praying, and had put them on her doorstep just to show her it was not the Lord who answered her prayers.

The woman's faith, however, was completely undisturbed

by this revelation. She squelched the unbeliever once and for all by saying, "I still believe the Lord answered my prayer and sent these things, even if He used the devil to deliver them!"

Miracle of the Water Turned to Wine

When considering this remarkable miracle, it is important, first of all, to determine what kind of wine Christ made. The Bible, as well as the dictionary, clearly shows that there are two kinds of wine.

Funk and Wagnall College Standard Dictionary says, "*Wine* — the expressed juice of grapes, fermented or *unfermented*."

Webster's New Collegiate Dictionary says, "Wine — the fermented or loosely the *unfermented* juice of fruit used as a beverage."

It is obvious for many reasons that the wine Jesus made was unfermented.

1. As the dictionary shows, wine may be fermented or unermented, just as cider may be sweet or hard. Why do some stubbornly insist it must have been fermented? In most cases, they take this view to excuse their own use of alcohol.

2. The Bible constantly disapproves of drinking alcoholic beverages (Prov. 23:31; Lev. 10:9, 10). Jesus would not disobey its injunctions.

3. It is incredible that the Lord would have manufactured a hundred gallons of alcoholic wine that probably would have resulted in a drunken scene among the wedding guests. Think of it — Christ starting newlyweds out in married life in the midst of a scene of intoxication for which He was responsible!

4. Christ drank unfermented wine, but refused the fermented wine (Mk. 15:23).

5. Jesus' attendance at the wedding was not an endorsement of drinking alcohol, as seen in His startling answer to His mother, Mary, when she told Him, "'They have no wine'" (Jn. 2:3). He replied in words that have been considered harsh, "'Woman, what does your concern have to do with Me? My hour has not yet come'" (ver. 2:4). Yet, in the light of the context, these were the very words demanded by the occasion. Christ, the Holy One, had reacted sharply to the implied sug-

gestion that He make more of the kind of wine the company had been drinking — alcoholic wine! So degrading are the results of drinking alcohol, that such a suggestion deserved a rebuke, even if His mother was the one who made it.

Then what kind of wine did Christ produce at the wedding feast? Jesus taught, if He taught anything at all, that people should live holy and sober lives. He warned them lest He come upon them in reveling and drunkenness. Perish the thought that He would overthrow all that He had ever taught on the subject by one act! Remember that the six water pots which held 18 to 27 gallons apiece were equivalent to about 100 gallons! This would be more than enough wine to intoxicate the whole party if the wine were the fermented kind.

But according to John 2:11, *the miracle brought glory to God.* He actually produced fresh wine, a delicious and wholesome beverage. Newly made wine is always nonalcoholic; it is not the intoxicating kind produced by the excretion of bacteria. Christ supplied a refreshing drink that left the guests for the better and not for the worse!

The Miracle of Feeding 5,000

There were two notable occasions in Christ's ministry when large multitudes were fed by miraculous means. These remarkable miracles were not the first of their kind. There is a lesser-known miracle recorded in II Kings 4:42-44, in which Elisha fed a large company of people with 20 loaves of barley bread. Let us now consider the miracle performed by Christ.

This remarkable incident occurred in an uninhabited region some distance from a town or village. Matthew tells us it was a "desert place." The people were so anxious to hear Jesus that they had journeyed this considerable distance far from available food supplies.

The disciples, realizing that the day was rapidly waning, suggested dismissing the multitude so they could go find food for themselves (Matt. 14:15). Apparently, Philip had become most concerned, for he discussed with Jesus how the people were to be fed. He said, "'Two hundred denarii worth of bread is not sufficient for them, that every one of them may have a little'" (Jn. 6:7).

Andrew called attention to the fact that the only food on hand was five loaves of barley bread and two small fish that had been brought by a little boy (Jn. 6:9). But Christ did not reject the offer.

Jesus instructed the disciples to have the people sit down in groups of 100s and 50s (Mk. 6:40). This was a matter of good judgment. When handling a large number of people, proper organization is important; it is advisable to employ methods that will avoid disorder and confusion.

Notice another beautiful symbol taught here — the giving of thanks before eating. "And Jesus took the loaves, and when He had given thanks He distributed *them* to the disciples" (Jn. 6:11). By this act, Jesus set the example that all Christians should offer grace before they begin their meals.

But more than that, in this situation, a miracle was about to be performed. God should always be sanctified before the people. *It is of urgent importance that when a miracle is performed, the attention of the people be directed Godward, not manward.* The Lord must always be the One Who receives the glory.

When the multitude was filled and satisfied, Jesus commanded the disciples, "'Gather up the fragments that remain, so that nothing is lost.' Therefore they gathered *them* up, and filled twelve baskets with the fragments ... " (Jn. 6:12, 13).

The benefits of a miracle should be carefully preserved. They are not to be treated carelessly. Those who think lightly of miracles may some day need one, but it will not be given them, even though they cry desperately for it.

The miracle of the loaves and fishes convinced the people that Christ was the prophet whom the Scriptures had promised would come into the world (Jn. 6:14). Unfortunately, the enthusiasm that the miracle produced was superficial. Some were ready to take Jesus by force, if necessary, and put a crown on His head. Had Jesus permitted this, it would have resulted in a bloody civil war — something completely alien to His purpose for coming into the world.

The Lord discerned their real motives and said, "'You seek Me, not because you saw the signs, but because you ate of the loaves and were filled'" (Jn. 6:26). Those who wanted to make Christ king were the "loaves and fishes" crowd. He warned them, "'Do not labor for the food which perishes, but for the food which endures to everlasting life, which the Son of Man will give you'" (ver. 27).

Miracle of Financial Provision

The children of Israel once asked the question, "Can God set a table in the wildernes" Ever since then a similar question has been asked by people, "Can God supernaturally provide for the financial needs of His children?"

When Jesus sent the disciples out, two by two, to prepare the way for Him, He told them to take neither silver nor gold in their money belt (Matt. 10:9). In this way, He showed them that God could miraculously provide for their needs. At the close of His ministry, He rescinded this command and told them that from now on, they should take their money belts (Lk. 22:35, 36).

What was Christ trying to teach His disciples? First, that God can take care of His people, even if they are absolutely penniless. Nevertheless, since His ministers were not to become objects of curiosity, living mysteriously without visible means of support, they were now to carry money with them. Furthermore, it is a fixed purpose in the divine plan that His people should regularly support the ministry. If preachers could be supported by a constant series of miracles, there would be no urgency for Christians to support the work of the Lord. However, God's ministers should never be at the mercy of another's generosity. Whether those who should support the ministry are faithful or not, ministers should have confidence that God will take care of them.

When Jesus and His disciples came to Capernaum, the city in which He had performed His greatest miracles, He was met with apathy and indifference. A mark of that apathy was the fact that the disciples had apparently not received enough money to pay the taxes assessed against them. How could they pay taxes without money?

Jesus taught His disciples that, regardless of the circumstances, God could at any time or place provide for their needs. He told Peter:

> "Nevertheless, lest we offend them, go to the sea, cast in a hook, and take the fish that comes up first. And when you have opened its mouth, you will find a piece of money; take that and give it to them for Me and you" (Matt. 17:27).

Here, the word of knowledge and the gift of miracles operated jointly to supply the need. Christ's knowledge that a fish had a coin in its mouth was an evident manifestation of the first gift. That the fish came to Peter's hook demonstrated the operation of the second gift.

Lesson: *As Peter found the coin in the fish's mouth, so God can provide miracles of finance to those who have faith.*

Chapter Thirty

Miracles Affecting Nature

In discussing miracles that affect nature, we should keep in mind that some of these were sovereign acts of God, and therefore, were not the working of the gift of miracles, which requires human participation. Some of these supernatural occurrences, involved judgments upon the wicked. Others were associated with special deliverances for God's people.

The Opening of the Red Sea

One of the first miracles involving nature was the opening of the Red Sea to permit the children of Israel to march through and escape the pursuing hosts of Pharaoh (Ex. 14). The Israelites were filled with fear because of the avenging Egyptian army, which was being urged in pursuit by Pharaoh who apparently had not yet learned his lesson. On either side, the people were hemmed in by rugged mountains, and before them was the open sea. They could expect no mercy from Pharaoh, who was maddened because his nation had been laid waste. Only a miracle could save them.

In this hour of extreme peril, Moses was on his face in prayer. The Lord, on this occasion, ordered Moses to stop praying, and to rise and stretch out his rod over the sea! (Ex. 14:15, 16). Miracles require action.

And so the children of Israel went forward. The pillar of cloud, indicating the presence of the angel of the Lord, which usually went before them, now moved to their rear, protecting them from the Egyptian army. The cloud, which was light for the children of Israel, became darkness for the pursuing Egyptians.

As Moses stretched out his rod, a strong east wind began to blow. This is typical of the way God works. He could have used a mysterious force to accomplish the same result, but instead, He caused the ordinary wind to accomplish His purpose. This strong movement of the atmosphere rolled back the sea and enabled the children of Israel to walk in the midst of the sea upon dry ground.

> So the children of Israel went into the midst of the sea on the dry *ground*, and the waters *were* a wall to them on their right hand and on their left (Ex. 14:22).

The rod of Moses was the key that controlled the unfolding drama. The moment the children of Israel reached the other side, the prophet stretched it forth again and the sea returned to its normal place, drowning the Egyptians in the midst of the sea (ver. 27).

The Breaking of the Drought

> Elijah was a man with a nature like ours, and he prayed earnestly that it would not rain; and it did not rain on the land for three years and six months. And he prayed again, and the heaven gave rain, and the earth produced its fruit. (Jas. 5:17, 18).

This was really two miracles. The first miracle was one of judgment — causing a drought. The second was the return of the rains after three-and-a-half scorching years. James tells us what I Kings 17:1 does not, that it was the result of Elijah's prayers that the drought came in the first place. He "prayed earnestly that it would not rain." And God answered his prayer.

Elijah had assurance as he stood before Ahab that he was in command of the situation. He told the king, "'*As* the LORD God of Israel lives, before whom I stand, there shall not be dew nor rain these years, except at my word'" (I Ki. 17:1).

Nevertheless, miracles of judgment are not performed at the whim of a prophet. Divine judgment is something altogether different from the mumbo-jumbo of a witch doctor who seeks to put a curse on others for profit. Personal vindication or retaliation has no place in the divine purpose. Jesus forbade the disciples to call down fire upon a Samaritan city simply because they had been refused hospitality. Even Elijah, to whom they referred as an example, had to move according to the Word of the Lord. When Elijah prayed before Israel on Mt. Carmel, he said, "'Let it be known this day that ... I have done all these things at Your word'" (I Ki. 18:36).

Ahab was under the influence of his wife, the notoriously wicked Jezebel. She had introduced the heathen religion of Baal worship into Israel, while at the same time, outlawing the worship of Jehovah. Those faithful to the Lord had to seek refuge in caves. It was largely the blasphemous and murderous acts of this execrable queen that brought the judgment of the drought.

Whether or not Ahab took the prophet's warning of the coming drought seriously is uncertain. The passage of time, however, made it abundantly clear that Elijah had not spoken in vain. However, neither Ahab nor Jezebel were brought to repentance by the drought. Apparently, they regarded the works of Elijah as a new kind of black magic, and thought that if they could find him and lay the law down to him, they could force him to break the magic spell. They sent searchers out into the nearby kingdoms, but all failed to locate the prophet. Eventually, Elijah showed himself to Ahab, and when the king accused him of bringing trouble to Israel, the prophet laid the blame squarely where it belonged:

> And he answered, "I have not troubled Israel, but you and your father's house *have*, in that you have forsaken the commandments of the LORD and have followed the Baals" (I Ki. 18:18).

There had been severe suffering in Israel as a result of the drought. But, before an alleviation could come, the cause of the evil had to be dealt with. As the writer of Proverbs says, "A curse without cause shall not alight" (Prov. 26:2). The inhabitants of Israel had to choose between Baal and the Lord. To the people gathered for the contest on Mt. Carmel, Elijah said, "'How long will you falter between two opinions? If the LORD *is* God, follow Him; but if Baal, follow him'" (I Ki. 18:21).

The fire of God fell in answer to Elijah's prayer and the people turned from Baal back to the God of their fathers. The way was now cleared for the ending of the drought. After the slaughter of the Baal prophets, Elijah said, "'*There is* the sound of abundance of rain'" (I Ki. 18:41). Then he went up on Mt. Carmel to pray.

The Fall of the Walls of Jericho

Much has been written on the supposed injustice of God in the destruction of the Canaanites. They contend that the Jehovah of the Old Testament was a vindictive God.

Actually, the overthrow of the Canaanites was an act of benevolence. They had thoroughly corrupted themselves and had become addicted to such abominable practices as human sacrifice. It was an act of kindness on the part of God to prevent further generations from growing up in an environment so wholly given to evil. "'But *it is* because of the wickedness of these nations *that* the LORD is driving them out from before you'" (Deut. 9:4).

The fall of Jericho, recorded in Joshua 6, involved one of the most dramatic miracles of judgment recorded in the Old Testament. The Lord explained to Joshua that the men of war were to participate in this event by marching around the walls of Jericho once each day for six days, and on the seventh day, they were to pass around it seven times, at which time they were to blow their trumpets and shout. At that moment, the walls of the city would fall flat.

Various explanations have been suggested by apologists regarding how the walls could have fallen by natural causes. Some suggest that the walls were weakened by the rhythmic tramping of the soldiers, or the sudden blast from the horns, and the shout of the people had a disintegrating effect. These ideas must be dismissed as unworthy of consideration. That such a thing would happen at just the right time, after they had circled the city 13 times is too ridiculous for comment. The event was a demonstration of the working of miracles in judgment.

The historical accuracy of the account has been proven by archaeologists. The modern city of Jericho was built on a hill, and the ruins of the old city lie just above Elisha's spring. Excavation and exploration of the site has gone on for a number of years, and all discoveries tend to confirm the biblical narrative.

It is to be noted that Joshua put a curse upon anyone who should attempt to rebuild the city.

> Then Joshua charged *them* at that time, saying, "Cursed *be* the man before the LORD who rises up and builds this city Jericho; he shall lay its foundation with his firstborn, and with his youngest he shall set up its gates" (Josh. 6:26).

Curiously enough, according to Bible chronology, just 666 years later, Hiel the Bethelite rebuilt Jericho, and Joshua's curse came upon him (I Ki. 16:34). The curse had apparently affected the water supply, resulting in the land becoming sterile. In response to the plea of the inhabitants, Elisha poured salt into the spring and the waters became sweet (II Ki. 2:21).

Today the waters from the spring are pure and wholesome. Women may be seen coming at all hours of the day bringing their pitchers and vessels to fill them with the water and take back to their homes.

Jericho witnessed both the miracle of a curse, and the miracle of a blessing.

The Miracle of the Sun Standing Still

> Then Joshua spoke to the LORD in the day when the LORD delivered up the Amorites before the children of Israel, and he said in the sight of Israel: "Sun, stand still over Gibeon; and Moon, in the Valley of Aijalon." So the sun stood still,

> and the moon stopped, till the people had revenge upon their enemies. *Is* this not written in the Book of Jasher? So the sun stood still in the midst of heaven, and did not hasten to go *down* for about a whole day. And there has been no day like that, before it or after it, that the LORD heeded the voice of a man; for the LORD fought for Israel (Josh. 10:12-14).

This is one of the most remarkable miracles in the Bible and one, of course, which has come under the ridicule of skeptics. Critics say that the story of Joshua commanding the sun to stand still could not possibly be true, or it would upset the whole course of nature. Moreover, they point out that it is not the motion of the sun which gives its apparent daily movement, but the rotation of the earth. Yet, everyone, including unbelievers and critics, uses the words "sunset" and "sunrise" in their conversation. Of course, they do not mean the sun actually rises or sets through its own movement! Such terms are used in the Bible in the same way we use them in everyday conversation.

Therefore, as far as we are concerned, what happened is that the sun "appeared" to stand still in the sky just as it ordinarily "appears" to rise and fall in the sky. God usually accomplishes His physical miracles through the most simple means. Obviously, the most simple method would not be for God to stop the rotation of the earth — although He could easily do that. The most simple method would be to temporarily change the refraction properties of light, so that the sun would appear to remain in one location.

It is a remarkable fact that early history has definite records of a long day. One of the historians who mentions it is Herodotus. Chinese writings state that there was such a day in the reign of their emperor Yeo, a contemporary of Joshua. The Mexican Indians also have a record of a long day.

Of course, the long day gave Joshua and his men the opportunity to pursue and overtake their enemies. God could have accomplished this with a much lesser miracle, but God can do anything. No miracle is too great for the Creator. Ordinarily, He does not suspend or supersede His physical laws. But when it serves His eternal purpose, He may and will, permit such to happen.

The Miracle of Stilling the Storm

The drama of a storm at sea has always caught the human imagination. Man is frail and helpless before the gigantic forces of the fierce winds that disturb the mighty deep.

Jesus had preached the Sermon on the Mount and performed a number of outstanding miracles of healing in the city of Capernaum, when He called His disciples into a ship to go over to the other side of the sea. Wearied with His labors, He fell asleep.

While Jesus slept, a terrible storm arose. His disciples tried everything to reach safety, but the violence of the storm seemed to indicate that unless it quickly stopped, their ship would be swamped and all lives lost (Matt. 8:23, 24).

Who is responsible for a storm? It is in the nature of things, during this present age, for storms, winds and cyclones to disturb the atmosphere. But Job 1:12, 19 indicates that Satan, "the prince of the power of the air," exercises a role in these storms at times. His power is limited, of course, but it seems clear that under certain circumstances, he can cause serious destruction and loss of life.

As the storm strengthened, the panicking disciples finally awoke Jesus saying, "'Lord, save us! We are perishing!'" (Matt. 8:25). But here they had made a great mistake. No ship has ever been built that would sink as long as Christ was in it! Although the storms of life can be very serious, we need never fear our boat will sink as long as Christ is in it! Should He not be in our boat, however, we can be sure that sooner or later, it will go down and all will be lost.

The Lord arose "and rebuked the winds and the sea, and there was a great calm" (ver. 26). The fact that the term "rebuke" is used *indicates that there was an active opposing agent*. We rebuke an evil spirit; we do not rebuke dead matter.

As soon as Christ uttered those words, the unleashed forces

of the sea became completely calm. He had shown His power over sickness by healing all manner of disease. He had shown His power over devils by casting them out, and His power over death itself by forcing it to give up its prey. And now, He revealed His dominion over the very forces of nature by calming the storm.

But was this power reserved only for the Son of God? This is not what the words of Jesus indicate. Instead, He turned to them and said, "'Why are you fearful, O you of little faith?'" (ver. 26). As if to say, "If you had the faith you ought to have, you would have been able to calm the sea yourselves."

This was in harmony with God's original decree giving man dominion over the earth (Gen. 1:26).

Chapter Thirty-one

Miracles of Divine Judgment

The incident of divine judgment on Korah and his confederates, recorded in Numbers 16, was an act of discipline against rebellious elements in the camp of the children of Israel. The judgment against Korah and his company was unusually severe because of the flagrant and serious nature of the insurrection. Had this corrective judgment not occurred, the nation of Israel probably would have broken into separate fragments and clans as the result of the selfish ambitions of some irresponsible, self-appointed leaders — some of whom were intent on going back to Egypt (Num. 14:4).

Korah and his conspirators rebelled against Moses, challenging his leadership. This disconcerting development caused the prophet to fall on his face before God. The Lord told Moses that the hour had come to invoke divine judgment on the rebels. But first, He would give them one last chance. Human life is precious in the sight of God, and He will try everything to bring the transgressor to repentance. God's patience, however, is not without limit. When He sees that mercy is spurned and further forbearance only emboldens men to commit more sins, He must, and will, establish His authority — even if it means using extreme measures.

Moses plead for two of the ringleaders of the rebellion, Dothan and Abiram, to meet him for a consultation. They curtly rejected the offer. They said, "'We will not come up!'" (Num. 16:12). That ended the day of grace for them. Their cup of impiety had reached its full.

As a final warning, Moses gave the people of the camp the opportunity to withdraw from these wicked men so they would not perish with them. Most of the people had now become alarmed by what was transpiring and they hastily withdrew. However, Korah, Dothan and Abiram, who had stiffened themselves in their rebellion, stood outside their tents, and assumed an impudent posture, indicating they considered Moses' words a bluff!

> Now it came to pass, as he finished speaking all these words, that the ground split apart under them, and the earth opened its mouth and swallowed them up, with their households and all the men with Korah, with all *their* goods. So they and all those with them went down alive into the pit; the earth closed over them, and they perished from among the assembly (Num. 16:31-33).

The divine judgment came in the form of an earthquake which caused the ground to split open and swallow up the rebels. At the same time, the fire of the Lord came forth and slew the 250 who had dared to usurp the priesthood and offer incense.

So deep-rooted and insolent had the spirit of rebellion become, that some of the people, even after these supernatural manifestations of the wrath of God, did not end their defiance. Some of the most stiffnecked had the audacity to accuse Moses, saying, "'You have killed the people of the LORD'" (Num. 16:41). But, a plague which broke out among the people quickly put an end to the diehards' rebellion. Moses' intercession, however, stopped the plague. He sent Aaron with a censor of incense into the middle of the people "and he stood between the dead and the living; so the plague was stopped" (Num. 16:48).

The lesson is this: God uses divine judgment as a last resort. Every possible means of persuasion and entreaty is used to secure repentance and submission to His authority. If, however, that authority is defied and mercy rejected, divine judgment is in order. God's leaders are commanded to secure obedience through supernatural discipline if all other means fail.

The Judgment of Fire From Heaven
Elijah had been given the herculean task of overthrowing

the Baal worship set up by Ahab and Jezebel. Severe measures were necessary to uproot this satanic religion. Ahab had died in the manner Elijah had predicted, and the dogs had licked up his blood "according to the word of the LORD which He had spoken" (I Ki. 22:38).

His son, Ahaziah, who succeeded him, was no better. He became ill as a result of an accident, and sent messengers to Baal-Zebub, the god of Ekron, to ask if he would recover from his disease. Elijah met the messengers and told them that because the king insisted upon seeking false gods, he would die of his disease. The messengers reported this to Ahaziah.

The king then sent a band of 50 soldiers to the top of the hill where Elijah was, and rudely demanded that he come down. This was the setting for the miracle of the judgment of fire from heaven.

Elijah answered the captain's demand with the ominous words, "'If I *am* a man of God, then let fire come down from heaven and consume you and your fifty men.' And fire came down from heaven and consumed him and his fifty" (II Ki. 1:10).

The stubborn king had not learned his lesson, so he sent another band of fifty with the same demand. Elijah answered the second captain as he did the first, "and the fire of God came down from heaven and consumed him and his fifty" (II Ki. 1:12).

When the king sent the third captain, the latter evidently had heard what had happened to the previous messengers. He came to Elijah begging for mercy, and Elijah granted his request.

This instance of calling down fire from heaven was different from the circumstances on Mt. Carmel, where fire fell upon the sacrifice and occurred at the express word of the Lord (I Ki. 18:36-38). The demonstration on Mt. Carmel had resulted in the people's acknowledgment that the Lord was God. Perhaps Elijah remembered that on Mt. Carmel he had called fire down upon the sacrifice, yet had panicked and fled in fear of Jezebel. Why should a man who has faith to call fire from heaven have to run from his enemies?

Now this son of the abominable Jezebel was ordering him

around. Elijah was in no mood to run this time. Thus the words, "'If I *am* a man of God, then let fire come down from heaven and consume you and your fifty men.'" This action, while not commanded of the Lord, was in conformity with the dispensation in which Elijah lived. This method of dealing with enemies, however, is not in accord with the spirit of the Sermon on the Mount (Matt. 5). The injunction to love our enemies guides the New Testament dispensation.

When the apostolic party tried to stop at a certain village of the Samaritans, they were rudely turned away. It occurred to James and John that they might call down fire from heaven on the village in retaliation for this flagrant lack of hospitality (Lk. 9:54-56). But Christ sharply rebuked the brothers for their impetuous suggestion, declaring it was completely out of order, for He had come to save lives, not to destroy them.

While the test of fire served very well on Mt. Carmel to prove to the people that the Lord was God, it does not always do so. For example, God permitted Satan to test Job by some very severe methods. In one instance, fire fell and burned up his cattle. This could have been a stroke of lightning, but Job's servant erroneously believed it was from God, and said, "'The fire of God fell from heaven'" (Job 1:16).

Now, since the Scriptures plainly state it was Satan who was responsible for the disaster, we see that the fire falling from heaven may not always be the fire of God. This fact is further demonstrated in Revelation 13, which tells us that the wicked Beast (False Prophet) has power to bring down fire out of heaven:

> Then I saw another beast coming up out of the earth, and he had two horns like a lamb and spoke like a dragon. ... He performs great signs, so that he even makes fire come down from heaven on the earth in the sight of men. And he deceives those who dwell on the earth by those signs which he was granted to do in the sight of the beast, telling those who dwell on the earth to

make an image to the beast who was wounded
by the sword and lived ... (Rev. 13:11, 13, 14).

The Scriptures plainly teach that both God and Satan have power to cause fire to fall from heaven. Therefore fire from heaven is not a perfect indication of God's hand.

The Judgment Against Jeroboam

Jeroboam, the first king of the 10 tribes of Israel, committed the serious sin of setting up golden calves at Dan and Bethel for people to worship (I Ki. 12:28, 29). For this presumptuous act, God sent a prophet to cry out against the altar and to prophesy that a king by the name of Josiah would arise (three centuries later) and destroy his altar. He gave a sign that same day saying, "'This *is* the sign which the Lord has spoken: Surely the altar shall split apart, and the ashes on it shall be poured out'" (I Ki. 13:3).

Jeroboam, who quickly became a tyrant after his ascension to the throne, attempted to take the prophet by force, probably intending to put him to death. But at that moment, his hand was paralyzed and the altar split apart (ver. 4, 5).

The astonished and greatly humbled king now begged the prophet to pray for his hand to be restored. And so he did. The man of God, however, refused the invitation to visit the king, for the Lord had forbidden him to eat or drink in the city, or to return the same way he had come. Obviously, God did not want this prophet to have any communication with the inhabitants of this wicked city which had come under the curse.

In a curious event that followed, an old prophet who lived at Bethel heard what had happened. By pretending that an angel had visited him, this man succeeded in persuading the prophet to disobey the Lord's instruction to have nothing to do with those in Bethel. The prophet returned to the old man's home. Strangely enough, the Spirit of the Lord came upon the old prophet, and he prophesied that because the man of God had disobeyed, he would die on his way home. The prophecy came true. On his return home, a lion came out and killed him (I Ki. 13:24).

Again we see the imperative importance that those who minister miraculous gifts walk in a straight line of obedience to God. Disobedience leads to the gravest dangers.

Uzziah Becomes a Leper

A similar miracle occurred in the case of Uzziah, King of Judah, who reigned as a good king for a time, and whom God prospered. "So his fame spread far and wide, for he was marvelously helped till he became strong" (II Chr. 26:15). Then, his prosperity went to his head, and he tried to perform the role of a priest (ver. 16).

Uzziah's actions were contrary to divine command, and the priests strongly protested. The king refused instruction and gave in to anger instead. But even while he was in his rage, leprosy rose up on his forehead and the priests hustled him out of the house of the Lord. Uzziah did not recover from leprosy, but carried it with him until death. It was a solemn object lesson to the people of Israel. It should also be a lesson to those today who seek to usurp positions which do not belong to them.

The Judgment of Ananias and Sapphira

The integrity of the body of Christ depends on the proper exercise of discipline among its members. The modern Church often witnesses flagrant violations of truth and honesty among its members. This indicates a lack of New Testament discipline.

Let us note an example of the operation of the working of miracles to execute judgment in the New Testament Church. For some time, the newborn Church experienced a beautiful, unselfish spirit among its members. People sold their possessions and brought in the proceeds, so the evangelization of the nation could proceed, and all the Church members would be taken care of during times of persecution. Then a sinister thing happened. A man and his wife, by the name of Ananias and Sapphira, conspired to bring evil into the assembly. They saw the miracles, and witnessed the tide of blessing. They saw others selling their property and bringing the proceeds to the feet of the apostles. No one had to do this, but Ananias and Sapphira thought they ought to follow suit in order to gain prestige as generous givers. They sold their property and brought the proceeds to Peter. However, they decided it would be prudent to reserve part of the money for themselves. When Ananias presented the money to Peter, he pretended that he had given the whole sum. But through the gift of discernment, Peter perceived Ananias' hypocrisy and rebuked him:

> But Peter said, "Ananias, why has Satan filled your heart to lie to the Holy Spirit and keep back *part* of the price of the land for yourself? While it remained, was it not your own? And after it was sold, was it not in your own control? Why have you conceived this thing in your heart? You have not lied to men but to God" (Acts 5:3, 4).

When Ananias heard these words, he fell down dead at Peter's feet. Later, the same judgment came upon his wife, Sapphira. Because the judgment took place immediately, we may say that the gift of the working of miracles was in operation.

This may seem like drastic punishment to be inflicted upon people who had merely lied to Peter, and who were giving a substantial portion of their goods to the Church. But, had this thing gone on, it would have eaten like a cancer into the integrity of the group. Instead, as a result of the judgment, "great fear came upon all the church and upon all who heard these things" (ver. 11). Hypocrites and the unconverted were afraid to join themselves to the company. On the other hand, "believers were increasingly added to the Lord, multitudes of both men and women" (ver. 14).

How different the result would have been if the discipline had been ordered by carnal means! Suppose a church committee had waited on Ananias and Sapphira and accused them of the act. Being liars, they no doubt would have denied it. Their friends might have believed their story and the unity and harmony of the Church would have been jeopardized. But because the discernment and infliction of punishment were supernatural, a holy fear was brought upon the Church and evil could gain no entrance into it.

Judgment of Elymas the Sorcerer

In the case we have just discussed, the punishment fell upon offenders within the Church. On other occasions, it was inflicted upon unbelievers who were seriously hindering the work of the Gospel. Such was the case in Acts 13:6-13. The proconsul of the country, Sergius Paulus, had been deeply stirred by the preaching of Paul. But, a false prophet and sorcerer named Elymas, attempted to turn him away from the faith. Paul, filled with the Holy Spirit, turned to the opposer and pronounced judgment upon him:

> Then Saul, who also *is called* Paul, filled with the Holy Spirit, looked intently at him and said, "O full of all deceit and all fraud, *you* son of the devil, *you* enemy of all righteousness, will you not cease perverting the straight ways of the Lord? And now, indeed, the hand of the Lord *is* upon you, and you shall be blind, not seeing the sun for a time." And immediately a dark mist fell on him, and he went around seeking someone to lead him by the hand (Acts 13:9-11).

The immediate result of this judgment was the conversion of the proconsul. Since these examples were recorded for our admonition, it is obvious that the Church should be exercising the gift of miracles in overcoming blatant and presumptuous opposition. In all likelihood, many of the wicked would be convinced and would repent of their sins if they witnessed such a manifestation.

This administration of divine judgment was done through the office of the working of miracles, and the results were swift and immediate. Divine discipline can also be administered through the gift of faith, where the results do not show as quickly, but come to pass just as certainly.

Chapter Thirty-two

Facts About the Gift of Prophecy

But he who prophesies speaks edification and
exhortation and comfort to men (I Cor. 14:3).

In the Old Testament, the prophetic ministry was essentially *foretelling*. In the New Testament, it shifts strongly to *forth-
telling*. As the above words of Paul indicate, the gift is for the
edification, exhortation and comfort of the Church of God.

As one studies the Old Testament prophecies, the amazing
accuracy with which the old prophets penetrated the distant
future is impressive. Nevertheless, knowledge and foreknowledge do not necessarily edify or make an individual more spiritual. People can speculate about the future and remain unconverted. The purpose of the New Testament gift, as exercised in
the public assembly, was to edify, exhort and comfort — in
other words, make people better and more useful Christians.
This is the usual manifestation of the gift which we see operating in the Church today.

When man was created and placed in the Garden of Eden,
God talked with him directly. Sin broke the communion. Nevertheless, there still remains a deep longing in the human spirit for direct communication with the Creator. This basic human
need is supplied in a measure through the operation of the gift
of prophecy, as manifested in the New Testament Church.
Congregations which do not have this gift operating are missing something vital to their worship.

Vehicle for the Operation of Other Gifts

By its nature, the gift of prophecy can be, and often is, a
vehicle for the operation of other gifts. Certain groups of gifts
function in close relation to each other. For example, the gift
of tongues and interpretation of tongues operate together. Pro-

phecy and interpretation, differ mainly in the way they operate in the assembly. The latter always follows speaking in tongues, while the other does not.

While New Testament prophecy is largely for edification, exhortation and comfort, it has a wider scope than this. For one thing, other gifts may work in cooperation and unison with it. The gift of interpretation may blend into the gift of prophecy. A short message in tongues may be followed by what appears to be a lengthy interpretation. Actually, what sometimes happens is when the interpretation is completed, the interpreter may move into the prophetic gift. This is an excellent example of three gifts working closely together.

Speaking in other tongues is valuable, chiefly, in that it gives the congregation opportunity to get into a prayerful attitude before the interpretation is given. Once this has been accomplished, there is not the same need for speaking in other tongues, since, as Paul said, speaking in an unknown tongue does not edify the Church. There is no given rule, however, that governs the operation of the three gifts. An experienced interpreter is guided in his proper manifestation by the circumstances of the moment.

The word of wisdom, the word of knowledge and the gift of discerning of spirits may, at times, be manifested through the gift of prophecy (I Sam. 10:1-7).

When we see how this gift and the gift of interpretation merge together so completely, we can understand how our gifts can relate very closely. It should be remembered, however, that there are a number of other ways in which the word of wisdom and the word of knowledge may be revealed — by dreams, visions, an angelic visitation, etc.

We are told that Philip the evangelist "had four virgin daughters who prophesied" (Acts 21:8, 9). Paul stopped at their home when he was on his way to Jerusalem. Tradition tells us that, a few years later, these women warned the Christians in Jerusalem to flee before the arrival of the Romans who, under Titus, were on their way to the city to lay siege against it. History confirms that, because of these warnings, the Christians left the city and fled to the safety of Pella.

Healing may occasionally be ministered in conjunction with the operation of this gift. An example of this was when Elisha told Naaman to go down and dip seven times in the Jordan River. He did as the prophet commanded him and was healed. Many times, people have been healed while sitting under the preaching of the Word, when it was given under a strong anointing. One example can be found in Acts 14:8-10. The anointed preaching of Paul had so built the faith of the lame man that he arose and "leaped and walked."

The Gift of Prophecy in Scripture

To understand the full range of the gift of prophecy, we must begin in the Old Testament. The first prophet recorded in the Bible was Enoch. We shall take particular notice of the main features of his prophecy since according to the law of first mention, the cardinal truths of a subject are given when it is *first* introduced. Incidentally, Enoch's prophecy is recorded, not in Genesis, but in the Book of Jude. Apparently, Jude had access to some inspired writings of the Old Testament period that we do not have. He refers to Enoch's prophecy in the following words:

> Now Enoch, the seventh from Adam, prophesied about these men also, saying, "Behold, the Lord comes with ten thousands of His saints, to execute judgment on all, to convict all who are ungodly among them of all their ungodly deeds which they have committed in an ungodly way, and of all the harsh things which ungodly sinners have spoken against Him" (Jude 14, 15).

1. Enoch was the *seventh* from Adam, indicating that he was a prophet chosen by God for a specific purpose and a specific time. Prophets are God-called, not man-chosen. God sets prophets in the Church. Enoch, we are told, "walked with God" (Gen. 5:22), indicating the type of individual who makes a true prophet.

2. The prophecy points forward to Christ. He is the One

around whom all prophecy revolves. "For the testimony of Jesus is the spirit of prophecy" (Rev. 19:10). So-called prophecies such as those of Nostradamus, who is alleged to have predicted certain modern inventions and wars, have little in common with true prophecy.

3. Enoch's prophecy referred to Christ's Second Coming. In a general way, all prophecy points forward to that great event, at which time Christ will return to reign on the earth.

4. The prophecy mentions Christ's coming with ten thousands of His saints. If He comes *with* them, He must have already come *for* them. This alludes to the rapture of the believers.

5. Enoch warned the ungodly so that they might be convinced of their evil deeds and repent. Prophecy is not given for the mere purpose of satisfying curiosity, but to awaken people to righteousness.

6. Enoch predicted that Christ's coming would bring judgment upon the unrepentant. "'Behold, the LORD comes ... to execute judgment on all.'"

7. As is often the case in Old Testament prophecy, Enoch was allowed to act out in drama, or type, his own prophecy. (Note that in Jeremiah 32:9-15, Jeremiah purchased a field just before the Babylonian captivity, to show his faith that God would again return the people to their land.) Enoch was translated, to become a type of those who would not see death, but be translated in the rapture (I Thes. 4:13-17). These will be the saints (along with those who have died in the faith), whom Christ will bring with Him.

In Enoch's brief prophecy, we have seven of the main elements which are involved in true prophecy. All these things show that while the New Testament prophecy usually functions as a separate gift, it may and often does, work closely with other gifts. Indeed, these gifts sometimes merge so closely in their operation, that it is difficult to know when one gift ceases its operation and another begins.

The Gift is Supernatural in Function
The gift of prophecy is not manifested in the ordinary teach-

ing or preaching of the Word. To say that it is, would be to rob the gift of its supernatural character. The word "preach" in the New Testament is different from the word "prophesy." It is true that some translators have made these two words to mean the same thing, so that they may plausibly lay claim to possession of the gift. But preaching and prophesying are two different things. The preaching of a pastoral sermon requires careful preparation. One does not *prepare* to deliver a message in prophecy, except to wait on the Lord for the anointing required for its manifestation.

A minister may, however, as the anointing increases, move from ordinary preaching into the realm of prophecy. If and when this occurs, the effect may be very powerful. Speaking in other tongues enables *man to speak to God supernaturally*. The gift of prophecy, on the other hand, enables *God to speak to man supernaturally*.

Various Kinds of Prophecies

Much of the prophecy in the Old Testament related to future events. The Patriarchal prophecies fit into this category. However, there were times when it was exhortational, such as the prophecy spoken by Moses in the Book of Deuteronomy, where the blessings for obedience and the curses for disobedience are recorded. There are many similar exhortational prophecies in the Psalms and the prophetic books of the Bible as well.

Many times, prophecies took the form of a song or poetry. There are other types of prophecies found in the Scriptures: Some predicting judgment, others which include lamentations over the suffering of God's people. There are also the apocalyptic prophecies of Daniel and John the Revelator. If we are to understand the function of the gift of prophecy today, we must take account of the rich variety of types of prophecy recorded in the Scriptures.

1. The Patriarchal Prophecies

By faith Isaac blessed Jacob and Esau concerning

things to come. By faith Jacob, when he was dying, blessed each of the sons of Joseph, and worshiped, *leaning* on the top of his staff (Heb. 11:20, 21).

The patriarchal prophecies are some of the first found in the Scriptures. They were given as a result of supernatural faith which was imparted to these men at the time. They spoke of events to occur many centuries in the future and were manifested by exercising faith with the laying on of hands. Isaac was not merely giving Jacob his paternal blessing. He knew that something supernatural which he could not invalidate, had taken place when he blessed Jacob, even though he had not been conscious at the moment of the identity of the son he had actually blessed (Gen. 27:33). More than supernatural faith was involved in Isaac's blessing; he spoke in the spirit of prophecy (Gen. 27:28, 29).

When Jacob blessed his sons, he spoke of events far in the future which concerned not only them, but their distant descendants. "'Gather together, that I may tell you what shall befall you in the last days'" (Gen. 49:1).

Noah also gave a patriarchal blessing concerning the destinies of his three sons, Shem, Ham and Japheth (Gen. 9:24-27).

Something similar to this type of prophecy is recorded in I Timothy 4:14 and II Timothy 1:6. A prophecy was given at the time Timothy received a gift, when hands were laid upon him by the elders.

2. *Prophecy in Song*

There are many passages in Scripture in which prophecy is in the form of a song. The song of the redeemed by Moses in Exodus 15 is an excellent example of this. This song is also referred to in the Book of Revelation:

And I saw *something* like a sea of glass mingled with fire, and those who have the victory over the beast, over his image and over his mark *and*

over the number of his name, standing on the sea
of glass, having harps of God. They sing the song
of Moses, the servant of God ... (Rev. 15:2, 3).

Another example of worship in prophetic song is the song
of Deborah and Barak:

> "Village life ceased, it ceased in Israel, until I,
> Deborah, arose, arose a mother in Israel. ... My
> heart *is* with the rulers of Israel who offered
> themselves willingly with the people. Bless the
> LORD. ... Awake, awake, Deborah! Awake,
> awake, sing a song! Arise, Barak, and lead your
> captives away, O son of Abinoam. ... They fought
> from the heavens; the stars from their courses
> fought against Sisera" (Judg.5:7, 9, 12, 20).

Many of the Psalms of David are among this type of prophecy. Almost every circumstance or problem involving human
need is touched upon in the Psalms. That is why they hold such
an important place in the believer's devotional reading.

3. Prophecy Edifies the Church
Edify means to build up. When people speak in tongues,
they edify themselves (I Cor. 14:4), but when they prophesy,
they edify the Church.

It was my good fortune, in the providence of God, to come
to Christ in a church where there was a beautiful manifestation of the gifts of prophecy and interpretation. The effect of
the operation of these gifts upon my spiritual life while still a
young convert can scarcely be overemphasized. I was deeply
convicted by the preaching of a man who had a strong ministry
of evangelism, and a powerful conversion resulted. But, it was
the operation of the gifts of the Spirit that gave me a great
awareness of God.

Before conversion, I had heard speaking in tongues a few
times, but it had always been followed by a rather mediocre
interpretation given by a foreigner, who actually needed his

own words interpreted into recognizable English. Naturally, this faulty manifestation of the gift made little or no impression upon me.

But, after I came to Christ, the splendid manifestation of the gifts of prophecy and interpretation that I witnessed in the assembly was very inspiring. We long to hear God speak to us, as He spoke to Adam in the Garden. God has made this possible through the gift of prophecy. The ministry of the gifts of the Spirit, combined with a powerful ministry of the Word, had a wonderful effect on my life.

Some say the gift of prophecy has ceased in the Church. It is notable that denominations which consider the gift of prophecy as obsolete are, in many cases, ready to take the next step and declare the Word of God as out-of-date as well.

The Psalms are a remarkable collection of devotional material that is similar to New Testament prophecy for edification, exhortation and comfort. The very first Psalm is an excellent example. It is not predictive prophecy, but is the poetry of prophecy.

In the Psalms, we find the whole range of prophecy as it instructs, edifies and comforts the people of God. Written nearly 1,000 years before Christ, these inspired passages still minister to the needs of the saints of God today.

Notice how the first, second and third person varies throughout the Psalms. At one time, God speaking to His people; at another, it is the Holy Spirit interceding for believers. At still other times, under inspiration, the Psalmist is speaking to the Lord under inspiration in worship.

4. *Exhortational Prophecy*

There are times when the spiritual fervency of the assembly drops in temperature, and its members fail to notice it. A church can become so engrossed in its organization, political events, business and social amenities, that it fails to notice the subtle cooling off. At such a time, the Spirit of prophecy may give a word of admonition to awaken the people. The words of Jesus to the Church at Ephesus are an example:

"Nevertheless I have *this* against you, that you have left your first love. Remember therefore from where you have fallen; repent and do the first works, or else I will come to you quickly and remove your lampstand from its place — unless you repent" (Rev. 2:4, 5).

Part of the words of Moses in Deuteronomy 28 may be considered exhortational prophecy, such as the conditions for blessings and curses in the land — blessings for obedience and curses for disobedience. The Psalms are filled with prophecies that speak of the blessing of God upon the righteous, and conversely, of judgment upon the wicked.

We find many similar exhortations given by various men of God throughout the Old Testament.

The Spirit of God is always gentle, however. I believe some messages of rebuke I have heard were out of order, and had their source mostly in the person's own spirit, rather than in the Spirit of God. Correction, when needed, is best given through the Word of God. When individuals attempt to correct an assembly through the gift of prophecy, they may put themselves in a vulnerable position and draw criticism upon themselves.

The Apostle Paul corrected the Church, not as a prophet, but as a teacher and instructor. God has ordained the Word to be applied to the problems in the Church.

5. Messianic Prophecy

The Psalms are not without the predictive element; these are generally referred to as the Messianic Psalms. Psalm 2 speaks of the establishment of the Kingdom of God. Psalm 16 tells about Christ's death and descent into Hades. The 22nd Psalm is a graphic picture of the crucifixion (ver. 14-18). The 23rd Psalm shows Christ as the Good Shepherd. The 45th reveals Him as the Bridegroom calling His Bride. The 68th shows Him in His ascension, leading "captivity captive." The 69th speaks of the Lord in His Messianic Kingdom. A number of other Psalms can be considered to be clearly Messianic in nature.

Many prophecies in other prophetic books are Messianic as well. Of these, Isaiah 53 stands out above all others.

6. Prophecies of Judgment

There are many Old Testament prophecies that foretell judgment. We have already noted the one given by Enoch. Moses' prophecy of judgment against Korah, Dothan and Abiram is another example (Num. 16:28-30).

The man of God from Judah who prophesied against Jeroboam's false altar is another example of a prophecy of judgment. In this case, the name of the king who would execute the judgment against the false altar was Josiah, who was born three centuries later.

> And behold, a man of God went from Judah to Bethel by the word of the LORD, and Jeroboam stood by the altar to burn incense. Then he cried out against the altar by the word of the LORD, and said, "O altar, altar! Thus says the LORD: 'Behold, a child, Josiah by name, shall be born to the house of David; and on you he shall sacrifice the priests of the high places who burn incense on you, and men's bones shall be burned on you'" (I Ki. 13:1, 2).

There are many prophecies like this in the Old Testament.

7. Prophecies of Lamentation

The Lamentations of Jeremiah are yet another form of prophecy. Their touching significance is found in the disclosure of God's love and sorrow for His people, who have gone into captivity because of their sins. The opening verse shows the Lord's grief. The literary form of Lamentations is worthy of note. In the original Hebrew, the lines are arranged in couplets and triplets, each of which begins with a letter of the Hebrew alphabet. In the third chapter, each line of the triplet begins with the same letter, so that the entire 66 verses are required to present the 22 letters of the Hebrew alphabet.

8. Prophecy Comforts

The gift of prophecy comforts Christians going through hard times (II Cor. 1:4). Jesus said, "'In the world you will have tribulation; but be of good cheer, I have overcome the world'" (Jn. 16:33). Every Christian will have a certain amount of tribulation and sorrow, but it has a purifying effect. Besides, we are not supposed to sorrow as do those without hope. Christians, to be at their best, should not be overcome with sorrow, but should be comforted in order to comfort others. Of the man in the Corinthian Church who had sinned, Paul said, "forgive and comfort *him*, lest perhaps such a one be swallowed up with too much sorrow" (II Cor. 2:7).

To those going through great troubles, the gift of prophecy may act as a healing balm, bringing wonderful solace through divinely-given words.

9. Prophecy Convicts the Sinner

> But if all prophesy, and an unbeliever or an uninformed person comes in, he is convinced by all, he is convicted by all. And thus the secrets of his heart are revealed; and so, falling down on *his* face, he will worship God and report that God is truly among you (I Cor. 14:24, 25).

Prophecy blesses believers, but it convicts sinners. It causes the unbeliever to become deeply conscious of the presence of God. Often, something in the prophecy will strike home like an arrow, and cause the sinner to feel that God is talking directly to him. However, conviction is not conversion. The manifestation of the gift of prophecy is not sufficient to convert sinners. The preaching of the Word is a necessary follow-up to secure a decision for Christ.

10. *Conditional and Unconditional Prophecies*

Many of the prophecies in the Bible are unconditional. The promises given to Abraham concerning the land of Canaan as an inheritance to his descendants, were unconditional. Thus, after 4,000 years, we see these prophecies now being fulfilled in the land of Israel. The judgments spoken against many of the ancient wicked cities were fulfilled exactly as predicted. Isaiah's prophecy of the future ministry and death of the Messiah (Isa. 53) was also unconditional. Prophecy may be said to be *His story* pre-written.

There are a number of prophecies in the Scripture which are clearly conditional. One was spoken by Isaiah to King Hezekiah, who was terminally ill. He told the king he would die (II Ki. 20:1), yet Hezekiah did not die! How can this be explained?

When Hezekiah heard the decree, he turned himself to the wall and poured out his heart to God. He knew that no medical skill nor help of man could save him. Yet, somehow, he believed God could change the order of events. His prayer and faith brought divine power into operation which overruled the power of death. So, Isaiah came to him again and announced the king's deliverance. The original prophecy was conditional, and Hezekiah's faith and determination in prayer changed it.

> "Return and tell Hezekiah the leader of My people, 'Thus says the LORD, the God of David your father: "I have heard your prayer, I have seen your tears; surely I will heal you"'" ...(II Ki. 20:5).

Another case of a conditional prophecy is the story of Jonah, who was commanded by God to go and pronounce judgment upon the wicked city of Nineveh. The word was, "'Yet forty days, and Nineveh shall be overthrown'" (Jon. 3:4). But, instead of obeying the command of God to go to Nineveh, Jonah went to Joppa and got into a ship to flee from the presence of the Lord. His act of disobedience got him into trouble. He was swallowed by a great fish prepared by the Lord. He cried to

God and was delivered, and was then ready to carry out his mission. The people of Nineveh took the warning to heart and repented. God, in His mercy, spared their city (Jon. 3:5-10).

This is a striking example of a conditional prophecy. The destruction of Nineveh had not been foreordained. But because of its wickedness, the city came under judgment. Repentance postponed the judgment. (A later generation ignored the lesson learned by their ancestors, and Nineveh came under judgment — never again to be restored as a city.)

A nation or a people can go so deep in sin that there is no remedy. When the hour of grace is ended, judgment is inevitable. This was the case in Israel just before the captivities. Despite God's repeated warnings, Israel committed such abominations that the day of mercy could no longer be extended.

> But they mocked the messengers of God, despised His words, and scoffed at His prophets, until the wrath of the LORD arose against His people, till *there was* no remedy (II Chr. 36:16).

The principle of God's forbearance is clearly seen in Ezekiel:

> "Again, when I say to the wicked, 'You shall surely die,' if he turns from his sin and does what is lawful and right ... none of his sins which he has committed shall be remembered against him; he has done what is lawful and right; he shall surely live" (Ezek. 33:14, 16).

God sometimes gives conditional prophecies, because it provides a period of warning during which people may change the situation if they choose. God allowed the above instances to be recorded so that we might understand the purpose of conditional prophecies.

Failure to understand these facts can result in serious confusion. God may promise something which is conditional. A prophecy of judgment, as we have seen, may be conditional.

God may promise a blessing, but the fulfillment may depend upon the obedience of the individual. Those who assume that a promise will be fulfilled without any real prayer or effort on their part, may discover that their hopes do not materialize. They may then conclude that the prophecy was false. But, the prophecy may actually have been a conditional one. This shows why it is so necessary to understand the nature of the gift and the rules which govern it. An experienced person can usually tell the difference between a conditional and unconditional prophecy, while a new convert often cannot.

11. Apocalyptic Prophecies

Prophecy in the Old Testament reaches a climax in its apocalyptic form. The 24th to 29th chapters of Isaiah are sometimes referred to as the "Little Apocalypse." However, Daniel 7-12 are the outstanding chapters of apocalyptic revelation in the Old Testament, and correspond to the Revelation of John in the New Testament. In these apocalyptic prophecies, we find the divine revelations given in an orderly sequence. They are given in symbolic form and the meaning is hidden from the understanding of the skeptic, but understood by the believer at the time appointed for their unfolding. These prophecies were usually delivered by angels — apparently to prevent any possibility of error in transmission. Daniel's prophecies were sealed from the people of his day (Dan. 12:4), but now both his, as well as those of the Book of Revelation, have been unsealed.

> Blessed *is* he who reads and those who hear the words of this prophecy, and keep those things which are written in it; for the time is near. ... And he said to me, "Do not seal the words of the prophecy of this book, for the time is at hand" (Rev. 1:3; 22:10).

Such is the varied panorama of the gift of prophecy in its different operations in the Old Testament. We find no prophetic operation in the New Testament that is not reflected in some way in the Old, except the special manifestation of prophecy in the form of tongues and interpretation. These latter gifts are unique to the New Testament Church.

The New Testament Gift of Prophecy

In Old Testament days, the prophetic office usually involved predictions of the future and giving divine guidance. In New Testament days, the change in the emphasis of the manifestation of the gift of prophecy is due to the change in the priesthood. In Old Testament days, one inquired of the Lord through a priest. In the current dispensation, all believers are part of a royal priesthood, and may approach the Lord individually.

> But you *are* a chosen generation, a royal priesthood, a holy nation, His own special people, that you may proclaim the praises of Him who called you out of darkness into His marvelous light (I Pet. 2:9).

Also, during Bible days, the Canon of Scripture had not yet been formed; it was not completed until about the third or fourth century A.D. Today, believers may go to the Bible for their spiritual guidance. This, of course, does not mean that one cannot go to a minister for counsel, or that guidance may not be given by the gift of prophecy (Acts 21:10-13). However, the believer no longer has to go to an oracle to meet with God, as in Old Testament days.

The New Testament begins by recording several prophecies given around the time of Jesus' birth. They were mainly prophecies of worship and adoration.

Elizabeth, the mother of John the Baptist, gave one of these prophecies. When her cousin, Mary, the mother of Jesus, came to visit her, Elizabeth was filled with the Holy Spirit. She began to bless Mary, saying, "'Blessed *is* she who believed, for there will be a fulfillment of those things which were told her from the Lord'" (Lk. 1:45).

Mary responded with a prophetic song that is often called the "Magnificat." She worshiped the Lord, saying:

> "My soul magnifies the Lord, and my spirit has rejoiced in God my Savior. For He has regarded the lowly state of His maidservant; for behold, henceforth all generations will call me blessed" (Lk. 1:46-48).

Zacharias, the father of John the Baptist, was made mute after he doubted the angel, Gabriel's, word (Lk. 1:18-22). But after the child was born, Zacharias received the ability to speak again, and he gave a prophecy of praise to the Lord in which he not only thanked God for His mercies to Israel, but also gave a brief preview of the ministry his son would have as the forerunner of Christ (Lk. 1:62-79).

Shortly after Jesus was born, Joseph and Mary took Him to the temple to be presented to the Lord. At that very moment, a man by the name of Simeon, came into the temple. It had been revealed to him that "he would not see death before he had seen the Lord's Christ" (Lk. 2:26). When he saw Jesus, he picked Him up and blessed him, saying:

> "Lord, now You are letting Your servant depart in peace, according to Your word; for my eyes have seen Your salvation which You have prepared before the face of all peoples, a light to *bring* revelation to the Gentiles, and the glory of Your people Israel" (Lk. 2:29-32).

Likewise, Anna the prophetess, who was over a 100 years of age, came and gave thanks to the Lord for the birth of the Savior. In each of these prophecies, we see the spirit of adoration and worship as the dominant theme.

1. Jesus' Prophecies

Much of Jesus' ministry was given to preaching and teaching. It is sometimes difficult to determine the exact gift operating at a given moment in His ministry. Certainly, all the gifts of the Spirit worked through Him, as they did with His disciples. We are clearly told that Jesus had to learn and increase in wisdom the same as others. Therefore, He was dependent upon the gifts of the Holy Spirit for His ministry (Lk. 2:40, 52).

We know that every word Christ spoke was inspired. "'The words that I speak to you are spirit, and *they* are life'" (Jn. 6:63). But, it is difficult to determine whether a particular utterance should be classified as prophecy, word of wisdom, word of knowledge, discerning of spirits or teaching. It is evident that these gifts work in very close relation to each other. However, there is no doubt that such passages as Matthew 11:21-27, can be considered the pure operation of the gift of prophecy.

2. The Prophecy of Caiaphas

There is a mysterious prophecy given by Caiaphas, the high priest — leader of those who condemned Jesus to die on the cross. It seems strange that the Holy Spirit would come upon this person, of all people, and cause him to give this remarkable prophecy. But that is exactly what happened.

> And one of them, Caiaphas, being high priest that year, said to them, "You know nothing at all, nor do you consider that it is expedient for us that one man should die for the people, and not that the whole nation should perish." Now this he did not say on his own *authority*; but being high priest that year he prophesied that Jesus would die for the nation, and not for that nation only, but also that He would gather together in one the children of God who were scattered abroad (Jn. 11:49-52).

This passage shows that the Holy Spirit may temporarily come upon a person who is completely out of God's will, and cause a gift to be manifested through him. It is evident, therefore, that the operation of a gift of the Spirit is not absolute proof that the person's heart is right with God. This is confirmed by the words of Jesus Himself in Matthew 7:22, 23, and Paul also brings out this thought:

> And though I have *the gift of* prophecy, and un-
> derstand all mysteries and all knowledge, and
> though I have all faith, so that I could remove
> mountains, but have not love, I am nothing (I
> Cor. 13:2).

These are serious matters to consider. A prophet may prophesy, yet in the end, lose his own soul. He may perform miracles, and yet be rejected on the day of judgment. Judas Iscariot healed the sick and cast out devils, for we are told that he "obtained a part in this ministry"(Acts 1:17). But there can be little doubt that, despite this, he lost his soul (Acts 1:25).

The Difference Between Edification and Revelation

As we have noted, with the founding of the Church there was an important change in the operation of the gift of prophecy. The emphasis of the gift is now on the edification of the Church, rather than on foretelling events. However, predictive prophecy *is* found in the New Testament also, although it is generally spoken of as "revelation."

I Corinthians makes a distinction between prophecies of revelation and prophecies of edification:

> But now, brethren, if I come to you speaking
> with tongues, what shall I profit you unless I
> speak to you either by revelation, by knowledge,
> by prophesying, or by teaching? (I Cor. 14:6)

Revelation and prophecy are mentioned separately, and are obviously not considered identical. Generally speaking, the gift of prophecy does not include revelation. This may be further seen in the fact that most prophecies given in our public services today are exhortational, rather than revelatory.

Revelation requires a much greater degree of yielding to the Spirit. A revelation may be given in a large public assembly, but it is more likely to be given to a smaller group. It is significant to note that, although Jesus told many things to all of His disciples, there were some special revelations that were reserved for the inner circle which included Peter, James and John. An example of this would be the things which they saw on the Mount of Transfiguration (Matt. 17:1-13).

Extreme caution must be exercised when revelatory prophecy apparently introduces a new doctrine. Doctrine is to be taught from the Word of God, not from "revelations." I recall a time when, as a young believer, I asked the Holy Spirit to give me information concerning a certain controversial doctrine. The Spirit rebuked me for asking the question, and directed me to the Scriptures, as all the answers are found there.

Experience over the years has shown that many of the false doctrines plaguing the Church today owe their origin to some supposed "revelation." Sometimes, they are so obviously false that little harm is done. There have been cases, however, in which the flock has been divided and havoc wrought in the Church as a result of such "prophecies." We cannot overemphasize that the Bible, not the gift of prophecy, is the proper source for developing doctrine. The possibility of the human mind entering into such a prophecy makes it too dangerous to allow the gift to be used for this purpose.

Yet, revelation does have a part in the New Testament Church. By means of revelation, the Early Church was able to prepare for a serious famine (Acts 11:27-30). Revelation also guided Paul to Macedonia to introduce the Gospel there (Acts 16:9, 10). Again, revelation warned Paul of what lay ahead for him in Jerusalem (Acts 20:23; 21:10-13).

I Corinthians 14:26 shows that revelation does have a place in the public assembly, but not to establish a doctrine. Notice how the apostles arrived at a conclusion concerning the matter of circumcision. They did not employ the gift of prophecy to determine the matter (Acts 15).

Prophecy is the Poetry of the Spirit

Speaking in tongues publicly does not have the same responsibility as giving a message in prophecy does. Nor is there the same responsibility when giving an inspirational prophecy as there is when giving a predictive prophecy or a revelation. Much greater yielding to the Spirit is necessary in the latter case. We are told that Peter was in a trance when he received the revelation to preach the Gospel of salvation to the gentiles (Acts 10:9-16). If Peter had not been so deeply in the Spirit, it is likely that his own mind, which was prejudiced against gentiles, would have dismissed the revelation.

However, it should be understood that inspirational prophecy is indeed supernatural. Some examples of prophesying or giving an interpretation that are seen today in public assemblies, are a far cry from the potential power and beauty of the gift when it is functioning at its best.

There are various explanations for these inferior prophecies. First, the person may be a novice who is just beginning to minister in public. Patience must be exercised in that case. There are also those who have not learned to yield to the Holy Spirit, or who are slow to get in the Spirit when needed. The Apostle John said that he "was in the Spirit on the Lord's Day" (Rev. 1:10). Therefore, he was ready to receive the great Revelation when it came. Those who minister in public should learn to stay in the Spirit, so that they are ready to interpret when a message in an unknown tongue comes forth.

Prophecy is the poetry of the Spirit. As Howard Carter once defined prophecy: "The thoughts expressed and the language which clothes them are raised above the level of the person's natural gift of speech."

While speaking in tongues is an important gift, it edifies only the person who speaks it. On the other hand, prophecy benefits the whole Church. Therefore, Paul said, "I wish you all spoke with tongues, but even more that you prophesied" (I Cor. 14:5).

According to I Corinthians 14:5, 24, the gift of prophecy is potentially available to all, to a certain degree. Yet, in actual practice, only a limited number manifest the gift in an acceptable manner in public.

Chapter Thirty-three

How the Gift of Prophecy Operates

The New Testament emphasizes exhortational prophecy. As we have seen, this is something quite different from revelatory prophecy, which is a deeper move into the mind of the Spirit. In I Corinthians 2:10 we are told that "the Spirit searches all things, yes, the deep things of God." In exhortational prophecy, the Spirit of God moves upon the person's subconscious mind. From this storehouse, the Holy Spirit anoints and brings forth truths which bless and edify the hearts of the hearers. Prophecy is "edification and exhortation and comfort" (I Cor. 14:3). These truths are arranged, energized and set forth by the Spirit of God.

The reason for the greater proportion of exhortational prophesying in the public assembly is obvious. It does not require the same degree of yielding to the Spirit as revelatory prophecy does; therefore, more people can exercise it. Also, exhortational prophecy is often more suitable to a congregation.

However, as they proceed, those who operate in exhortational prophecy may move deeper into the Spirit and into revelatory prophecy. When revelatory prophecy begins to come forth, the rhetorical flow is often so rapid, and so distinctly supernatural, that it would be impossible for a human to form the thoughts and sentences on their own.

Today there is a great hunger among God's people for revelatory prophecy, and the Church should pray and expect such operations of the Spirit to be manifested more. However, because of the complexity of the gift, it requires certain safeguards. Special teaching and instructions are important if the manifestation of the gift is to be kept within divine order.

Prophecy: Merging the Human Mind with the Holy Spirit

The gift of prophecy involves the merging of the human

and the divine, the finite with the infinite, the imperfect with the perfect. It is commonly understood that when a prophecy or an interpretation is given, that God, Himself, is speaking. In a real sense this is true, but if the gift of prophecy were entirely an operation of God without man's participation, there would be no need for instruction in its exercise.

The inspirational and revelatory gifts *are a product of both God and man.* God is infallible, but man is fallible. When the person is fully yielded to the Spirit of God, the utterances are infallible, but people are not always fully yielded. Even when the individual *is* fully in the Spirit, the imprint of the individual's personality is upon what is said. Prophecy is the result of the merging of the divine and the human.

Because of this, Paul said, "The spirits of the prophets are subject to the prophets" (I Cor. 14:32). The Holy Spirit is not subject to the prophets; it is the other way around. But, God works in a variety of ways; therefore, the number of combinations is as great as the number of prophets. No two prophets have the same style. Although the prophecies of both Isaiah and Hosea are divinely and verbally inspired, they are markedly different! The personality of Isaiah, under divine anointing, resulted in a book of prophecies of surpassing beauty and depth. It is recognized even by secular scholars as being among the finest literature ever produced.

The physical and mental freshness of the person prophesying has an effect on the richness of the prophecy. Weariness can prevent him from flowing in the Spirit. The anointing that comes as a result of special prayer and fasting may be another factor. Daniel received his greatest revelations during the times he had set aside for prayer and fasting.

We really know little about the nature of the Holy Spirit. All other things we see or know about have been created, but the Spirit of God is eternal. We know also that He is omnipresent, omniscient, omnipotent, and fills the bounds of space. The Holy Spirit not only has all power, but also has access to all the wisdom of God. This wisdom is made available to man only through the exercise of faith.

But God has revealed *them* to us through His Spirit. For the Spirit searches all things, yes, the deep things of God. For what man knows the things of a man except the spirit of the man which is in him? Even so no one knows the things of God except the Spirit of God (I Cor. 2:10, 11).

The analogy is clear. Just as people search their memories for stored away knowledge, so, in the operation of the gift of prophecy, the Spirit of God searches the infinite reservoir of divine knowledge for what He desires to reveal at the time.

The Limits of Prophecy

One of the most obvious facts about the operation of the gift of prophecy is its scrupulous faithfulness to the Scriptures. The Holy Spirit recognizes the Bible as complete and sufficient to bring people to spiritual perfection.

All Scripture *is* given by inspiration of God, and *is* profitable for doctrine, for reproof, for correction, for instruction in righteousness, that the man of God may be complete, thoroughly equipped for every good work (II Tim. 3:16, 17).

Since this is true, though He has infinite stores of wisdom and knowledge at His command, the Holy Spirit does not add to the canon of Scripture. Although the gift of prophecy does clarify, unfold and emphasize the truths that are specifically important at the time, it rarely, if ever, reveals what could be considered completely new information. In this connection, we should keep in mind the warning given by John the Revelator:

For I testify to everyone who hears the words of the prophecy of this book: If anyone adds to these things, God will add to him the plagues that are written in this book; and if anyone takes away from the words of the book of this prophecy, God shall take away his part from the Book of Life, from the holy city, and *from* the things which are written in this book (Rev. 22:18, 19).

"The Testimony of Jesus is the Spirit of Prophecy" (Rev. 19:10). The above words of the angel who was a guide to John the Revelator are deeply significant. They briefly sum up the purpose of the gift of prophecy. True prophecy always centers around and points to Christ — to His deity, His purpose in coming into the world, His ministry and His return to earth.

Any alleged prophetic gift which is engaged mainly in foretelling future events, telling fortunes, divining mysteries, entertaining people with supernatural demonstrations, but which leaves out Christ as the central and dominant theme, is clearly suspect. Such "revelations" have lured many unwary souls into confusion, doubt and spiritual shipwreck. All utterances which claim to be prophecy, but which do not focus or relate in some way to the truth and person of the Lord Jesus Christ, are counterfeit.

Laying on of Hands

Do not neglect the gift that is in you, which was given to you by prophecy with the laying on of the hands of the eldership (I Tim. 4:14).

Therefore I remind you to stir up the gift of God which is in you through the laying on of my hands (II Tim. 1:6).

Twice, Paul refers to his act of laying on of hands, and the simultaneous impartation of a gift to Timothy, in connection with the operation of the gift of prophecy. Concerning this, we make the following observations:

1. Since Paul repeated the statement twice, it appears that there is a definite operation of the gift of prophecy in connection with the laying on of hands.

2. However, the laying on of human hands *is only mean-*

ingful if the hands of God are laid upon the individual first.
The action of man is a confirmation of what God has already
done.

3. The Apostle Paul did not lay hands indiscriminately
upon everyone. His warning to Timothy was to "not lay hands
on anyone hastily" (I Tim. 5:22). Before mentioning the fact
that he had laid hands on Timothy, Paul refers to the young
man's spiritual background — the faith of his mother, Eunice,
and his grandmother, Lois. *Paul knew he was not laying hands
on a novice.*

It is unfortunate that people so often tend toward excess.
On one occasion, in my experience, a minister guaranteed in a
newspaper advertisement that 95 percent of those who attended his meeting would receive a certain gift! Sometimes, people
were told that they had received several gifts of the Spirit. In
the course of time, they learned that the ceremony performed
on them was meaningless. It is unscriptural to minister gifts
wholesale to a congregation in this way, and is certain to
produce confusion in their minds.

4. Gifts of the Spirit are not given by the will of man, but
by the Holy Spirit.

> But one and the same Spirit works all these
> things, distributing to each one individually as
> He wills (I Cor. 12:11).

> God also bearing witness both with signs and
> wonders, with various miracles, and gifts of the
> Holy Spirit, according to His own will? (Heb.
> 2:4).

In view of these Scriptures, those who minister the laying
on of hands to impart a gift must be clearly led by the Holy
Spirit and not by their own spirit.

5. The Holy Spirit divides the gifts as He desires. It appears
that God may ordain prophetic gifts to people before their
birth. Such was the case of Jeremiah:

> "Before I formed you in the womb I knew you; before you were born I sanctified you; I ordained you a prophet to the nations" (Jer. 1:5).

However, this does not mean that the individual will automatically enter into the prophetic office. There are things he or she must do before the gift will operate. Even after the gift has been manifested, the person may fail to exercise it as he/she should. Therefore, Paul admonished Timothy not to neglect the gift, but to stir it up. Jeremiah decided to withhold his gift due to the severe persecution he was receiving:

> Then I said, "I will not make mention of Him, nor speak anymore in His name." But *His word* was in my heart like a burning fire shut up in my bones; I was weary of holding *it* back, and I could not (Jer. 20:9).

Jeremiah went back to prophesying.

The Gifts Are to be "Stirred Up."

From what we have just learned, we see that many people have an inadequate view of the operation of the gifts of the Spirit. They suppose that the gifts operate by the sovereign will of God. It is not unusual for someone who gets out of order in the assembly to defend himself by saying, "The Holy Spirit compelled me to do what I did."

The truth is, the gifts of the Spirit are given according to the sovereign will of God, *but the exercise of them according to scriptural lines, depends upon the individual.* A prophet can get out of order, and if and when he does, he is not only responsible to God, but he is subject to judging by other prophets (I Cor. 14:32).

While it is true that the Holy Spirit gives the gifts, it is the individual who is responsible for manifesting them. He may be tempted to settle back into a natural sphere of ministry and neglect to stir up the gift. The Early Church evangelized with great power during the first centuries. But, after the time of

Constantine, they lapsed into a human-oriented ministry, and the gifts of the Spirit were gradually set aside. The Dark Ages followed as a result, with its monasteries, nunneries, hierarchies, ecclesiasticism, counting beads, awe of relics and spiritual death.

God is calling for the modern Church to stir up the gifts He has given it. And this includes the office and ministry of the prophet.

Is Prophecy Manifested in Preaching the Word?

Many present-day writers do not consider any kind of preaching to be a manifestation of the gift of prophecy. Howard Carter, in his *Questions and Answers on the Gifts of the Spirit* says:

> Prophecy is not preaching. If this were actually so, preparation for preaching would be unnecessary, as one might wait for the anointing of the Spirit without any premeditation. The one who ministers should wait on his ministry. Scripture affirms that God saves men by the foolishness of preaching, and not by the manifestation of prophecy.

Harold Horton in *The Gifts of the Spirit* declares:

> These translators who give the word "preach" instead of "prophesy" in English, in these chapters, must know well that they are taking liberties with the text. Their idea is, of course, so to translate the Word that they may plausibly lay claim to the possession of the gift of prophecy. To do so, they must, since they do not believe in the miraculous, strip the Word of every vestige of the miraculous.

I believe what these brothers have said is true. Indeed, much that passes under the name of preaching is neither prophecy nor even preaching in the scriptural sense. A lecture on philosophy, psychiatry, current events, sociology, book reviews, etc., is not preaching the Gospel. Nor is the ordinary ministry of the Word a manifestation of the gift of prophecy. We are encouraged to study the Scriptures in order to have a well of knowledge from which to draw when we minister to people. A rambling, ill-prepared sermon that has neither head nor tail, is not likely to edify the hearers.

While the ordinary teaching and preaching of the Word, even by the most skillful of preachers, should not be considered the manifestation of the gift of prophecy, I do believe there are times when the anointing of God comes so mightily upon speakers that they minister in the spirit of prophecy.

Consider the matter of prayer. Most praying is not an operation of the gift of prophecy, but there are occasions when prayer moves out of the natural realm and into the supernatural.

> Likewise the Spirit also helps in our weaknesses.
> For we do not know what we should pray for as
> we ought, but the Spirit Himself makes interces-
> sion for us with groanings which cannot be ut-
> tered (Rom. 8:26).

Apparently, both the gift of tongues and prophecy are being referred to here. Paul said, "I will pray with the spirit, and I will also pray with the understanding" (I Cor. 14:15). When he spoke of the Spirit making intercession for us (Rom. 8:26), it could mean an unknown tongue, or the spirit of prophecy. Such prayers of the Spirit are found throughout the Psalms. Although prayer is normally the expression of the human spirit, the Holy Spirit can, and often does, pray through the person who knows how to yield to Him.

Preachers of the first generation of this latter day Pentecostal revival, commonly understood that, at times, when a special anointing of the Spirit came upon them, the gift of prophecy was manifested through them while they were preaching. Some of these ministers prayed day and night for this anointing, and we must remember that it was this very ministry which broke through the centuries of denominationalism, to bring the apostolic experience back to the Church.

I feel there is an important truth being lost concerning this gift. While we are teaching young ministers how to preach, how to outline their sermons, how to make their sermons homiletical, we are shutting them off from the possibility of bringing the supernatural into their preaching.

Chapter Thirty-four

Prophecy and Guidance

> Now when they had gone through Phrygia and
> the region of Galatia, they were forbidden by the
> Holy Spirit to preach the word in Asia. After
> they had come to Mysia, they tried to go into
> Bithynia, but the Spirit did not permit them. So
> passing by Mysia, they came down to Troas. And
> a vision appeared to Paul in the night. A man of
> Macedonia stood and pleaded with him, saying,
> "Come over to Macedonia and help us" (Acts
> 16:6-9).

It is evident that, at times, guidance was given to the Early
Church through the gift of prophecy. But, it is also clear that
it was only one of the means for obtaining guidance, and was
used to warn God's people to avoid doing certain things as often
as to give a go-ahead signal.

The above passage demonstrates that the Lord has given us
various methods of guidance, and that we are not to restrict
ourselves to just one. Paul had been visiting the churches in
Asia Minor which he had established, giving "them the decrees
to keep, which were determined by the apostles and elders at
Jerusalem" (Acts 16:4). We are not told that Paul received any
special guidance in this particular task. His own good judgment showed that giving the churches these instructions was
necessary, and the providence of God made it possible for him
to do this at that particular time.

But, after completing this mission, Paul was uncertain
about what to do next. In his own mind, he thought he should
go deeper into Asia on another missionary journey. But, before
he could set the plan into operation, the Holy Spirit definitely
forbade him to do this.

Paul and his companions then decided to go into Bithynia, but "the Spirit did not permit them" to go there either (Acts 16:7). It is quite likely that the gift of prophecy was exercised by some members of the group in warning them that they were not to go in this direction.

It was still unclear where God wanted them to go. We may confidently assume that Paul's team was making it a matter of much prayer. In the meantime, they made their way down to the seaport of Troas. God was actually preparing the missionary team for a new project which was to have an immeasurable impact on world history. It was while they were at Troas that Paul had a vision of a Macedonian man, who said, "'Come over into Macedonia and help us'" (Acts 16:9).

Divine guidance was imparted in several ways when the Macedonian call was given. Although the gift of prophecy may have been manifested, it was not the only means of guidance by which Paul and his companions were led. Divine providence, sanctified judgment, the gift of prophecy, a God-given vision and a gradual elimination of alternatives all entered into the final decision.

The Gift of Prophecy and Paul's Journey to Jerusalem

During Old Testament days, it was common for people to inquire of a prophet for instruction when they needed divine guidance. A prophet or priest was the accepted intermediary between God and mankind. But the coming of the New Dispensation made all believers priests (I Pet. 2:9). All may go to God directly and receive instruction from Him without any human mediator.

And yet, all the gifts of God have a place in His plan. One of these is the gift of prophecy. But there are dangers if the biblical pattern is not followed. This is clearly brought out in the story of Paul's journey to Jerusalem. The Holy Spirit, through certain prophets in the Church, warned Paul that if he went to Jerusalem, he would be arrested, imprisoned and his very life would be endangered.

"And see, now I go bound in the spirit to Jerusalem, not knowing the things that will happen to me there, except that the Holy Spirit testifies in every city, saying that chains and tribulations await me" (Acts 20:22, 23).

We see that prophecy is not to be taken blindly, but its meaning must be weighed in light of all other evidence. If the Bible must be thoroughly and prayerfully studied in order to understand its meaning, certainly the gift of prophecy must be given the same consideration. Above all, what is revealed must be spiritually evaluated. The natural mind, without spiritual aid, can very easily get wrong impressions.

According to the prophecies that Paul received, it appeared that he should not go to Jerusalem.

And finding disciples, we stayed there seven days. They told Paul through the Spirit not to go up to Jerusalem (Acts 21:4).

Concerning this same matter, another prophecy was given to Paul by the prophet Agabus who had previously and accurately predicted a great drought would come upon the world. He bound himself with Paul's girdle and said: "'So shall the Jews at Jerusalem bind the man who owns this belt, and deliver *him* into the hands of the Gentiles'" (Acts 21:11).

After these warnings, those in Paul's company begged him to change his plans. And yet, the apostle went anyway! Did Paul disobey the Lord? How do we understand Paul's decision to go to Jerusalem in the light of these prophecies?

Unless we are to assume that Paul stepped out of the will of God, we cannot interpret these prophecies as actually forbidding Paul to go to Jerusalem. Rather, we must believe that the Spirit was showing the apostle what would happen to him if he did go.

1. There are times when advance information is of great value. It helps to prepare us for the things which will happen. Paul, knowing what would happen, was evidently prepared in his spirit for the hardships of the imprisonment which he

would soon face. Of this, he said, "'I am ready not only to be bound, but also to die at Jerusalem for the name of the Lord Jesus'" (Acts 21:13).

2. By giving these warnings, the Holy Spirit showed compassion for His servant who had endured so many sufferings for Him. God was not requiring that Paul make this hazardous trip. He was now in his 60s, nearly at the age when men ordinarily think of retirement. He would still be in God's will should he not go to Jerusalem. If he went, it would be "above and beyond the call of duty."

3. Of course, Paul did not go to Jerusalem just to be put into prison. That would have been totally foolish. Sacrifice without a purpose has no merit. God never recommends self-inflicted punishment. Paul had a mission to perform in Jerusalem. In Romans 15:25, he writes to the Romans concerning this trip, saying, "Now I am going to Jerusalem to minister to the saints." In his letter, he explains that he is carrying "a certain contribution for the poor among the saints who are in Jerusalem" (ver. 26).

4. Now notice this: Paul did not believe that his imprisonment was foreordained. He understood the prophecy to mean that unless the situation changed, imprisonment awaited him. He believed it was in the realm of possibility that if the saints stood with him in faith and prayer, he might be delivered from this, as he shows in Romans:

> Now I beg you, brethren, through the Lord Jesus Christ, and through the love of the Spirit, that you strive together with me in prayers to God for me, that I may be delivered from those in Judea who do not believe, and that my service for Jerusalem may be acceptable to the saints (Rom. 15:30, 31).

5. Paul had a deep affection for his own countrymen. (Rom 9:1-5). He was even willing to be "accursed from Christ" for their sake. He evidently hoped that by bringing the gifts he had gathered for the poor Christians in Jerusalem, it would open

the hearts of the Law-bound believers. Very likely, his trip to Jerusalem did have this effect.

6. As we know, Paul did go to prison, just as the prophecy indicated. God was able to take Paul's willingness to suffer for Christ and use it for His glory. Many people do not realize that a large number of the New Testament epistles were written while Paul was in prison. The busy apostle might never have found time to put in writing the great truths God had revealed to him had he not spent those years in prison. Those letters written to the various churches have become one of the most priceless treasures of the Church.

It is clear that the prophecies given to Paul were accurate, but he did not interpret their meaning in the same way others did. This incident reveals an important lesson on how prophecies should be evaluated when used for guidance. They are not to be acted upon blindly or upon how others interpret them. They are a part of a composite picture and should be considered in proper perspective when ascertaining God's will. When all methods of divine leading have been considered and a decision has been reached, there will be a deep peace of mind regarding whatever the future may hold.

Prophecy in Counseling and Forewarning

The gift of prophecy should be used sparingly when counseling those who are untaught in the Scriptures. People should not look for additional means of guidance when they have not taken advantage of what God has already provided. Daniel was a great prophet, but before He asked God for additional information, he studied the Scriptures to learn what He had previously revealed (Dan. 9:2).

People who are thoroughly acquainted with the Bible are better able to evaluate a prophecy. Just as young believers have a tendency to stumble over or misunderstand the Scriptures, they are also likely to stumble over and misinterpret a prophecy. Once a novice gets a wrong meaning from a prophecy, it is very difficult to change his or her mind, especially if they consider the prophecy an approval of what they wish to do.

Prophecies given in the Spirit must be interpreted by a spiritual mind and in the light of other leadings. This, as we have seen, is clearly brought out in the prophecies which were given to Paul at the time he was going up to Jerusalem.

One of the operations of the gift of prophecy is to foresee and forewarn concerning future events. The Old Testament is filled with such incidents, but the New Testament does not record as many, mainly because we have, apart from the Gospels, only one historical book in the New Testament. Of course, Jesus' ministry was full of incidents in which supernatural foreknowledge manifested, and in the Book of Acts, there were a number of incidents in which the Spirit of prophecy alerted the Church of dangers ahead.

The operation of the gift of prophecy in foretelling and warning concerning imminent danger still continues today. One such experience occurred on my trip to Japan in February, 1966:

The Crash on Mt. Fuji

A week before I left on my trip to visit our mission centers around the world, I received a phone call from Anna Schrader, a wonderful woman of prayer. She had been praying, and said, "I have just had a vision, and I see trouble on the Tokyo-Hong Kong flight." But she seemed to see me landing safely in Hong Kong. Then, in a further word that seemed rather mysterious at the time, she said, "There is danger at your right at the Hong Kong airport." Knowing that when Mrs. Schrader saw a vision, it should be taken seriously, I prayed a lot about the Tokyo-Hong Kong flight, but said nothing to my wife because I did not want her to worry. I left for Tokyo on Tuesday as planned.

It had been my desire for a long time to visit Hiroshima, the city upon which the first A-bomb fell in 1945, and I had made definite plans to visit the place while in Japan. I intended to complete my business of setting up our Japanese literature program with Kin Ichiro Endo on Thursday, then go by train to Hiroshima Thursday night, return Friday night, and take the 12 p.m. BOAC flight to Hong Kong on Saturday. I asked

Mr. Endo if he could accompany me to Hiroshima, but he was unable to go.

The next few hours, I was unsure of whether or not I should make the trip alone. I had learned a long time prior to this to put all plans in the hands of God, since only He can foresee the future. I had no presentiment of any danger, for at that moment, what Mrs. Schrader had said about the Tokyo-Hong Kong flight did not enter my mind. After wavering in indecision for some time, I finally decided to cancel the Hiroshima trip.

I called Lufthansa and made reservations to leave on Friday at 11 a.m., instead of taking the Saturday flight on BOAC. The next morning, I boarded the plane, and as it taxied out to the end of the runway, I thought of the plane which had plunged into the bay, killing all 133 passengers only a few days before. I did not know that a drama was about to unfold that would mark the next 24 hours as "the darkest day in all commercial airline history."

Although the fog was bad, our plane was able to take off successfully, and passing by Mt. Fuji — the suicide mountain — we were on our way south within a few minutes. Four-and-a-half hours later, we landed at the Kowloon Airport, across from Hong Kong. Looking out the window on my side of the plane, I saw a large Canadian Pacific jet. It was 2:30 p.m. Some passengers were standing around ready to board, for it was scheduled to take off at 3 p.m.

We went swiftly through customs, and as I looked ahead I saw Mr. S.K. Sung waiting for me. I remembered Mrs. Schrader's words, and I looked to the right to see what was in that direction. I saw only passengers who were hurrying through the exits to the Canadian Pacific plane ready for boarding. Dismissing this from my mind, I hurried forward to meet Mr. Sung. The next morning, I looked at the newspaper headlines. A Canadian plane coming into Tokyo Harbor had undershot the runway, crashed and exploded into a pillar of fire that killed 64 passengers. It dawned on me that the passengers boarding their plane at whom I had glanced so casually, were the victims of the disaster.

After a busy day in Hong Kong, I went to the home of Mr. Sung to spend the night. The next morning when I picked up a newspaper, the headlines blazed of another terrible air crash near Tokyo. The BOAC jet had exploded over Mt. Fuji, killing all 124 passengers. *It was the plane I almost took!* This crash, plus the Canadian Pacific tragedy, made it the worst day in the history of commercial aviation.

But to me, the strangest thing of all was the warning 10 days earlier that there would be trouble on the Tokyo-Hong Kong flight. Only because of a last-minute change of plans, did I escape being one of those passengers that perished on Mt. Fuji.

I might add that after I left Dallas, Mrs. Schrader had become so burdened with the premonition of danger, that she had called for three days of prayer and fasting by my family. It is obvious that such warnings are not given to satisfy mere curiosity, but that we might avoid disaster through prayer.

Chapter Thirty-five

False Prophets and Prophecies

> Beloved, do not believe every spirit, but test the
> spirits, whether they are of God; because many
> false prophets have gone out into the world. By
> this you know the Spirit of God: Every spirit
> that confesses that Jesus Christ has come in the
> flesh is of God, and every spirit that does not
> confess that Jesus Christ has come in the flesh is
> not of God. And this is the *spirit* of the Antichrist,
> which you have heard was coming, and is now
> already in the world (I Jn. 4:1-3).

Much as we would like to think otherwise, we need not go
far to find prophecies that do not meet the biblical test for genuineness. The Old Testament records numerous examples of
psuedo and backslidden prophets who gave false prophecies.
In some cases, they prophesied out of their own hearts. In other
instances, the false prophecies were the work of evil spirits.

Prophets with a true prophetic ministry will agree that they
must always be on guard against their own mind injecting
thoughts into a prophecy. When the anointing is strong, this is
not a serious problem. When it is weak, there is the possibility of the human expressing itself. That is why Paul tells the
prophets to speak one by one and let the others judge (I Cor.
14:29). Prophecies need to be judged. But note this: *They are
best judged by another prophet.*

When encouraging the development of prophecy in the
Church, we must recognize that when an inexperienced person
begins to manifest the gift, it is possible for him to make mistakes. Therefore, the pastor or the one guiding the service must
have patience with such people, or they may completely discourage them from manifesting the gifts.

People should refrain from critical discussion regarding a prophecy given in public. However, in extreme cases where obvious error has been spoken that might lead souls astray, it may be necessary for correction to be given by the pastor. A congregation should be taught to have a reverent and sympathetic attitude toward the manifestation of the gifts. Nevertheless, they should also understand that prophecies are never to be considered infallible. Those who have a prophetic gift are obligated to secure a good understanding of the Scriptures.

Some who make mistakes in the use of the gift are very sincere, and patient teaching will enable them to learn to manifest the gift in the proper way. On the other hand, it is a fact that a few individuals actually speak from their own mind, willfully misusing the gift for their own purposes. God overlooks unintentional mistakes made by those who minister the gift of prophecy, but calculated or premeditated misuse of the gift is a very serious matter, and can bring severe judgment upon those who commit such sacrilege.

The False Prophecy of Hananiah

An example of a prophet who prophesied out of his own mind is found in Jeremiah 28. Hananiah, the son of the prophet Azur, spoke to the people in the temple, saying:

> "Thus speaks the LORD of hosts, the God of Israel, saying: 'I have broken the yoke of the king of Babylon. Within two full years I will bring back to this place all the vessels of the LORD's house ...'" (Jer. 28:2, 3).

This was in flat contradiction to what Jeremiah had predicted in chapters 26 and 27. Jeremiah's prophecy of judgment had been very unpopular, and in fact, was considered treason. The priests were so incensed against him that they "seized him, saying, 'You will surely die!'" (Jer. 26:8). Jeremiah did not resist, telling them to do what seemed good and proper to them, but that if they carried out their plans, they would bring blood on themselves and the city (Jer. 26:14, 15). Jeremiah had many friends among the princes and the people who restrained the priests. A lesser known prophet, Urijah, was not so fortunate. King Jehoiakim sent a detachment of soldiers who captured Urijah and brought him to the king, who then had him executed (Jer. 26:20-23).

Hananiah who had prophesied the captivity would end in two years, persisted in his prophecy despite Jeremiah's warning that it was false. As a result, Hananiah died that year according to Jeremiah's word (Jer 28:13-17).

When Moses gave the amazing prophecy of the Messiah (Deut. 18:15-19), Whom he said would be a prophet like himself, he also gave a way to test whether or not a prophet is true.

> When a prophet speaks in the name of the LORD, if the thing does not happen or come to pass, that *is* the thing which the LORD has not spoken; the prophet has spoken it presumptuously; you shall not be afraid of him (Deut. 18:22).

We regret to say that there are also those who have risen up in our day, and in order to create a sensation and draw disciples to themselves, they have made fantastic predictions.

Others have laid their hands on ignorant laymen, and prophesied over them that they would receive all nine gifts of the Spirit. Of course, such prophesies were not of God, and came out of the heart of the speaker, who, by rejecting the teachings of the Scripture, had probably deceived himself into believing that his words were true.

Deuteronomy 13 also refers to false prophets who speak out of their own minds. The penalty for this presumption, under Mosaic Law, was death (ver. 5).

Jeremiah had to continually contend with false prophets who spoke out of their own hearts, prophesying good things to the people, when actually destruction was moving toward the land like a whirlwind (Jer. 14:13, 14).

Prophecies of Seducing Spirits

The Apostle John gives a solemn warning regarding these false spirits. He declares that many lying and deceiving spirits have gone out into the world (I Jn. 4:1-3) deceiving and deluding the unwary. Anyone who has been engaged in ministry for any length of time will sooner or later come into contact with such spirits. If their real identity were known, few, if any, would listen to them, so these deceiving spirits naturally pretend to be the Spirit of God.

Not only unbelievers, but even Christians sometimes fall for these deceptions. Not long ago, a man who claimed to be a prophet gave several startling demonstrations of his extrasensory power. He gave a warning to a group of men who were about to make a missionary trip. He told them that they should not make this trip under any circumstances, or they would all be killed. Being mature Christians, they decided after some reflection, to disregard the "prophecy." They made the trip with God's richest blessing, and returned safely. A few months later, it was not only discovered that the man was a fraud, but also a communist agent!

Honest people who are sincere before God do not need to be afraid of receiving a false spirit. However, those who live a double life are open to such spirits, and when possessed with one, are often convinced that the spirit is of God! I know of a young man who would attend prayer meetings and manifest what all believed was the gift of prophecy. Yet, he was secretly a heavy drinker. It was soon proved that he was possessed by a lying spirit. While in a state of drunkenness, a familiar spirit had taken possession of him.

The mediums of spiritism are, without exception, possessed by familiar spirits. Although many things that take place in seances are only tricks, some of the phenomena are genuine spirit manifestations. Spiritists' greatest hold on the gullible, is in their pretended communication with the dead. The "control spirit" of the medium calls up other spirits which imitate the voices of the dead. All Christians are warned to have absolutely nothing to do with spiritist mediums. Attempted communication with the dead by means of familiar spirits is condemned by the Scriptures (Lev. 19:31; I Chr. 10:13).

Lying Spirits

One of the most outstanding demonstrations of lying spirits in operation is found in I Kings 22:6-39. Ahab was a wicked king of Israel who made an alliance with King Jehoshaphat of Judah. Evil as he was, Ahab was religiously inclined. His plan was to go up against Ramoth Gilead, so he called about 400 prophets together and asked them to bless the endeavor (I Ki. 22:6). Without exception, these paid prophets told Ahab that the Lord would deliver the city into his hands.

Nevertheless, the godly Jehoshaphat was not satisfied with these glib promises. He asked if there was a prophet of Jehovah from whom to inquire. He was informed that there was a prophet by the name of Micaiah who had refused to identify himself with Ahab's prophets. Ahab said that he had dealt with him before, and his complaint was that Micaiah always prophesied evil against him. Therefore, the king had not invited Micaiah to join the party. Ahab apparently believed that if he could get enough prophets to predict victory, he would win the battle!

Jehosphaphat insisted that Micaiah be brought. He came, but was not at all pleased by the situation in which he was placed. At first, he pretended to go along with the other prophets, but even Ahab saw he was not speaking what he believed, and asked, "'How many times shall I make you swear that you tell me nothing but the truth in the name of the LORD?'" (I Ki. 22:16). Then Micaiah gave his strange revelation concerning the lying spirit, which God had permitted to come into the mouths of Ahab's prophets (I Ki. 22:17-23).

We should study this passage carefully, for it throws a revealing light on the operation of seducing spirits. When an individual, such as Ahab, yields to evil, God permits lying spirits to deceive him. Paul also brings this out in II Thessalonians 2:9-12.

Micaiah's prophecy was fulfilled. In the ensuing battle, Ahab was mortally wounded by an arrow, and by the time they had taken him back to Samaria, he was dead. The dogs licked up his blood when they washed his chariot, just as Elijah had proclaimed (I Ki. 21:19).

How Evil Spirits Come on Prophets

How do evil spirits get control of people? Consider the words of Jesus in Luke 11:

> "When an unclean spirit goes out of a man, he goes through dry places, seeking rest; and finding none, he says, 'I will return to my house from which I came.' And when he comes, he finds *it* swept and put in order. Then he goes and takes with *him* seven other spirits more wicked than himself, and they enter and dwell there; and the last *state* of that man is worse than the first" (Lk. 11:24-26).

Here, we see the operation of a certain law in the spiritual world. Within every human heart there is a spiritual void that can never be satisfied unless it is filled with God. Many people deny their souls the fulfillment of this inherent longing, all the while trying to fill that emptiness, but nothing else suffices.

King Saul had been mightily anointed by the Holy Spirit; he had prophesied, and had been numbered among the prophets (I Sam. 10:6-12). But, because of his insane jealousy, he left the door open for evil spirits to enter. The Spirit of the Lord departed from Saul and an evil spirit took its place (I Sam. 16:14). Later, Saul was delivered and healed from the power of this evil spirit (ver. 23).

Surely, this deliverance was an act of God's mercy. But, Saul did not appreciate his healing, and he allowed the same monster of jealousy to possess him again. Saul saw David only as a rival to his throne and therefore, was determined to kill him. So, it was not long before the evil spirit came upon Saul again. This time, the murderous spirit actually *prophesied* through Saul!

> And it happened on the next day that the distressing spirit from God came upon Saul, and he prophesied inside the house. So David played *music* with his hand, as at other times; but *there was* a spear in Saul's hand. And Saul cast the spear, for he said, "I will pin David to the wall!" But David escaped his presence twice (I Sam. 18:10, 11).

Here we see Saul prophesying under the influence of an evil spirit! Naturally, he supposed that the prophecy was of God.

People who have once had the true spirit of prophecy, may still prophesy even if evil emotions have taken over, but it may be the prophesying of a seducing spirit! Such a person becomes the victim of delusion, no longer comparing the teaching of the spirit which possesses him with the Scriptures. He and his followers go blindly to their fate, just as Saul and those who followed him went on to doom.

The time may come when the victim realizes he has been deceived, but in the case of Saul, it was too late.

> And when Saul inquired of the LORD, the LORD did not answer him, either by dreams or by Urim or by the prophets (I Sam. 28:6).

In desperation, Saul visited the Witch of En Dor, a demon-possessed woman, for instructions. Poor Saul! He went to inquire about his fate from a demonic spirit which had all along been scheming for his destruction. The Witch of En Dor told him that his doom was sealed: The next day about that time, he and his sons would be dead (I Sam. 28:15-17, 19).

The lesson is clear: Those to whom God has given the gift of prophecy must learn to live in the Spirit. Like Enoch, the first prophet, they must always walk with God.

Wrong Uses of the Gift

Great care should be taken so that the gift of prophecy is exercised only in the scriptural way. For example, I have heard of people entering into marriage based on a prophecy indicating that it was God's will. Certainly, it is a great mistake to choose a marriage partner in this fashion. Of course, we should take God into consideration when making such an important decision, but the first step is to search the Scriptures and learn what they teach about marriage. Half of the ill-fated marriages of Christians would never have happened if the two people concerned had followed scriptural advice on marriage. Some people are amazingly ignorant of what the Bible teaches about a union between believers and unbelievers, or concerning divorce and remarriage, as well as other basic laws governing this divinely-ordained institution.

We should not expect any further revelation from God on matters about which He has already revealed His will. After one has ascertained that there is no scriptural objection to entering a proposed union, then there should be a complete committal of the matter to God. If such a marriage is not in His will, He will permit the circumstances which are against it to be brought to light.

God works through His divine providence to guide His people, and nowhere is this method more suited than when seeking a marriage partner. But seeking guidance concerning marriage through the gift of prophecy is inviting the possibility of marital disaster.

Not for Introducing New Doctrines

The gift of prophecy is given for "edification, exhortation, and comfort," not for the purpose of introducing new doctrines. There is no comfort or edification in hearing Christians squabble over some new doctrine. The Apostle Paul had difficulty with certain people who brought division into the Church with teachings they claimed came by divine revelation, but which contradicted what had been taught by the apostles. One of the doctrines which was being propagated was that the resurrection had already passed. Paul turned these offenders over to Satan so they might be taught not to blaspheme.

The Scriptures came by men of God who spoke as they were moved by the Holy Spirit.

> For prophecy never came by the will of man, but
> holy men of God spoke *as they were* moved by
> the Holy Spirit (II Pet. 1:21).

Peter warns us that there will be false prophets arising with "destructive heresies" (II Pet. 2:1). As the Scriptures have been given by true prophets, so Satan uses false prophets to bring in doctrines which are erroneous. People are more easily deceived if they suppose the new doctrine has been given by revelation.

Perhaps, the most vulnerable part of the revelatory gifts is this temptation to use them to establish new doctrine. The worst of it is that the victim usually becomes closed to what the Scriptures have to say on the matter. In fact, direct statements by Jesus on the subject have little or no effect upon them. Moreover, the belief becomes a fixation and they cannot rest, but must continually try to persuade others of its supreme importance.

It is sad, but true, that some prominent Christians have been vulnerable to Satan's attacks by becoming sidetracked from the mainstream of Evangelical Christianity, into an area in which they are ill-qualified to participate, and from which they are usually unable to extract themselves.

The Gift is Not to be Used to Settle Arguments

> Then one from the crowd said to Him, "Teacher,
> tell my brother to divide the inheritance with
> me." But He said to him, "Man, who made Me
> a judge or an arbitrator over you?" (Lk. 12:13,
> 14).

This man wanted Jesus to settle a dispute he had with his brother over an inheritance. Jesus refused to act on this request, and sharply rebuked him instead. The Spirit of God is peaceful and easily grieved, and is not to be drawn into petty disputes or arguments over material matters.

A serious dispute developed in the Early Church when certain teachers in Judah took a doctrinal stand for circumcision, saying, "'Unless you are circumcised according to the custom of Moses, you cannot be saved'" (Acts 15:1). A controversy arose in Antioch over the matter. The Jews seemed to have a strong argument to back up their case. Paul stood against them, pointing out that the Old Testament ordinances had passed away, but the advocates of circumcision were not persuaded. It appeared that the controversy, if not settled, would destroy the unity of the Early Church.

The question was not solved by getting a word from the Lord by means of the gift of prophecy; it was taken before the apostles who were in Jerusalem. The matter was given very careful consideration. After it had been thoroughly weighed in light of the Scriptures, they reached a decision that the rite of circumcision was not to be imposed upon the gentiles.

Although the Church had numerous prophets within its ranks, the apostles did not turn to them to settle doctrinal controversies. Unfortunately, some in recent times have not been so wise. Serious heresies have arisen because some self-appointed prophets claim to have received some "new revelation" or "a deeper truth." On this basis, they draw followers, in some cases causing them to become extreme bigots focused mainly on proselytizing others to their peculiar views, rather than reaching lost sinners for Christ.

God gave us His complete Bible, which has long been recognized by the whole Church. From it, doctrine is to be established — not from the "revelations" of a self-styled prophet.

Not Designed to Satisfy Mere Curiosity

It is true that God often reveals important information through the gift of prophecy, and the general meaning of any such revelation is in harmony with the dignity and holiness of God. The contrast between divine revelation and the pseudo-revelations obtained by people controlled by seducing spirits is strikingly apparent. Divine revelation is not given to satisfy curiosity seekers or those possessed by an inquisitive spirit. Those who turn from the Scriptures and set themselves up as an authority on what is truth and what is not, are often the first to become victims of seducing spirits.

Chapter Thirty-six

True and False

The very existence of the Bible is supreme evidence of the value of the gift of prophecy, a gift which has been a God-ordained channel of communication to mankind. Nevertheless, the Scriptures have forewarned us that there are false spirits and prophets in the world. We must be on the alert against them.

Some people have little scriptural instruction concerning the ways of evil spirits, and may be led into fanaticism and sometimes into actual sin. Like Eve in the Garden, they fail to recognize the voice of Satan.

Prophets Who Speak Out of Their Own Hearts

It seems strange that any prophet would attempt to speak out of his own heart. It would hardly seem possible that anyone would be guilty of such sacrilege, but Satan is sometimes able to lead people to commit such an act, under the guise of promoting the Gospel. This is different from a prophet being a victim of delusion and prophesying in his delusion — although it may lead to it.

The case of a prophet deliberately lying is recorded in I Kings 13. There was an old prophet who lived in Bethel. He had sons who apparently joined with King Jeroboam in ministering at a false altar he had erected in order to keep the people from going to Jerusalem for worship. The family of the prophet, no doubt, was aware that Jeroboam's false altar was out of divine order, but they decided to conform, as a matter of policy, to Jeroboam's new mode of worship. Apparently, they wanted to retain the patronage of the king. When a strange prophet came, prophesied against the altar and performed the miracle of judgment upon Jeroboam, the old prophet probably saw that his standing was endangered. He likely felt that he had to meet this man and determine what effect these events would have on his own position.

God knew that the people of Bethel had gone into apostasy, and He did not want His messenger to have any communication with them. So He gave him strict orders to leave the city:

> But the man of God said to the king, "If you were to give me half your house, I would not go in with you; nor would I eat bread nor drink water in this place. For so it was commanded me by the word of the LORD, saying, 'You shall not eat bread, nor drink water, nor return by the same way you came'" (I Ki. 13:8, 9).

The old prophet heard about the matter from his sons, but by that time, the man of God had already left the city. The old prophet saddled his donkey and followed after the man of God in an attempt to persuade him to return to his house. When the man of God refused the invitation, the old prophet declared that he, too, was a prophet, which was true, and that an angel had told him to ask him to return with him, which was not true.

> He said to him, "I too *am* a prophet as you *are*, and an angel spoke to me by the word of the LORD, saying, 'Bring him back with you to your house, that he may eat bread and drink water.'" (He was lying to him.) (I Ki. 13:18).

In this way, the old prophet succeeded in getting the man of God to disobey. Nevertheless, while they sat at the table, the word of the Lord came to the old prophet, and he prophesied that because the man of God had disobeyed God's instructions, death would meet him on the way home. The prophecy came to pass just as the old man said.

It may seem strange that after the aged prophet had lied, the word of the Lord would still come through him, but the gifts and callings of God are without repentance. The incident teaches us that true prophecy will never contradict previous instructions given us by the Lord, and that it is possible for a prophet who is under strong motivation, to deliver a false prophecy. This circumstance is, no doubt, an unusual one, but the Scripture has given us this example as a warning not to be led astray by a prophecy which plainly conflicts with the Word of the Lord.

While there are a few who are bold enough to prophesy out of their own mind, there are others who are clearly victims of seducing spirits. This kind of prophet is the most dangerous, for they are usually sincere in their beliefs. Jesus warns us of these:

> "For false christs and false prophets will rise and show great signs and wonders to deceive, if possible, even the elect" (Matt. 24:24).

Prophecies are to be Judged

We are not to despise prophesies, but they must be weighed in the light of the Scriptures. As Isaiah the prophet spoke concerning any prophecy that appears to be questionable: "To the law and to the testimony! If they do not speak according to this word, *it is* because *there is* no light in them" (Isa. 8:20).

One of the warnings the Holy Spirit gave me years ago was as follows:

> For my people are sometimes intemperate in the things that I have given unto them and they have gone far over what I have spoken. And they have spoken words of their own voices. The people must know when the speaking of the Spirit comes forth and when the words of men come forth to my people. They must know this and discern. They must differentiate between the voice of the Lord and the voice of the people. Even though the words of the Lord come through my servants, there are times when my servants shall speak their own words, even as my servant Paul spoke of his

words. So I would have you to note the difference. For they are in confusion over this.

For there are sometimes prophetic utterances which are not according to the Scriptures of understanding. But my people first have spoken out, and then read the Word of the Lord. That is the chaff in the wheat. And the Lord would have that blown away by the precious wind of the Holy Ghost that came down on the day of Pentecost.

When a prophecy requires judging, it is best that it be done by another prophet. Carnally-minded people are likely to be hostile to admonitions that step on their toes. Worldly Christians are apt to resent any judging of what they feel are their liberties. Refusal to heed admonitions and checks of the Spirit may lead to disaster.

Those who hear a prophecy that seems out of line are not necessarily called upon to judge it publicly, or to keep record of it. There are times when it is wise not to speak. However, this does not mean we are to blindly accept all that we hear.

Don't Despise Prophesies

While we are not to despise prophesies, we have the right to compare them with the Scriptures.

Do not quench the Spirit. Do not despise prophecies. Test all things; hold fast what is good (I Thes. 5:19-21).

The Scriptures warn us against false prophets, false spirits and false prophesies, yet the true gift has a very important place in the Church. If the scriptural safeguards are heeded, and the spirits are tested, the gift of prophecy can be, and should be, a tremendous blessing to the people of God.

Because of the Gift of Prophecy:

1. We have the Bible.
2. We have the great prophecies of the Savior's birth.
3. We have the promise that Christ will come again.
4. We have absolute proof of the divine authorship of the Scriptures.
5. We have a means of direct communication with God.
6. Communion, which was lost in the Garden of Eden, is restored.
7. We have certain other gifts of the Spirit in operation.
8. The Church receives exhortation, edification and comfort.
9. Within certain bounds, we have guidance through difficult situations.
10. We have the testimony of Jesus as the Spirit of prophecy; the gift honors Christ.
11. We have the promise of "things to come."
12. Honor is paid to the Scriptures (which were originally given through the gift).
13. We are warned of dangers ahead and how to avoid them.
14. The Church is given a new consciousness of God's presence.

Part IV

The Baptism in the Holy Spirit, Speaking in Tongues and Interpretation of Tongues

Chapter Thirty-seven

21 Reasons Christians Should Speak in Tongues

1. Speaking in other tongues is foretold in the Old Testament prophecies.

For with stammering lips and another tongue He will speak to this people, to whom He said, "This *is* the rest *with which* you may cause the weary to rest," and, "This *is* the refreshing"; yet they would not hear (Isa. 28:11, 12).

It has been well said that the Old Testament is the New concealed, and the New Testament is the Old revealed. The great truths of the New Testament all have their roots in the Old. It is not surprising, therefore, that the phenomenon of speaking in other tongues is clearly foretold in Isaiah, a book written some 800 years before the Church Age began.

Isaiah chapters 24-28 have often been called the "Little Apocalypse." These brief chapters reveal a moving portrayal of the whole scope of events that will occur at the end-time. They tell of the Great Tribulation, the destruction of the gentile powers, the resurrection of the dead, the restoration of Israel, the establishment of the millennial kingdom and the binding of Satan. But the inspired writer does not complete this panoramic preview of end time events until he records that along with these world judgments, God would also give His people a great blessing, a "rest" and "refreshing" — the mighty baptism in the Holy Spirit with the attending phenomenon of speaking in other tongues.

As previously noted, the law of first mention involves the peculiar fact that when a great truth first appears in Scripture, the most important aspects of that truth are mentioned or touched upon in the passage. In the present instance, the following important points are alluded to in the prophecy:

• This prophecy would take place in its fullness just before the end of the age. (Notice that it is associated with the great end-of-the-age prophecies.)

• Speaking in other tongues will be a special method God will use to reach people of that time period.

• Speaking in other tongues would include "stammering lips," inferring that at first the utterances may be halting and broken, before the clear flow of the language takes place.

• The phenomenon of speaking in other tongues will be directly associated with a special refreshing and rest that God will give to His people — a blessing which is none other than the baptism in the Holy Spirit.

• Despite the manifestation of this divine phenomenon, many will harden their hearts, reject it and in turn, be rejected by God. The extreme danger of such unbelief is shown in chapter 28:

> Yet they would not hear. But the word of the LORD was to them, "Precept upon precept, precept upon precept, line upon line, line upon line, here a little, there a little," that they might go and fall backward, and be broken and snared and caught (Isa. 28:12, 13).

2. The New Testament declares that speaking in tongues is a fulfillment of this Old Testament prophecy.

> In the law it is written: "*With men of other tongues and other lips I will speak to this people; and yet, for all that, they will not hear Me,*" says the Lord (I Cor. 14:21).

The prophecy mentioned in Isaiah was not overlooked in the New Testament. When the Apostle Paul discussed the various gifts of the Spirit in his first epistle to the Corinthians, he pointed out that this prophecy foretold the coming of the gift of tongues to the New Testament Church. He added that the prophecy also mentioned one of the great purposes of the gift — that it should be a sign to unbelievers. In other words, it would be the means of convincing unbelievers of the reality of the supernatural Gospel.

Paul further noted, however, that despite the startling impressiveness of the sign, there would be those who would not believe it or the prophecy which foretold its coming. Nevertheless, speaking in other tongues was foretold in prophecy and therefore belongs to the Church.

3. In the Great Commission Christ said that believers should speak in tongues.

> And He said to them, "Go into all the world and preach the gospel to every creature. He who believes and is baptized will be saved; but he who does not believe will be condemned. And these signs will follow those who believe: In My name they will cast out demons; they will speak with new tongues ..." (Mk. 16:15-17).

One of the most important passages in the whole Bible is Mark 16, where Christ gave the Great Commission to the Church. These were the last words of our Lord before He went back to heaven. Their tremendous importance has been universally recognized by the Church down through the centuries.

First, the Church was instructed to go into all the world and preach the Gospel to every creature. Though we have lagged sadly behind in carrying out this command, the Church does generally recognize the importance and urgency of fulfilling it as soon as possible.

Next, Jesus commanded that we make disciples of all nations. Those who believe the Gospel will be saved and those who reject it will be lost.

So far, the evangelical Church is in agreement, but that is not all of the Great Commission. At the same time, Christ spoke of certain signs that would identify true believers. Among these signs are casting out demons and speaking in tongues (ver. 17). That Jesus included speaking in other tongues in the Great Commission emphatically calls attention to the sign's importance.

4. The original 120 disciples who were filled with the Holy Spirit on the Day of Pentecost spoke with other tongues.

The charter members of the Early Church were the 120 who obeyed the Lord's command, "'Tarry in the city of Jerusalem until you are endued with power from on high'" (Lk. 24:49). These 120 believers included the apostles, perhaps the 70, Mary the mother of Jesus and certain others. "These all continued with one accord in prayer and supplication, with the women and Mary the mother of Jesus, and with His brothers" (Acts 1:14). Then came the Day of Pentecost, and while they were in the upper room praising and blessing God, the Holy Spirit suddenly fell upon them and each person began to speak in other tongues!

> When the Day of Pentecost had fully come, they were all with one accord in one place. And suddenly there came a sound from heaven, as of a rushing mighty wind, and it filled the whole house where they were sitting. Then there appeared to them divided tongues, as of fire, and *one* sat upon each of them. And they were all filled with the Holy Spirit and began to speak with other tongues, as the Spirit gave them utterance (Acts 2:1-4).

Notice that as they were filled with the Holy Spirit, the apostles, Mary the mother of Jesus and the others all spoke in other tongues. This is the original pattern for receiving the Holy Spirit — with the infilling, each person speaks in other tongues as the Spirit gives utterance.

This supernatural visitation in Jerusalem drew together a multitude of people. Their wonder was turned to sheer amazement as they heard the 120 disciples speaking in various languages, including the native languages of the visitors who were in Jerusalem. This phenomenon caused them to give serious attention to Peter's sermon, as he explained the meaning of what had happened. A revival broke out that day, and before night, 3,000 people accepted Christ. Many things could be said concerning this epochal event, but the point to be made in connection with our study is that each one of these original believers spoke in other tongues as they received the Holy Spirit.

5. The first gentiles to be saved received the Holy Spirit and spoke in other tongues.

The story of how Cornelius and his household were saved and received the Holy Spirit holds a prominent place in the Book of Acts. Although the apostles did not understand it, God's plan was for both Jews and gentiles to share in the blessings of the New Testament dispensation that were obtained through Christ's death and resurrection. In accordance with this purpose, an angel appeared to Cornelius and said to him, "'Your prayers and your alms have come up for a memorial before God. Now send men to Joppa, and send for Simon whose surname is Peter'" (Acts 10:4, 5).

God had to do some persuading to get Peter to go to this gentile home and preach the Gospel to them, but He succeeded, and Peter and his friends went to the house of Cornelius. While Peter was still preaching to them, the Holy Spirit fell upon all who heard the Word:

> While Peter was still speaking these words, the Holy Spirit fell upon all those who heard the word. And those of the circumcision who believed were astonished, as many as came with Peter, because the gift of the Holy Spirit had been poured out on the Gentiles also. For they heard them speak with tongues and magnify God (Acts 10:44-46).

The gentiles received the Holy Spirit as well as Jews, but

how did Peter and his friends know that they had received the Holy Spirit? The answer is, "For they heard them speak with tongues and magnify God." This was exactly the same as what had happened to the Jews at Pentecost! Peter, reporting back to the other apostles, said, "'And as I began to speak, the Holy Spirit fell upon them, as upon us at the beginning'" (Acts 11:15). Both Jews and gentiles had now received the Holy Spirit, and both groups spoke in tongues when they received! Receiving the Holy Spirit with speaking in other tongues became a pattern for other gentiles.

6. The Apostle Paul spoke in other tongues.

The outstanding figure of the Early Church was Paul. His conversion was perhaps the most unusual one recorded in the New Testament. Brought up a strict Pharisee at the feet of Gamaliel, his intellectual powers promised a brilliant future for the Jewish religion. Even more zealous than his colleagues, he not only participated in the stoning of the first Christian martyr, Stephen, but he was also active in a persecution designed to wipe out Christianity completely. This was all before his notable experience on the Damascus Road. There, in a blinding light that outshone the midday sun, the Lord Jesus appeared to him. At that moment, his whole life was changed. From that point onward, he proved to be Jesus' most devoted follower.

As he arose from the ground where he had fallen, Paul was told by the Lord to go into Damascus. Being blinded by the vision, he had to be led into the city, where he prayed for three days and nights, taking neither food nor drink. Then Ananias, came in and laid hands upon him, as God had commanded him, and Paul received the Holy Spirit and was delivered from blindness.

In this account recorded in Acts 9, nothing is said about Paul speaking in tongues. But when he wrote to the Corinthian Church, he said, "I thank my God I speak with tongues more than you all" (I Cor. 14:18).

Why is Paul's experience significant to us? He said that he

was to be a pattern for all Christians who should afterward believe in Christ:

> However, for this reason I obtained mercy, that
> in me first Jesus Christ might show all longsuf-
> fering, as a pattern to those who are going to be-
> lieve on Him for everlasting life (I Tim. 1:16).

That Paul, whose life was supposed to be a pattern for all
believers, spoke in tongues is one more reason why all Christians should speak in tongues.

*7. More than 25 years after Pentecost, those who received the
Holy Spirit spoke in other tongues.*

More than 25 years had passed since the Day of Pentecost,
and Paul had gone to Ephesus on one of his many missionary
journeys. Upon meeting some disciples from that city, he asked
them, "'Did you receive the Holy Spirit when you believed?'"
(Acts 19:2). Perhaps their lack of spiritual power prompted
this question; at any rate, their answer showed they knew nothing about the experience. They replied, "'We have not so much
as heard whether there is a Holy Spirit'" (Acts 19:2). Upon
further inquiry, Paul found that they knew only about John's
baptism.

This reply moved Paul to preach a sermon on the Holy
Spirit. He pointed out that John not only preached about the
baptism of repentance, but that he spoke also about One who
would come after him who would baptize with the Holy Spirit
and fire (Matt. 3:11). These disciples, upon accepting Paul's
report, were baptized in Jesus' Name. Then Paul laid hands
upon them, and they received the Holy Spirit and spoke in
other tongues!

> And when Paul had laid hands on them, the Holy
> Spirit came upon them, and they spoke with ton-
> gues and prophesied (Acts 19:6).

Is it not apparent that a pattern is emerging?

- The 120 received the Holy Spirit, and all spoke in other tongues.
- The gentiles received the Holy Spirit at the house of Cornelius and they, too, spoke in other tongues.
- Paul received the Holy Spirit and spoke in other tongues.
- The men at Ephesus were filled with the Holy Spirit, and they spoke in other tongues.

"By the mouth of two or three witnesses the matter shall be established" (Deut. 19:15). Here are four cases in which people received the Holy Spirit, and in each instance, the recipients spoke in other tongues.

8. Did the believers who received the Holy Spirit in Samaria speak in other tongues?

There is only one other time in the New Testament where it is recorded that people received the Holy Spirit. Philip the evangelist went down to Samaria and conducted a healing revival. Did these people who received the Spirit also speak in other tongues?

> And the multitudes with one accord heeded the things spoken by Philip, hearing and seeing the miracles which he did. For unclean spirits, crying with a loud voice, came out of many who were possessed; and many who were paralyzed and lame were healed (Acts 8:6, 7).

News of the revival reached the ears of the apostles in Jerusalem. They were pleased, of course, to hear of the revival, but they were a little disturbed because no one had received the Holy Spirit. When Peter and John, who had a special ministry in this respect, went to Samaria and laid their hands on them, they received the Holy Spirit (Acts 8:17).

Nothing is specifically said here about speaking in other tongues, but notice what happened. A sorcerer by the name of Simon had attended the revival and had become interested, though he apparently supposed the whole thing was just another kind of sorcery. The healings and miracles impressed him, but not to the point that he would part with his money. But when he saw the people receive the Holy Spirit as Peter and John laid their hands on them, he considered this such great "magic" that he was willing to give money to obtain it. Peter gave him the scathing rebuke he deserved for thinking he could secure the gift of God through money.

What did Simon see that impressed him so much that he was willing to part with his money? Neither the miracles nor the healings had moved him to make such an offer. A possible answer is that when the people were filled with the Holy Spirit they spoke in other tongues. It was probably this phenomenon that astonished Simon, just as it had amazed the people in Jerusalem.

9. Speaking in other tongues is a gift given by God to the Church, the body of Christ.

In I Corinthians 12, Paul lists nine gifts given by the Holy Spirit to the Church. Among these gifts is speaking in *"different kinds of tongues"* (I Cor. 12:10).

Despite tradition which teaches the contrary, God has never withdrawn these gifts from the Church. The only Scripture even offered in an effort to substantiate such a position is found in I Corinthians 13:8: "Love never fails. But whether *there are* prophecies, they will fail; whether *there are* tongues, they will cease; whether *there is* knowledge, it will vanish away." It is contended by some that this statement means that "tongues" have already ceased. The context, however, clearly shows that this is not the meaning. Paul is referring to the time "when that which is perfect has come" (I Cor. 13:10).

Paul adds that when that which is perfect is come, prophecies will fail and knowledge will vanish away. As anyone knows, we have not come to perfect knowledge, neither have we entered the perfect age. Until that time, we will need prophecy, knowledge, speaking in other tongues, and all the other manifestations of the Holy Spirit.

The gifts of the Spirit are sorely needed in the Church today.

We need them just as the Corinthian Church needed them.

Paul also promised that God would not withdraw them, but that He would confirm His people through these gifts, until Christ returns.

> So that you come short in no gift, eagerly wait-
> ing for the revelation of our Lord Jesus Christ,
> who will also confirm you to the end, *that you
> may be* blameless in the day of our Lord Jesus
> Christ (I Cor. 1:7, 8).

Since Christ will confirm His Church until His coming, the gifts should be in operation now. Believers should speak in tongues just as Jesus said in the Great Commission.

10. God has set "different kinds of tongues" in the Church.

So far we have observed that all believers have the privilege of speaking in other tongues, and that this sign apparently follows as the initial evidence of the baptism in the Holy Spirit. However, beyond this, we find that God gives to some believers a more varied manifestation of the gift — the ability to speak in more than one tongue. Thus in I Corinthians 12:10, we are told that some are given "different kinds of tongues." Verses 7-10 show that one particular gift is given to one individual and another gift is given to another. The 11th verse declares:

> But one and the same Spirit works all these
> things, distributing to each one individually as
> He wills (I Cor. 12:11).

Again in the 28th verse, we are told that God has appointed "varieties of tongues" in the Church. Although, in each case recorded in the Scripture, those baptized in the Holy Spirit spoke with other tongues, it is evident that the gift of "varieties of tongues" is not for everyone. The specialized gift is for certain individuals chosen by the Spirit. This is made clear in verse 30, which refers to verse 28 saying that all do not speak with these "varieties of tongues." Only a limited number of those baptized in the Holy Spirit speak in more than one language.

11.   *Those who speak in other tongues speak to God.*

> For he who speaks in a tongue does not speak to men but to God, for no one understands *him;* however, in the spirit he speaks mysteries (I Cor. 14:2).

Many people wonder about God's purpose in speaking in other tongues. The fact that those who speak in an unknown tongue speak to God, would be a sufficient reason if it were the only one!

At the time of conversion, God speaks to us in our own language and says, "Child, you are now a member of My family." But when we are baptized in the Holy Spirit, we are able to speak to God in His language — a language only He understands.

If God chooses, He can give us a language that not even the devil can understand — a way of communicating with God that neither man nor devil can intercept. In time of war, nations have codes for secret communication. Sometimes the enemy is able to break that code, but we may be sure that not even the devil can break God's code!

12. *The believer who speaks in tongues edifies himself.*

> He who speaks in a tongue edifies himself, but he who prophesies edifies the church (I Cor. 14:4).

This is something that a person on the outside usually does not understand. They hear someone speak in tongues and cannot see any blessing in it. This is not surprising, for Paul declares that speaking in other tongues is not for the purpose of edifying the listener. (We are not referring to certain unusual manifestations of the gift like what happened on the Day of Pentecost, resulting in the conversion of 3,000.) Speaking in other tongues is a spiritual exercise designed to edify the speaker. For this reason, Paul taught that speaking in tongues in the assembly, unless accompanied by interpretation, was to be discouraged (I Cor. 14:5, 6).

Naturally, until some speak in tongues they cannot understand how it can be a blessing to them, or how they will be edified by it. But once they receive it, they find it a supernatural experience carrying with it a rich spiritual blessing.

13. Paul said, "I wish you all spoke with tongues" (I Cor. 14:5).

Not all gifts of the Spirit are for every member of the Church to exercise. The gift of miracles, for example, might result in disaster if someone unqualified used it. Even the apostles were once ready to use the gift in a manner that was out of the will of God (see Lk. 9:52-56).

Most of the gifts are intended for the edification of the Church and need to be exercised by people having certain qualifications. But no special qualification is needed for edifying oneself. Where an unlearned person might disturb the order of a religious service through lack of wisdom, there is no such difficulty presented when he/she edifies themself. If one feels like speaking in tongues for several hours, it is all right, and good is done rather than harm. Paul found the gift highly profitable in his devotions and prayer life. He said, "I will pray with the spirit, and I will also pray with the understanding. ... I thank my God I speak with tongues more than you all" (I Cor. 14:15, 18).

14. If interpreted, speaking in tongues is equal to prophecy.

I wish you all spoke with tongues, but even more that you prophesied; for he who prophesies *is* greater than he who speaks with tongues, unless indeed he interprets, that the church may receive edification (I Cor. 14:5).

Although speaking in tongues is principally for private edification, it does have some very important uses. The unintelligible spoken mysteries in the Spirit are not edifying to the audience unless there is some way to interpret them. Occasionally, the unknown tongue is in the native language of someone present and he/she can interpret what has been said. Usually, however, there is no one present who understands the language which has been spoken. For this reason, God has also given the gift of interpretation to the Church. If the Holy Spirit enables either the one who speaks in tongues, or another person present, to interpret the message given, then the church is edified. When these two gifts function together, they are equal to the gift of prophecy.

The person who gives a public message in an unknown tongue must be very sensitive to the Spirit's leading. Though there may be exceptions, the Holy Spirit will rarely lead them to interrupt when a message is being preached. He will not attempt to give two messages at the same time, either (I Cor. 14:23, 27). Prophets may only speak one at a time (I Cor. 14:31). They should watch for an appropriate time in the service for giving a message. If the time is properly chosen, the whole audience senses that God has come on the scene and is speaking to them, and the church is edified. Of course, if there is no interpreter in the church, they should remain silent (I Cor. 14:28).

How many messages may be given during a single service? Verse 27 indicates that two or three are generally sufficient. A long series of tongues and interpretations could make the gift common and weaken its effect.

Although the speaking in other tongues and the interpretation of tongues are to be exercised only according to the scriptural order, they have a definite place in the church and should be encouraged.

15. One may pray in the Spirit through an unknown tongue.

> Likewise the Spirit also helps in our weaknesses. For we do not know what we should pray for as we ought, but the Spirit Himself makes intercession for us with groanings which cannot be ut-

tered. Now He who searches the hearts knows
what the mind of the Spirit *is* because He makes
intercession for the saints according to *the will
of* God. (Rom. 8:26, 27).

In the above Scripture, the apostle tells us that none of us
knows how to pray as we should, but we have a powerful ally
in the Holy Spirit, Who will, if permitted, make intercession for
us. Moreover, since the Holy Spirit always knows the mind of
God, He will always pray for us according to God's will.

But how does the Holy Spirit pray through us? We may be
sure that the Spirit seeks to help us, no matter how we pray,
but that is not what the apostle means. He is referring to prayer
in the Spirit through an unknown tongue. In such a case, the
Holy Spirit prays through the believer. Paul said he prayed
with the Spirit and with the understanding — both ways. It is
good to pray with understanding, but also it is good to pray in
the Spirit, for when we are at loss for words and unable to
express ourselves in prayer, the Holy Spirit will, in the unknown tongue, take the need and lift it up to God. With the
Holy Spirit praying through us, all things will work for our
good.

And we know that all things work together for
good to those who love God, to those who are
the called according to *His* purpose (Rom. 8:28).

16. Speaking in tongues is a sign to unbelievers.

In the law it is written: "*With men of other tongues and other lips I will speak to this people;
and yet, for all that, they will not hear Me,*" says
the Lord. Therefore tongues are for a sign, not to
those who believe but to unbelievers; but prophesying is not for unbelievers but for those who
believe (I Cor. 14:21, 22).

Although some people resent speaking in other tongues,

there are many who can testify that they were first spiritually awakened by the manifestation of this sign. Though they did not understand it, they sensed that God was in it. Others have heard a message in tongues with the interpretation that followed, and knew it was God's voice speaking to them.

Paul, quoting from Isaiah, declares that speaking in other tongues is a sign to unbelievers. The prophecy adds, however, that many will not believe or accept the sign as a divine phenomenon. In rejecting it, God rejects them according to the prophecy. Nevertheless, there are many who have heard speaking in other tongues and through this sign, have turned to God.

17. Speaking in other tongues has sometimes been in the native language of one present, thereby convincing him/her of the reality of the gift.

The effect speaking in other tongues has on unbelievers is multiplied many times when, as sometimes happens, the language used is known to one or more of the listeners. In almost every case like this, the listeners are astonished to hear a message in their own language from the lips of someone they know has never learned the language.

It was an event of this nature that astonished the people on the Day of Pentecost. Some of them had come from distant lands and spoke languages totally unfamiliar to the Galileans, yet they heard these Galileans speaking and glorifying God in their own languages (Acts 2:5-6).

Though some of the crowd that had gathered scoffed and accused Peter and the other apostles of being drunk, many believed as the result of what happened that day. Approximately 3,000 accepted Christ, were baptized and admitted into the newly-formed Church.

It should be observed, however, that the gift of languages that amazed the multitude on the Day of Pentecost did not take the place of preaching. After an audience gathered, Peter preached in the ordinary language of the country. However, God may occasionally do the unusual. A few instances have been reported in which a person has been enabled to preach in a foreign language without learning it by natural methods, but such cases are rare.

18. God said that with stammering lips and another tongue He would speak to the people.

When the prophetic word in Isaiah 28 mentioned speaking in other tongues, it also included the sign of "stammering lips" (ver. 11). This sign has been a stumbling block to some people. But note that the prophet declared this would be! He said, "That they might go and fall backward, and be broken and snared and caught" (ver. 13). Verse 14 shows that religious rulers would be numbered among the scornful. They can see no purpose in speaking in other tongues, and they certainly see no place for "stammering lips."

"If it is of God," they say, "would it not come forth perfect and in full bloom at once?" They do not realize that just as a child learns to speak, so the first utterances of those who speak in tongues may be with "stammering lips." And just as a child gradually learns to speak fluently, so the person who stammers will, as he yields to the Spirit, begin to speak a clear tongue.

In this same prophecy (ver. 9) the Lord likens a believer's spiritual development to the natural development of a child. For a time, children nurse at their mother's breast. They can only take milk, and their first words are halting and imperfect. Later, they are weaned and develop in wisdom and utterance. The scornful person sees only imperfection in the lives of those who speak in tongues, but God sees them as they will be when they reach perfection.

Some people come close to a scriptural experience but fail to fully enter in, because they hear themselves begin to speak with stammering lips and they become fearful. They think, "Maybe this is just me." They are partly right. It is their own lips and voice speaking, but it is the Holy Spirit giving the utterance. That is the way it was on the Day of Pentecost. They "began to speak with other tongues, as the Spirit gave them utterance" (Acts 2:4).

Therefore, when the Holy Spirit comes upon you, do not fear. Do not quench the Spirit, or stifle the stammering lips. Let

God have His way. As you learn to speak, as He gives utterance, and as you yield to His Spirit, you shall find that the stammering lips will become a beautiful, fluent flow of language.

19. Speaking in other tongues is an indication of the "rest" and "refreshing" promised by the Lord.

The Holy Spirit must have been speaking about something of great importance when He said, "'This *is* the rest *with which* you may cause the weary to rest,'" and, "'This *is* the refreshing'" (Isa. 28:12). It is evident that this verse is a reference to the previous one which says, "For with stammering lips and another tongue He will speak to this people" (ver. 11).

The Holy Spirit Who comes and gives the utterance is the "rest" and the "refreshing," not speaking in other tongues in itself. The Holy Spirit is a person. When He comes, He speaks. The manifestation and presence of the Holy Spirit thus becomes the great blessing.

Thus it was that immediately after the Day of Pentecost, when the Early Church was in the flush of its great Pentecostal experience, Peter called the people of God to repent and receive the blessing in "times of refreshing ... from the presence of the Lord" (Acts 3:19).

Let no one minimize the experience of speaking in other tongues, for it indicates the presence of the Holy Spirit, Who has come to make His home in the believer's life.

20. Paul commanded the Church not to "forbid to speak with tongues" (I Cor. 14:39).

Paul knew there were problems connected with the exercise of the gift in public. He also knew that undisciplined people would sometimes misuse the gift, like they had done in the Corinthian Church. In his letter, He gave several admonitions against abuses that could have had adverse effects. Yet, he did not consider these possible dangers sufficient cause to rule out the speaking in other tongues. Doing that would cause the Church to suffer great loss. Instead, he admonished those who had charge of the services to guide them with discretion. He showed those who spoke with tongues that they must also have the love of God, or their speaking would be as "sounding brass or a clanging cymbal" (I Cor. 13:1).

Yet after giving this warning, instead of belittling the gift, Paul gave detailed instructions on how it can be the blessing God intended. He closed his remarks by saying, "Do not forbid to speak with tongues." Therefore, those who will not allow this manifestation in the Church violate the direct commandment of the Scriptures, and label themselves as ignorant:

> But if anyone is ignorant, let him be ignorant. Therefore, brethren, desire earnestly to prophesy, and do not forbid to speak with tongues. Let all things be done decently and in order (I Cor. 14:38-40).

21. *The contrast between the Tower of Babel and Pentecost.*

At the Tower of Babel, God sent judgment on the builders by confusing their languages (Gen. 11:5-9). Because of their rebellion, they were scattered over the face of the earth.

On the Day of Pentecost, God gave the gift of speaking in other tongues to the Church so that people from the scattered nations could hear and understand the wonderful works of God. Among these people were "those dwelling in Mesopotamia," the very land where the Tower of Babel was built! (Acts 2:9).

At Babel, the builders were confused and forced to stop building their pagan temple. But, at Pentecost, God began building a new structure — the church of the living God, with Jesus Christ as the chief cornerstone.

The Tower of Babel was left unfinished. Stones prepared for it were never set in place, and today it lies in total ruin on the deserts of Babylon, as a monument to the folly and presumption of mankind.

The structure created by what happened at Pentecost is still being built today. And the stone (Christ) that would have been rejected is now the head of the corner.

"This is the *'stone which was rejected by you builders, which has become the chief corner-stone'*" (Acts 4:11).

Thank God for this gift. It has become one of the great channels by which man is united to God. "For he who speaks in a tongue does not speak to men but to God" (I Cor. 14:2).

Chapter Thirty-eight

Facts About the Holy Spirit

Much of our knowledge concerning the Holy Spirit is found in John 14-16, where Christ reveals the Holy Spirit as the Paraclete, which translators have rendered as the "comforter." The Greek is a very rich language and the word implies even more than "comforter," including advocate, governor and caretaker. Jesus speaks of Him as the Spirit of Truth, implying that there are also false spirits. The one is called the Holy Spirit, while the others are known as evil spirits.

The Holy Spirit Deity

The Holy Spirit (also called the Holy Ghost), being a part of the Godhead, possesses all the attributes of deity. The Spirit of God brooded over creation and brought order out of the primeval chaos. He has the power to give life, and it was by Him that Christ was raised from the dead (Rom. 8:11). He is the Spirit of Truth. He never lies; and "is not a God of disorder but of peace" (I Cor. 14:33 NIV).

God the Father is also spoken of as a Spirit (Jn. 4:23, 24), and as far as we know, He does not have a physical form. We are told that His appearance is like a consuming fire (Ex. 24:17). The Holy Spirit has no form or shape, and is invisible to the eye. Although the Greek word for "spirit" is a neuter word and therefore is neither male nor female, Jesus refers to the Spirit as "Him" and "He." Because the Holy Spirit is more than an influence, but is a personality, the apostles could say, "For it seemed good to the Holy Spirit, and to us" (Acts 15:28). Agabus said, "'Thus says the Holy Spirit'" (Acts 21:11). Jesus said, "'He will guide you into all truth; for He will not speak on His own authority'" (Jn. 16:13).

The Holy Spirit is not subject to natural laws and limitations. Since He does not have a material body, He is free from all physical limitations. He can influence the physical universe, but is not Himself influenced by it. Gravity and natural laws have no effect upon Him. Having no dimensions, no place is too small or too large for Him to fill. He can dwell in the body of the believer or He can occupy the entire universe. He can manifest His presence in the home, in a church, outside, in an airplane, or on a ship at sea. No physical walls can hinder His movement.

The Work of the Spirit in Conviction and Conversion

When considering the Holy Spirit's ministry, we should first consider His work upon the sinner. There is no other agency of which we have any knowledge that can produce conviction of sin. Neither men, angels, principalities nor powers can do it. Jesus refers to this work of the Spirit in the Book of John:

> "And when He has come, He will convict the world of sin, and of righteousness, and of judgment: of sin, because they do not believe in Me; of righteousness, because I go to My Father and you see Me no more; of judgment, because the ruler of this world is judged" (Jn. 16:8-11).

The Holy Spirit's work on the sinner is a subject not well understood by a large part of the Church. Yet, it is one of the Spirit's greatest manifestations. The Church's recruits cannot become true members of the body of Christ, until they are converted. This does not take place until the Spirit gives them a real conviction of sin. Due to the absence of the Holy Spirit in a large section of the nominal Church, many of its members are unregenerated.

Because of this lack of the Spirit's presence, people have busied themselves by seeking substitutes to attract people into their churches. All such substitutes are worthless counterfeits. Individuals joining a church without true conviction of sin usually entertain a false hope that they are converted, when actually they are unsaved and lost.

True conviction takes place when the person has sorrow of

heart because he/she has lied, stolen, mistreated family and rejected Christ. There must be godly sorrow over sin before there can be real salvation. This comes as the result of the Spirit's work upon the sinner's heart. He takes the Word of God and lays it to the heart like a sword (Heb. 4:12).

The innermost thoughts of a person's heart are revealed through the Word of God. Therefore, the preaching of the Word is necessary in order to bring about conviction. The Spirit will use all means possible to reach a person's heart. But eventually, there is a limit to these avenues, and when the Spirit has tried them all and found the doors closed, there is nothing more He can do. Such a person then becomes hardened to the Gospel. It is a sad day indeed for that individual when the Spirit leaves him/her.

The natural man, however gifted, moral or refined, must be born again — that is, regenerated. It is an actual revolutionary work of the Spirit that changes the person's very nature. Paul states it beautifully:

> Therefore, if anyone *is* in Christ, *he* is a new creation; old things have passed away; behold, all things have become new (II Cor. 5:17).

When conviction of the Spirit reaches a point where the individual is willing to surrender to God, he repents of his sins and accepts Christ as Savior. The invisible work of the Spirit then begins. The person is born-again in a moment of time, but the Spirit's work is not completed at that instant. The Holy Spirit continues, as He is permitted, to work in a person's life, bearing the fruit of the Spirit and gradually changing the person's life into the image of Christ.

The Work of the Spirit Upon the Believer

The work of the Spirit upon the believer is quite different from His work upon the sinner. His ministry is essentially centered not around Himself, but around Christ.

"However, when He, the Spirit of truth, has come, He will guide you into all truth; for He will not speak on His own *authority*, but whatever He hears He will speak; and He will tell you things to come. He will glorify Me, for He will take of what is Mine and declare *it* to you" (Jn. 16:13, 14).

The Holy Spirit's first work with the believer is to reveal Christ as God's great and unspeakable gift to His people. Upon conversion, the Spirit baptizes the believer into the body of Christ (I Cor. 12:13) — a related work, but not to be confused with the baptism in the Holy Spirit.

New converts are usually asked to join some church or a denomination, and of course this is right. But joining a church must not be confused with being baptized by the Holy Spirit into one body, the body of Christ. People can profess faith in Christ, but if they isolate themselves and do not seek to work in harmony with other members of the body, it is difficult to understand how they can consider themselves belonging to the true Church.

The Spirit of God takes the things of Christ and reveals them to us. The importance of this is seen in the fact that while Jesus was on earth, He could minister only to a limited number at a time. The Holy Spirit, however, can deal individually with every person living in the world at the same time and with the greatest of ease.

It should be understood that we do not use the Holy Spirit, rather the Holy Spirit uses us. Different individuals have different capacities to be used by the Spirit. Great natural ability without the Spirit's anointing is not as valuable as a lesser ability with a powerful anointing of the Holy Spirit. However, where natural ability is yielded to God, there are greater results. The Apostle Paul, with his education, religious training, keen mind and remarkable natural talents, became a powerful tool in the Spirit's hand, launching the great missionary movement of the Early Church.

The Holy Spirit must have a body through whom He can

work. The consecrated believer becomes a channel through which the Spirit of God flows. The Holy Spirit prays, preaches, prophesies, interprets and heals the sick through yielded instruments.

An early writer sums up the work of the Spirit as follows:

> This is none other than the power of God and the Holy Spirit. This great power not only works in us and through us, but also for us. As children of God we are in the world but not a part of it, and against us are arrayed mighty and powerful spiritual hosts of wickedness in the heavenly places (Eph. 6:12). These fight against us for the purpose of hindering us from obtaining our inheritance, and stunting our growth as Christians, but most of all in order to make fruitless our efforts toward furthering the cause of the kingdom of heaven. Against these, our comparatively puny physical and mental abilities and knowledge do not go very far. But the One Who is in us, the Spirit of Jehovah, is greater than the one who is in the world, and through Him we have the victory. He not only blesses the physical and spiritual man to make him effective, but He also arranges the conditions and environment under which we labor. He goes before and opens the way for our efforts. He nullifies the activities of others who as Satan's direct tools and emissaries are trying to resist our endeavors. Through His knowledge He knows, and by His great power He sets at nought the best laid plans of the enemy.

The Holy Spirit vs. False Spirits

We are living in a day when the whole world is in a state of perplexity, religiously as well as politically. Great care is needed to avoid becoming ensnared in anything that is demonic in origin. The apostle John tells us to test the spirits. However, caution can go too far and cause one not only to refuse the false, but also the genuine. With some people, everything supernatural is of God. We must avoid both extremes. If we follow carefully the biblical instructions, we shall be able to distinguish and differentiate between the two.

> Beloved, do not believe every spirit, but test the spirits, whether they are of God; because many false prophets have gone out into the world. By this you know the Spirit of God: Every spirit that confesses that Jesus Christ has come in the flesh is of God, and every spirit that does not confess that Jesus Christ has come in the flesh is not of God. And this is the *spirit* of the Antichrist, which you have heard was coming, and is now already in the world (I Jn. 4:1-3).

Any spirit that denies, degrades or annuls Christ is the spirit of the Antichrist and is of the devil. Spiritualism, for example, traffics in these false, impersonating spirits.

On the other hand, some attribute all supernatural phenomenon to the devil, and that is a grave danger. The Pharisees claimed the miracles Christ performed were accomplished by the power of Beelzebub (Matt. 12:24). Jesus warned that by making this charge, they were in danger of committing the unpardonable sin. To give Satan credit for the work of the Holy Spirit is blasphemy against the Spirit — a sin that cannot be forgiven. There is little excuse for people to commit this sin when they have an open Bible before them.

Jesus said of an unknown miracle worker, "... for no one who works a miracle in My name can soon afterward speak evil of Me" (Mk. 9:39). This is still true today.

Chapter Thirty-nine

Why Every Christian Should Receive the Holy Spirit

Jesus' great gift to His followers was the baptism in the Holy Spirit. As He stood with His little band of disciples on the Mount of Olives just before His departure for heaven, His instructions were, "to wait for the Promise of the Father, 'which,' He *said*, 'you have heard from Me; for John truly baptized with water, but you shall be baptized with the Holy Spirit not many days from now'" (Acts 1:4, 5).

Upon speaking these words, Jesus ascended to heaven and the disciples returned to Jerusalem where they spent the next 10 days in prayer and worshiping God, after which the Holy Spirit fell as tongues of fire and a mighty rushing wind. He filled all the house where they were sitting, and they all began to speak in tongues as the Spirit gave them utterance. This wonderful gift they received revolutionized their lives and set them on fire for God. Though unlearned laymen (Acts 4:13), they went forth and preached a message that changed the world.

What is the baptism in the Holy Spirit and why would one desire to receive Him? Here are 10 reasons why every Christian should receive the baptism in the Holy Spirit:

1. If Christ and the apostles needed the Holy Spirit, then we need Him, too.

Christ, the Son of God, emptied Himself of His glory, came down from heaven and became man. In this human role as the Son of man, He was subject to suffering (Heb. 5:7-9) and He needed the Holy Spirit baptism. Therefore, before the first act of His public ministry, He received the Holy Spirit while He was being baptized by John in the Jordan River (Matt. 3:16).

The 12 apostles and every one of the 120 in the upper room received the Holy Spirit (Acts 2:4). The 3,000 who heard Peter preach his sermon on the Day of Pentecost, were given the promise of the gift of the Holy Spirit (Acts 2:38, 39).

As the Scripture states, this mighty gift of the Holy Spirit is for all (ver. 39).

2. *The Holy Spirit gives power to witness.*

> "But you shall receive power when the Holy Spirit has come upon you; and you shall be witnesses to Me in Jerusalem, and in all Judea and Samaria, and to the end of the earth" (Acts 1:8).

We need power to attain a victorious Christian life. We continually meet the forces of evil and face strong temptations against which the human will cannot successfully stand. We need not only to defend ourselves against evil, but to take the offensive.

We also need power in order to witness effectively to others and to carry out our chief function as Christians. We need power to influence others for Christ; the purpose of the baptism in the Holy Spirit is to give us that power.

The most amazing proof of the truth of Christianity is the fact that a band of lowly fishermen, uneducated and untrained (Acts 4:13) according to the standards of the religious leaders of that day, were able to go out, under God, against severe opposition, and become instruments to bring into existence the most powerful religious movement in all history.

And the story is repeating itself in this latter-day outpouring. A half century ago, Pentecost was preached in tents, store buildings and abandoned churches. Yet today, Pentecost has become a powerful movement throughout the world.

When the Lord spoke to Zerubbabel who helped rebuild the temple after the return from Babylon, He said, "'Not by might nor by power, but by My Spirit,' says the LORD of hosts. 'Who *are* you, O great mountain? Before Zerubbabel *you shall become* a plain!'" (Zech. 4:6, 7). No human power could level the mountain before Zerubbabel, but by the power of the Spirit, the mountain became a plain. So today, the believer meets mountains which he cannot climb in his own strength, but these can be moved by the power of the Holy Spirit.

3. The Holy Spirit gives power to live a holy life.

> *There is* therefore now no condemnation to those who are in Christ Jesus, who do not walk according to the flesh, but according to the Spirit. For the law of the Spirit of life in Christ Jesus has made me free from the law of sin and death. ... For if you live according to the flesh you will die; but if by the Spirit you put to death the deeds of the body, you will live (Rom. 8:1, 2, 13).

Here, we are told that the Holy Spirit frees us from the law of sin and death. Without the Spirit, human attempts to live a holy life are futile and vain. We cannot, in our own strength, live an overcoming life. Man will fail again and again, as Paul describes in his autobiographical experience in Romans 7:18-25. Indeed, man's self-righteousness is as filthy rags in the sight of God.

Now, every Christian has the Spirit of Christ to some degree — otherwise he/she is not a follower of the Lord at all. But the experience, as received on the Day of Pentecost, represents a fuller measure of the Spirit. He was with the believer, but now He is in the believer.

It should be pointed out, however, that the baptism in the Holy Spirit does not automatically make someone holy or an ideal Christian. The saints in the Corinthian Church received the Holy Spirit, yet they were very carnal, requiring stern discipline and correction by the Apostle Paul. While the infilling of the Spirit gives the believer power to live a holy life, people are free moral agents. Therefore, it cannot be guaranteed that every believer will live up to that responsibility.

4. The Holy Spirit is a comforter Who will abide forever.

"And I will pray the Father, and He will give you

another Helper, that He may abide with you forever" (Jn. 14:16).

What a thrilling thought that this glorious Holy Spirit who
moved on the darkness at the dawn of creation and caused the
light to shine, comes to abide, not for a day, a month, or a year,
but forever! A million years from now, He will still be with us
to guide, comfort and give us eternal fellowship with God.

How all material blessings pale into utter insignificance beside this great Comforter! Solomon spoke the truth when he
said, "All things *are* full of labor; man cannot express *it*. The
eye is not satisfied with seeing, nor the ear filled with hearing"
(Eccl. 1:8). Earthly pleasures can satisfy only for a little while,
and in time satiate the appetite. How sad to see great people,
as they near the end of their lives, suddenly realize that all the
honors of this world they have gained are worthless. Death
rings down the curtain and hustles them out into the great
unknown. No wonder Solomon, as he came to the end of his
soliloquy in Ecclesiastes, drew the conclusion that he did:

> Remember now your Creator in the days of your
> youth, before the difficult days come, and the
> years draw near when you say, "I have no plea-
> sure in them" (Eccl. 12:1).

But he who has the mighty Comforter never needs fear the
evil days. The glorious Holy Spirit's infilling is the only power
that can fully satisfy the human soul. We are made so that by
ourselves we are incomplete. There is a spiritual vacuum in our
souls, and if it is not occupied with God, it will eventually be
filled with that which is evil (Lk. 11:24-26).

*5. The baptism in the Holy Spirit is "the refreshing" spoken of
in prophecy.*

As the human race wanders away from God, it finds itself
in a state of unrest and unfulfillment. But there is one satisfying experience that can never sate the soul. God has promised
the Holy Spirit to whomever desires Him. "'And it shall come

to pass afterward that I will pour out My Spirit on all flesh'" (Joel 2:28). "'If anyone thirsts, let him come to Me and drink'" (Jn. 7:37). The infilling of the Holy Spirit with the speaking in unknown tongues is as the prophecy declares — the "rest" and the "refreshing." And to this truth, many thousands will testify.

6. The Holy Spirit will quicken our mortal bodies.

> But if the Spirit of Him who raised Jesus from the dead dwells in you, He who raised Christ from the dead will also give life to your mortal bodies through His Spirit who dwells in you (Rom. 8:11).

We know that divine healing is accomplished by the power of the Spirit. But God's purpose goes further than healing. It includes divine health, as III John 2 declares:

> Beloved, I pray that you may prosper in all things and be in health, just as your soul prospers.

The supreme event of history was the resurrection of Christ from the dead. This great miracle was made possible by the Spirit of God. But the Apostle John adds that the same Spirit that raised Christ from the dead has been given to believers to quicken their mortal bodies. He is not talking about the future resurrection, for the context shows that he is referring to the life we are living now.

The time of the resurrection has not yet come, but, in the meantime, the Spirit will quicken our physical bodies so that we shall have the strength necessary to perform the work God has called us to do.

Of course, any blessing given by the Holy Spirit must be appropriated by bold faith in the same way any other blessing is obtained. Many have experienced this quickening, and it is one more of the great benefits which is given by the Holy Spirit. Jesus said that He came to give life, and life more abundantly (Jn. 10:10).

7. The Holy Spirit will guide the believer into all truth.

> "I still have many things to say to you, but you cannot bear *them* now. However, when He, the Spirit of truth, has come, He will guide you into all truth; for He will not speak on His own *authority*, but whatever He hears He will speak; and He will tell you things to come" (Jn. 16:12, 13).

Some denominations that deny the experience of the baptism in the Holy Spirit have been drifting into rationalism and unbelief. They deny the virgin birth, the miraculous, the born-again experience and some have even been ensnared in such Bible-dishonoring teachings as the theory that man evolved from brute beasts.

Of course, it is possible for a believer to receive the Holy Spirit and still be subject to mistakes. We can choose error, since God never takes away our free will (I Tim. 1:19, 20; II Tim. 2:17, 18). But if we are obedient to the light we have, the Spirit of the Lord will keep us from serious error.

A Spirit-filled person usually becomes conscious that a Christian's walk is a holy one. Hundreds of people testify that without a sermon being preached on the subject, and without anyone saying a word on the matter, the Holy Spirit caused them to drop such hindrances as smoking, drinking and worldliness.

It should be understood, however, that believers have a measure of the Holy Spirit, even before they receive the full baptism. Before Pentecost, Jesus told the disciples "He dwells with you and will be in you" (Jn. 14:17). And Paul said, "Now if anyone does not have the Spirit of Christ, he is not His" (Rom. 8:9). In fact, the Holy Spirit's work of guiding people into truth begins even before their conversion (Jn. 16:8).

However, the Spirit is able to lead men into "all truth" more effectively after they receive the baptism in the Holy Spirit. For example, before the Day of Pentecost, the disciples could not understand why Christ needed to go to the cross. But after Pentecost, it became clear (Acts 2:22-36).

8. The Holy Spirit will help you to pray supernaturally.

We do not have to receive the baptism in the Holy Spirit in order to pray. Because God is gracious, the convicting power of the Holy Spirit will help the sinner pray. The new convert, too, has a measure of the Spirit and will be able to receive many answers to prayer.

But there is something more. When the full baptism in the Spirit comes, and we yield to Him, we will find that the Spirit of God within us will intercede and help us to pray and get answers to difficult problems (Rom. 8:26). As this verse indicates, none of us knows how to pray as we should, but if permitted, the Spirit of God will make "intercession for us with groanings which cannot be uttered." The Apostle Paul tells us that he prayed both with the Spirit and with the understanding (I Cor. 14:15).

9. One should have the Holy Spirit in order to exercise the gifts fully.

It appears that in some cases, God gives a gift to a person even before birth (Jer. 1:5). Even so, it is necessary for the Spirit of God to anoint the person, at least in a measure, before the gift can properly operate. Some of the gifts were manifested in the ministry of the apostles even before they received the full baptism in the Spirit, for Jesus commanded them to heal the sick and cast out devils (Matt. 10:8). It is clear that the disciples did not have the baptism at that time, making it evident that the gifts may operate in a measure with a partial anointing of the Spirit.

However, the manifestation of certain gifts in Peter's ministry became evident only after he received the baptism in the Holy Spirit. For example, neither Peter nor any of the other disciples, knew that Judas was intending to betray Jesus (Mk. 14:17-21). And even when Jesus practically told them who it was, they still did not see the significance of His words. Yet, after Peter received the baptism in the Holy Spirit, he instantly discerned the hypocrisy of Ananias and Sapphira (Acts 5:1-11).

When the storm arose on the Sea of Galilee, the disciples showed only a human faith (Matt. 8:23-26). But after they had received the Holy Spirit, they had faith for great miracles, even for raising the dead (Acts 5:12; 9:36-42). As for speaking in other tongues, none of the disciples manifested that gift until after the Day of Pentecost.

10. The Holy Spirit produces the fruit of the Spirit.

> But the fruit of the Spirit is love, joy, peace, long-suffering, kindness, goodness, faithfulness, gentleness, self-control. Against such there is no law (Gal. 5:22, 23).

We have mentioned that the Holy Spirit gives power to live a holy life, but, He does more than this. He bears the fruit of the Spirit — resulting in a positive change of nature and personality.

The fruit of the Spirit is love.

Jesus said, "By this all will know that you are My disciples, if you have love for one another" (Jn. 13:35). Love does not harm its brother. Love is the fulfillment of the whole law.

The fruit of the Spirit is joy.

Puritanical religion held the view that a Christian should always wear a long face. Christ strikes at this false conception by declaring that even when men are fasting and denying the flesh, they are not to be "'like the hypocrites, with a sad countenance'" (Matt. 6:16). Many think of Christ as a sad, melancholy man. This picture is quite misleading. Although Christ was a man of sorrows and acquainted with grief, the sorrow He bore was for the world — not for Himself. As He went to Calvary, He was able to say: "'These things I have spoken to you, that My joy may remain in you, and *that* your joy may be full'" (Jn. 15:11).

The fruit of the Spirit is peace.

The world is restless, frustrated and disillusioned. "The eye is not satisfied with seeing, nor the ear filled with hearing"

(Eccl. 1:8). One of the greatest purposes of the indwelling Spirit is to produce peace in the heart of the believer — the peace that passes all understanding.

The fruit of the Spirit is longsuffering.

Who, but the Spirit of God, can give us understanding of, and patience with, less spiritual saints? Those who claim to have great spiritual gifts, but lose their tempers when things don't go their way, only betray their own carnality and inconsistency.

The fruit of the Spirit is gentleness.

A person does not show greatness by pompous language or domineering others. Although, by His infinite power, the Holy Spirit brought creation into existence, He is gentle as a dove and easily grieved. God is not only all-powerful; He is also gentle. The Psalmist said, "Your gentleness has made me great" (Psa. 18:35).

The fruit of the Spirit is goodness.

What greater reputation could one have than the one that Barnabas had? "For he was a good man, full of the Holy Spirit and of faith" (Acts 11:24).

The fruit of the Spirit is faith.

Not all have the special gift of faith, but if they are full of the Spirit, their faith will grow into supernatural faith.

The fruit of the Spirit is meekness.

Here, we really have a supernatural quality. The natural man seeks to impress others, constantly compares himself with others, and seeks his own advantage. But, the fruit of the Spirit causes us to seek the lower place and give honor to others. Humility is the true path of exaltation. "Humble yourselves in the sight of the Lord, and He will lift you up" (Jas. 4:10).

The fruit of the Spirit is temperance.

Only the Spirit of God can give us balance. Mankind is naturally given to extremes and excesses. If God blesses one person more than others, there is a strong possibility that he/she will become puffed up. But the Holy Spirit seeks to give us balance and temperance in all that we do.

Opposed to the beautiful fruit of the Spirit are the fruits of the flesh. Paul lists them in Galatians 5:19-21. They are an evil list. The purpose of the baptism is for the Holy Spirit to come into our lives and destroy the works of the flesh, thus permitting the fruit of the Spirit to grow and mature.

Chapter Forty

The Holy Spirit Baptism Foreshadowed in the Old Testament

The Scriptures make it clear that the baptism in the Holy Spirit is distinctly a New Testament experience. It is something different from anything the prophets received in Old Testament days, but, there were Old Testament experiences which were similar to the Holy Spirit baptism, and in fact, actually foreshadowed it. Three events recorded in the Old Testament are of special importance:

1. The Spirit being given to the 70 elders.
2. Elisha receiving the double portion by being with Elijah when he was taken.
3. The dedication of Solomon's temple, and the coming of the Shekinah glory.

These incidents have certain remarkable circumstances associated with them, and a careful study of them is helpful in understanding certain things about the baptism in the Holy Spirit.

Moses' Anointing

While the children of Israel were wandering in the wilderness, Moses told the Lord that the burden of caring for the spiritual problems of the people was more than he could bear. God answered him by saying He would take of the Spirit that was upon Moses and put it on the 70 elders. These men would then share the burden with him (Num. 11:17).

The question arises as to when Moses received his special measure of the Holy Spirit. He may have received this great experience during the 40 days he spent on Mt. Sinai communing with God and receiving the Ten Commandments and the Law (Ex. 24:16-18).

On the other hand, Moses may have received this great experience the second time he was on the mountain — this time fasting and making intercession for the people's sin. Toward the end of those 40 eventful days, God hid Moses in the cleft of the rock, and as He passed by, permitted Moses to witness His glory (Ex. 33:18-23). The Lord put His hand over Moses so he would be able to see His glory and still live. During those brief moments, while his eyes beheld the divine brilliance, Moses' physical body absorbed so much glory that he had to put a veil over his face to keep from blinding the people when they looked at him (Ex. 34:29-35).

Moses knew he could never accomplish the task set before him unless the Spirit of God went with him.

> And He said, "My Presence will go *with you*, and I will give you rest." Then he said to Him, "If Your Presence does not go *with us*, do not bring us up from here" (Ex. 33:14, 15).

The 70 Elders Receive the Spirit

If 70 elders were to receive the Holy Spirit, it would not be because of their own faith. Therefore, the Lord said to Moses, "'I will take of the Spirit that *is* upon you and will put *the same* upon them'" (Num. 11:17).

Here, we see the foundation of the doctrine of laying on hands for receiving the Holy Spirit. On the Day of Pentecost, the Holy Spirit came directly from heaven upon the 120 who had been waiting before the Lord. But in most other cases in the New Testament, the Spirit was given through the laying on of hands.

We have a hint here that those who lay hands on individuals to receive the baptism, must be Spirit-filled themselves. Moses had a portion of the Spirit that he could share with the 70.

One of the traditions of the nominal Church has been that people receive the Holy Spirit by faith (which is true), but that they will not feel anything, or have any evidence that they have received (which is not true).

The Holy Spirit manifests His presence when He comes upon a person. In the case of the 70 elders, when the Spirit of the Lord came upon them, they prophesied:

> Then the LORD came down in the cloud, and spoke to him, and took of the Spirit that *was* upon him, and placed *the same* upon the 70 elders; and it happened, when the Spirit rested upon them, that they prophesied, although they never did *so* again (Num. 11:25).

This was a foreshadowing of the New Testament experience, as shown in Acts 19:6:

> And when Paul had laid hands on them, the Holy Spirit came upon them, and they spoke with tongues and prophesied.

There is an interesting sequel to this event. Two of the 70 who had been set apart were Eldad and Medad. They did not go to the tabernacle where the other elders were, but remained in the camp. When the 68 received the infilling, these two who were still in the camp also received. This indicates that God will pour out His Spirit on the hungry any place, at any time.

The prophesying of Eldad and Medad caused quite a commotion in the camp. Joshua, who was jealous for Moses, suggested that Moses command them to stop prophesying. But Moses' gracious reply was that he wished the Lord would put His Spirit upon all His people. Moses' words were prophetic, for when Christ fulfilled redemption by His death on the cross, God began to pour out His Spirit "on all flesh" (Acts 2:16, 17).

Elisha's Double Portion of the Spirit
It is remarkable that the phrase "Spirit of the Lord" is mentioned only twice in connection with the ministry of Elijah. But there is no doubt that the Spirit of the Lord was responsible for the mighty works performed by Elijah. Certainly, Obadiah and the sons of the prophets knew the source of his mighty

power. Twice, there is reference to his being transported supernaturally by the Spirit of God (I Ki. 18:12, II Ki. 2:16).

Elijah is an Old Testament character who immediately attracts attention, yet he was very much human, as James points out (Jas. 5:17). The day after his victory over the prophets of Baal, in a moment of weakness, Elijah fled from Jezebel into the wilderness, and there under a juniper tree, prayed to die.

But God still had a ministry for Elijah. For 40 days, he fasted as he journeyed to the same mount as Moses did, to see the fire and the shaking mountain that Moses saw (Ex. 19:17, 18; I Ki. 19:11, 12), and to hear the same voice of God. At Sinai, the Lord revealed himself to Elijah through that still small voice, and there he received his new instructions which included commissioning and anointing his famous disciple, Elisha.

The time came when God was going to take the prophet to heaven. Elijah knew, Elisha knew, and the sons of the prophets knew what was going to happen as these two prophets journeyed together beyond the Jordan River. On the other side of the river, Elijah said to Elisha, "'Ask! What may I do for you, before I am taken away from you?'" (II Ki. 2:9). The quick response was, "'Please let a double portion of your spirit be upon me.'"

A small "s" is used for Spirit. But obviously, the text does not mean that Elijah's human spirit was going to come upon Elisha. It meant that a double portion of the Holy Spirit that rested on Elijah would come upon Elisha.

From this we see there is a difference in the degree to which the Holy Spirit rests upon different individuals. The Spirit of God came upon the prophets and the sons of the prophets (II Chr. 15:1), but not in the degree that He came upon Elijah and Elisha. Likewise, there is a difference in the degree to which individuals receive the Spirit in the present New Testament dispensation.

Elisha had to desire this double portion more than anything else in the world. He had to be able to press through into the spiritual world where the double portion could be obtained. When the chariot of fire came sweeping down to pick up Elijah, Elisha was alert, and seeing everything he cried out, "My father, my father, the chariot of Israel and its horsemen!" (II Ki. 2:12).

This remarkable event teaches us that there is such a thing as a double portion experience. Not all baptisms are the same. Some people have not prepared their hearts as others have, or exercised their faith to the same degree. They receive a portion, but not a double portion. God grant that there will be many who will reach out and take the double portion like Elisha did.

There is one more important truth taught in the event of Elijah's translation. The story is a beautiful type of Christ's ascension to heaven. The Holy Spirit could not be poured out until Christ was glorified and had returned to heaven (Jn. 16:7). The Spirit of God came upon Elisha in double power at the point of Elijah's translation. So, while Christ was on earth, the Holy Spirit was not given. But upon His ascent to heaven, He received the promise of the Father and gave it as a gift to His disciples. As Elisha saw Elijah when he was taken away, by faith we can see Christ as ascended to heaven and receive the Spirit.

The Coming of the Shekinah Glory Into Solomon's Temple

The dedication of Solomon's Temple was a wonderful type of the coming of the Holy Spirit on the Day of Pentecost. It will help us to understand certain things about the baptism in the Holy Spirit by noting the remarkable analogy between the two events.

The dedication of Solomon's Temple did not take place until it was finished and ready for the Ark of the Covenant (II Chr. 5:1). There was also a period of preparation by Christ's disciples, as they awaited the coming of the Comforter (Lk. 24:49; Acts 1:4).

On the day of dedication, the glory of the Lord came suddenly and filled the temple (II Chr. 7:1). So there need be no long period of waiting, once the heart is prepared and purified by faith.

We are told that the Levites were dressed in white linen for the dedication of the temple. This is very significant, for the Scriptures inform us that white linen is the righteousness of the saints (Rev. 19:8).

White linen is to be given to the Bride of Christ and it is not her own righteousness, but the "righteousness of God." Those who would receive the infilling of the Holy Spirit must depend entirely upon the righteousness imputed through Christ. The Holy Spirit is not given as the result of human goodness or good works. To try to make one's self good enough to receive the Holy Spirit is a snare and a delusion, and is absolutely futile.

The number of priests, 120 (II Chr. 5:12), is strikingly significant — this is the exact number of those who received the Holy Spirit on the Day of Pentecost! One hundred and twenty, in Scriptural symbolism, is the number of a new era.

It is significant that just as there were 120 priests employed in the dedication of the temple when the Shekinah glory came and inaugurated a new era, so there were 120 disciples in the upper room when the Holy Spirit fell. The outpouring of the Spirit on the Day of Pentecost marked the beginning of a new era — the era of the Church.

It has always been a difficult matter to bring God's people into unity. There appears to be something perverse in the fallen nature which promotes division rather than harmony. That weakness is projected into the Christian life too often. But the people of Israel were in gladness of heart that day, because the great temple was finished and ready for dedication. The worshipers and singers had become as one (II Chr. 5:13).

We see this beautiful unity of the people of God on the Day of Pentecost as well. "When the Day of Pentecost had fully come, they were all with one accord in one place" (Acts 2:1). This is an essential element in the outpouring of the Spirit — God's people must be one in spirit and heart. Discord and contention are elements which seriously interfere with the moving of the Spirit.

The Lord dwells in the praises of His people. Worship is the divine method of producing an atmosphere conducive for the outpouring of the Holy Spirit. It was during worship and praise that the Spirit came and filled the temple (II Chr. 5:13, 14).

As the 120 waited, they "were continually in the temple praising and blessing God" (Lk. 24:53). So, too, should those who desire to receive the baptism in the Spirit, learn to worship the Lord in song and praise.

While the priests were worshiping the Lord, a wonderful event took place. "The house of the LORD, was filled with a cloud, so that the priests could not continue ministering because of the cloud; for the glory of the LORD filled the house of God" (II Chr. 5:13).

Likewise, on the Day of Pentecost as the disciples worshiped the Lord and were in one accord, "there came a sound from heaven, as of a rushing mighty wind, and it filled the whole house where they were sitting" (Acts 2:2). In addition to filling the house, the Holy Spirit also filled the people. "And they were all filled with the Holy Spirit and began to speak with other tongues, as the Spirit gave them utterance" (Acts 2:4).

Chapter Forty-one

The Holy Spirit During the Church Age

Irenaeus was the first theologian of distinction in the history of the Early Church. He was reared in Smyrna under the ministry of Polycarp, who in turn, sat under the ministry of the Apostle John. Thus, there was only one link between this champion of Christianity and the apostles. His great work was to defend Christianity against error. He began also the compilation of the New Testament canon and wrote the distinguished work *Against Heresies*, which effectively demolished the position of the the Gnostic heretical sect. What did this noted theologian have to say about the gifts of the Spirit and speaking in other tongues? Irenaeus said in his books V and VI:

> For this reason does the apostle declare, "We speak wisdom among them that are perfect" (I Cor. 2:6), terming those persons "perfect" who have received the Spirit of God, and who through the Spirit of God do speak in all languages, as he used himself also to speak. In like manner we do also hear many brethren in the church who possess prophetic gifts, and who through the Spirit speak all kinds of languages, and bring to light for the general benefit the hidden things of men, and declare the mysteries of God.

Here are some quotations from the writings of a few other of the Early Church fathers:

> For the prophetical gifts remain with us, even to the present time. And hence you ought to under-

stand that (the gifts) formerly among your nation have been transferred to us. — Justin, *Ante-Nicene Fathers, Vol. I*, p. 240.

For apostles have the Holy Spirit properly, who have Him fully, in the operations of prophecy, and the efficacy of (healing) virtues, and the evidences of tongues; not partially as all others have. — Tertullian, *Ante-Nicene Fathers Vol. IV*, p. 52.

This is He who places prophets in the church, gives powers and healings, does wonderful works, offers discriminations of spirits, affords powers of government, suggests counsels, and orders and arranges whatever other gifts there are of Charismata; and thus makes the Lord's Church everywhere, and in all, perfected and completed. — Origen, *Ante-Nicene Fathers, Vol. IV*, p. 254.

For the Holy Spirit is not only given by the laying on of hands amid the testimony of temporal, sensible miracles, as He was given in former days to be the credentials of a rudimentary faith, and for the extension of the first beginnings of the church. For who expects in these days that those on whom hands are laid that they may receive the Holy Spirit should forthwith begin to speak with tongues? — *On Baptism, Against Donatists*, p. 443, Augustine, Vol. IV.

Many more quotations might be made to show that down through the Church Age, various groups within and without the Church received the baptism and spoke in other tongues. Probably one of the best-known testimonies is that of the powerful evangelist, Charles G. Finney, who tells the story of his baptism in the Spirit in his memoirs:

As I turned and was about to take a seat by the fire, I received a mighty baptism of the Holy Ghost. Without any expectation of it, without ever having the thought in my mind that there was any such thing for me, without any recollection that I had ever heard the thing mentioned by any person in the world, the Holy Spirit descended on me in a manner that seemed to go through me, body and soul. I could feel the impression like a wave of electricity, going through and through me. Indeed it seemed to come in waves and waves of liquid love, for I could not express it in any other way. It seemed like the very breath of God. I can recollect distinctly it seemed to fan me like immense wings.

No words can express the wonderful love that was shed abroad in my heart. I wept aloud with love and joy; and I do not know but I should say I literally bellowed out the unutterable gushings of my heart. These waves came over me, and over me, and over me, one after another, until I recollect I cried out, "I shall die if these waves continue to pass over me." I said, "Lord, I cannot bear any more," yet I had no fear of death.

How long I continued in this state, with this baptism continuing to roll over me and go through me, I do not know.

It seems obvious that the "unutterable gushings" of his heart was the Spirit speaking through Charles Finney in tongues.

D.L. Moody's testimony of receiving the Holy Spirit is also very striking:

At the close of a service two women whom he frequently noticed in attendance came forward and said to him they were praying for him, as they felt he needed "the power of the Spirit." "I need power! Why," said he in telling of the interview, "I thought I had power! I had the largest congregations in Chicago, and there were many conversions. I was, in a sense, satisfied. But right along these two godly women kept praying for me, and their earnest talk about "anointing for special service" set me thinking. I asked them to come and talk with me, and they poured out their hearts in prayer that I might receive the filling of the Holy Spirit. There came a great hunger into my soul. I did not know what it was. I began to cry out as I never did before. I really felt that I did not want to live if I could not have this power of service.

I was crying all the time that God would fill me with His Spirit. Well, one day in the city of New York — oh, what a day — I cannot describe it. I seldom refer to it; it is almost too sacred an experience to name. Paul had an experience of which he never spoke for fourteen years. I can only say that God revealed Himself to me, and I had such an experience of His love that I had to ask Him to stay His hand. I went to preaching again. The sermons were not different; I did not present any new truths; and yet hundreds were converted. I would not now be placed back where I was before that blessed experience if you should give me all the world.

These experiences, however, were not universal. It was not until New Year's Day, 1901, that an event took place marking the beginning of the latter-day Pentecostal movement. A large building in Topeka, Kansas had been rented by some individuals for the purpose of studying the Word of God, and to find out what the scriptural baptism in the Holy Spirit was. In their studies they came to the conclusion that the biblical evidence of the baptism in the Holy Spirit is speaking in other tongues as the Spirit gives utterance.

The first person of the group to receive the Holy Spirit was Miss Agnes Ozman. Her personal story is quoted in Stanley Frodsham's book *With Signs Following*:

> It was in October, 1900, that I went to this school, which was known as Bethel College. We studied the Bible by day and did much work downtown at night. Much time was spent in prayer every day and all the time. Prayer was offered night and day continually, in a special upper room set apart as a prayer tower. I had many blessed hours of prayer in this upper room during the night watches. As we spent much time in the presence of God, He caused our hearts to be opened for all that is written.
>
> I had had some experiences with the Lord and had tasted the joy of leading some souls to Christ. I had had some marvelous answers to prayer for guidance and in having my needs supplied. I was blessed with the presence of the Lord, Who, in response to my prayer, healed some who were sick. Like some others, I thought I had received the baptism with the Holy Ghost at a time of consecration, but when I learned that the Holy Spirit was yet to be poured out in greater fullness, my heart became hungry for the promised Comforter and I began to cry out for an enduement with power from on high. At times I longed more for the Holy Spirit to come in than for my necessary food. At night I had a greater desire for Him than sleep.
>
> We were admonished to honor the blood of Jesus Christ to do His work in our hearts, and this

brought great peace and victory ...

As the end of the year drew near, some friends came from Kansas City to spend the holidays with us. On Watch Night, we had a blessed service, praying that God's blessing might rest upon us as the new year came in. During the first day of 1901, the presence of the Lord was with us in a marked way, stilling our hearts to wait upon Him for greater things. The spirit of prayer was upon us in the evening. It was nearly eleven o'clock on the first of January that it came into my heart to ask that hands be laid upon me that I might receive the gift of the Holy Ghost. It was as hands were laid upon my head that the Holy Spirit fell upon me and I began to speak in tongues, glorifying God. I talked several languages, and it was clearly manifest when a new dialect was spoken. I had the added joy and glory for which my heart longed, and a depth of the presence of the Lord within that I had never known before. It was as if rivers of living water were proceeding from my innermost being.

The following morning I was accosted with questions about my experience of the night before. As I tried to answer, I was so full of glory that I talked in tongues. Others were made hungry to receive the Holy Spirit, and I pointed out to them the Bible references, showing that I had received the baptism according to Acts 2:4 and 19:1-6.

After Miss Ozman's experience, many of the students received the baptism with speaking in tongues. Soon the work spread to Texas, where remarkable manifestations of the Holy Spirit occurred. Then, in 1906, the famous Azusa Street Mission outpouring occurred, where thousands received the baptism in the Holy Spirit. From there, workers went out all over the world.

Chapter Forty-two

Does the Holy Spirit Baptism Occur at Conversion?

Where faith is present and those who possess a ministry of the Spirit are ministering, the baptism in the Holy Spirit may follow conversion almost immediately. The account of Cornelius' family receiving the Holy Spirit is an excellent example of this (Acts 10:44-48).

But in this case, much spiritual preparation had taken place beforehand. Cornelius had been fasting and praying, and his household was devout and eagerly seeking the truth. Their hearts were hungry for God, and He filled them with the Spirit while Peter was still preaching!

Normally, however, there is an interval, though sometimes brief, between the work of salvation in the life of an individual, and the full infilling of the Holy Spirit.

1. Christ taught that believers should ask for the Spirit.

> "If you then, being evil, know how to give good gifts to your children, how much more will *your* heavenly Father give the Holy Spirit to those who ask Him!" (Lk. 11:13).

In this first mentioning of the gift of the Holy Spirit, Jesus reveals a principle which runs through the whole superstructure of redemption: Although God has purchased complete salvation for everyone, it is necessary for the individual to ask for these blessings. Christ is not speaking of sinners or rebels outside the Kingdom, but of children — His children. Christians do receive some measure of the Spirit's presence at conversion, but it is evident from this Scripture that we do not automatically receive the fullness that is divinely intended until we ask for Him.

2. *Christ told the disciples to wait for the promise of the Father.*

If there was to be any change in the significance of Christ's words concerning receiving the Holy Spirit, He certainly would have made it known when He gave the Great Commission. At that time, He did indeed speak to His disciples concerning the Holy Spirit and He breathed upon them saying, "'Receive the Holy Spirit'" (Jn. 20:22). Afterwards He said for them to, "wait for the Promise of the Father, 'which,' *He said*, 'you have heard from Me; for John truly baptized with water, but you shall be baptized with the Holy Spirit not many days from now'" (Acts 1:4, 5). This great event took place on the Day of Pentecost as the second chapter of Acts records.

The fact that the baptism in the Holy Spirit is a subsequent experience is revealed again in Luke 24:49, where Jesus mentioned the endowment of the Spirit which the disciples received later.

3. *The Scriptures show that the baptism in the Holy Spirit follows conversion, even after Pentecost.*

Philip, the evangelist, went down to Samaria and preached Christ to the people. Then, he had a great healing service. It was because of the miracles that "multitudes with one accord heeded the things spoken by Philip" (Acts 8:6). Notice the order of events:

- Philip preached Christ.
- Miracles of healing strengthened their faith and con firmed the message.
- There was great joy in the city.
- They believed in Jesus.
- They were baptized.

But, notice that the Samaritans had not yet received the Holy Spirit. This is so plainly declared that there can be no further doubt that the baptism in the Holy Spirit is normally an experience that follows conversion (Acts 8:14-17). Then, Peter and John, who had a ministry of imparting the Holy Spirit, went to Samaria, prayed for these people, laid hands on them and they received the Holy Spirit.

4. Paul received the Holy Spirit after his conversion.

Paul's experience is significant. The apostle specifically states that God's great purpose for him was that he should be "a pattern to those who are going to believe on Him for everlasting life" (I Tim. 1:16). Paul received the Holy Spirit three days after his conversion during prayer and fasting (Acts 9:8-17). Ananias came to him, prayed for his healing and for him to receive the Holy Spirit (ver. 17). Thus, we see the cumulative evidence is overwhelming that receiving the Holy Spirit normally follows conversion.

5. Paul taught that receiving the Spirit follows believing in Jesus.

When Paul came to Ephesus, he met some disciples. His first question was, "'Did you receive the Holy Spirit when you believed?'" (Acts 19:2). This indicates that Paul knew that the Holy Spirit does not automatically fall on individuals when they first believe in Jesus. If it was automatic, then he never would have asked such a question. No instructed person would ever ask a new convert if they received pardon when they repented and believed in Jesus! This always takes place. But, that is not the case with the infilling of the Holy Spirit. There is ordinarily an interval, during which time the person is instructed in the need and purpose of the Holy Spirit baptism. However, it is true that the divine plan includes receiving this experience as soon as possible after conversion.

6. Common experience substantiates this truth.

The baptism in the Holy Spirit is an experience of such a nature that everyone knows when it has occurred. A careful reading of the passages of Scripture in Acts 2,8,9,10 and 19 indicates that certain manifestations attend the receiving of the gift. God's Word has not changed. All who hunger for the Holy Spirit will find that God will give Him to them as He has promised.

Everyone who has been converted has received the Spirit in a certain measure (I Cor. 12:3; Rom. 8:9). As one stated it, "You have the Holy Spirit but the Holy Spirit doesn't have you." The Lord defined the difference between the Holy Spirit's presence in salvation, such as the disciples had received before Pentecost, and what they experienced afterward, by saying, "'He dwells with you and will be in you'" (Jn. 14:17). These are the rivers of living water spoken of by Jesus in John. 7:37, 38, which every Bible believer should earnestly desire to receive.

It is the power of the Holy Spirit within the believer that quickens the mortal body and gives divine health and dominion over sin (Rom. 8:11-13). Therefore, it is of extreme importance that believers receive the baptism in the Spirit immediately after their conversion.

Chapter Forty-three

On What Basis Do We Receive the Holy Spirit?

The late J.E. Stiles, admirably stated some of the truths brought out in this chapter in his excellent book, *The Gifts of the Holy Spirit*. Years ago, Brother Stiles held a campaign for us while we were pastoring. His teaching was tremendously effective in helping those who had sought the Holy Spirit for some time and failed to receive. Almost all the so-called "chronics" in that part of the country received the Holy Spirit during the time he was there.

Some people accused him of introducing a new method to receive the Holy Spirit, inferring that they received a different kind of baptism. Observation afterward showed that the overall results from the meeting were as great or greater than the old method of tarrying hour after hour, week after week, and sometimes years for the baptism.

There are two schools of thought regarding the basis for receiving the Holy Spirit. One school particularly emphasizes the need for holiness in order to receive. The other declares that the baptism is not given on the basis of personal holiness, but on the basis of grace. What is the truth regarding this matter? Is the Holy Spirit given on the basis of our holiness, and must we have a certain number of merits before we can receive?

We must get the matter straight. Many people suppose that holiness is conformity to a set of standards arbitrarily set up by mankind. One may outwardly conform to these things and still have the sins of pride, self-will and self-righteousness in his/her heart.

The fact is, one doesn't receive the Holy Spirit because of great spiritual achievements, or because strong Christian character has been developed. To tell people they must meet a certain standard before they can receive the Holy Spirit may shut them off from the very source by which they can live a victorious life. Also, we must be very careful in judging others, for they may not have the same light we have.

We should bear in mind that there is a difference between our standing before God (righteousness through Christ) and our actual state. A young convert can stand before God absolutely justified, yet have many things that need to be worked out in his/her life. Many sincere Christians are distressed because they find they have a carnal nature which dominates them. They are anxious to live a victorious life, but struggling in one's own strength can be very disappointing and usually unfruitful.

The fact is, we need the Holy Spirit in order to bear the fruit of the Spirit. J.E. Stiles, in his splendid book, makes an excellent comment on this subject:

> Sad to say, God has many children who have never gone very far forward in developing into the likeness of Christ. If only they could realize that they can do nothing by struggling against their natural evil tendencies to make themselves more holy or good, then they might throw themselves unreservedly upon the Lord and trust Him to do in them and for them, by His Spirit, that which they never could do in and for themselves. The universal testimony of all great Christians of the past or present is that the fullness of blessing and spiritual development comes only to those who will make a complete consecration to God, putting themselves entirely in His hands, and then trusting Him recklessly to receive what they have committed to Him, and to shape them into the likeness of Christ. Oh! that we might learn to trust Him for righteousness instead of trying to produce it by the efforts of the natural man. All our efforts will produce are the works of the flesh. (See Gal. 5:19-21.)

Failure to understand this has caused thousands of people who have earnestly sought the Holy Spirit to fail to receive. They feel they have not attained a high enough degree of holiness in order to receive the baptism. And so it becomes a vicious cycle. Of this, J.E. Stiles further says:

> We all admit that any saved person would go to be with the Lord if he should die, and yet multitudes of saved people have been told that they were not spiritually prepared to receive the Holy Spirit. How utterly inconsistent is such teaching. Which is the greater experience; standing uncondemned in the presence of God and the glories of heaven, or receiving the Holy Spirit here on earth? Certainly to enter the glories of heaven, clothed in the righteousness of Christ, is an incomparably greater experience than to receive the Holy Spirit here, which is one of the means God has given to fully prepare us for heaven. To put the means above the end is contrary to all logic and sense. Any saved person is ready to receive the Holy Spirit if he knows what the Word teaches.

We must understand that the Holy Spirit is a gift (Acts 2:38, 39). If we earned this gift, or deserved it, it would not be a gift. Christ, in Luke 11:13, makes this clear. He says:

> "If you then, being evil, know how to give good gifts to your children, how much more will *your* heavenly Father give the Holy Spirit to those who ask Him!"

In Galatians, Paul emphasizes that the Holy Spirit is not given by the works of the law, but by faith:

> This only I want to learn from you: Did you re-

ceive the Spirit by the works of the law, or by the hearing of faith? (Gal. 3:2).

Paul then shows that it is a gift ministered by faith. That was what Ananias did for him at Damascus, and Peter and John did for believers at Samaria. The Holy Spirit is not given when people believe they have become holy enough, or when they have reached a certain spiritual level. Actually, the Scriptures indicate that God is almost over-eager for people to receive His Spirit. The proper order is to "repent and be baptized." But, in two cases in the Book of Acts, the people received the Holy Spirit before they were baptized in water!

The average person who has earnestly tried to receive the Holy Spirit and has failed, is confused and uncertain of what to do next. It seems that the very conscientiousness of some individuals hinders them from receiving. They want to be absolutely sure they are holy enough, and this hinders their faith. But, God said He would pour out His Spirit upon all flesh. The result is that the unstable and erratic type of person will often push forward and receive before the solid Christian does. Frequently, the latter becomes the "chronic seeker."

There is another serious result that has come about because of the teaching that the giving of the Holy Spirit is based on achievement. Superficial people who speak in tongues may arrive at the conclusion that they are especially holy. This may make them proud and unteachable. Of this, J.E. Stiles says:

> Another tragedy ... is that when the seeker for the Holy Spirit does receive Him, and speaks with tongues supernaturally, he very often assumes that his character is fully pleasing to God. His reasoning is as follows: "If the Holy Spirit is given on the basis of my having arrived at a high degree of consecration and holiness, then I must have arrived at that level of spirituality which is fully pleasing to God." He is very often proud, arrogant and unteachable, because he feels he has arrived at the pinnacle of Christian experience.

Now where is he to go? Many times he becomes slack and careless in his Christian life and is less useful after he received the Holy Spirit than he was before. He must look behind him to see the apex of his Christian experience, and that is tragic in anyone's life. Surely, our Christian life should be a steady growth, ever ascending to greater heights of faith, holiness and Christlikeness as the years go by. The person who feels he has passed the greatest experience of his Christian life cannot possibly have the correct viewpoint. He does not realize that the receiving of the Holy Spirit is on the basis of grace, and therefore no credit is due him whatever. ... The actual fact is that the individual has no more character immediately after he has received the Holy Spirit than he had before, but he has a source of help and power to build Christian character which cannot be overestimated.

The idea that people receive the baptism because of their own holiness has further consequences. When certain members of the church do not receive, they may come under suspicion. Although they are ideal Christians, and busy in every good work, the thought is that there must be some hidden sin in that person's life or they would receive. When such suspicions are whispered around, it can only cause heartbreak for the individual in question, especially since he knows it isn't true.

This unscriptural teaching can have still another serious result. Sooner or later, a truth which is presented in an unbalanced way invites a reaction in the Church. People may come to think that speaking in tongues is not genuine, but an illegitimate experience. Since it has not produced genuine Christian character, there must be something wrong with it.

Certainly this view of the baptism in the Holy Spirit is completely out of line with the teaching of the Scriptures. Balaam had a beautiful gift of prophecy and died under the judgment of God. Saul received the Holy Spirit, but because of self-will and disobedience, an evil spirit came into his life (I Sam. 16:14). Samson was mightily anointed of God, but let fleshly lusts dominate him. Even David, who was mightily used in writing the Psalms, fell into adultery and was later guilty of murder.

The possession of the Holy Spirit and His gifts gives us a much increased responsibility to live a godly life, but it is not proof that we are meeting the responsibility.

The Lord felt this was a matter of such importance that He gave a special warning to His disciples. He said there would be those who would come to Him on the Day of Judgment, saying they had healed the sick, cast out devils and performed great miracles. But, the Lord would tell them that He never knew them. The real proof of holiness is not the gifts, but the fruits. "'Therefore, by their fruits you will know them'" (see Matt. 7:15-23).

Still, one more unfortunate result from the teaching that receiving the Holy Spirit is based on personal holiness is that the attention of seekers is fixed on the poorest and most unworthy examples in the Church, leading to the conclusion that all are hypocrites. They don't understand that God, in His graciousness and love for mankind, has made His Holy Spirit available to all — even though He knows that unstable and erratic people who receive the Spirit will perhaps bring reproach on the message. Jesus said, "'For offenses must come, but woe to that man by whom the offense comes!'" (Matt. 18:7).

There is, of course, no excuse for those who live a shallow Christian life. Yet, we are all free moral agents and at liberty to use, or fail to use, what God has put at our disposal to build our Christian character.

Failure to understand the basis upon which the Holy Spirit is given has caused some ministers to become discouraged and even to retreat from preaching the message of the baptism. They have been led to believe that those who receive the baptism should live an exemplary Christian life, and when they see those who do not, they become confused. If these ministers had only realized that the Holy Spirit is given on the basis of grace alone, they would not be taken by surprise when certain Spirit-filled Christians fail.

Their mistake is that instead of talking about the high state of holiness people must attain to receive the baptism, they should teach the way of holy living after having received the Holy Spirit. It is not the Holy Spirit that causes these individuals to fail, but it is the result of the teaching they receive — the mistaken belief that because they received the baptism, they have a character fully pleasing to God.

God gave the Holy Spirit to His people on the Day of Pentecost. His part in the matter is finished. The Holy Spirit is ready to come into any life that will receive Him. He does not come in because we have reached a high state of achievement, but because He wants to provide the means by which we can reach that goal.

Chapter Forty-four

Preparation to Receive the Holy Spirit

There are conditions to receiving salvation and divine healing (although both are received through grace), and there are also certain conditions to receiving the Holy Spirit.

One of the fundamental truths of Scripture is that divine healing is a gift of God to His people. We have the right to healing and health not on the basis of merit, but solely because Christ took our sickness upon Himself (Matt. 8:14-17). But, to say that because healing is given through grace there are no conditions attached, is a serious error. There are definite conditions to receiving the Holy Spirit. Since a special state of spiritual achievement is not the condition for receiving the Holy Spirit, what is?

There is a basic principle involved in receiving any of God's blessings. We are never to take God casually, and there must be a deep desire in our hearts to live wholly for Him. The Holy Spirit is given to those who will obey Him, according to the light that has been received (Acts 5:32). A person in a state of conscious disobedience to the Lord is not a fit candidate to receive the Holy Spirit.

It is important that candidates receive some instruction about the purpose of the Holy Spirit in their lives. New converts always need instruction. If it is essential to give instruction to people who come to receive healing, then certainly those who are to receive the Holy Spirit need instruction.

Bring Forth Fruits of Repentance

Those who desire to receive the Holy Spirit should fully repent of their sins. Peter told the people this in his sermon on the Day of Pentecost:

Then Peter said to them, "Repent, and let every one of you be baptized in the name of Jesus Christ for the remission of sins; and you shall receive the gift of the Holy Spirit" (Acts 2:38).

People may not have victory over all bad habits, but they can give up loving them, and in their hearts, turn from what they know is evil. Anyone who still loves sin is not ready to receive the Holy Spirit; instead, they should be candidates for repentance.

John the Baptist preached the baptism of repentance and told people to prepare for the One Who was to come, Who would baptize them in the Holy Spirit and fire:

"I indeed baptize you with water unto repentance, but He who is coming after me is mightier than I, whose sandals I am not worthy to carry. He will baptize you with the Holy Spirit and fire" (Matt. 3:11).

When the Pharisees came to John, he said, "'Therefore bear fruits worthy of repentance'" (ver. 8). Those who are true candidates, even for water baptism, must show evidence of repentance. How much more, those who come to receive the Holy Spirit!

John gave the people more instructions. He told them to share their material blessings with the poor (Lk. 3:11). He required the tax collectors to stop their crooked dealings, saying, "'Collect no more than what is appointed for you'" (ver. 13). He commanded the soldiers saying, "'Do not intimidate anyone or accuse falsely, and be content with your wages'" (ver. 14).

Prepare the Way of the Lord

But, John went even further than this. He said, "'*Prepare the way of the LORD; make His paths straight*'" (Lk. 3:4). There is such a thing as preparing the way of the Lord; Christ cannot walk with those who follow crooked paths.

441

God commended Jehoshaphat saying, "'Nevertheless good things are found in you, in that you ... have prepared your heart to seek God'" (II Chr. 19:3). But, the Lord did not commend the people, who had permitted the high places to remain:

Nevertheless the high places were not taken away,
for as yet the people had not directed their hearts
to the God of their fathers (II Chr. 20:33).

It is significant that John the Baptist, who was the first preacher to teach about the baptism in the Holy Spirit, so strongly emphasized that people should prepare their ways before the Lord. We cannot change our nature by ourselves, but we can repent of our sins.

Unworthy Candidates for the Holy Spirit

Observe what happened at the first Holy Spirit service the apostles conducted. It is obviously a pattern for us to follow. Though Philip, the evangelist, had had a great revival in Samaria, and certainly had preached to the people about the Holy Spirit, none had received Him. Then Peter and John came down and prayed with them. No doubt these apostles gave them instruction, although what they told the people is not recorded. Finally, they laid hands on them and they received the Holy Spirit (Acts 8:14-17).

At this time, a man by the name of Simon Magus came to Peter. He offered money, indicating that he would like to have the power to impart the Holy Spirit through laying on hands. This was enough to alert Peter to the fact that this man was in no state even to receive the Holy Spirit, let alone lay hands on others! The apostle rebuked him, charging that his heart was not right with God, and that only true repentance could save him from the consequences of his evil ways.

The first work of the Spirit is not to baptize candidates, but to bring upon them conviction of sin. As Jesus said, "'And when He has come, He will convict the world of sin, and of righteousness, and of judgment'" (Jn. 16:8).

Waiting Before the Lord

I believe that people can and should receive the Holy Spirit instantly. Nevertheless, there is a time to wait on God to prepare the heart. When hearts are ready, the blessing can come without delay. Such was the case in the great revival that occurred in the days of Hezekiah.

> Then Hezekiah and all the people rejoiced that God had prepared the people, since the events took place so suddenly (II Chr. 29:36).

There is no need to wait weeks for the baptism in the Holy Spirit. It is God's plan, if the heart has been prepared, for us to receive immediately.

Jesus told His followers, "'Tarry in the city of Jerusalem until you are endued with power from on high'" (Lk. 24:49). And so they waited in prayer before the Lord.

When Paul was converted on the Damascus Road, he was permitted to spend three days and nights in prayer. It was a time of heart-searching and getting his bearings for the new life before him. The Lord told Ananais to go and lay hands on him so he would receive the Holy Spirit. When hands were laid on Paul, he received the Holy Spirit instantly.

When the angel of the Lord appeared to Cornelius giving him instructions on how to have a relationship with God, he said, "'Your prayers and your alms have come up for a memorial before God'" (Acts 10:4). Cornelius had already prepared his heart, and when the Word was preached, the Holy Spirit fell upon his whole household. It is important that a person's soul be open to receiving the Holy Spirit before their attention is focused on speaking in other tongues.

Some Advice to the Candidate

How can we help those who have prepared their hearts to receive the Holy Spirit, receive the baptism?

Again, I have taken the liberty to quote a few paragraphs from J.E. Stiles' excellent book, *The Gift of the Holy Spirit*, which includes certain instructions for the candidate. If a person's heart has been prepared to receive the Holy Spirit, these instructions will be of great help:

1. Help him see that God has already given the Spirit, that it is up to him to receive the *gift* now, and above everything he is not to beg God to fill him with the Holy Spirit. All begging is in unbelief.

2. Tell him that when hands are laid on him, he is to receive the Holy Spirit. A little explanation is needed here. It is quite evident from the Scripture and from our experience that all do not have a ministry along this line, as God gives various ministries to His various servants. At Samaria (Acts 8:5-17) none received the Holy Spirit under Philip's ministry, but when Peter and John arrived and laid hands on them, they all received. Today some have this ministry and others do not, but we believe many more would have it if they asked God for it and believed. If you have no one at hand who has this ministry, call in someone to help you who has (Acts 10:5).

3. Tell the candidate that he is to expect the Spirit to move his vocal organs, and put supernatural words on his lips which he is to speak out in cooperation with the Spirit. Remember, the *man* speaks (lifts his voice) by an act of the will.

4. Tell him to throw away all fears which he has gotten from foolish teachers that he may get something false and spurious. Point out to him Luke 11:11-13, and help him to see that God promises he will not receive a substitute for the Holy Spirit, Whom he has come to receive.

5. Tell the candidate to open his mouth wide and breathe in as deeply as possible, at the same time telling God in his heart, "I am receiving the Spirit right now by faith." Absolutely insist that he shall not speak a single word of his natural language. Then, when you see the Spirit moving on his lips and tongue, after he has taken several deep breaths, tell him to begin recklessly speaking whatever sounds seem easy to speak, utterly indifferent as to what they are. That is faith, as the person is lifting his voice and trusting God for the guidance. When he begins speaking, tell him to go right on doing so, praising God with those supernatural words until a free clear language comes, and he has confidence and assurance that he has received the Holy Spirit. Some may say it is foolish to tell the candidate to open his mouth. If you feel this way, then read Psalms 119:131; 81:10. Also see Job 29:23 where there is a statement directly applying to the receiving of the Holy Spirit.

6. Don't have a crowd around, all giving instructions and getting the individual confused. If all present will either pray in the Spirit (i.e., in other tongues, I Cor. 14:14, 15), or pray quietly so as not to disturb the candidate, they will greatly help him rise in faith. It is easy to see that with a dozen men all praying aloud in their natural language at once, the candidate hears a lot of things which he understands, and often it is not productive of unity. On the other hand, if the same twelve men are praying aloud in other tongues, the praying is absolutely in unity, since One (the Holy Spirit) is guiding it, and it creates an atmosphere of faith in which it is easy for the candidate to rise in faith, and expect to do the same things. The result is that almost always he

will receive the Holy Spirit under these conditions.

In recent years, we have had hundreds receive the Holy Spirit when we gave them correct instructions, and stated conditions around them which aided faith. We do not allow a lot of haphazard instructions and so-called help when we are in charge. We tell people to either pray in the Spirit or keep still, and a great many have thanked us for this kind of help and instruction, which enabled them to joyfully enter into the blessed experience of being filled with the Holy Spirit.

We repeat again, the all-important instruction that the candidate shall cast aside all thought of speaking his own natural words, which are a product of his own mind. Because of deep-rooted tradition, we find that many will begin to talk in their natural language as soon as they feel the moving of the Spirit upon them, even after they have been shown that this is not the position of faith. If they do this, we call everything to a halt, and tell them that they must stop even the whispering of their own words if they are to speak with other tongues without a lot of struggling. A person can no more speak his natural language and also speak with other tongues at the same time than he can speak two earthly languages at once. No one would be foolish enough to try to speak English and French at the same moment. He would put away all thought of speaking one when he began to speak the other. Why not use the same common sense in regard to speaking with other tongues?

Chapter Forty-five

Two Ways the Holy Spirit is Imparted

It is a matter of practical interest to determine not only how the Holy Spirit is received, but how it is imparted. Some say it is received by waiting — without the laying on of hands. Others declare that the only scriptural way to receive the Holy Spirit is through the laying on of hands. Actually, the Holy Spirit may be received either way, although the laying on of hands is the more general method used by the New Testament Church. At the risk of some repetition, we shall show that God has not restricted Himself to any one method.

Receiving Without the Laying on of Hands

Obviously, the apostles had to receive the Holy Spirit directly, since there was no one who possessed the Holy Spirit to lay hands on them. Some wrongly deduce that except on this one occasion, the Holy Spirit was always given through the laying on of hands. However, He fell upon the household of Cornelius without anyone laying hands on them (Acts 10:44). If God had regarded laying on hands as the superior method, He would have baptized the 12 apostles and then let them lay hands on the other 108. God did not do this, which indicates that He has not restricted Himself to any one method.

In Luke 24:49, the disciples were told not to leave Jerusalem, but to wait until they were endued with power from on high. In Acts 1:4, the same command is repeated — "to wait for the Promise of the Father."

Some believe that the only purpose for the disciples having to wait during this period, was that the Day of Pentecost had not come and that God had to wait for the calendar to roll around so He could send the Spirit on this day to fulfill Old Testament prophecy. It is true that the falling of the Holy Spirit on the Day of Pentecost fulfilled a prophecy, but we should remember that God usually arranges things so that more than one purpose may be fulfilled. Waiting for 10 days in the upper room in worship and prayer served an important purpose. The disciples had time to search their hearts and prepare themselves for the tremendous responsibilities that would soon be put upon them.

If our baptism is to be really effective, there must be a time of waiting upon God. If not before, then certainly afterward. If one receives the Holy Spirit immediately following conversion, it is very important that they set aside a time afterward for waiting upon God. The law of the spiritual world is, "Draw near to God and He will draw near to you" (Jas. 4:8). Many men of God, both in the Old and New Testaments, gave themselves to special seasons of waiting upon God. This is sorely needed today if we are to have more than superficial experiences.

It is true that the Holy Spirit may be, and should be, received instantly. We do not receive this experience by merit, long prayers, or because we have fasted. The Holy Spirit is a gift and cannot be earned. Nevertheless, there is a preparatory work that needs to be accomplished in our hearts.

We are told the disciples were in the temple praising and blessing God during the waiting days. They were not on their knees praying when the Holy Spirit came. Apparently, they were relaxed and sitting in an attitude of expectation when the hour came for God to meet them. Certainly, there should be no need for long weeks of agonizing in order to receive the Holy Spirit.

Peter began his sermon at Cornelius' house by saying, "'In truth I perceive that God shows no partiality. But in every nation whoever fears Him and works righteousness is accepted by Him'" (Acts 10:34, 35). Why did God choose to pour out His Spirit on the household of Cornelius and not on some other household? Though he was a Roman officer and a gentile, Cornelius was obedient to the light he had received. The Scriptures describe him as "a devout *man* and one who feared God with all his household, who gave alms generously to the people, and prayed to God always" (Acts 10:2).

While we do not receive the gift of God by reason of our works, nevertheless, obedience to God is important. When the angel appeared to Cornelius, he told him, "'Your prayers and your alms have come up for a memorial before God'" (ver. 4). Is it not clear that God regarded his prayers and devotion as opening the way for him to become a candidate for the baptism of the Holy Spirit? We are practically told that it was because of these things that God chose to reveal Himself as He did.

Nevertheless, it was necessary for Peter to preach the Word and to make known the fact that God's gift is given, not through good works, but solely through the merits of Jesus Christ. It was necessary for Cornelius to know that he had received remission of sins through the Name of Jesus, so as Peter was still speaking, "the Holy Spirit fell upon all those who heard the word" (Acts 10:44).

Thus we see that in two instances, the Holy Spirit fell without the intermediacy of laying on of hands.

Receiving Through the Laying on of Hands

Hebrews 6:2 informs us that the laying on of hands is one of the fundamental doctrines of Christ and is associated with such important doctrines as faith, repentance, resurrection of the dead and eternal judgment. We may therefore infer that the laying on of hands is a doctrine of unusual importance, for though the Holy Spirit was given at Pentecost and at the house of Cornelius directly, laying on hands is actually the more common method recorded in the Scriptures.

During the first evangelistic campaign held outside Jerusalem, Philip preached Christ and demonstrated the power of the Gospel through an unusual healing ministry in the city of Samaria (Acts 8:6, 7). There is no record that any of the Samaritans received the Holy Spirit through Philip's ministry. When the apostles heard about the stirring revival in Samaria, they sent Peter and John, and through their ministry, they received the Holy Spirit (ver. 14-17).

It would seem from the Scriptures that there had been an expectation that the Holy Spirit would have fallen on at least some of them. Since this had not yet occurred, they did two things: First, they prayed for them to receive the Holy Spirit, and second, they laid their hands on them — and they received the Holy Spirit.

Notice that the apostles prayed before the laying on of hands. The laying on of hands is valid only if God lays hands on the candidate also. Second, a spirit of discernment is necessary in the effective operation of this ministry. Paul gives warning to "not lay hands on anyone hastily" (I Tim. 5:22). In other words, there needs to be a preparation in the hearts of those who are to receive, before hands are laid on them.

Simon the sorcerer had seen what had happened, and he, too, wanted the power to lay hands on individuals that they might receive the Holy Spirit. He offered the disciples money, doubtless mentally calculating how much he would charge those who came to him to receive the Holy Spirit. Certainly, Simon intended to get his money back!

It is not necessary to assume that Simon was so bold as to come right out and bargain with Peter in the matter of buying this power. He may have thought that it was the opportune time to give Peter a substantial offering. Some people hand the preacher an offering when they are about to ask for a special favor.

However, it was the insinuation that the Holy Spirit could be purchased with money that shocked Peter and caused him to severely rebuke the pseudo-religionist. The incident is a warning that money cannot enter into any transaction in which the Holy Spirit is concerned. As Peter said to Simon, "Your money perish with you" (Acts 8:20).

The chief lessons taught in this incident are:

1. The Holy Spirit is given through the laying on of hands.
2. Certain ones have the ministry of laying on hands.
3. There must be some preparation in the hearts of the candidates before hands are laid on them to receive the Holy Spirit.
4. Ministers should exercise discernment as upon whom they lay hands.

The story of how Paul was converted and received the Holy Spirit is an instructive one. He had been a dangerous enemy of Christianity, but on the Damascus Road, as he was on the way to carry out persecution against the Christians, he was suddenly stopped by a blinding light from heaven. Christ appeared to him in a vision, and at that precise moment, Paul was converted. Paul was led into the city to the house where a man named Judas lived. Then, for three days he prayed, fasted and waited on the Lord.

Two things are notable about this incident. God permitted Paul to spend 72 hours in prayer. He could have sent Ananias the next day, but God waited three days, obviously because Paul needed the time for real soul-searching. Second, the Lord could have baptized Paul with the Holy Spirit without having Ananias perform the act of laying on of hands, but He chose to do it this way. God Himself endorsed the laying on of hands for giving the Holy Spirit.

> And Ananias went his way and entered the house; and laying his hands on him he said, "Brother Saul, the Lord Jesus, who appeared to you on the road as you came, has sent me that you may receive your sight and be filled with the Holy Spirit" (Acts 9:17).

Since Paul received the Holy Spirit through the laying on of hands, it is not surprising that he should employ this same method in his own ministry. In his travels, he met a group of disciples at Ephesus. Perhaps discerning that something was lacking in their experience, he asked them if they had received the Holy Spirit. Their answer was that they had "not so much as heard whether there is a Holy Spirit" (Acts 19:2). This led Paul to preach a sermon to them, explaining that John had baptized with the water of repentance, but that Christ, Who came after him, baptized in the Holy Spirit. These disciples then submitted to Christian baptism.

After that, "when Paul had laid hands on them, the Holy

Spirit came upon them, and they spoke with tongues and prophesied" (Acts 19:6).

Summing Up

The Holy Spirit may fall directly on the candidate, or may be imparted through the laying on of hands. The following facts seem to be clearly taught:

1. God is not restricted to a certain time, place, or method, of pouring out His Spirit. The laying on of hands was apparently the most common way in apostolic times. This same method was also used in Old Testament days. Moses laid hands on Joshua in order for him to receive the Holy Spirit (Deut. 34:9).

2. Prayer and soul-searching seem to be important before receiving of the Holy Spirit. The 120, "all continued ... in prayer and supplication" before the Holy Spirit fell on the Day of Pentecost (Acts 1:14). The apostles prayed for the Samaritans before they laid hands on them (Acts 8:15). Cornelius' prayers and fasting came up as a memorial before God prior to the angel being dispatched to give the instructions that led to the Holy Spirit falling upon his household (Acts 10:2-4). Paul was permitted to spend three days in prayer and fasting before hands were laid upon him to receive the Holy Spirit.

3. It appears that some spiritual preparation is therefore in order before candidates may receive the Holy Spirit to the best advantage. It is a fact that some receive with very little instruction, yet we are instructed not to lay hands on anyone hastily. Hypocrites, such as Simon the sorcerer, should be detected and brought to repentance before hands are laid upon them.

4. When the simple, scriptural conditions are met, hands may be laid on the candidates and they should receive instantly.

Chapter Forty-six

Why People Receive Different Measures of the Spirit

"For He whom God has sent speaks the words of God, for God does not give the Spirit by measure" (Jn. 3:34).

The above Scripture is the key to the subject which we shall consider in this chapter: Do all people receive the same measure of the Spirit? We are told that Christ received the Spirit of God without measure, that is, He received an inexhaustible supply of the Spirit.

The fact that John 3:34 declares that the Holy Spirit was given to Christ without measure, implies that it is given in a lesser measure to some. In other words, some receive a larger measure than others. Indeed, all evidence goes to show that this is true with most believers — they have a measure of faith, a measure of the Spirit, and a "measure of Christ's gift" (Rom. 12:3; Eph. 4:7). This circumstance is important for us to keep in mind if we are to understand certain facts about the baptism in the Holy Spirit.

As we have seen, there is a measure of the Spirit that moves upon the hearts of the unconverted to bring them to repentance. It should be noted, however, that when the Spirit strives with people to forsake their sins, He does this only for a limited time. If they resist the Spirit, their hearts get harder and harder until finally they become impenetrable to the Spirit's influence. "And the LORD said, 'My Spirit shall not strive with man forever, for he *is* indeed flesh ...'" (Gen. 6:3).

The Spirit Upon Moses

Moses, who was a singular type of Christ, received the Spirit without measure. The Spirit of God came upon him in such power that his face shown with a transfiguring light. He had such an abundant measure of the Spirit that the Lord could take part of what was upon him, put it upon the 70 elders, and there was no apparent decrease in the supply. This event in Moses' life foreshadowed the Christian dispensation, when God-anointed individuals would so overflow with the Spirit that they could minister it to others. The reason some have an almost infinite supply of the Spirit is because He comes as "rivers of living water" — a river that flows endlessly.

In this connection, it may be noted that the measure of the Spirit that was upon the 70 elders was in a considerably lesser degree than it was upon Moses. In fact, we are told that the Holy Spirit was grieved with that generation in the wilderness, and He swore they would not enter into His rest (Heb. 3:7-11). This included 68 of the 70 elders. Only two, Joshua and Caleb, entered into Canaan — Canaan is generally considered a type of the full baptism in the Holy Spirit.

There were also other children of Israel, beside the 70 elders, who received the Spirit — undoubtedly in the same manner they had received. In Exodus 28:3, God declared to Moses that He had given the "spirit of wisdom" to the "gifted." One craftsman, by the name of Bezalel was singled out, in particular, to build the tabernacle. God said, "'And I have filled him with the Spirit of God, in wisdom, in understanding, in knowledge, and in all *manner of* workmanship'" (Ex. 31:3).

The Measure of the Spirit Upon the Prophets

> And the Spirit of the LORD began to move upon him at Mahaneh Dan between Zorah and Eshtaol (Judg. 13:25).

The above verse portrays the typical working of the Spirit as He moved upon the prophets in Old Testament days. We are told that the Spirit of God "moved" Samson at times. On such occasions, Samson had superhuman strength. He had received a measure of the Spirit, but it was not the full New Testament experience. We might add that Samson's erratic conduct eventually crossed over the line of God's patience. When Samson revealed the secret of his strength to Delilah and permitted his hair to be cut, the Spirit departed from him. He arose and said to himself, "'I will go out as before, at other times, and shake myself free!' But he did not know that the LORD had departed from him" (Judg. 16:20). King Saul's circumstances were similar to Samson's:

> "Then the Spirit of the LORD will come upon you, and you will prophesy with them and be turned into another man" (I Sam. 10:6).

God's purpose in giving the Spirit to Saul was to change him into "another man," but his disobedience resulted in the Spirit of God leaving him and an evil spirit taking His place. Saul was delivered for a time through David's faith, but in time he fell back again into his stubborn ways (I Sam. 16:14-16, 23).

A Double Portion of the Spirit

"Elisha said, 'Please let a double portion of your spirit be upon me'" (II Ki. 2:9). Elisha recognized that there are different measures of the Spirit. This point has extreme significance in our consideration of the baptism in the Holy Spirit: Different people receive different measures of the Spirit.

The difference depends on two main factors. The first is related to the degree of faith and anointing of the one who does the ministering. Elisha received the double portion, partly because of the great anointing upon Elijah. Some ministers are especially anointed to minister the Spirit. Paul speaks of those who minister the Holy Spirit by faith (Gal. 3:5). Not everyone possesses this special gift. But Peter and John did (Acts 8:14-17). So did the Apostle Paul (Acts 19:6) and Ananias (Acts 9:12,17). Those specially anointed with the ministry of the laying on of hands will have greater results than those who do not.

The other factor, and a very important one, which determines the measure of the Spirit people receive, lies within the people themselves. There is a great difference in the way people react. Although the same person may be ministering, some seekers will remain unresponsive, while others will be strongly anointed by the Spirit, receiving a satisfying baptism. There may be one or two who will receive a "double portion." A powerful baptism of the Spirit often foreshadows a special ministry for that individual. Yet, this does not always tell the story. Some seem to stumble along, gaining a little ground at a time, but by the force of persistence and prayer, overcome all hindrances, and finally pass others who seemed to have had a much better beginning.

Elisha received the double portion because he had a great hunger for God. He would not leave Elijah. He pressed on, determined that he would attain the desire of his heart. And he did. Jesus' words apply to those who receive the double portion: "'Blessed *are* those who hunger and thirst for righteousness, for they shall be filled'" (Matt. 5:6).

Rivers of Living Water!

On the last day, the great *day* of the feast, Jesus stood and cried out, saying, "If anyone thirsts, let him come to Me and drink. He who believes in Me, as the Scripture has said, out of his heart will flow rivers of living water." But this He spoke concerning the Spirit, whom those believing in Him would receive; for the Holy Spirit was not yet *given*, because Jesus was not yet glorified (Jn. 7:37-39).

The double portion Elisha received is actually a type of the full baptism in the Holy Spirit that God intends for New Testament believers to have. Because of various hindrances in individual's lives, some will have a mere trickle of the Spirit. With others, His indwelling will be like a great river of living water, freely flowing out to bless others. The experience of being filled with the Holy Spirit can be like that of Moses and Elisha — a mighty, immeasurable anointing of the Spirit's power, or it can be like that of the 70 elders, who had to depend entirely on someone else's faith for their blessing.

Differences Between the Old and New Testament Experiences

Now, we are ready to consider the two main differences between the Old and New Testament experiences of receiving the Holy Spirit. Jesus said:

> "And I will pray the Father, and He will give you another Helper, that He may abide with you forever — the Spirit of truth, whom the world cannot receive, because it neither sees Him nor knows Him; but you know Him, for He dwells with you and will be in you" (Jn. 14:16, 17).

Even before Pentecost, the disciples had the Spirit. John 20:22 declares that Jesus "breathed on *them*, and said to them, 'Receive the Holy Spirit.'" There is no doubt that they already had a measure of the Holy Spirit, but it was not the full measure. The Holy Spirit was with them, but on the Day of Pentecost, He came and dwelt in them. And when He came, it was not temporarily, like in Old Testament days. Nor was it only until death; it was forever!

The other important difference between receiving the Holy Spirit in Old Testament times and in the New, is speaking in other tongues. This experience was exclusively for New Testament saints. Isaiah foresaw it and declared it to be something very wonderful that would accompany the baptism, and which would be the "refreshing" that would cause "the weary to rest" (Isa. 28:11, 12).

Isaiah's language shows us that this was to be something very important. Speaking in other tongues is not just a sign, or something added onto the baptism; it is an essential part of the baptism in the Holy Spirit. People may receive the Spirit without the speaking in other tongues, like in Old Testament times, but they do not have the full New Testament baptism.

Chapter Forty-seven

The Two Phases of the Holy Spirit Baptism

And they were all filled with the Holy Spirit and began to speak with other tongues, as the Spirit gave them utterance (Acts 2:4).

In the familiar Scripture quoted above, we see the two phases of the baptism in the Holy Spirit. The first phase of the baptism is receiving the Holy Spirit. The other is the articulate expression of the Holy Spirit through the lips of the filled person. Some have stressed the anointing and the infilling of the Spirit, and have disregarded the speaking in tongues. Likewise, others have focused so much attention on speaking in tongues that they have failed to emphasize that the infilling must come first.

In a normal baptism, the Holy Spirit comes on the person in surging waves of power, varying in intensity with different individuals. It is a thrilling and distinctive experience that one can never forget. Because it is so wonderful, some who have received it disregard speaking in other tongues, which is also wonderful and is an important part of the baptism. In so doing, they make a great mistake.

Speaking in Other Tongues

As most of us know, the tongue is the most difficult member of the body to control. It is usually the last member for the Holy Spirit to conquer. Even when people begin to speak in other tongues, they may unconsciously resist the Holy Spirit and revert back to speaking in their familiar vernacular. But if they are reassured and encouraged to yield their tongue to these unfamiliar sounds, there will come forth a few inarticulate words or phrases that are often repeated, and then different words, and finally sentences. Invariably, these words are languages unknown to the person. When heard by one who knows the language, or has the gift of interpretation, they are found to be words of praise and adoration to God. Sometimes, a person newly baptized will preach a short sermon or give an exhortation in the unknown tongue. They may have a vision of the Lord, although very seldom do they lose consciousness.

It is essential for the believer to speak in the unknown tongue. Jesus said, "And these signs will follow those who believe ... they will speak with new tongues" (Mk. 16:17). It is a supernatural experience. In a sense, it is a continuous miracle that Christians can take with them for a lifetime.

It is entirely in order to instruct candidates to yield their tongues to the Spirit when the anointing of the Holy Spirit comes upon them. Human nature is stubborn; it requires every gift of persuasion that a minister has to get some people to yield their lives to God. It is not surprising that we have to encourage and even persuade people to yield their tongues to Him. Although the Holy Spirit has all power, He is mild and gentle, and forces no one. The Spirit leads men, but never drives. He guides into truth, but never forces.

Many individuals have received wonderful anointings of the Spirit, and all they lack to enjoy the full baptism is some instruction on yielding their tongues. Often such people, when properly instructed, will begin speaking in a clear language within only a few minutes, although they may have been seeking the baptism for years.

At this point, I will take the liberty to speak of my own experience in receiving the Holy Spirit:

One night, only a week or two after the campaign in which I was saved had ended, I was at the altar, asking God to give me the baptism in the Holy Spirit. Suddenly, while I was praying, a mighty wave of power began to sweep over me. As I continued, that vibrating, surging force began to permeate every part of my body. Each moment it went deeper and deeper, until this mighty power, like pulsating electricity, only something more wonderfully pleasant, had taken control of every part of my being. How long this continued I cannot say, but I knew that

I had received something out of this world — something intensely real. It was a heavenly experience beyond human ability to describe. It brought me into such a close relationship with God, that all I could think of at that moment was to devote my whole life to His service. Several other times, the Spirit came upon me, and each time this occurred, I was more convinced that God had something special in store for my life.

I had received a wonderful anointing of the Spirit, and it was glorious. Nevertheless, I had not spoken in other tongues as I had seen others doing who had received the Holy Spirit. This was a disappointment to me, and although I continued to seek God earnestly from night to night, and received many wonderful and repeated anointings of the Spirit, I did not speak in tongues.

Then one Saturday afternoon while I was waiting before the Lord, a lady came and knelt nearby. While I was praying, my tongue seemed to get a little thick. I began to speak a few words that were not clear English. I quickly recovered myself, however, and began again to pray in English, thinking that my tongue had become twisted. Is it not strange that many of us are so obsessed with the idea that God is going to use brute force to make us speak in tongues, that we fail to see He is trying to use our tongues? Fortunately, the lady kneeling nearby recognized what I did not — that the Spirit was attempting to speak through me. She told me to let the words come out any way that they would, for it was the Spirit of God. May that lady's memory be blessed! Rather timidly, I did as she said — the words, however, sounded very strange to me. But in a very few minutes I was speaking clearly and powerfully in the unknown tongue! I did not stop, but continued for about two hours.

And what a blessing speaking in tongues has been over the years. My own experience makes it clear to me that many who have received the anointing of the Spirit need only a little instruction to cause them to yield their tongues to God.

Thus, we see that the baptism in the Holy Spirit has two distinct phases. First, the anointing and presence of the Holy Spirit that comes upon us to dwell with us forever. Hallelujah!

How could death or the grave cause us to fear when the Spirit of Life dwells within us! The other part of the baptism is speaking in other tongues by the Spirit. This is important, too, for we must have this to receive the full baptism.

Chapter Forty-eight

How to Receive the Holy Spirit Baptism

(By Mrs. Gordon Lindsay)

Life is filled with complex problems. That is a fact that no one would challenge. What is the answer? Has God created mankind upon this earth to be continually molested and buffeted by the enemy? No, God has given us an appropriate weapon — the baptism in the Holy Spirit.

Who is to receive the Holy Spirit? Paul says in Ephesians 5:18, "Be filled with the Spirit." This includes every boy and girl, every man and woman. The Lord told us in Joel:

> "And it shall come to pass afterward that I will pour out My Spirit on all flesh; your sons and your daughters shall prophesy, your old men shall dream dreams, your young men shall see visions. And also on *My* menservants and on *My* maidservants I will pour out My Spirit in those days" (Joel 2:28, 29).

It sounds as if God didn't leave anybody out. We have been witnesses to this fact. God's Spirit is being poured out, around the world, on men — great men, and also upon servants. We have seen the Lord baptize children at three years of age, and we have witnessed Him fill people 100 years of age. We have seen Him fill those who believe from various backgrounds — the Lutheran, Methodist, Baptist, Pentecostal, Muslim, Hindu, Mormon, Indian and Catholic. God is no respecter of age, denomination or race. Jesus said, "'If you then, being evil, know how to give good gifts to your children, how much more will *your* heavenly Father give the Holy Spirit to those who ask Him!'" (Lk. 11:13).

The infilling of the Holy Spirit is an experience subsequent to salvation. It is a distinct and separate gift, as shown in Acts 19:1-6.

Saul of Tarsus was converted on the Damascus Road. Three days later, Ananias said to him, "'Brother Saul, the Lord Jesus, who appeared to you on the road as you came, has sent me that you may receive your sight and be filled with the Holy Spirit'" (Acts 9:17). Whether it is one, two or three days after your conversion, the important thing is to be filled with the Spirit now.

What is the initial evidence of the Holy Spirit? Let me give you five instances from the book of Acts:

1. Acts 2:4 says that "they (the 120 Christians including Christ's own mother and His brothers, Acts 1:14) were all filled with the Holy Spirit and began to speak with other ton-gues, as the Spirit gave them utterance."

2. Acts 8:17, 18 points out the fact that Simon saw that they received the Holy Spirit. Comparing other Scriptures, the only logical conclusion is that he saw that the people began to speak in tongues when hands were laid upon them.

3. Acts 9:17 tells us that hands were laid on Paul to receive the Holy Spirit. We know he spoke in tongues, for he himself said, "'I thank my God I speak with tongues more than you all'" (I Cor. 14:18).

4. Acts 10:46 declares that Peter heard the gentiles speak in tongues.

5. Acts 19:6 shows us that when Paul laid his hands on the Ephesians, "they spoke with tongues and prophesied." Tongues have not been done away with, as some teach from I Cor-inthians 13:8, 9. "Whether *there are* tongues, they will cease; whether *there is* knowledge, it will vanish away." There has never been a time when there was as much knowledge as there is today!

What is the purpose of the Holy Spirit?

1. Acts 1:8 informs us that we receive power after the Holy

Spirit comes upon us: Power to live an overcoming life, power to pray for the sick, power for the service of our Master.

2. Acts 1:8 also tells us that the Holy Spirit makes us witnesses. He is a flame within us that drives us to witness of this glorious Gospel.

3. I Corinthians 14:4 shows us that when we pray in tongues we are "edified" — built up, benefitted or charged up like a car battery.

4. I Corinthians 14:2 says that "in the spirit he speaks mysteries." In other words, we have a secret code between us and God, which the devil will never be able to crack! While the devil can even intercept our thoughts and inject his own diabolical doubts, he never knows what we are saying when we pray in tongues! Praise God!

5. John 14:26 reveals another attribute of the Holy Spirit. It calls Him "the Helper." In this world of death and sorrow, what a joy to possess this wonderful Comforter.

6. John 14:26 also tells us that the Holy Spirit will "bring to your remembrance all things." That is to say, He will quicken our minds for the particular work the Lord calls us to do, be it secular or spiritual. I have seen this happen many, many times. God takes someone, seemingly without the qualifications for a particular work, and greatly multiplies their abilities and talents. Those who were already leaders in their field before their infilling, He has advanced to even greater heights. Our God-given, natural abilities find their highest expression and greatest reward as we yield our lives completely to the Holy Spirit.

7. The infilling of the Holy Spirit broadens our prayer lives. When we pray with our understanding, we pray only for things we understand. But when we pray in the Spirit, God is able to lay upon our hearts, burdens for individuals around the world. People we have never met or known will benefit by our ministry of intercession. Paul admonishes us to pray both with our understanding and in the Spirit (I Cor. 14:13-15). Praying becomes more pleasurable, and a new joy wells within us.

8. Another tremendous asset of being filled with the Spirit is the "rest" and "refreshing" it brings (Isa. 28:12). How much

better to possess the Holy Spirit than to have to rely on tranquilizers to relax us! God has made every provision for us — body, soul and spirit.

9. The Holy Spirit is a divinely appointed guide (Jn. 16:13). Life does not need to be a hit-and-miss comedy of errors. We can commit our lives daily to the Master in prayer, and let the Holy Spirit guide us. Natural wisdom is not enough; it may lead us up blind alleys and down dead-end streets, but never so the Holy Spirit.

How can one be filled with the Holy Spirit?

Let's begin with the most quoted Pentecostal Scripture, Acts 2:4: "And they were all filled with the Holy Spirit and began to speak with other tongues, as the Spirit gave them utterance." Who began to speak? Some answer, "The Holy Spirit." But that is not what the Scripture says. Read the verse again. It says, "they ... began to speak." One might object, "If I do the speaking, it will be the flesh speaking." That's right. Joel 2:28 says He will pour out His Spirit on all flesh. As long as you have a mortal body, you will be speaking in the flesh. Once you are taken to heaven, you won't need to speak in tongues.

"As the Spirit gave them utterance" indicates that speaking in tongues is supernatural. If you had to think up the words to say, then there would be nothing supernatural about it; but the Spirit gives you the words to say. After you have centered all your thoughts on the Lord in worship, you speak out, in faith, the words that are in your heart. You don't need to understand them, for the words will sound strange. They may at first sound like a child learning to speak. Isaiah 28:11 says, "For with stammering lips and another tongue He will speak to this people." Don't be afraid of your voice and don't hesitate. Speak out the words distinctly. Express what God has put in your heart.

Take a deep breath and begin to speak in tongues. Remember, if you are saved, you have Christ, and Colossians 2:9 says, "For in Him dwells all the fullness of the Godhead bodily." Believe that you have the Holy Spirit in you. He is waiting for you to do something for Him.

When I speak in English, I use my tongue, lips, teeth and

my voice. You must do exactly the same when you speak in tongues — use your lips, your teeth, your tongue, your voice. Yet, I have seen many who are expecting to be filled with the Spirit become very tense. Their upper lip becomes rigid, and they can't even speak in their own language in this fashion! Rest in the Lord. Relax and watch the beautiful Holy Spirit move in your life.

If you are capable of conversing in English, French, Spanish and German, you can only speak in one language at a time, right? Likewise, if you insist on continuing to speak in your native language, you will never speak in tongues. Praise the Lord for a few minutes until you feel the Holy Spirit moving in your soul. Then stop speaking in your native language, and in faith begin to speak in the unknown tongue. As you become obedient to the moving of the Holy Spirit, great joy will flood your soul, for the Bible says that "the disciples were filled with joy and with the Holy Spirit" (Acts 13:52). That joy may come the day you receive the Holy Spirit, or it may come later, as you learn to submit yourself to Him.

Where can one best receive the Holy Spirit? Most individuals receive in church because there, the presence of the Lord is conducive to bringing a worshipful attitude into one's heart, which is a requirement for receiving. On the other hand, one truck driver testified that he was baptized in the Holy Spirit while driving down the highway. He said he got so happy he pulled his truck off the road, and just jumped up and down beside it for sheer joy. Another man said he received while shaving, and yet another, while lying in bed. Some have written to say that they were baptized while serving sentences in prison. A lady said she received while washing her dishes. The 120 in the upper room were apparently sitting (Acts 2:2). God is no respecter of posture or of place.

When we first took the pastorate in Ashland, Oregon, one of the finest men we ever met, a railroad man by the name of Ben Pedersen, was on the church board. One family, in particular, felt he was not qualified to serve on the board unless he had the baptism in the Holy Spirit. When we approached Brother Pedersen, he said he had been "seeking" for many years, but had not received. So we gave him the instructions, and in half-an-hour or so, he was gloriously speaking in a language he hadn't learned.

My own wonderful mother had "tarried" for perhaps 25 years. She begged and pleaded with God to fill her. Tears streamed down her face, as she prayed by the hour. After 25 years, she was no doubt further from receiving than she was the day she first believed in the Acts 2:4 experience. Then a rugged evangelist held a series of meetings in the church she faithfully attended. Many received the Holy Spirit each night, but my mother was not among them. Night after night, the evangelist watched her praying in desperation. One evening, after she had given up, the evangelist came over to her. "How long have you been seeking the Holy Spirit?" he asked.

"Twenty-five years," she replied.

"Sister, you can pray another 25 years, just as you have, and you'll get nowhere," he told her. She was really jarred!

He continued, "You're begging and trying to coax God into giving you something He has already given you. Acts 2:38 tells us that the Holy Ghost is a gift. God is extending the gift to you. Now, if I were offering you a gift in my hand, and you refused to take it, but kept right on pleading for me to give it to you, you'd insult my integrity. I'd feel that you didn't trust me. God is the same. He gave you the Holy Ghost 2,000 years ago. Quit your begging, my sister, and accept."

All the next day, my mother pondered these words — torn at times between a wounded pride and a deep hunger to be filled. Needless to say, before the campaign came to a conclusion, she was one of the 200 who were filled.

When anyone asked my dear father-in-law, for years a school teacher, and later a high school principal, if he had received the Holy Spirit, he would always answer, "Do all speak with tongues?" Usually, those who take this attitude don't believe it is necessary to speak in tongues in order to receive. Actually, this verse in I Corinthians 12:30 refers to one of the nine gifts, as the context clearly shows. True, not all have the gift of tongues. But this certainly does not refer to the initial evidence of receiving the Holy Spirit. Finally, after reaching the ripe age of 70, my father-in-law accepted Acts 2:4, and was baptized by the Spirit. He lived another 20 years and what a joy it was to hear him pray in the unknown tongue during our daily devotions.

I'm a firm believer that if I Corinthians 14:4, is true, that if "he who speaks in a tongue edifies himself," then every Spirit-filled believer ought to pray in tongues every day. Praying in tongues will build us up in the way of God. Each morning, before I leave my bed, I raise my hands in thanks to God. And during the day, as I go about my work, I pray in tongues — sometimes audibly, but often to myself. I would be utterly lost without the presence of this wonderful Holy Spirit.

While it is scriptural to lay hands on individuals to receive the Holy Spirit, as Paul did in Acts 19:6, it is not always necessary. We have seen thousands receive through the laying on of hands, but also many who have not had hands laid on them.

How long should it take to receive the Holy Spirit? It should only take as long as it takes you to touch God. With some, it's five seconds, with others, it's half an hour and for others, it is longer.

I vividly remember a tent campaign we were jointly holding with the T.L. Osborns in Athens, Tennessee. I had been announced to speak at the service the following afternoon to help those who wanted to receive the Holy Spirit. When Brother Osborn gave his call for those who wanted to accept the Lord as Savior, I went to the rear of the tent to pray with some of the candidates. After the last convert had left, and Brother Osborn had begun to pray for the sick, a fine-looking young man approached me. He said, "I'm a student from Cleveland, studying for the ministry. I have been in Bible school for a couple of years, but have never received the baptism. I'm in school, so I won't be able to come tomorrow afternoon. Can you help me now?"

I sat down with him on a bench, and gave him the simple instructions. When I finished, he turned to me with the following question, "Do you mind if I receive tonight?" I told him, "Not in the least." He knelt on the sawdust while I walked to the end of the bench to put on my coat, for it was getting cool. I returned to where he was kneeling, so I could pray for him to receive, but I was too late! By the time I returned to where he was, he had his hands in the air, and was already speaking in tongues. He didn't need my mighty prayer! In fact, in a matter of minutes, he got so loud that a number of the boys with whom he attended Bible school came running in from the main tent, as they recognized the voice of their "chronic seeker" speaking in tongues. To say they all had a camp meeting is putting it mildly! How wonderful to see young people and those of every age and level of society yield to the mighty moving of the Holy Spirit. To God be the praise! You can have your portion today.

Chapter Forty-nine

30 Objections to Speaking in Tongues and the Biblical Answers

OBJECTION 1:

The passage of Mark 16:9-20, in which are included the words, "they will speak with new tongues" is a counterfeit addition to the Book of Mark.

ANSWER:

While a few manuscripts omit this passage, many more with as great an authority include it. Moreover, the Vatican manuscript, which is the one most often cited as leaving out the passage, has a blank space between Mark 16:8 and the book of Luke, as if the copier were not sure whether or not to include it. With a few exceptions, all the uncial manuscripts retain these twelve verses. The cursive manuscripts unanimously recognize the passage as genuine.

The Vulgate version prepared by Jerome (347-419 A.D.) includes the disputed verses. Many of the Early Church fathers quote from the passage in their writings, thus further indicating its genuineness. (See Iranaeus A.D. 177 AVD. Haer III 10.)

The internal evidence strongly indicates that the passage is a part of the 16th chapter of Mark. Certainly, the stark abruptness of the ending of the eighth verse is almost overwhelming proof that there was more text after it. Can we imagine Mark, the forceful evangelist, ending his book with the words, "for they were afraid"?

Some have strongly defended the Bible against agnostics who have taken a position against the authenticity of Mark 16:9-20. The agnostics then demanded that they give an explanation of Mark 16:15-18. When these embarrassed defenders tried to explain that the passage was not genuine, the agnostics mockingly agreed with them.

However, the authenticity of the Mark 16:15-18 passage is ultimately attested to by the fact that it agrees perfectly with the rest of the teaching of the New Testament.

OBJECTION 2:
If we are to accept Mark 16:15-18 as genuine, then Christians must handle snakes to show they are true believers. For it reads, "They will take up serpents."

ANSWER:
We must let the Bible explain its own statements. The passage in question first declares that believers will cast out demons. The fulfillment of this promise is demonstrated in Acts 16:18 where Paul cast the spirit of divination out of a girl.

In the passage, Jesus also said that believers would lay hands on the sick and they would recover. There is no difficulty in understanding what is meant by that. Jesus and the apostles laid hands on the sick and healed them.

What, then, is meant by the statement, "they will take up serpents"? Does it mean that Christians are to go out and literally pick up deadly snakes to prove they are believers? Again, we must let the Bible explain the Bible. When Paul picked up a snake by accident (Acts 28:3-5), he did not wave it around to show he was a believer, but shook it off into the fire. God protected him from its deadly bite and he "suffered no harm."

Since Satan is typified by a snake, Jesus' reference to them in the Great Commission has a further symbolic meaning. This is evidenced in the promise given to the 70:

> And He said to them, "I saw Satan fall like lightning from heaven. Behold, I give you the authority to trample on serpents and scorpions, and over all the power of the enemy, and nothing shall by any means hurt you" (Lk. 10:18, 19).

The meaning of the third sign is seen in the fourth, "And if they drink anything deadly, it will by no means hurt them" (Mk. 16:18). The word "if" explains what the passage means. People are not to drink deadly poisons and pick up snakes to prove they are believers. But if by mistake or accident they should do so, then they may claim the promise of immunity.

The promise of divine protection for those who believe is entirely consistent with the Scriptures (see Psalm 91).

OBJECTION 3:

Assuming the passage of Mark 16:15-18 is genuine, the words, "They will speak with new tongues," must mean that, after conversion, one's speech will be from a renewed spirit. That is, instead of cursing and speaking evil as they did in the past, they will bless others after salvation.

ANSWER:

It is true that God does put a new song in the mouths of His people when they are converted. But the signs listed in the context — divine healing and casting out devils — are supernatural signs. All rules of logic require that this sign be supernatural also.

There are others who contend that speaking in new tongues refers to ministers who are anointed with the Holy Spirit and receive power to preach with new fluency and fervor. Few commentators take this position, and the vast majority of Bible students agree that the gift was in active operation in the Early Church. The Book of Acts definitely shows that these "new tongues" refer to actual languages.

However, some teach that God withdrew this gift as well as others from the Church on the basis that they had served their purpose. But, there are no biblical grounds for this view.

OBJECTION 4:

There is no such thing as "the unknown tongue." One writer says, "In every instance where the gift of tongues was granted, the onlookers or believers included foreigners who spoke different languages and could, therefore, understand what was spoken."

ANSWER:

Few expositors hold this view, for it is in flat contradiction to the Scriptures. It is, of course, well-known that on the Day of Pentecost, people from 17 countries heard the 120 disciples speaking in their respective languages. Similar incidents have occurred in our own time, as attested to by numerous witness. Nevertheless, the understanding of a message in other tongues by someone who happens to know the language, only happens occasionally. Such an occurrence is recorded only once in the Bible — in Acts 2.

Ordinarily, tongues is not understood by anyone present. This is so clearly stated by Paul that it cannot be denied. The apostle said in I Corinthians 14:2, "For he who speaks in a tongue does not speak to men but to God, for no one understands *him*; however, in the spirit he speaks mysteries."

When speaking in other tongues occurs in the public assembly, the people ordinarily do not understand what is said. The gift of interpretation of tongues is needed to make known what is said (I Cor. 14:13, 27).

OBJECTION 5:

Pentecostals teach that everyone should speak in tongues, but Paul asks the question, "Do all speak with tongues?" (I Cor. 12:30) which implies that they do not. Therefore, the teaching that speaking in other tongues always accompanies the baptism in the Holy Spirit is erroneous.

ANSWER:

A good test of any interpretation of Scripture is whether it works out in practice. If the Bible speaks of the necessity of water baptism, and those who interpret it never baptize anyone, something is wrong with the interpretation. If the Scriptures teach repentance and faith in Christ, and those who interpret it never have anyone repent or accept Christ, it can hardly be said that their theology is correct. In other words, if an explanation is right, those responsible for teaching it must have some practical results to show that their view is not just theory.

The words, "Do all speak with tongues?" imply that at least

some people should speak with tongues. But the fact is, those who use this Scripture to argue against the Pentecostal experience rarely, if ever, have anyone speaking in tongues! Indeed, if someone in their midst does speak in tongues, they usually try to make them stop. In practice, they make the words, "Do all speak with tongues?" mean that "none should speak in tongues." Something is wrong with this explanation, which is obviously being used to discourage speaking in tongues.

What then is the real meaning of the words, "Do all speak with tongues?" I Corinthians 12 and 14 plainly refer to the gifts of the Spirit as they operate in the Church. The gift of tongues is actually "*different* kinds of tongues" (I Cor. 12:10, 28). It is clear that all do not have the gift of "varieties of tongues" nor are "*different* kinds of tongues" associated with the infilling of the Spirit.

There is, however, a level of speaking in tongues that is directly associated with receiving the Spirit. Thus on the Day of Pentecost, every one of the 120, when filled with the Spirit, began to speak in other tongues.

It is to be noted that Peter associated this phenomenon with Joel's promise. When the people said in Acts 2:12, "'Whatever could this mean?'" (speaking in other tongues), Peter related it to the promise that God would pour out His Spirit upon all flesh (Acts 2:16-18).

When Peter went to Cornelius' house and preached to them, we are told that the hearers received the Holy Spirit. How did Peter and those who were with him know this? How were the prejudiced Jews convinced? The answer is, "For they heard them speak with tongues and magnify God" (Acts 10:46). This makes it evident that speaking in other tongues had become recognized by the Early Church as the initial physical evidence of the infilling of the Spirit. Again, in Acts 19:6, we see that speaking in other tongues related to receiving the Holy Spirit.

Differences in the operations of the Spirit are seen in Christ's words in the Great Commission. He said, "These signs will follow those who believe ... they will lay hands on the sick, and they will recover" (Mk. 16:17, 18). All believers may pray for the sick, but this is not the same as the gifts of healings spoken of in I Corinthians 12 which were restricted to certain individuals.

Jesus also said that believers, "will speak with new tongues." This promise is for all believers, but the gift of "varieties of tongues" is not. Speaking in other tongues, as referred to in the Great Commission (which is available to all believers), is obviously not the same as the gift of "different kinds of tongues," which is not available to all.

The gift of "different kinds of tongues" is subject to definite restrictions which are explained in I Corinthians 14. But those speaking at Pentecost, at the house of Cornelius and at Ephesus, were not under these restrictions. Why not? Because in these cases, the speaking in other tongues indicated the arrival of the Holy Spirit. Paul said that in the regular operation of the gift, only one should speak at a time. But on the Day of Pentecost, the whole 120 spoke at once. Why? There is only one answer: There are obviously two levels of speaking in tongues. One is the initial evidence of the baptism; the other is the gift as listed in I Corinthians 12.

Some not only try to modify Paul's words, but they attempt to obliterate their meaning altogether. Were the same rules of exegesis followed with other parts of the Bible, we would soon cancel out every truth in it. In fact, this is the very method Satan used when he took the words, "You shall not eat it ... lest you die," and told Eve they meant, "You will not surely die" (Gen. 3:3, 4). Poor Eve learned, to her great loss, that God meant exactly what He said.

OBJECTION 6:

Paul stated that tongues are a sign, not to those who believe, but to those who do not. But Pentecostals make it a sign to those who believe.

ANSWER:

Speaking in other tongues is indeed a sign to unbelievers. "'*And yet, for all that, they will not hear Me,*' says the Lord" (I Cor. 14:21). It is obviously a sign of judgment to unbelievers. Those who oppose speaking in other tongues do not accept it as a sign from the Lord, and are unknowingly fulfilling the very prophecy which they do not believe!

In the days of Belshazzar, the fingers of a man's hand appeared and wrote the words "MENE, MENE, TEKEL UPHARSIN" on the wall. They were written in an unknown tongue, which could only be interpreted by Daniel the prophet, in whom dwelt the Spirit of God. When interpreted, the words spoke of judgment. "You have been weighed in the balances, and found wanting" (Dan. 5:27).

In the days of the Early Church, speaking in other tongues was a sign of coming judgment, not to believers, but to unbelievers. The prophet Isaiah pointed out that the sign would not be accepted by the nation as a whole, "that they might go and fall backward, and be broken and snared and caught" (Isa. 28:13). And that is what happened to the unbelieving Jews. Forty years after Pentecost, Titus and his armies invaded the land and, after destroying the city of Jerusalem, took the inhabitants into captivity.

We can draw a parallel and say that speaking in other tongues is, again, a sign of impending judgment. God is speaking to this fateful generation and saying, "You have been weighed in the balances and found wanting." The Laodicean Church, as a whole, rejects the sign of speaking in tongues. As the Scripture says, "'And yet, for all that, they will not hear Me,' says the Lord."

The fulfillment of the prophecy that tongues is a sign to unbelievers does not nullify the fact that it is obviously scriptural evidence of the infilling of the Holy Spirit. The apostles knew those at the house of Cornelius had received the Holy Spirit, "for they heard them speak with tongues and magnify God" (Acts 10:46). One Scripture cannot be interpreted to contradict another.

OBJECTION 7:

Certain Scriptures state that one cannot be a Christian unless he has the Holy Spirit. There are many who have felt the regenerating and sanctifying power of the Spirit, and have never spoken in other tongues.

ANSWER:

All believers have a measure of the Spirit, as Paul declares:

> Therefore I make known to you that no one speaking by the Spirit of God calls Jesus accursed, and no one can say that Jesus is Lord except by the Holy Spirit (I Cor. 12:3).

> But you are not in the flesh but in the Spirit, if indeed the Spirit of God dwells in you. Now if anyone does not have the Spirit of Christ, he is not His (Rom. 8:9).

It is clear from these Scriptures that one cannot be a Christian without having the Holy Spirit. But Christ made a clear distinction between having the Holy Spirit and having the Spirit dwell within you.

> "The Spirit of truth, whom the world cannot receive, because it neither sees Him nor knows Him; but you know Him, for He dwells with you and will be in you" (Jn. 14:17).

It is readily agreed that all saved people have the Holy Spirit, but that does not mean there is not an additional experience of the baptism in the Spirit. The fullness of the Spirit is described in John 7:37-39.

The Scriptures plainly teach that there is another operation of the Spirit which energizes the person for special service in witnessing and which has an outward supernatural expression.

As Robert Chandler Dalton says in his *Tongues Like As of Fire*:

> In a general way Paul refers to this outward expression as the "manifestation of the Spirit" (I Cor. 12:7) perhaps in contrast to the quiet and secret operations of the Spirit. In the New Test-

ament this experience is designated by such expressions as falling upon, coming upon, being poured out, being filled with. These expressions convey the thought of suddenness and supernaturalness. All these terms are connected with the experience known as the baptism in the Holy Spirit. The operation of the Spirit described by these terms is so distinct from His quiet and ordinary manifestations that scholars have coined a word to describe it. The word is "Charismatic" for a Greek word frequently used to designate a special impartation of spiritual power.

Mr. Dalton then quotes from A.B. Bruce, a Presbyterian scholar:

The Spirit's work was conceived of as transcendent, miraculous, and charismatic.

The power of the Holy Ghost was a power coming from without, producing extraordinary effects that could arrest the attention of even a profane eye like that of Simon the sorcerer.

While acknowledging that the early Christians believed also in the sanctifying operations of the Spirit and His inspiring of faith, hope, and love within people, he concludes that the gift of the Holy Spirit came to mean the power to speak ecstatically and to prophesy enthusiastically, and to heal the sick by a word of prayer.

The point we desire to emphasize is the following: the Baptism in the Holy Spirit, which is a baptism of power, is charismatic in character, judging from the description of the results of impartation.

Now while freely admitting that Christians have been born of the Spirit and workers anointed with the Spirit, we maintain that not all Christians have experienced the charismatic operation of the Spirit, followed by a sudden, supernatural utterance.

That there are different degrees in which the Holy Spirit moves in an individual's life is the clear teaching of Christ and the other New Testament writers.

OBJECTION 8:

Speaking in other tongues is referred to in only one epistle. If the gift were important, Paul would have mentioned it in other epistles. That it is referred to only in I Corinthians — a letter written to a carnal church — proves that Paul puts a low value upon it.

ANSWER:

The Lord's Supper is given great emphasis by most denominations, yet it is mentioned in no other epistle except I Corinthians, and in only one place. In contrast, speaking in other tongues is referred to no less than 18 times in the same book!

Many writers, however (some outside Pentecostal circles), believe that speaking in other tongues is referred to in some of the other epistles. They consider Ephesians 5:19 and Colossians 3:16 which speak of "spiritual songs" as referring to a special kind of speaking in tongues. Paul indicates that the gift assumes that form of operation occasionally and calls it singing with the Spirit (I Cor. 14:15).

Many commentaries consider that I Thessalonians 5:19, 20 which says, "Do not quench the Spirit. Do not despise prophecies," refers partly to the speaking in other tongues. Paul equates speaking in other tongues to prophesying if the former be interpreted. The Pulpit Commentary says, "By the Spirit here, is usually understood the miraculous gifts of the Spirit — speaking with other tongues or prophesyings: and it is supposed that the apostle here forbids the exercise of these gifts being hindered or checked."

The gifts of the Spirit, which include speaking in other tongues, are directly referred to in Hebrews:

> God also bearing witness both with signs and wonders, with various miracles, and gifts of the Holy Spirit, according to His own will? (Heb. 2:4).

We know that speaking in other tongues occurred in the Ephesian Church, for the charter members all spoke in other tongues and prophesied (Acts 19:6).

Paul speaks of praying in the Spirit (I Cor. 14:14, 15). Romans 8:26 says, "The Spirit Himself makes intercession for us with groanings which cannot be uttered." This is apparently a reference to the Holy Spirit praying through believers in sounds that we cannot utter in our own language.

But we need not go further, for Paul tells us that God appointed "varieties of tongues" in the Church, not just in the Corinthian Church (I Cor. 12:28). And Jesus said, "'These signs will follow those who believe ... they will speak with new tongues'" (Mk. 16:17).

OBJECTION 9:

Paul said, "Yet in the church I would rather speak five words with my understanding, that I may teach others also, than ten thousand words in a tongue" (I Cor. 14:19). According to this, the preaching of the Word is 2,000 times as desirable as speaking in an unknown tongue.

ANSWER:

The above verse must be considered in context. Paul says in the fifth verse "he who prophesies *is* greater than he who speaks with tongues, unless indeed he interprets, that the church may receive edification." This puts a completely different light on the matter. What Paul is saying, is that there is to be no speaking in tongues in the public assembly except with interpretation. However, if there is interpretation, it is equated with prophecy. To isolate a Scripture from its context is not a fair way to interpret God's Word.

OBJECTION 10:

Speaking in tongues is placed last in both lists of gifts and gift-ministries; therefore, it is the least of the gifts.

ANSWER:

We have never heard anyone contend that speaking in tongues is better than other gifts, but that does not mean it does not deserve full recognition. The Apostle Paul compares these gifts, including speaking in other tongues, to the members of the human body. He declares that those members which are the most feeble are also necessary.

> But now God has set the members, each one of them, in the body just as He pleased. And if they *were* all one member, where *would* the body *be*? But now indeed *there are* many members, yet one body. And the eye cannot say to the hand, "I have no need of you"; nor again the head to the feet, "I have no need of you." No, much rather, those members of the body which seem to be weaker are necessary (I Cor. 12:18-22).

It should be added that just because speaking in tongues is enumerated last, does not necessarily mean it is the least. When Paul speaks of faith, hope and love in the next chapter, he mentions love last, yet he says it is the most important. When Peter lists the fruits of the Spirit, he mentions love last (II Pet. 1:5-7). In I Corinthians 13, tongues is mentioned before prophecy, but this does not mean it is greater than prophecy. The fact that the gift of tongues is mentioned last in inconsequential.

OBJECTION 11:

Speaking in other tongues on the Day of Pentecost was to

assist the rapid evangelization of the world. God gave the disciples these various languages so that they could quickly carry the Gospel to the nations. When this work was completed, the gift of tongues was no longer necessary.

ANSWER:

It is true that this particular manifestation of the gift of tongues occurred on the Day of Pentecost. Similar cases, with hearers being able to understand a certain language spoken (because it was their native language), have occurred from time to time. However, this is not the principal purpose of speaking in other tongues; in fact, its occurrence in this manner is the exception and not the rule. When Paul explains the varied purposes of the gifts of the Spirit in I Corinthians 14, he does not even mention it. Instead, he begins his discussion by saying that "he who speaks in a tongue does not speak to men but to God, for no one understands *him*" (I Cor. 14:2).

Actually, when the 120 began speaking in tongues, there were no (or certainly very few) outsiders present. The disciples were worshiping and praising God in tongues among themselves. But as the news gradually spread, a multitude came, heard and were amazed. While they were in this state of wonder, Peter began to preach to them. There is not a word to indicate that he preached in tongues. Peter could not have preached to them in the 17 different languages of those present; he preached to them in the popular language of Israel — Aramaic. Hearing their native languages spoken by the power of the Spirit, amazed the multitude, but it was Peter's preaching in a common language that caused them to repent and be converted.

It is a historical fact that Greek, Aramaic and Latin were the principal languages spoken in the Roman world; so, it was possible for the Early Church to evangelize the nations with a minimum of language barriers.

OBJECTION 12:

The gifts of the Spirit, including speaking in other tongues, were needed to establish Christianity. After this was accomplished, they were no longer needed.

ANSWER:

To imply that the world now believes in Christianity, and that the ministry of the supernatural is no longer needed, is to merely shut one's eyes to reality. Missionaries are meeting tremendous opposition in the foreign fields. Islam is having a revival. Buddhism and Confucianism have vast followings. If anything, the need for the supernatural is greater now than ever before. In the days of the apostles, there were only a few hundred million unsaved people. Today there are billions.

When Elijah preached to the people on Mt. Carmel and called for a decision, the people were so confused that they did not answer. They did not know who was God — Jehovah or Baal. But when the supernatural fire fell in answer to Elijah's prayer, the people cried out, "'The LORD, He *is* God! The LORD, He *is* God!'" (I Ki. 18:39).

The ministry of the supernatural has never lost its power to impress the human spirit. Huge crowds have assembled in foreign lands to hear the preaching of the Word with signs following. A miracle is the universal language. Despite the fact that many have rejected speaking in other tongues as one of the miraculous signs to follow believers, it has captured the attention of others, and they have given their hearts to Christ, as happened on the Day of Pentecost.

OBJECTION 13:

Even though the sign-gifts did appear in the Early Church, historically, their manifestation did diminish greatly near the end of the first century. This indicates that God's purpose for them was largely fulfilled, and He was withdrawing them.

ANSWER:

The argument that the Lord was responsible for the disappearance of the Church's spiritual gifts is without scriptural foundation. Gideon did not regard the absence of miracles in his day as an indication of God's favor. He said, "If the LORD is with us, why then has all this happened to us? And where *are* all His miracles which our fathers told us about ...?'" (Judg. 6:13). The Pharisees believed in the miracles of Moses' day, but not in those of their own time. Fundamentalists of today believe in the miracles of the days of the apostles, but not in those occurring now. And so it goes, each one professing to believe in miracles, but not in the miracles that take place in his day.

When Jesus gave the Great Commission to the apostles, He said that signs would follow those who believe. John Wesley declared that the reason the ministry of the supernatural had declined was "because the love of many, almost all Christians so-called, waxed cold. That was the real reason why the extraordinary gifts of the Holy Ghost were no longer to be found in the Christian church."

The Church of Ephesus began with a revival in which speaking in tongues was manifested. When the gifts declined in the church, was it because the people had become too spiritual to need them? No! Instead, the Lord had to rebuke that church for its backslidden condition (Rev. 2:4, 5).

The real reason the gifts of the Spirit stopped functioning in the Church is because natural methods superseded the supernatural. Worldliness crept into the Church. God's people entered into an affinity with the world. Christianity became a state religion and was soon infused with heathenism and evil. Lukewarmness, not spirituality, is the reason the gifts disappeared from the Church.

The idea that there was one Gospel for the apostles and another for the present day Church is untrue. In the Great Commission, Jesus told the disciples that they were to preach the Gospel to every creature. He instructed them to, "'Go ... teaching them to observe all things that I have commanded you.'" And lest it be thought that he was speaking only to that generation, He added, "'Lo, I am with you always, *even* to the end of the age'" (Matt. 28:19, 20).

OBJECTION 14:

The apostle Paul says in I Corinthians 13:8, 10, that "whether *there are* tongues, they will cease. ... But when that which is perfect has come, then that which is in part will be done away." This means that when the New Testament canon was completed, there was no further need for this gift.

ANSWER:

In this passage, we are told that prophecy, tongues and knowledge shall vanish away. Those who oppose speaking in tongues advance the idea that the words "when that which is perfect has come" refer to the New Testament canon. But a careful look at the context shows that Paul is not referring to the New Testament canon at all, but to the perfect age. "For now we see in a mirror, dimly, but then face to face. Now I know in part, but then I shall know just as I also am known" (I Cor. 13:12). The word "then" clearly refers to the time when we shall see Christ face to face.

The gifts of the Spirit have not stopped. Nor has speaking in tongues or the gift of prophecy stopped. Only "when that which is perfect has come," will they cease being necessary. In the beginning, everyone spoke one language (Gen. 11:1). But because of man's apostasy, the Lord dispersed the people from the Tower of Babel by giving them different languages. Therefore, when God's redemption plan is complete, everyone will return to a "pure language" (Zeph. 3:9). The divine judgment given at Babel, will be lifted then, and at that time, speaking in tongues will cease.

If we were to be facetious, we might say of those who declare that "tongues have ceased," that it looks very much on their part like "knowledge has vanished away!"

OBJECTION 15:

One of the groups of people who heard the disciples speaking in other tongues on the Day of Pentecost, lived in Judea. Since the disciples, who were Galileans, spoke the same language (Aramaic) as the Judeans, it follows that some of the disciples must have spoken supernaturally in their own language instead of in other tongues. That being true, not all of the 120 spoke in other tongues.

ANSWER:

To say the Galileans spoke in their own dialect is to contradict the Scriptures, which state that all spoke in other tongues. The Galileans had a distinctly different dialect from the Judeans. This was seen when Peter tried to hide his identity when he denied Jesus. His accusers said to him, "'You are a Galilean, and your speech shows *it*'" (Mk. 14:70). It was impossible for the Galileans to speak without their peculiar accent. That they spoke in the Judean vernacular is what amazed the Judeans. The Scripture says, "And they were all filled with the Holy Spirit and began to speak with other tongues, as the Spirit gave them utterance" (Acts 2:4). That means that all of the 120 spoke in other tongues.

OBJECTION 16:

Pentecostals refer to speaking in tongues as the initial evidence of the baptism in the Holy Spirit. But the baptism in the Holy Spirit occurred at Pentecost when the Spirit fell upon the Church. Never again do the Scriptures speak of anyone being baptized in the Spirit. It occurred once and for all at Pentecost.

ANSWER:

This statement is incorrect. The Scriptures refer to those at the house of Cornelius receiving "the same gift" (Acts 11:17) the disciples received at Pentecost, and even speak of their experience as "baptized with the Holy Spirit" (Acts 11:16).

Those accompanying Peter to Cornelius' house knew that the gentiles had received the Holy Spirit, "for they heard them speak with tongues and magnify God" (Acts 10:46). Nevertheless, the Jews did not receive this news with pleasure. They argued strongly with Peter for eating with the uncircumcised. He then explained what had happened:

> "And as I began to speak, the Holy Spirit fell upon them, as upon us at the beginning. Then I remembered the word of the Lord, how He said, 'John indeed baptized with water, but you shall be baptized with the Holy Spirit.' If therefore

God gave them the same gift as *He gave* us when we believed on the Lord Jesus Christ, who was I that I could withstand God?" (Acts 11:15-17).

We can see several things from this passage: The gentiles spoke with tongues, proving to the Jews that they had received the Holy Spirit, and they received Him in the same way the 120 did "at the beginning," on the Day of Pentecost. Peter said it was that which the Lord spoke of, saying, "'John indeed baptized with water, but you shall be baptized with the Holy Spirit'" (ver. 16). It was also said to be the same gift which the apostles had received.

OBJECTION 17:
Nothing is said about the Samaritans speaking in tongues when they received the Holy Spirit (Acts 8:1-25).

ANSWER:
Carl Brumback, in his classic *What Meaneth This?*, answers this question so clearly that it can scarcely be improved upon. I take the liberty to quote from it:

> Verses 18 and 19 tell us, "And when Simon saw that through laying on of the apostles' hands the Holy Ghost was given, he offered them money, saying, 'Give me also this power, that on whomsoever I lay hands, he may receive the Holy Ghost.'" No one can doubt from these words that there was an outward evidence of the reception of the Spirit. It does not seem plausible that a man of Simon's caliber would offer money for the ability to produce an invisible effect.

> What, then, did Simon see? It is our conviction that Simon witnessed the glossolalia. This miracle of utterance was entirely new to him, and would arrest his attention as nothing else. How he would covet the power to impart this gift!

"The voice they uttered was awful in its range, in its tones, in its modulation, in its startling, almost penetrating power; the words they spoke were exalted, intense, passionate, full of mystic significance." With this power he could again take his place before the people as at least the equal of Philip. The multitudes would wonder at him, and acclaim him again as "the great power of God!"

I believe Mr. Brumback has proven his case. He also gives considerable documentation to show that the most revered commentators and expositors of the Church believed the Samaritans spoke with tongues when they received the Holy Spirit.

Adam Clarke (1762-1832) a Methodist:

"They prayed and laid their hands on the disciples, and God sent down the gift: so, the blessing came from God by the apostles, and not from the apostles to the people. But for what purpose was the Holy Spirit given? Certainly not for the sanctification of the souls of the people: this they had on believing in Christ Jesus; and this the apostles never dispensed. It was the miraculous gifts of the Spirit which were thus communicated — the speaking with different tongues, and these extraordinary qualifications which are necessary for the successful preaching of the Gospel."

Thomas Scott (1747-1821), Episcopalian:

"Many teachers, and probably private Christians, wrought miracles and spake with tongues, as the Spirit gave them utterance, but the honor of communicating those gifts by the imposition of hands and prayer, was, generally at least, restricted to the apostles. When Simon, therefore, saw the effects which followed from the laying on of their hands, he concluded that they could, if they chose, impart to him a similar power, supposing that the whole power was at their disposal (note II Cor. 13:7-10). This he supposed would admirably subserve his purpose of obtaining honor and wealth: for by enabling men at his own will to speak foreign languages, without the trouble of learning them, and to cure disease by word, he would not only carry on a most lucrative trade, but be almost adored as a deity."

Joseph Benson (1748-1821), Methodist:

"Then laid they their hands on them ... And they received the Holy Ghost — in answer to the prayers of the apostles; that is, these new converts spoke with tongues, and performed other extraordinary works."

William Burkitt (1650-1703), Episcopalian:

"They prayed and laid their hands on them and they received the Holy Ghost. Whereby the Holy Ghost is not to be understood as the sanctifying graces of the Holy Ghost, which the apostles never did nor could dispense, but the extraordinary gifts of the Holy Ghost, the gift of tongues and prophecy, and the power to work miracles."

Charles John Ellicott, Episcopalian:

"When Simon saw that through laying on of the apostles' hands ... The words imply that the result was something visible and conspicuous. A change was wrought: and men spoke with tongues and prophesied."

H.B. Hackett (1808-1875), Baptist:

"They received the Holy Spirit as the Author of the endowments conferred on them. Among these many have been the gift of tongues (see Acts 2:4; 10:46), and also that of prophecy as well as the power of working miracles" (*Commentary on the Original Text of the Acts of the Apostles*, 1858).

M.F. Sadler, *Commentary on the New Testament* (12 Vols.):

"It is clear from this that the manifestations of the presence of the Spirit were in outward gifts, such as healing, or speaking with tongues. If they had only been gifts of spiritual grace and holiness, Simon would not have discerned them, or would have held them in no account."

OBJECTION 18:
Paul did speak about the gifts of the Spirit in I Corinthians 12, but he concluded by saying, "And yet I show you a more excellent way" (ver. 31). This means that while tongues were temporarily in the Early Church, Paul now would have them discard the gift and choose a more excellent way — the way of love.

ANSWER:
If that was Paul's intent in writing the 12th chapter of I Corinthians, his words certainly contradict it. He began the chapter by telling the people he did not want them to be ignorant "concerning spiritual *gifts*" (ver. 1). He did not downgrade the gifts, but said that God desires that they should be manifested through everyone. "But the manifestation of the Spirit is given to each one for the profit *of all*" (ver. 7). He followed this by listing the gifts. He then compared them to the various members of the human body, and declared that even those which "seem to be weaker are necessary" (ver. 22).

Paul did not conclude the chapter by implying that the gifts were temporarily useful, and that now they should be discarded in favor of love. He said, "But earnestly desire the best gifts. And yet I show you a more excellent way" (ver. 31). The gifts and the fruits are not in competition; they supplement one another. Paul was emphasizing that with the gifts, it is absolutely necessary for believers to have the fruits. He said, "Though I speak with the tongues of men and of angels, but have not love, I have become sounding brass or a clanging cymbal" (I Cor. 13:1). Likewise, he said if one had the gift of prophecy and understood all mysteries, and had not love, it would profit nothing.

It is ridiculous to hold that these statements should cancel out everything else Paul said. The gifts of the Spirit were given for the edification and profit of the Church. God placed them in the Church. The 12th chapter describes the gifts, while the 13th shows the spirit in which they are to be exercised. The 14th chapter sums it all up with the words, "Pursue love, and desire spiritual *gifts*" (ver. 1). Surely, this statement cannot mean the exact opposite of what it says!

OBJECTION 19:

Love is the only real evidence of the baptism in the Holy Spirit, not speaking in other tongues.

ANSWER:

While it is true that speaking in other tongues can be counterfeited, so can love. There is so-called physical love which, in a moment, can turn to hatred and murder (II Sam. 13:15). On the other hand, there is a love that lays down its life for another. Most young people who get married believe they are in love, yet a large number of such cases end in the divorce court with charges and counter charges of cruelty and mistreatment. To determine the genuineness of love, it must be observed over a period of time.

On the other hand, the disciples immediately knew that the people at Cornelius' house had received the Holy Spirit, "For they heard them speak with tongues and magnify God" (Acts

10:46). It is true that some who receive the Spirit, fail to walk in the Spirit, and thus discredit their experience, as did some in the Corinthian Church. But that is a different matter.

OBJECTION 20:

The Pentecostal message appeals mainly to the ignorant and illiterate. One critic says: "I found — and this was true in every meeting of this type I attended — that the appeal was almost one hundred percent to human emotion. The 'Pentecostal' ministers were obviously quite proficient at mass psychology — especially when directed, in this case, toward the backward or uneducated types of people."

ANSWER:

In every major revival of the Church Age, there have been elements of extremism. Martin Luther sorrowfully discovered that a considerable part of his following was being influenced by radicals and extremists who went so far as to take the law into their own hands. This action culminated in the bloody Peasant's War, during which tens of thousands perished. The Catholics blamed Martin Luther for these excesses, although he stood strongly against those who were responsible for them. Nevertheless, despite the fanaticism unhappily associated with the revival in Luther's day, the Reformation saved the Church from total apostasy and ruin.

To imply that those having the Pentecostal experience include only the ignorant and uneducated is false. True enough, not all Pentecostal ministers have had the advantage of a college education, and many people they serve are common people. The rulers of the Jews held this against the apostles. "Now when they saw the boldness of Peter and John, and perceived that they were uneducated and untrained men, they marveled" (Acts 4:13). Nevertheless, many people have been called to high service and have given themselves to study without a college education. Abraham Lincoln is one example. Peter and John must have done so too, for the books they wrote in later years are not only well written, but they have changed the lives of multitudes. Today, the most highly-educated scholars study their writings for pleasure and profit.

On the other hand, many who have received the baptism in the Holy Spirit are highly-educated people. Thousands of college graduates and professionals have received the experience. Today, many of America's most prominent ministers in the historic denominations have received the baptism in the Spirit and are earnestly advocating it to others. As an example of how far this has gone, Yale, Princeton and Union Theological seminaries have actually permitted lectures to be given to their students on speaking in other tongues, and many have received the experience in their halls.

OBJECTION 21:

In I Corinthians 14:20, Paul suggested that the gift of tongues was for the Church only during the days of its infancy, when he said, "Brethren, do not be children in understanding; however, in malice be babes, but in understanding be mature." The Church received the gift of tongues in the beginning, but it was not intended to become a permanent part of the worship service.

ANSWER:

Although this is the position taken by those who oppose the Pentecostal experience, it certainly does not represent the position of the Scriptures. The Apostle Paul said, "I thank my God I speak with tongues more than you all" (I Cor. 14:18). Is he, therefore, to be considered immature or a babe? What would happen if the Apostle Paul were to visit some churches today which take this view? What would be their attitude if they found that when he came to their church he spoke in tongues more than all others?

OBJECTION 22:

No responsible leaders of the historic churches believe in speaking in other tongues.

ANSWER:

That statement is not valid. Actually, many responsible and learned men from the historic churches are now speaking and writing in favor of the experience. A masterpiece entitled *Tongue Speaking* was written by Morton T. Kelsey, an Episcopal clergyman and student of Jungian psychology. Before its publication by Doubleday, Rev. Kelsey presented his manuscript to the well-known skeptic Upton Sinclair, whose wife was a member of Rev. Kelsey's church. Doubleday had requested Mr. Sinclair to peruse the manuscript. Only because his wife was a member of Rev. Kelsey's church was the famous writer persuaded to read it. The book had a profound effect upon Mr. Sinclair, and he wrote in the foreword of the book the following words:

> Now there could be no subject named in which this author would have expressed less interest than the practice known as "glossolalia," or speaking in other tongues; and never before had he received a full-length manuscript with less expectation of pleasure. But he found that he was mistaken; he found himself reading a precise and careful study of a strange and fascinating subject competently written and worthy of all praise.

He went on to say that while "the rich churches of America grow respectable," this book tells how the Christian religion began and "how it still works among the poor and lowly."

As to the statement that no responsible leaders of historic churches believe in speaking in other tongues, let us note that the following was taken from a tract published by the National Council of Churches on the subject of speaking in other tongues:

> And God appointed in the church ... speaking in tongues and interpreters (Read Acts 2:4-11). As you pray, think of the meaning of these verses as they apply to your own particular congregation,

remembering the significance of the unusual and the extraordinary in the Christian church as opposed to the normal and the mediocre.

— Of the witness which does not come only from the intellect and transcends the understanding of man.

— Of the "speakers in tongues" who can continually challenge and disturb the church which all too easily becomes complacent and self-satisfied and contented to remain as it is.

This remarkable tract was printed shortly after David Du Plessis and I were invited to meet leaders in historic churches of America and present the Pentecostal message to them. Their reception of the message was reflected in the above words.

OBJECTION 23:
Speaking in other tongues is merely psychic ejaculations by people who are in a state of delirium or religious frenzy.

ANSWER:
To this, we must sharply object. The Scriptures declare that the apostles spoke in other tongues as the Spirit gave them utterance. Therefore, to attribute such utterance to psychic ejaculations is dangerously close to the sin of attributing the work of the Holy Spirit to that of Beelzebub — a sin for which there is no forgiveness (Matt. 12:24-32).

The inspired writer of Acts said that speaking in other tongues came forth as the Spirit gave utterance. That is the true explanation of the glossolalia, as found among those who have received the baptism in the Spirit.

OBJECTION 24:
Speaking in other tongues is a gibberish and unintelligible babble that does not follow the rules of any known language. Others who speak in tongues appear to have nothing but stammering lips.

ANSWER:

The great majority of those who publicly speak in other tongues speak fluently, and sometimes do so in several languages. Often, each language is strikingly different from the others spoken. The actual gift mentioned by Paul is "varieties of tongues" (I Cor. 12:28). There have been many cases in which speaking in other tongues has been recognized and understood by someone who knew the language, thus proving conclusively that what was spoken was an actual language.

There are some dialects, however, which are of a rudimentary nature and may sound like gibberish. Although spoken by primitive tribes, they are definite languages. Certainly, those who spoke on the Day of Pentecost spoke true languages. But though many were convinced and led to repentance, there were others who mocked, saying, "'They are full of new wine'" (Acts 2:13).

There are instances of those who appear to give forth a stammering tongue. These are generally individuals who have just received the baptism in the Spirit. They usually come forth later with a clear tongue. While no one with a stammering tongue should attempt to use it in public ministry, the Scriptures do not disown even this (Isa. 28:11, 12).

OBJECTION 25:

Why do some people speak with stammering lips? If God has all power, should not the gift He gives be clear and perfect?

ANSWER:

We have to let God set the rules. The Holy Spirit does not overwhelm people and force them to speak in tongues. In contrast, Satan operates by compulsion. As a rule, spiritualist mediums must lose consciousness in order for "control spirits" to speak through them. On the other hand, those who receive the baptism in the Holy Spirit rarely lose consciousness, and their faculties are fully retained. The candidates must yield their tongues, for the Spirit will not force His way.

It is not unusual for people to stammer when they first begin speaking in other tongues. But after they fully yield to the Spirit, they will begin speaking with a clear tongue. That "stammering lips" would prove to be a stumbling block to some, is noted by the prophet who says, "Yet they would not hear" (Isa. 28:12).

OBJECTION 26:

There are people whose lives fail to measure up to the Christian standard, but claim to speak in other tongues. Surely, God would not pour out His Spirit upon people who are so imperfect.

ANSWER:

Peter preached to people on the Day of Pentecost who had committed the greatest sin of all time — murdering the Son of God. He said, "'Men of Israel, hear these words ... Him, being delivered by the determined purpose and foreknowledge of God, you have taken by lawless hands, have crucified, and put to death'" (Acts 2:22, 23).

Yet, Peter offered these arch sinners the promise of the Holy Spirit upon their repentance and acceptance of the Gospel. He said the promise was to them and their children, to those who were afar off, and for as many as the Lord would call (Acts 2:39). As a basis for his words, Peter quoted from Joel 2:28-32, saying that God would pour out His spirit upon all flesh.

Not all who joined the apostolic company show the marks of sanctified people. Ananias and Sapphira actually lied to the Holy Spirit. Although the gifts of the Spirit functioned in the Corinthian Church to a notable degree, Paul said that these people were carnal (I Cor. 3:1-4). Paul declared that they occasionally used the gifts in ways that were not proper, but he never challenged the genuineness of the gifts. Instead he reproved them sharply for their moral laxity.

OBJECTION 27:

Some who speak in tongues live on a low Christian standard. Is it not presumptuous for Pentecostals to claim these people have the Holy Spirit, while some of the world's leading soulwinners, who have won thousands to Christ, do not have the experience?

ANSWER:

Those who raise this objection forget that most denominations claim that their communicants not only were saved but received the Holy Spirit when they became members of their church. Pentecostals teach the baptism in the Spirit is subsequent to salvation.

While it is true that every Spirit-filled person ought to live an exemplary Christian life, and indeed it is a serious matter not to do so, the Scriptures do not indicate that this will always be the case. Joel said that God would pour out His Spirit upon all flesh. The carnal Corinthians received the Holy Spirit because they believed it was for them, not because they were exemplary Christians.

It is unfair to compare a few great leaders of the non-Pentecostal world with unfortunate misfits and neurotics who may attach themselves to the Pentecostal movement. Such people are often an embarrassment to the movement, since opposers are quick to claim they are typical of all Pentecostal believers. However, it is not completely against the movement that it welcomes the weak and underprivileged. The wealthy churches are prone to turn such people from their doors.

A true test is to take the Pentecostal people as a whole and compare them to the general membership of the denominational world. Practically all Pentecostal believers can give a definite testimony of a born-again experience. This isn't true of many members of the formal churches.

OBJECTION 28:

Even though speaking in other tongues is scriptural, it causes too many problems in the Church. Note the difficulties Paul faced with those who spoke in tongues in the Corinthian Church. Considering all these problems and complications, would it not be safer to eliminate it altogether?

ANSWER:

This is man's solution to the matter, but not God's. The fact is that the preaching and propagation of the Gospel has always involved problems. When believers professed Christianity in the early centuries, it often led to martyrdom. Surely, that was a problem! A compromise was to worship both Christ and Caesar. Many did not take the easier route, but chose death instead.

Naturally, speaking in tongues presents problems. If God, by means of His omnipotence, controlled the use of the gift, there would be no problems. But then man would become an automation; he would not have a free will. This free will of man is implied in Paul's statement that "the spirits of the prophets are subject to the prophets" (I Cor. 14:32). Since the proper use of the gift depends partly on the individual, instructions are necessary regarding how it should be used.

Naturally, some do not want to be bothered with problems. It is easier to forbid speaking in tongues. That is one way to get rid of problems, but it is not God's way. Paul apparently met people in his day who thought to solve the problem in that way, but he stood against this saying, "Do not quench the Spirit. Do not despise prophecies" (I Thes. 5:19, 20).

There are those who fear that if they allow speaking in tongues in church it will get out of control. It is not dangerous, however, if the pastor follows the instructions of I Corinthians 14. Certainly, he must not attempt to solve the problem by forbidding speaking in other tongues and prophesying!

OBJECTION 29:

If speaking in other tongues accompanies the full experience of the baptism in the Holy Spirit, why did no one speak in tongues during the centuries prior to the 20th century?

ANSWER:

The Bible shows that speaking in other tongues was not a phenomenon that occurred only on the Day of Pentecost and shortly after. For example, toward the end of Paul's ministry when he was at Ephesus, he laid his hands on some disciples and they spoke in tongues (Acts 19:1-6).

Of course, speaking in tongues was only one of the nine gifts of the Spirit that distinguished apostolic ministry. The Church at Ephesus was noted for its well-rounded ministry. Paul said that he held back nothing during the three years he ministered to that church. Some 35 years later, however, the Lord spoke to the Church at Ephesus — which prophetic scholars declare typifies the apostolic church — warning that, because it had left its first love, it was in danger of being removed from its place (Rev. 2:4, 5).

History records that the supernatural ministry of the Early Church declined rapidly after the death of John. The apostolic church, as far as its peculiar ministry was concerned, gradually vanished from view.

Nevertheless, the gifts of the Spirit, including speaking in other tongues, were manifested in some degree during the early centuries and throughout the whole Church Age. (See chapter 41.)

Below, are quotes from some of the Early Church fathers. Tertullian, in defending orthodox Christianity, challenged Marcion to produce anything among his followers that occurred among his people.

> Let him exhibit prophets such as have spoken, not by human sense, but the Spirit of God, such as have predicted things to come, and have made manifest the secrets of the heart. Let him produce a psalm, a vision, a prayer, only let it be by the Spirit in an ecstasy, that is in a rapture, whenever an interpretation of tongues has occurred to him (*Smith's Dictionary of the Bible*, Vol. 4, page 3,310).

St. Augustine, the noted theologian and author of the famous *City of God* wrote:

We still do what the apostles did when they laid hands on the Samaritans and called down the Holy Spirit on them by laying on of hands. It is expected that converts should speak with new tongues.

Chrysostom, another of the Early Church fathers wrote:

Whoever was baptized in apostolic days, he straightway spake with tongues, for since in their coming over from idols, without any clear knowledge of training in the ancient Scriptures, they at once received the Spirit; not that they saw the Spirit, for He is invisible, but God's grace bestowed some sensible proof of His energy, and one straightway spoke in the Persian language, another in Roman, another in Indian, another in some other tongue, and this made manifest to them that were without it that it was the Spirit in the very person speaking. Wherefore, the apostle calls it "the manifestation of the Spirit which is given to every man to profit withal."

The *Encyclopedia Britannica* states that the glossolalia (or speaking in tongues) "recurs in Christian revivals of every age, e.g. among mendicant friars of the thirteenth century, among the Jansenists and early Quakers, the persecuted Protestants of the Cevennes, and the Irvingites" (Vol. 27, pages 9, 10, Eleventh Edition).

In *History of the Christian Church* by Philip Schaff (Vol. 1, page 232), the author gives a considerable record of speaking in other tongues in various revivals over a period of many centuries.

In a German work, Souer's *History of the Christian Church* (Vol. 3, page 406), the following is found concerning Martin Luther:

Dr. Martin Luther was a prophet, evangelist, speaker in tongues, and interpreter, in one person, endowed with all the gifts of the Spirit.

Francis Xavier, according to Schaff and *The Catholic Encyclopedia*, "Possessed a remarkable exercise of the gift of tongues."

When F.B. Meyer visited Estonia, he wrote to the *London Christian* of the wonderful work of the Holy Spirit that he saw among the peasants:

It is very remarkable, at a time when the Lutheran church of this land has lost its evangelistic fervor, and is inclined to substitute forms and rites for the living power of Christ, that God raised up a devoted nobleman, Baron Uxhall, to preach the Gospel in all its simplicity, and is renewing among the peasantry these marvelous manifestations which attended the first preaching of the Gospel when God bore witness to the message of salvation with signs and wonders and gifts of the Holy Ghost. To have come across a movement like this is intensely interesting. The gift of tongues is heard quite often in meetings, especially in the villages, but also in the towns. Here at Reval, the pastor of the Baptist church tells me that they often break out in his meetings. They are most often uttered by young women, less frequently by men. When they are interpreted, they are found to mean, "Jesus is coming soon; Jesus is near. Be ready; be not idle." When they are heard, unbelievers who may be in the audience are greatly awed. A gentleman who was present on one occasion was deeply impressed by the fact that those who spoke were quite ordinary people until they were uplifted as it were by a trance and then they spoke with so much fluency and refinement.

Regarding D.L. Moody, Rev. R. Boyd, D.D., a Baptist, says on page 402 of *Trials and Triumphs of Faith*:

> When I got to the rooms of the Young Men's Christian Association, Victoria Hall, London, I found the meeting on fire. The young men were speaking with tongues, prophesying. What on earth did it mean? Only that Moody had been addressing them that afternoon. What manner of man is this, I thought? ... I cannot describe Moody's great meeting: I can only say that the people of Sunderland warmly supported the movement, in spite of their local spiritual advisors.

The facts are simply that the great truths of the Gospel were gradually lost, one at a time, and the traditions of men were substituted by the Church of Rome, so that by the time of Luther, almost all evangelical truths were lost or distorted by papal decrees and encyclicals. Therefore, just as there was a successive loss of these truths, so the restoration came gradually. The Reformation which began under Luther was carried on by Knox, the Wesleys, Fox and many others. Luther brought back the truth that "'the just shall live by faith'" (Rom. 1:17). The Wesleys emphasized holiness. Others were raised up by God to bring back the various truths of the Gospel.

It was toward the close of the life of the noted leader and founder of the Christian Missionary Alliance, Dr. A.B. Simpson, that the great Pentecostal outpouring came. The following is a comment he made on the Pentecostal movement in one of his annual reports:

> We believe there can be no doubt that in many cases remarkable outpourings of the Holy Spirit have been accomplished with genuine instances of the gift of tongues and many extraordinary manifestations. This has occurred both in our own land and in some of our foreign missions.

Many of these experiences appear not only to be genuine, but accompanied by a spirit of deep humility and soberness, and free from extravagance and error. And it is admitted that in many of the branches and States where this movement has been strongly developed and wisely directed, there has been a marked deepening of the spiritual life of our members, and an encouraging increase in their missionary zeal and liberality. It would therefore be a serious matter for any candid Christian to pass a wholesale criticism or condemnation upon such movements, or presume to limit the Holy One of Israel.

OBJECTION 30:

Speaking in other tongues, as practiced by the Pentecostals, has its source in sorcery and demon activity.

ANSWER:

It is true that there are false prophets in the land, including spiritists who speak under the unction of a power other than the Spirit of God. There were false prophets in Bible days, and there are false prophets today. If an evil spirit can speak through a false prophet in a known language, it is theoretically possible that it could speak in an unknown language, although in my many years of experience, I have rarely run into such cases.

Satan has counterfeits for a number of God's works. Remember that Pharaoh's magicians matched many of God's miracles (Ex. 7 and 8). However, did this nullify God's miracles? Should Moses have rejected the miracle power of God simply because Satan performed some of the same feats?

On the exact same premise, no Christian should turn against any of the gifts of the Holy Spirit as clearly outlined in the Bible, specifically the speaking in other tongues, simply because Satan has tried to counterfeit it through the mouths of false prophets and spiritualists. On the contrary, the Bible says that we should be "wise as serpents and harmless as doves" (Matt. 10:16) and not ignorant of Satan's devices.

The Word of God says, "'If a son asks for bread from any father among you, will he give him a stone? Or if *he asks* for a fish, will he give him a serpent instead of a fish? ... If you then, being evil, know how to give good gifts to your children, how much more will *your* heavenly Father give the Holy Spirit to those who ask Him!'" (Lk. 11:11, 13). God's integrity and Word confirm that He can be trusted to give the Holy Spirit and not a demon to His true born-again children.

To say that all supernatural manifestations of speaking in tongues are the work of evil spirits is to take a daring and dangerous stand. The Pharisees were the fundamentalists of Christ's day, and they attributed His works to the power of the devil (Matt. 12:22-24). Jesus not only rebuked such accusations but said, "... every sin and blasphemy will be forgiven men, but the blasphemy *against* the Spirit will not be forgiven men" (Matt. 12:31).

Speaking in other tongues, as the Holy Spirit gives utterance, is clearly outlined in the Bible. The question rests on this: Is God's Word true or false? Those who deny it are saying that the Scriptures are false — it is a decision every individual must make.

Chapter Fifty

Interpretation of Tongues

I wish you all spoke with tongues, but even more that you prophesied; for he who prophesies *is* greater than he who speaks with tongues, unless indeed he interprets, that the church may receive edification (I Cor. 14:5).

Most of what was said in earlier chapters about the gift of prophecy applies to the gift of interpretation. Indeed, since the two gifts are similar, interpretation is equated by the Scriptures to prophecy. The obvious exception is that speaking in tongues always precedes an interpretation. It will be noticed in the above verse that those who prophesy in the public assembly are greater than those who speak in tongues unless they interpret the message. The inference is that prophecy and interpretation are equivalent gifts.

The Reason for the Gift of Interpretation

The fact that the two are equivalent gifts raises such questions as, "What is the purpose of the gift; why not use only prophecy in the assembly?" There are various reasons:

First of all, without the gift of interpretation, there would be no speaking in other tongues in a public congregation, for the speaker is instructed to be silent unless there is an interpreter present. Speaking in tongues is a sign "to unbelievers" (I Cor. 14:22). But if speaking in tongues was never allowed, how could it be a sign to unbelievers? Some have rejected the sign in unbelief, as the Scriptures declared (ver. 21), but others have been awakened to the reality of the supernatural as a result of the manifestation of the gift.

Another very important reason for the manifestation of the gift of tongues is that it alerts the congregation that the Holy

Spirit is about to speak. It gives the people time to get into a reverent attitude of prayer before the interpretation is given. If the message was given in prophecy without the introductory speaking in tongues, the audience might not be prepared to receive it.

When a message is spoken in an unknown tongue and then skillfully interpreted, the effect is greatly enhanced upon the listener to whom this ministry is new. It is an excellent demonstration of two or more members of the body of Christ working together.

It is not uncommon for someone present, when a message in the unknown tongue is given, to recognize the language spoken as their own vernacular. Such an occurrence naturally leaves a very deep impression upon that person, as it did upon the hearers on the Day of Pentecost. Summing up, the manifestation of the gift of tongues and the accompanying interpretation, given under a strong anointing, usually results in great edification and blessing to the listeners.

An Interpretation is Not Usually a Translation

An interpretation of a message in tongues, as a rule, is not a translation. A translation is a literal word-for-word rendering from one language into another. An interpretation has far more latitude of action than a translation. For example, the interpretation may only give the main point of what was said in the unknown tongue, just as a professional language interpreter sometimes does. If the speaking in tongues was overly long, then the interpretation may sum up what has been spoken. It is worthy of notice that when the Holy Spirit quoted passages from the Old Testament into the New, He often used what is called a free translation. The general message was always retained, but a different phrasing was often used. This being the case, we may understand that the Holy Spirit reserves the right to interpret His own words in the unknown tongue into English words that may vary in phrasing from the original.

Yet, on the other hand, the Spirit may translate word for word what was said in the unknown tongue. There have been occasions when I personally observed that the repetitions made in the unknown tongue were faithfully repeated in English at the appropriate place — showing the interpretation was following an exact translation. The Holy Spirit binds Himself to no hard and fast rule.

The Different Types of Interpretation

Those who have witnessed and studied the working of the gift of interpretation over a number of years, will agree that interpretations differ widely in character and quality. Some are excellent, some fair, others mediocre. The subconscious mind becomes a receiving station in the operation to intercept the mind of God, and thus convey to the people the message the Holy Spirit desires to give. There is, however, a very wide range of yieldedness to the Spirit between different people, which is obvious to anyone who has been a regular attendant at charismatic meetings.

Those used in the ministry of interpretation fall into rather definite classifications.

First of all, it must be conceded that there are those whose interpretations are so poor that it is doubtful the messages they give result in edifying the service at all. Indeed, it is quite possible that in certain cases they do harm. Paul asks, "Do all interpret?" (I Cor. 12:30). The fact is, not all who attempt to interpret have the gift. This may include some people of a limited intelligence who are obviously unfit for public ministry at all. This is especially evident in those who give tiresome repetitions when speaking, such as, "My children, my children, I say unto you ..." There is no message and therefore no one is edified.

Those who deny that the gifts are operating in the Church today delight in pointing out such poor examples. Of course, they are not typical at all. When a situation of this nature arises, correction is obviously needed. But a pastor must exercise great wisdom at this point, so that he does not cause others to be afraid to manifest their gifts. Yet if one continues to attempt to manifest a gift in an unedifying manner, they should be taken aside and gently shown what is necessary before they can acceptably minister in public.

There are others who actually have a gift, but because of a lack of proper instruction, they manifest it so poorly in public that instead of edifying the people, it has the opposite effect. For example, some individuals have a burden to preach. Lacking such an opportunity, they go on for perhaps 10 or 15 minutes when giving an interpretation. What began acceptably was carried to such length that the good effect was lost. Strangers who do not understand the working of these gifts might even wonder if God were in the message at all. God may have been in the message, but it lost its impact because of the lack of wisdom on the part of the interpreter.

We are told in I Corinthians 14:32 that "the spirits of the prophets are subject to the prophets." There is a time to speak and a time to stop speaking. There are occasions when God reveals things to a person which would be out of order to reveal at the moment (ver. 30).

Others may give a message at a time in which the spirit of the service is moving in a different direction. If the speaker is at a crucial place in the sermon, an interruption at that time might divert attention from the point the speaker has been laboring to build. Worse still, is one who gives a message which is completely irrelevant to the service. The Lord never anoints a person to bring that type of message.

Still others do not know how to let the Spirit speak through them to the people in an acceptable manner. Some will boom out in deafening tones so loud that even the members of the congregation are startled, let alone strangers who might be present. Or, they might accompany their speaking with violent demonstrations which divert attention from what is being said. Also, their enunciation may be poor so that no one can understand them. All these things detract from the effectiveness of the gift.

Interpretations That Edify or Reveal

Fortunately, there are many excellent interpreters in the Church — although not nearly as many as there should be.

Included with them are those who know just when to give a message in tongues. Usually, the best time is when the people are in the spirit of worship — perhaps after a good devotional song has been sung. Someone is then moved to give a message in the Spirit, and the interpretation naturally follows. If, however, the one speaking in tongues is out of order, the interpreter will usually feel a check in his/her spirit about giving an interpretation.

Ministers generally do not wish to be interrupted while preaching the Word. Yet, if the going is a little hard and they are having trouble collecting their thoughts, they may welcome assistance. A message at such a time may enable them to get a fresh hold of the audience. Or, if an altar call is difficult, a message in tongues and interpretation may be effective in getting sinners to the altar.

In the public service, the prophecy or the interpretation will generally be as I Corinthians 14:3 declares, "edification and exhortation and comfort." There are occasions, however, when revelation may come forth. The person giving this type of interpretation, or prophecy, must be deep in the Spirit, and usually should have considerable experience ministering in the gift. Bringing forth actual revelation, requires being deeper in the Spirit than giving an exhortation. It is also more apt to be manifested in smaller gatherings in which the people are in close unity.

Instruction Concerning the Gift of Interpretation

The Apostle Paul took time to lay down a number of instructions concerning how the gift of interpretation should operate in the service. We shall briefly review his instructions:

1. Speaking in other tongues is not permitted in the public assembly when there is no interpreter. However, tongues with interpretation is acceptable, and is equivalent to prophecy (I Cor. 14:5).

2. If there is no interpreter present in the congregation, then the person speaking in an unknown tongue should pray to interpret the message themselves. Until then, they should keep silent (I Cor. 14:13).

In I Corinthians 12:31, Paul said to "desire the best gifts." In I Corinthians 14:39 he says, "desire earnestly to prophesy." Evidently, we should understand that the gift of prophecy is one of the best gifts. Since interpretation is equated to prophecy, we must place this gift on the list also. Certainly, when properly manifested, it is of great value and usefulness to the Church.

3. Paul limited the number of messages in the unknown tongue.

> If anyone speaks in a tongue, let *there be* two or at the most three, *each* in turn, and let one interpret (I Cor. 14:27).

These are very vital instructions. The number of messages should ordinarily be one or two, but three at most. Why is this instruction given? The answer is obvious. There is a limited amount of time available, and if it is all used for tongues and interpretation, there is no time left for other important things in the service, such as prayer, worship, preaching, altar services, etc. There can be too much of anything.

Even if each message is only two minutes long, the tongues and interpretations for three messages would take twelve minutes. Paul said not to permit more than three messages.

4. While several people may speak in the unknown tongue, only one should interpret. Otherwise, there might be the spectacle of two people attempting to interpret at the same time. That would be very confusing.

We might state here, however, that often when the Spirit is moving mightily in a service, and a message in tongues is given, several people may begin to feel the quickening of the Spirit for the interpretation. It is then very necessary to wait quietly for a specific "go ahead" to interpret. Sometimes, it is best "in honor preferring one another" to let another give it. If prophecy is to represent God speaking, people would rightly wonder why He would interrupt Himself by attempting to speak through two people at the same time.

Paul recognized that this was possible, because of the

nature of the gift. It is God speaking, but the directing comes from man. God is infallible; mankind is fallible. In prophecy and interpretation, we have the merging of the fallible with the infallible, the blending of God's conscious mind with man's subconscious mind.

For this reason, Paul said, "The spirits of the prophets are subject to the prophets" (I Cor. 14:32). If prophecy and interpretation did not come through the vehicle of a human, no instruction would ever be needed, and the manifestation would be perfect at all times. But since these utterance gifts represent the fusing of the human mind with the divine mind, the human will is involved and becomes an active factor in the manifestation of the gift. Therefore, it is important that those who manifest these gifts receive teaching and instruction concerning their use.

In light of this, Paul's instructions make sense. As an example, a fourth person might feel that they ought to give a message, but the Scripture says three messages are sufficient, so they should refrain from giving it. Some ignore this instruction and give six or seven messages. This not only takes more time than is available, but makes the things of God appear common.

Again, one might feel an anointing to give a message while another is still speaking. However, if they are instructed, they will wait until the other is through. The Scripture says to do it in turn. Common sense also would dictate this procedure. "For you can all prophesy one by one" (ver. 31). "For God is not *the author* of confusion but of peace" (ver. 33).

5. Prophecies and interpretations are to be judged. "Let two or three prophets speak, and let the others judge" (I Cor. 14:29).

When the gift of prophecy is operating properly, it is indeed God speaking to His people, and His words should be listened to prayerfully and with reverence. Yet there are times when a prophecy must be judged. We are not to blindly accept anything, especially if it appears to be out of harmony with the Word of God. There have been occasions in which someone has come into an assembly and spoken things that did not line up with the Scriptures. There have been prophecies given which advocated strange doctrines, or teachings that were unsound. These, if left unanswered, might result in serious division in the Church. The public judging of prophecies under suspect should, if possible, be done by another prophet, or at least by one who has the gift of prophecy or interpretation of tongues.

Spiritual things need to be spiritually discerned. It is possible even for true prophecy to be misconstrued by those who are novices. When Jesus said to His disciples, "'Take heed and beware of the leaven of the Pharisees and Sadducees,'" they thought He was speaking of bread (Matt. 16:6, 7). Jesus had to patiently explain to them that He was not speaking of bread, but of false doctrines (ver. 11, 12).

Despite these possibilities, the manifestation of the gifts of interpretation and prophecy, when they conform to their scriptural place in the assembly, can be a blessing of inestimable value. The advantages far outweigh any risks involved. Let us always remember Paul's injunction in this respect, which though brief, is to the point. He said, "Do not quench the Spirit. Do not despise prophecies. Test all things; hold fast what is good" (I Thes. 5:19-21). These are sound instructions, and we would do well to heed them.

CREATION SCIENCE

SERIES

**Vol. 1
Foundations for
Creation Science
$9.95**

**Vol. 2 Harmony of
Science and
Scripture
$9.95**

**Vol. 3 The Origins
Controversy:
Creation or Chance
$6.95**

**Vol. 4
The Canopied Earth:
World That Was
$7.95**

Vol. 5 The Genesis
Flood: Continents in
Collision
$7.95

Vol. 6 The Original
Star Wars and the
Age of Ice
$8.95

Vol. 7 The Dinosaur
Dilemma: Fact or
Fantasy
$9.95

Vol. 8 The Birth of
Planet Earth and
the Age of the
Universe
$8.95

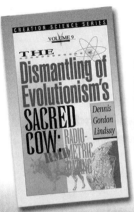

Vol. 9 The Dismantling of Evolutionism's Sacred Cow: Radiometric Dating

$8.95

Vol. 10 The ABCs of Evolutionism

$9.95

Vol. 11 The Glory of the Genesis Man: The Biblical View of Early Man

$7.95

Vol. 12 Joshua's Long Day and Jonah's Long Night: Fact or Fairy Tale?

$9.95

Soon to be released: **Vol. 13**
Lucifer's Illusions:
Pyramids, Crystals and
the New Age Mirage

Vol. 14   The Genesis
Man & His Amazing
Accomplishments:
Part 1 The Old World
                     $9.95

Soon to be released: **Vol. 15 The**
Genesis Man & His Amazing
Accomplishments: Part 2 The
New World and the Isles of
the Pacific

Complete Set of 13 Available Books
$108.00